MW00332653

LANDSCAPE AND CHANGE IN
EARLY MEDIEVAL ITALY

This innovative environmental history of the long-lived European chestnut tree and its woods offers surprising perspectives on the human transition from the Roman to the medieval world in Italy. Integrating evidence from botanical and literary sources, individual charters, and case studies of specific communities, the book traces fluctuations in the size and location of Italian chestnut woods to expose how early medieval societies changed their land use between the fourth and eleventh centuries, and in the process changed themselves. As the chestnut tree gained popularity in late antiquity and became a valuable commodity by the end of the first millennium, this study brings to life the economic and cultural transition from a Roman Italy of cities, agricultural surpluses, and markets to a medieval Italy of villages and subsistence farming.

PAOLO SQUATRITI is Associate Professor of History and Romance Languages and Literatures at the University of Michigan. He specializes in the study of the pre-industrial environment and has published on ecological and landscape change in the "Dark Ages."

LANDSCAPE AND CHANGE IN EARLY MEDIEVAL ITALY

Chestnuts, Economy, and Culture

PAOLO SQUATRITI

CAMBRIDGE
UNIVERSITY PRESS

CAMBRIDGE
UNIVERSITY PRESS

University Printing House, Cambridge CB2 8BS, United Kingdom

Cambridge University Press is part of the University of Cambridge.

It furthers the University's mission by disseminating knowledge in the pursuit of education, learning and research at the highest international levels of excellence.

www.cambridge.org
Information on this title: www.cambridge.org/9781316633205

© Paolo Squatriti 2013

This publication is in copyright. Subject to statutory exception and to the provisions of relevant collective licensing agreements, no reproduction of any part may take place without the written permission of Cambridge University Press.

First published 2013
First paperback edition 2016

A catalogue record for this publication is available from the British Library

Library of Congress Cataloguing in Publication data
Squatriti, Paolo, 1963–
Landscape and change in early medieval Italy : chestnuts, economy, and culture /
Paolo Squatriti.
pages   cm
Includes bibliographical references and index.
ISBN 978-1-107-03448-8 (hardback)
1. Chestnut–Italy–History–To 1500.   2. Chestnut–Social
aspects–Italy-History–To 1500.   3. Chestnut–Economic
aspects–Italy-History–To 1500.   4. Landscapes–Italy–History–To 1500.
5. Landscape changes–Italy–History–To 1500.
6. Land use–Italy–History–To 1500.   7. Italy–History–476-1268.
8. Italy–Economic conditions.   9. Italy–Environmental conditions.   I. Title.
SD397.C5S78   2013
712.0937–dc23   2012047924

ISBN 978-1-107-03448-8 Hardback
ISBN 978-1-316-63320-5 Paperback

Cambridge University Press has no responsibility for the persistence or accuracy of URLs for external or third-party internet websites referred to in this publication, and does not guarantee that any content on such websites is, or will remain, accurate or appropriate.

For Cristina

CONTENTS

MAPS

PREFACE

Above the olives began the woods. At one time the pines must have dominated the whole area, for they still intruded in pockets and tufts of woodland down the slopes as far as the beaches, just like the spruces. The oaks then were more frequent and thicker than appears today, for they were the first and most valuable victims of the axe. Further uphill pines gave way to chestnuts, the woods climbed the mountain, and you could not see their bounds. This was the world of sap within which we, inhabitants of Ombrosa, lived, almost without noticing it.

Italo Calvino, *Il barone rampante* (1957)

Since 2006, the year when I began to study the history of chestnut trees, many people have asked me why I was doing it, or how I came to such study. The answers are various and complicated and perhaps not fully satisfactory. To begin with, as one ages one finds oneself increasingly in sympathy with *all* trees, and a growing admiration for how trees endure life's indignities may well be where this book began. No other organism has trees' stolid grace, their capacity to weather adversity. No other organism manages to stay in one place and become part of the place, generally improving it, quite like trees. Their stoical resolution and indifference to the toing and froing of mobile life become more appealing when one's own mobility declines. One begins to notice and to appreciate more deeply what Calvino called the "world of sap" ("universo di linfa") and the quiet dignity that keeps the sap circulating, often for the benefit of other organisms, year after year, rooted in one locality.

But beyond this all too personal attraction to trees (and to chestnut trees in particular), I have found that chestnuts are an excellent field of study for historians interested in how past environments in Italy evolved. In the peninsula, chestnuts retain peculiar ecological and economic importance still today, even if over the past few human generations their profile has changed rapidly in response to new diseases, global market demands, and local labor conditions. As this book argues, such shifts are inherent in all Italian environmental histories. Italy's sharp relief, its fragile soils and wobbly tectonic plates, its mosaic of climatic zones, all contribute to pronounced environmental instability. Yet in the long, meandering, and necessarily dynamic history of environment in Italy a decisive conjuncture took place during the early Middle Ages, the period on which this study focuses, and involved chestnut trees, whose special ability to grow wood fast and regularly to make fruit people like to eat became trump cards at that time. Thus if one notices them, as Calvino urged, trees that might seem mere curiosities, marginal to the grander flows of history, begin to look like protagonists in the Italian theater of the great transformation that fashioned a medieval world out of an ancient one.

Early medieval chestnuts furthermore facilitate good thinking about one of the great preoccupations of the twenty-first century, environmental change, and not just in Italy. Chestnuts permit the realization that not all was a hoary wilderness in the post-Roman world, and that early medieval woodlands included carefully stewarded chestnut stands that stabilized land- and waterscapes while delivering "sustainable" sustenance to people, something no other tree could do as well. In this way, chestnut history corrects overly catastrophist versions of the end of antiquity. It also suggests how medieval environmental history might contribute to current debates about land use in areas where depopulation has brought drastic changes in the past two generations.[1] For the hillsides of the Mediterranean, but also for other wooded areas, the story of post-classical chestnut woodlands suggests that the outcome of human involvement with trees is not always deforestation, erosion, and destruction. The latter are, naturally, always possible, but chestnut history, and particularly medieval chestnut history, offers some important correctives to environmental narratives that too starkly distinguish between nature and culture and imagine the relations between the two as inevitably corrosive.

Chestnuts furthermore satisfy the microhistorian's requirement of a seemingly small and particular subject that opens unexpected vistas onto supposedly familiar historical terrain, and locates agency where none had been seen.[2] European chestnuts are thus a peculiarly useful lens through which to observe the early Middle Ages. They reveal the most basic workings of early medieval societies and show changes in their productive landscapes to have been less purely human than we imagined. This

---

[1] On the ecological effects of the emptying of Mediterranean mountain regions after 1945, see J. McNeill, *The Mountains of the Mediterranean World* (Cambridge, 1992). But the desolation of late-twentieth-century Detroit is also relevant here.

[2] See J. Brooks, C. DeCorse, and J. Walton, "Introduction," in *Small Worlds: Method, Meaning, and Narrative in Microhistory* (Santa Fe, 2008), 3–6.

unfamiliar, slightly less anthropocentric version of early medieval history is one benefit of noticing what can seem a mere tree. But the historiographical utility of chestnuts transcends this microhistorical surprise. For, more even than olive trees, European chestnuts live phenomenally long lives, sometimes thousands of years. Thanks to this unique long duration that binds past, present, and future together, chestnuts also allow us to see things from a different perspective than the ephemeral ones of armies and emperors, or monks and conversions.[3] From the point of view of chestnuts, late antiquity and the early Middle Ages are times of transformation, perhaps more than most times are, but the changes are part of a longer story of ecological shifts and thus look much less abrupt and cataclysmic than do shifts measured in purely human terms.

To take seriously the conditions that cause this plant to flourish or wilt, and to consider them historically relevant, turns out to be a powerful investigative tool. Pondering the chestnut, a plant with quite strict requirements for health and growth, as it diffused itself across Italian and European landscapes in late antiquity, raises the question of how social and cultural conditions came into being that were so perfectly congruent with the ecological needs of this species. Study of chestnuts, in other words, reveals important clues about important transformative mechanisms at work among human communities of the first millennium AD.

Considering the role of a particularly productive tree like the chestnut clarifies first-millennium patterns of economic change most of all. Fluctuations in the size and location of Italian chestnut woods remind us of how dynamic landscapes are, but understanding what drove fluctuations in land use between the fourth and eleventh centuries, and popularized chestnuts, uncovers the fundamental productive processes whereby people lived. It turns out that chestnuts grow mostly where and when people have them grow, so chestnuts are a very useful indication of the strategies and choices of people, especially of those who worked on the land: in the early Middle Ages, the vast majority. Chestnuts, and human willingness to tend to them, illuminate the economic reorientations whereby a Roman Italy of cities, agricultural surpluses, and markets turned into a medieval Italy of villages and subsistence farming. Chestnuts therefore indicate how people actually may have coped with the decline and fall of the Roman empire, and permit much less lachrymose versions of early medieval history to emerge than those Gibbon made canonical.

These are some of the reasons that brought me to consider chestnuts, and finally to write a book about them. Writing any book, perhaps more

---

[3] Microhistory generally eschews longues durées: E. Muir, "Introduction," in *Microhistory and the Lost Peoples of Europe*, ed. E. Muir and G. Ruggiero (Baltimore, 1991), vii–xxviii (vii).

so a book like this (despite kindly curiosity about its motives), is a solitary exercise, but the writer's solitude elicits so much solidarity and companionship that one can sometimes forget it. I am very thankful to many people who helped me understand chestnuts better, and write more clearly about them, over several years. After enquiring about why I was doing research on the history of chestnuts, some actually read portions of this book, and generously suggested numberless improvements to it. Among them, in alphabetical order, are Bill Bamberger, Sueann Caulfield, Alison Cornish, Hussein Fancy, Richard Hoffmann, Sue Juster, Rick Keyser, Val Kivelson, Peggy McCracken, Massimo Montanari, Leslie Pincus, Helmut Puff, Ray Van Dam, and Chris Wickham. Oliver Rackham and two anonymous readers for Cambridge University Press read the whole manuscript and contributed signally to making it a better book than it would have been.

I am grateful to Hendrik Dey, Joachim Henning, Helena Kirchner, Federico Marazzi, Fabio Saggioro, and Robyn Veal who kindly supplied useful references; to Ben Graham for rewarding conversations about trees and history; and to Noah Blan for teaching me about the Plan of St. Gall. Many inspiring botanical conversations with Jack Ullman, and many trips among trees with him, contributed much to this book. So did Vangelis Zournatjis, who drew the maps with care and flair. My comprehension of ancient chestnuts was enriched both by Mimmo Piegari who in 2007 took me for a memorable visit to a chestnut grove in the Alburni mountains above Buccino (and to an equally memorable lunch afterwards), and who sadly has died since, and by the Santini family, who took time off from their busy lumber business at Santa Restituta to instruct me in the niceties of modern chestnut-husbandry.

Audiences at York University, Western Michigan University, and the University of Michigan heard attempts to make sense of the chestnuts with unwarranted benignity, and pointed me in useful directions with their questions, including the usual one about how I had gotten interested in the nuts to begin with.

I am also grateful for support from the University of Michigan's Humanities Award, and to the local history department, which allowed me time to write about chestnuts. The Ecole française de Rome and the Istituto storico italiano per il medioevo deserve my thanks for providing excellent places in their libraries to read and write about chestnuts. Further thanks are due to the staff at the University of Michigan's Hatcher Library, who efficiently procured materials, no matter how obscure, when I needed them, including when I was not in Ann Arbor.

Finally, I dedicate the book to Cristina, who did very little for it, beyond always noticing trees and being an avid consumer of chestnuts. But she asked for it, and for her that is enough.

ABBREVIATIONS

CDA	*Codice diplomatico amalfitano*, 2 vols., Vol. 1, ed. R. Filangieri di Candida (Naples, 1917)
CDB	*Codice diplomatico del monastero di S. Colombano di Bobbio*, 3 vols., Vol. 1, ed. C. Cipolla (Rome, 1918)
CDC	*Codex diplomaticus cavensis*, 10 vols., ed. M. Morcaldi, M. Schiani, S. De Stefano, *et al.*, Vols. I–III, VIII (Naples, 1873; Milan, 1875–76, 1893)
CDL	*Codice diplomatico longobardo*, 5 vols., ed. L. Schiaparelli, C. Brühl, and H. Zielinski (Rome, 1929–33, 1981, 1983)
CDLang	*Codex diplomaticus Langobardiae*, ed. G. Porro Lambertenghi (Turin, 1873)
CDV	*Codice diplomatico verginiano*, 13 vols., Vol. 1 ed. P. Tropeano (Montevergine, 1977)
CISAM	Centro italiano per lo studio dell'alto medioevo
CLA	*Chartae latinae antiquiores*
CP	*Il codice Perris, cartulario amalfitano*, 5 vols., Vol. 1, ed. J. Mazzoleni and R. Orefice (Amalfi, 1985)
CSMN	*Le carte dello archivio capitolare di Santa Maria di Novara*, 3 vols., ed. F. Gabotto (Pinerolo, 1913)
MGH	Monumenta Germaniae historica
MPL	Patrologia latina, ed. J.-P. Migne

INTRODUCTION: TREES, WOODS, AND CHESTNUTS IN EARLY MEDIEVAL ITALY

In the early Middle Ages, trees were seldom just trees, simple clumps of cellulose and chlorophyll. People loaded them with meaning. A rare Latin saint's life, probably produced in the south Italian metropolis of Benevento, shows this double identity of trees as matter and construct clearly.

Somewhat unusually for early medieval hagiography, the *Life of Barbatus, the Beneventan Bishop* begins in the thick of things, bypassing the traditional preliminaries about the holy man's holy birth, upbringing, and rise to prominence. The anonymous hagiographer, who seems to have written late in the Carolingian era, launched his account with the decisive event in Barbatus' career, one that took place in 663 when Barbatus was already in his sixties, a very old man.[1] In fact, Barbatus' great deed constitutes virtually the whole composition, for the *Vita* says almost nothing about the life of Barbatus, either as a young man, or as bishop, *after* he had successfully turned the Beneventan Lombards from their lamentable pagan rituals. The moment of conversion instead deserved the full attention of writer and audience, and was described graphically, beginning with the "primitive rite of paganism" ("priscum gentilitatis ritum") that male Lombards practiced around Benevento in the mid seventh century. In the *Vita*, the "beastly" barbarians worshipped a beast, more exactly a viper, in unspecified ways. Near the city they also worshipped a "sacred tree" on designated holidays, in ways the

---

[1] *Vita Barbati* quotes Paul's *History of the Lombards* so presumably post-dates it. J. Martin, "A propos de la *Vita* de Barbatus," *Mélanges de l'Ecole française de Rome* 86 (1974), 137–64, dated the text to the late 800s. Its death scene, set in 682, says the saint was eighty, so the opening events occurred when he was about sixty. S. Gasparri, *La cultura tradizionale dei Longobardi* (Spoleto, 1983), 69–91 comments extensively and cites the bibliography.

author specified lavishly.[2] The *Vita's* opening scene reveals how the tree cult worked: an animal's skin was hung from the tree's branches, then all present turned their backs on it and rode their horses hard away from the trunk, as if in a race. At a designated moment they swerved around and charged back at the skin-festooned tree. As they reached it the worshippers struck the suspended skin and tore small bits off it to eat "superstitiously."[3]

Such strange and (as far as I know) unparalleled exercises were "offerings" (*vota*) and to the hagiographer explained the Lombards' choice of a name for the place where the tree grew, Votum.[4] But if the tree's name was so deeply imprinted onto the hills of the southern Lombard world that two centuries after the ritual an erudite hagiographer needed to explain how a local church got its puzzling epithet (S. Maria de Voto), the tree itself proved much less solidly rooted. In the *Vita's* narrative Barbatus exploited the panic caused in Benevento by a Byzantine siege of 663, led by the first Roman emperor seen in Italy since 476, to win over to orthodoxy the tree-worshipping, viper-loving unbelievers. As soon as the Emperor Constans II had obligingly marched his Byzantine troops off to Naples, Barbatus personally hacked down the "abominable tree" with an axe, then dug up the roots and piled up earth over the stump "so no-one could find even a trace of the tree" thereafter. Barbatus' victory over the tree was completed when, in the very next sentence of the *Vita*, the locals unanimously elected him bishop of Benevento.[5]

Barbatus' arboricide is an extraordinary episode in early medieval religious and arboreal history, interesting in itself for many reasons. For

---

[2] *Vita Barbati episcopi Beneventani*, ed. G. Waitz, in *Scriptores rerum Langobardicarum et Italicarum saec. VI–IX*, MGH, Scriptores rerum Langobardicarum (Hanover, 1878), 557–64 (Chapter 1, 557):

> sicut bestiali mente degebant, bestiae simulacro, quae vulgo vipera nominatur, flectebant colla … non longe a Beneventi menibus quasi sollempnem diem sacram colebant arborem, in qua suspendentes corium, cuncti qui adherant terga vertentes arbori celerius equitabant, calcaribus cruentantes equos, ut unus alteri possit prehire; atque in eodem cursu retroversis manibus corium iaculabant, iaculatoque particulam modicam ex eo comedendi superstitiose accipiebant.

[3] The animal might have been a goat: A. Pratesi, "Barbato," in *Dizionario biografico degli Italiani*, 76 vols., Vol. VI (Rome, 1961), 128–30. On the rising suspicion of goats in post-classical times: J. Voisenet, *Bêtes et hommes dans le monde médiéval* (Turnhout, 2000), 32.

[4] Waitz, the editor (557 n. 2) recorded another manuscript's version, wherein the site was called Votum "until today" because "of the offering of the tree." The irony of the hagiographer undermining the saint's attempt to erase the tree from earth was manifestly intended. Like any "damnatio memoriae," to be effective this one could not obliterate all memory of the object of oblivion. On Benevento's early churches: S. Carella, *Architecture religieuse haut-médiévale en Italie méridionale: Le diocèse de Bénévent* (Turnhout, 2011), 19–70.

[5] *Vita Barbati*, Chapter 7, 560: "Repente beatissimus Barbatus securem accipiens, Votum pergens, et suis manibus nefandam arborem … defossa humo a radicibus incidit, ac desuper terrae congeriem fecit, ut nec inditium ex ea quis valeat repperire. Recesso igitur hoste, uterque sexus et aetas ad beatissimi Barbati episcopatus electionem unanimiter confluxerunt …" After the election, Duke

my purposes here, however, what matters most is the power of the tree. To Barbatus, to his hagiographer, and to the audiences of the *Vita*, it was self-evident that a tree could have a magnetic pull on the souls of people, and that it could be central to the identities of unbelievers in the region of Benevento. The tree's excision demonstrated Barbatus' authority and was the climax in an (otherwise undocumented) seventh-century struggle between Roman Christianity and the "sacrilegious" ancestral paganism of the Lombards. Without the tree to support them and their rituals, age-old error rapidly receded and the Lombards became observant believers, willing to submit to a bishop. The tree, in other words, was literally and metaphorically the hub around which spun the spokes of local religion and community, enacted by the horse charges. For this reason it had to be utterly destroyed, stump and all.

Barbatus' holy tree did not stand alone in the religious landscape of early medieval Europe. The links between trees, communal identity, and pagan religiosity were well known to the first Christian emperors, who sought to staunch the flow of unbelief in the empire from the late fourth century by depriving temples of their financing, pagans of their right to worship in public, and sacred trees and groves of their frequenters: the *Theodosian Code* included a stipulation of 392 rendering it illegal, and punishable by the confiscation of one's house, to loiter in the sacred glens or deck the empire's holy trees with garlands.[6] If the prescriptions of the late Roman state were not enough, the private enterprise of zealous Christians supplemented them. St. Martin, perhaps the most successful western Christian holy man of late antiquity, famously made short work of a holy pine to which peasants near Tours had been showing excessive respect at around the time when the Theodosian law was drawn up.[7] Unlike Barbatus, Martin got the pagans to chop the tree down themselves, in hopes of its crushing him, and unlike Barbatus, did not worry at all about the stump. But the similarities remain: Barbatus' axe-wielding exertions in effect lifted a hitherto obscure south Italian holy man to parity with the West's most exalted saint, for chopping down trees meant a lot in the decline of the Roman empire.

In fact, if the *Life of Barbatus* was written in the 800s its readers would have had fresher examples of meaningful tree-cutting to mull over and compare with that of Barbatus in the 660s. Clerical anxieties about marginal locations in the landscape, such as those exhibited in the Beneventan biography, are also visible in Anglo-Saxon England, where non-Christian

---

Romuald offered the bishopric jurisdiction over the holy cave of St. Michael in the Gargano, a proper destination of religious mobility, unlike the tree. Asserting Beneventan rights in the Gargano probably motivated the author: Carella, *Architecture*, 218–19.

[6] *Codex Theodosianus* 16.10.12.2. See R. Trifone, *Storia del diritto forestale in Italia* (Florence, 1957), 4.

[7] Sulpicius Severus, *Vita Martini* 13.

tree cults persistently called into question the depth of Christian commitment in places removed from episcopal surveillance.[8] In the early eighth century the success of the English missionary Boniface in Hesse had a lot to do with his divinely mediated destruction of an oak tree sacred to the divinity of thunder and fertility, Jupiter or Thunor, thereby rendering the region fit for Christian habitation.[9] Shortly thereafter the monastic writers of the *Royal Frankish Annals* celebrated Charlemagne as destroyer of the Irminsul, a tree or tree trunk somewhere in Germany that some people supposed (erroneously, as it turned out) held up the heavens: this was a decisive event in the Frankish effort to subdue the Saxons and eradicate paganism in the Carolingian East.[10] A few decades after this, far beyond the furthest reaches of Carolingian rule, in the Crimea of the 860s, St. Cyril-Constantine too stamped out heathenism by eliminating its arboreal bulwark, according to a story that may well have circulated in Rome, an early center of devotion to the "apostles of the Slavs."[11] Even centuries after the fall of the Roman empire and the Christianization of its territories, people understood very well the religious potency of trees. It added poignancy to human interactions with them.[12]

In early medieval Italy, as in Carolingian Saxony, ninth-century Crimea, or late antique Gaul, trees were mighty things, far greater than the sum of their leaves, branches, and root stocks. The biography of Barbatus therefore offers a privileged peek into a landscape where trees were simultaneously physical, botanical facts, and cultural artifacts. Trees, and their associations in stands like groves, woods, and forests,[13] enjoyed a special form of double citizenship as things and ideas that other forms of vegetation – say prairie grasses or kelp beds – never quite attained. More than other plants, real trees

[8] C. Cusack, *The Sacred Tree: Ancient and Medieval Manifestations* (Newcastle upon Tyne, 2011), 121–46; A. Walsham, *The Reformation of the Landscape* (Oxford, 2011), 11, 22–25, 37–42. Walsham shows nicely how the landscape and the trees in it sustained the "economy of the sacred" in ancient Britain, as well as Reformation England.

[9] Willibald, *Vita santi Bonifatii*, ed. W. Levison, MGH, Scriptores rerum Germanicarum in usum scholarum 57 (Hannover, 1905), 1–58 (31).

[10] *Annales regni Francorum*, AD 772, supplemented by Rudolf of Fulda's *Translatio S. Alexandri* 2–3, ed. G. Pertz, *MGH* Scriptores 2 (Hanover, 1829), 673–81 (675–76). See Cusack, *The Sacred Tree*, 101–12. In Lombard Italy, eighth-century "rustici" had to be restrained from trees they called "holyfied" ("sanctivus") by fines: "Leges Liutprandi regis," ed. F. Blühme, in *Leges Langobardorum*, MGH, Leges 4 (Hanover, 1868), 96–182, Chapter 84 (142).

[11] *The Vita of Constantine and the Vita of Methodius*, trans. M. Kantor and R. White (Ann Arbor, 1976), Chapter 12, 41–43. Constantine personally hacked the tree down, but its dismemberment, uprooting, and burning were collective activities.

[12] C. Higounet, "Les forêts de l'Europe occidentale du ve au xie siècle," in *Agricoltura e mondo rurale in occidente nell'alto medioevo*, Settimane del CISAM 13 (1966), 343–98 (383), noted tree cults still worried eleventh-century clergymen. See also Gasparri, *La cultura*, 76–78.

[13] A distinction based on size, complexity, and density. A grove is smaller and likely more open, with fewer species; a wood is bigger, less open, more varied; a forest or wildwood is large and likely quite thick with diverse trees.

sprouted alter egos in people's consciousness and the two grew together, becoming indivisible to human observers. Early medieval writers noted particularly how trees spread up and down, uniting by their verticality different components of the world, and noted too deciduous trees' apparently endless ability to spring back to life each year and indeed to never stop growing, a consolation for human mortality and certainly a feature that set trees apart from "annual" vegetation.[14] Indeed, it helps to explain why Carolingian monks planted their cemeteries with trees.[15]

Such observations were by no means uniquely early medieval, or even European. Frazer's enormous *Golden Bough* catalogued a dizzying array of European, Asian, and American creeds built on the vegetative properties of trees.[16] Thus, if there may have been a special early medieval willingness to ascribe dangerous supernatural power to trees, thinking trees remarkable forms of life, thinking about and with trees, and classifying trees apart from other plants was normal. For instance, trees have seemed to many different people to join disparate realms of existence, aerial, terrestrial, and subterranean.[17] Furthermore, anthropological studies show how the most disparate communities assign meaning to trees' vitality, and Maurice Bloch has speculated that trees attract so much attention, and end up doing so much cultural work for people, because trees' tenacious attachment to living somehow reminds people of themselves.[18] Manifestly alive and subject to the same processes of birth, growth, maturity, and degeneration that humans undergo, trees offer powerful analogues to the human condition.

But if the life cycles of trees are rather human, trees are nevertheless quite different from people. Their durability, seasonality, and immobility set trees apart, as does the fact that trees continue to grow even in maturity. The resulting ambiguous situation of trees, simultaneously like and unlike people, is what makes them perfect symbolic tools.[19] Often enough, the self-reliance of trees and their capacity to outlive humans has contributed to their adoption as representations of human communities'

---

[14] D. Hooke, *Trees in Anglo-Saxon England* (Woodbridge, 2010), 5; S. Schama, *Landscape and Memory* (New York, 1995), 14–15; H. Birkhan, *Die Pflanzen im Mittelalter* (Vienna, 2012), 8–9.

[15] C. Frugoni, "Alberi in *paradiso voluptatis*," in *L'ambiente vegetale nell'alto medioevo*, Settimane del CISAM 37 (Spoleto, 1990), 725–62 (756).

[16] The general index to Frazer's classic contains three columns of entries on tree cults and beliefs. J. Frazer, *The Golden Bough*, 12 vols., Vol. II (London, 1913), Chapters 9 ("The Worship of Trees") and 20 ("The Worship of the Oak") are most pertinent, but Frazer delineated Christian accommodation to ancient arboreal beliefs in Chapter 10 ("Relics of Tree Worship in Modern Europe").

[17] Cusack, *The Sacred Tree*, 1–3, 9.

[18] L. Rival, "Trees, from Symbols of Life and Regeneration to Political Artefacts," in *The Social Life of Trees*, ed. L. Rival (Oxford, 1998), 2–3, 7–9; M. Bloch, "Why Trees, Too, Are Good to Think With," in Rival, *The Social Life of Trees*, 39–55 (40–44).

[19] Bloch, "Why Trees," 48–52. Birkham, *Die Pflanzen*, 9 compares trees' ceaseless growth to that of animal horns and human nails.

historical continuity, for people know their trees have been and will be around much longer than they will. Since trees stretch comfortingly between past, present, and future, perhaps especially where a community seeks to give concrete expression, in a specific place, to its relationship with time, trees can carry meaning.[20] That, after all, is what happened outside Benevento, where the "abominable tree" permitted Carolingian hagiographers to connect present with past inhabited space.

Dark Age men, then, and not just Barbatus and his hagiographer, assigned to trees a special ability to communicate meanings to people. Barbatus in particular made a brilliant career for himself by recognizing trees' liminal status, and by challenging the cultural might and physical presence of the Beneventan tree. But we should recall that such antagonistic relations with trees were only one of many ways early medieval people could interact with the taller plants, and in Christian culture some trees were highly praiseworthy and had positive roles to play in God's creation.[21] Either way, the point remains the same: in order to understand the early Middle Ages we must take seriously the arboreal landscape of that time, both as a physical reality and as an agent in early medieval imaginations.

SCALE AND MEANING IN THE WOODS

Trees and treed landscapes had peculiar cultural importance in the early Middle Ages, and have attracted historians' attention in consequence.[22] Very much related to this cultural evaluation of Europe's arboreal vegetation have been discussions of the actual prevalence of medieval woodlands, for their extent and their significance in European culture go together. In the case of Italy, divergent reconstructions of post-Roman woodland history actually seem to converge around the opinion that the Italian peninsula became more wooded after antiquity.

For in some analyses the waning of classical civilization coincided with irresponsible and even catastrophic mismanagement of woodland; this profligate behavior is held to have led to denuded hillsides, topsoil erosion, loss of agricultural productivity, excessive deposition in river

---

[20] Rival, "Trees," 17–19.

[21] Frugoni, "Alberi," 725–62, surveys early medieval Christian thinking on the trees of Eden. See also for later developments P. Dronke, "*Arbor caritatis*," in *Medieval Studies for J. A. W. Bennet*, ed. P. Heyworth (Oxford, 1981), 207–53.

[22] A benchmark of the scholarly acceptability of the topic is the Spoletan "Settimana di studio" about "the vegetative environment" organized in 1989. The resulting publication included seven major articles focused on early medieval trees, arboriculture, and forestry, and several others giving prominence to trees: Settimane del CISAM 37.

valleys, and outbreaks of deadly disease.[23] In other evaluations the end of Rome's hegemony corresponded to a frightful surge in the number of trees and the area they occupied, at the expense of human habitation.[24] Yet this is an apparent opposition only, for even the "catastrophic deforestation thesis" rests on the assumption that post-classical peoples' wanton destruction occurred because of a superabundance of trees and woods that allowed a wasteful, myopic mentality to develop.[25] In the end it seems fair to say that the idea of woodland increasing across Italy from the fifth century on enjoys a scholarly consensus.

This view may have some empirical grounding, but certainly it is an aspect of the trope that sees everywhere in the early Middle Ages a "return of nature," a version that holds on even as the naturalness of the early medieval wilderness comes into question (a topic to be addressed below). For instance, Jacques Le Goff's great *Civilization of the Medieval West* describes Europe in the wake of Rome's demise as cloaked by thick woods, very much seen as the corollary to barbarity, and effectively characterizes concurrent civilization as "the world of wood."[26] Half a century after that magisterial effort, the advance of forests, the retreat of arable fields, and the rise of Rome's barbarian successor states continue to appear as synchronous and related phenomena.[27] Indeed, with only slight exaggeration one could say that a favorite scholarly measure of the "transformation of the Roman world" during late antiquity is the relentless forward march of forest. Such a conceptualization held sway throughout the twentieth century. In Italy the magisterial writings of the academic geographer Arrigo Lorenzi set the tone at the end of World War I: his lectures and articles proved that the early medieval forest surged

[23] G. Marsh, *Man and Nature* (Seattle, 2003 [1864]), 7–13 and esp. Chapter 3 first articulated such views. See also J. Hughes, *Pan's Travail: Environmental Problems of the Ancient Greeks and Romans* (Baltimore, 1994), 73–90, 188–91; and J. McNeill, *The Mountains*, which applies the same idea (depopulation leads to ecological cataclysm) to the 1900s. C. Watkins and K. Kirby, "Historical Ecology and the European Woodland," in *The Ecological History of European Forests* (Wallingford, 1998), ix–xx (xi), astutely note historians' obsession with deforestation as opposed to forest management practices.

[24] Higounet, "Les forêts"; C. Wickham, "European Forests in the Early Middle Ages," in *L'ambiente vegetale nell'alto medioevo*, Settimane del CISAM 37 (Spoleto, 1990), 479–545; B. Andreolli and M. Montanari, eds., *Il bosco nel medioevo* (Bologna, 1988); A. Giardina, "Allevamento ed economia della selva in Italia meridionale: Trasformazioni e continuità," in *Società romana e produzione schiavistica*, 3 vols., ed. A. Giardina and A. Schiavone, Vol. 1 (Bari, 1981), 87–113 (106–09).

[25] A. Lorenzi, "L'uomo e le foreste," *Rivista geografica italiana* 25 (1918), 141–65, 213–42; 26 (1919), 47–57 (25: 238–39) gives a classic exposition of the "familiarity-breeds-contempt" theory. See also Trifone, *Storia del diritto*, iii–iv, 29; M. Montanari, *Campagne medievali: Strutture produttive, rapporti di lavoro, sistemi alimentari* (Turin, 1984), 16.

[26] *La civilisation de l'Occident médiéval* (Paris, 1964), 169 ("un grand manteau de forêts"), 258 ("le monde du bois"). Cf. R. Doehard, *Le haut moyen âge occidental* (Paris, 1971), 94–109.

[27] J. Devroey, *Économie rurale et société dans l'Europe franque (VIe–IXe siècles)*, Vol. 1 (Paris, 2003), 312 (but cf. 27). Hooke, *Trees*, 113–18, shows how Anglo-Saxon studies lately qualify the late ancient "return of nature" and forest.

forward across the Roman agricultural landscape from the third century, facilitated by barbarian settlers and their woodsy culture.[28] To Lorenzi, the most reliable allies of the barbarian hordes were arboreal.

As the biography of Barbatus already adumbrated, there are sound cultural reasons for the scholarly penchant to link afforestation and "the barbarian invasions." The Germanic people who settled inside the western empire's provinces from the fourth century onwards are thought to have been related to those the first-century Roman aristocrat Tacitus wrote about in his ethnographic polemic *Germania*. In Tacitus' treatise the northern barbarians are tightly bound both culturally and economically to trees and forests. Simon Schama has luminously illustrated this Tacitean symbiosis between barbarians from Germany and their woodland home, and how it became a fixture in early *and* fully modern texts, to the point that a first-century literary concoction seems to have inspired and motivated sixteenth-century patriotic diatribes, nineteenth-century scientific forestry, and twentieth-century combat operations.[29] Ironically, then, the *Germania*, a Roman text utterly ignored during the Middle Ages, gave a decisive nudge to Renaissance and later interpretations of the early medieval period as especially woodsy. It is by no means the only ingredient, but Tacitus' account of forest-based noble savagery has leavened conceptions of post-Roman landscapes and the people in them until today.

Ultimately, the early medieval forest in modern accounts is as loaded with meaning as Barbatus' tree in his *Vita*. The Dark Age forest signifies something more than just trees. To modern observers it tends to mean primitive, barbarous, perhaps even Germanic times.[30] The tradition is venerable and extends past Tacitus: in sedentary agrarian societies, like the Roman or modern ones, woods often imply economic underdevelopment and cultural backwardness, no matter what people actually did in those woods. Shady forests are an inscrutable opposite of open-sky agriculture and bright cultural productivity in a way that neither scrublands nor swamps or any other land form can quite equal.[31]

Thus the Roman man of letters Varro, a contemporary of Cicero, postulated that there had been (or could be) exactly three stages of human economic and cultural development, beginning with hunting (in forests); moving through herding (in forest clearings); and finally attaining the loftiest stage of human engagement with nature, agriculture (without forests).[32]

---

[28] Lorenzi, "L'uomo," 224, 48–52.

[29] Schama, *Landscape*, 83–116.

[30] For instance P. Dutton, *Charlemagne's Mustache* (New York, 2004), 44, who excellently deconstructs the cultural associations of animals, but not of trees.

[31] Watkins and Kirby, "Historical Ecology," xi.

[32] Varro, *De agri cultura* 2.3–5.

In Varro's teleological scheme, as in other ancient developmental sequences like the fifth book of Lucretius' *De rerum natura*, the first humans had consorted with trees and lived among them and from them. Then, as civilized practices took hold, so did arable agriculture, and trees subsided in consequence. At the very inception of the ancient literary tradition, Hesiod imagined the earliest people living from oak trees' bounty, something Roman authors such as Pliny the Elder readily accepted while noting that in more recent times no one ate acorns any more, save as a desperate measure when grain harvests failed.[33] Similarly, the Roman architectural writer Vitruvius suggested that huts of tree branches and nests of twigs, the first human habitations, had (rightly) given way to masonry constructions in the forward progress that led straight to the happy times of Augustus, whose subject Vitruvius was. Whether gastronomic, architectural, or economic, ancient culture consistently presented an emancipation from the forest and from trees as the great leap forward in human history.[34]

As Barbatus' adventures show, the ancient literary convention that consigned the woods to archaic times and considered them the locus of primitive ignorance lived on after antiquity. In the early 600s the encyclopedist bishop of Seville, Isidore, postulated that the first humans subsisted on woodland products, especially nuts, before discovering the advantages of agriculture and moving on, in an evolutionary narrative clearly based on classical Latin antecedents.[35] Later the Varronian tripartite division of early time into hunting, herding, and farming found numerous champions, including many who studied prehistory before the mid 1900s, though criteria for the subdivision of periods based on slightly different things (inert materials like stone or iron, for example) also became fashionable.[36] In all these accounts, the woods and wood-based economies always remained at the very beginning of reconstructions of the process that led to greater material plenty and intellectual sophistication.[37]

---

[33] Pliny the Elder, *Historia naturalis*, ed. J. André (Paris, 2003), 16.15.

[34] Vitruvius, *De architectura* 2.1.2–7. On forest primitivism, see T. Allsen, *The Royal Hunt in Eurasian History* (Philadelphia, 2006), 1–3; W. Logan, *Oak: The Frame of Civilization* (New York, 2005), 36–37. For context, see A. Lovejoy and G. Boas, *Primitivism and Related Ideas in Antiquity* (Baltimore, 1935), esp. Chapter 12.

[35] Isidore of Seville, *Etymologies* 17.7.26 in fact ascribes the notion to Virgil. See 17.7.28 for the claim that beech mast was early humans' preferred food; and G. Duchet-Suchaux, "Les noms des arbres," in *L'arbre: Histoire naturelle et symbolique de l'arbre, du bois et du fruit au Moyen Age* (Paris, 1993), 13–23 (21).

[36] D. Harris, "Domesticatory Relationships of People, Plants, and Animals," in *Redefining Nature*, eds. R. Ellen and K. Fukui (Oxford, 1996), 437–63 (440–46); G. Daniel, *The Origins and Growth of Archaeology* (Harmondsworth, 1967), 90–106. J. Radkau, *Wood: A History* (Cambridge, 2012), 14–18, points out that the Stone Age was actually another wood age, though prehistoric wooden implements have failed to survive as well as flints.

[37] Economic evolutions with three phases, the boskiest first, are imagined by M. Gadgil and R. Guha, *This Fissured Land: An Ecological History of India* (Berkeley, 1992), 34–37.

Most evolutionary schemes presume unlikely watertight periods following smoothly from each other without commingling their characteristics. Thus, any period when trees increased their physical and cultural presence could only be an anomaly, especially if it came *after* a period of intensified agricultural exploitation, like the Roman one. As a result, the early Middle Ages look like an interruption to European history's natural flow (forward), a throw-back to prehistoric conditions – in a word, a Dark Age. Save in an epochal cataclysm, a "sylvo-pastoral" economy like the early medieval one should not succeed an "agro-pastoral" one like the Roman. Any economy that relies heavily on or fails to reduce the incidence of woods is inferior to economies founded on sown crops and open fields. This hierarchy is also reflected in the cultures produced by each economy.[38]

This intellectual association of economic primitiveness, barbarians, and woodlands in ancient and medieval historiography is extremely solid. Even the revolutions in how history is written and how the "decline and fall of the Roman empire" is framed that occurred during the 1900s seem unable to topple it. The advent of abundant and precise archaeological data that probably did the most to change early medieval history in the late twentieth century likewise has not severed the ties between "Germanic" post-Roman societies, backward economies, and vast, thick forests, though it offers the best prospects for achieving this.

One curious but revealing dimension to this enduring association between underdevelopment and trees has been archaeologists' lively debates about post-Roman housing. The abandonment of the enormous and often luxurious villas of imperial or late Roman date that is a salient feature of sixth-century rural archaeology can indeed seem a clear marker of the decline and fall of the empire.[39] An empire whose capital the first emperor had reinvented made of bricks and marble, and whose most famous artifacts were all of masonry and clay, might rightly be pronounced dead when wooden constructions sprouted across its former provinces, and the majority of ceramic roof tiles or fired bricks in circulation were spoliated.[40] Indeed, in Italy, by the seventh century a lot of rural dwellings, and some urban ones too, seem to have been built exclusively

---

[38] R. Delort and F. Walter, *Histoire de l'environnement européen* (Paris, 2001), 192, suppose the shift from sylvo- to agro-pastoralism depended on demography.

[39] G. Brogiolo and A. Chavarría Arnau, *Aristocrazia e campagne nell'Occidente da Costantino a Carlomagno* (Florence, 2005), 34–7, 47–51.

[40] G. Brogiolo, "Nuove ricerche sulle campagne dell'Italia settentrionale tra tarda antichità e alto-medioevo," in *Castrum 5: Archéologie des espaces agraires méditerranéens au Moyen Age*, ed. A. Bazzana (Madrid, 1999), 153–65 (158), equates wood use and "segnali di decadenza."

from the products of the woods, with timber frames, thatch roofs, and light walls of wood whose fissures were sealed with mud.[41]

Though the archaeological footprint of such structures is understandably minimal (a few post-holes only, in some cases), the ancient traditions that classified woods and wood as primitive have made their cultural impact much deeper. The rise (and surprisingly late fall, in the twelfth and thirteenth centuries[42]) of wooden construction techniques in Italy becomes another sign of the barbarization of early medieval societies, probably because those techniques seem closer to forest-dwelling simplicity than those based on the kiln (ironically, a technology that was itself highly dependent on woodland resources).[43] Following this logic, the fashion for wooden houses and sheds archaeologists have uncovered in deposits from the post-classical centuries looks like a result either of the new and barbaric ubiquity of trees that rendered lumber cheaper and easier to deploy, or of a cultural shift (and technological impoverishment) brought about by Germanic settlers, whose atavistic predilection for wood, forests, and related products Tacitus established once and for all.[44] Either way, it is a decline, and either way another triumph for the linkage of trees and their bounty to specific cultural contexts. Anyone who has attempted to deal with lumber knows that building anything out of wood depends on highly

[41] Exceptionally fine data on such buildings come from Tuscany, where the University of Siena's excavations (at Scarlino, Montarrenti, Miranduolo, etc.) have been exemplary. See for instance M. Valenti: "Edilizia nel villaggio altomedievale di Miranduolo (Chiusdino, SI)," *Archeologia medievale* 35 (2008), 75–97; "Architecture and Infrastructure in the Early Medieval Village," in *Technology in Transition: AD 300–650*, ed. L. Lavan, E. Zanini, and A. Constantine Sarantis (Leiden, 2007), 451–89; and "La Toscana tra VI e IX secolo," in *La fine delle ville romane*, ed. G. Brogiolo (Mantua, 1996), 81–106. For Latium, see L. Sadori and F. Susanna, "Hints of Economic Change during the Late Roman Empire Period in Central Italy," *Vegetation History and Archaeobotany* 14 (2005), 386–94.

[42] In Latium, masonry only re-established itself in the 1200s: E. Hubert, "Maisons urbaines et maisons rurales dans le Latium médiéval," in *Castrum 6: Maisons et espaces domestiques dans le monde méditerranéen au moyen âge*, ed. A. Bazzana and E. Hubert (Rome, 2000), 89–103 (94–95); in Apulia, not known for trees, in the twelfth century: J. Martin, "Quelques données textuelles sur la maison en Campanie et en Pouille (xe–xiie siècle)," in *Castrum 6: Maisons et espaces domestiques dans le monde méditerranéen au moyen âge*, ed. A. Bazzana and E. Hubert (Rome, 2000), 75–87 (78–80). V. Fronza, "Strumenti e materiali per un atlante dell'edilizia altomedievale in materiale deperibile," in *IV congresso nazionale di archeologia medievale*, ed. R. Francovich and M. Valenti (Florence, 2006), 539–45 (543), proposes a shorter chronology.

[43] Schama, *Landscape*, 87, 95, traces the development of Tacitean tropes of wood versus marble, iron versus gold, furs versus silk, forest austerity versus urbane luxury.

[44] Both "cultural" arguments (barbarians liked wood) and "functional" ones (it was easier to get) have enjoyed currency: see P. Galetti, *Abitare nel medioevo* (Florence, 1997), 34, 80, 86; Valenti, "La Toscana," 92 and "Architecture," 459; M. Valenti, "L'insediamento altomedievale," in *Poggio Imperiale a Poggibonsi*, ed. R. Francovich and M. Valenti (Florence, 1996), 79–142 (381). C. Citter, "L'Italia centrale tirrenica in età carolingia," in *V congresso nazionale di archeologia medievale*, ed. G. Volpe and P. Favia (Florence, 2009), 302–05 (304), interestingly linked wood construction with peasant submission. Hubert, "Maisons," 96, pointed out lumber's extremely *high* value in medieval documents.

sophisticated techniques of management, procurement, and assembly, yet the new-style late antique and early medieval structures built of wood receive little dispassionate attention as reflections of the choices or strategies of the peasants who inhabited them.[45] The "world of wood" seems to confirm the spread of dark forests and the involution of civilization.

Just as superior excavation techniques have given scholars access to the "world of wood" in Italy and its characteristic timber huts in the last few decades, so too have much more refined excavation techniques opened dazzling prospects on real late antique woodlands, their extent, and their composition. Yet the emergence of new scientific disciplines within archaeology, and their application to post-classical sites, have so far failed to revolutionize the standard narratives about the "return of nature" and large-scale afforestation. Of course there *have* been sites in Italy where careful and technologically refined studies point to increased arboreal cover in the centuries after 500 or so, in some way confirming the traditional notions of chaotic afforestation after Rome's fall. The bones of the animals eaten at Monte Gelato, near Rome, in the centuries between 550 and 950, suggest the locals had access to reliable woods where the animals could shelter and feed: the bank vole (*Chlethrionomys glareolus*), in Italy now found only in a few remote recesses of the Gargano and Sila forests, was a popular snack in early medieval Monte Gelato, just north of Rome.[46] The very consistent presence of the remains of pigs and sheep in early medieval Italian middens, for example in Milan, Florence, and Rome, has suggested to most scholars the abundant availability of wooded pasture where these domestic animals could flourish.[47] Several of the exceptionally well-excavated and well-published early medieval sites in southern Tuscany appear to have arisen in wooded landscapes. For instance, judging from pollen deposits, Maremman Scarlino's coastal forests recovered vigor after Roman exploitation of Elba's ironworks subsided.[48] Meanwhile, in Piedmont, around Alba, pine, fir, and spruce forests asserted themselves in late antiquity where, earlier, fields had lain.[49]

---

[45] C. Wickham, *Framing the Early Middle Ages* (Oxford, 2005), 516, is an exception.
[46] A. King, "Mammal, Reptile, and Amphibian Bones," in *Excavations at the Mola di Monte Gelato*, ed. T. Potter and A. King (Rome, 1997), 383–403 (389, 393, 397, 399).
[47] M. Biasotti and R. Giovinazzo, "Reperti faunistici," in *Scavi MM3* 3.2, ed. D. Caporusso (Milan, 1991), 167–84 (167); C. Corridi, "Dati archeozoologici dagli scavi di Piazza della Signoria a Firenze," in *Atti del 1 Convegno nazionale di archeologia* (Florence, 1995), 331–39 (331–33); J. De Grossi Mazzorin and C. Minniti, "L'allevamento e l'approvvigionamento alimentare di una comunità urbana," in *Roma dall'antichità al medioevo*, 2 vols., ed. M. Arena and L. Paroli, Vol. 1 (Milan, 2001), 69–78 (69–70, 72–73).
[48] C. Cucini, "Topografia del territorio delle valli del Pecora e dell'Alma," in *Scarlino 1: Storia e territorio*, ed. R. Francovich (Florence, 1985), 147–320 (163).
[49] R. Caramiello and A. Zeme, "Analisi palinologiche," *Alba Pompeia* 13 (1992), 43.

It stands to reason that the collapse of urban demand for wood after about 500 was good for Italy's trees, and it seems probable that on balance woodland grew as people dwindled and agriculture retreated.[50] But if there was one general characteristic to the post-Roman landscape, this would have to be its extreme heterogeneity. For each archaeological study proving more trees filled more space in the early Middle Ages than at the height of Rome's hegemony, there are others where it appears the Dark Age forests actually receded. For example, a particularly ingenious archaeobotanical reconstruction linked the feeding patterns of owls, visible in their fossilized pellets found in a Corsican cave, to the evolution of arboreal vegetation and the kinds of prey it made available to the nocturnal predators: in this case late antique forest cover diminished, as the owls then ate creatures that live in open spaces.[51] Meanwhile, just across the Tyrrhenian Sea, at Prato Spilla, an upland Apennine site between Parma and the Ligurian Sea, between the late sixth and late seventh centuries major shifts in vegetation occurred after centuries of stability. Palynologists detect significant deforestation there around 600 (a date that stands out in their 12,000-year spectrum), with beech trees favored at the expense of other species. The object was to form clearings where hay would grow, pasturage that the leaves and mast of the beeches supplemented. Prato Spilla's settlers are unlikely to have spent their winters at the site, which lies at an altitude of 1,350 m and so is under snow for some time each year, but they opened up the woods to support their cattle, and thereby themselves. In effect, an area Roman shepherds had crossed only occasionally began to be exploited *more* intensively in the darkest Dark Ages.[52] Nor was Prato Spilla just a highland eccentricity. The low-lying woods near Vercelli in the Po plain receded between about 500 and 750 in a quite similar pattern wherein pasturage strategies were paramount.[53]

In 2001, Grove and Rackham reminded everyone that, all told, the early medieval evidence for resurgent forests drawn from pollen deposits, the best indicator of real vegetation change, is inconclusive.[54] More than ten

---

[50] N. Christie, *From Constantine to Charlemagne* (Aldershot, 2006), 485–92, has sensible things to say on late ancient afforestation.

[51] J. Vigne, "Small Mammal Fossil Assemblages as Indicators of Environmental Change in Northern Corsica during the Last 2,500 Years," *Journal of Archaeological Science* 23 (1996), 207–11.

[52] C. Davite and D. Moreno, "Des 'saltus' aux 'alpes' dans les Apennins du nord (Italie)," in *L'homme et la nature au moyen âge*, ed. M. Colardelle (Paris, 1996), 138–42; J. Lowe, "Holocene Pollen Stratigraphy and Human Interference in the Woodlands of the Northern Apennines, Italy," *The Holocene* 4.2 (1994), 153–64.

[53] M. Negro Ponzi Mancini, "Ambiente e risorse alimentari: Data archeologici," in *San Michele di Trino (VC): Dal villaggio romano al castello medievale*, 3 vols., ed. M. Negro Ponzi Mancini, Vol. II (Florence, 1999), 549–73 (549).

[54] A. Grove and O. Rackham, *The Nature of Mediterranean Europe* (New Haven, 2001), 177.

years later, in the absence of any resounding archaeological confirmation that Italy's tilled fields vanished after the fourth century swallowed by the all-encompassing dark forest, the idea of a generalized, disorderly "naturalization" of the landscape, of massive uncontrolled afforestation, must remain a hypothesis, and one of whose ideological roots in classical classifications of economic activity we are aware. If it seems likely that, on the whole, woodland advanced from at least the fifth century, it is also likely that it did so opportunistically, and not everywhere, creating a mosaic effect of more and less wooded zones across the Italian peninsula. At least for now, the totally overwooded early medieval landscape must remain a metaphorical one.

PEOPLING THE WOODS

The imaginary woods that always accompany the real ones tend to seem wild, not at all anthropogenic, dominated by metaphors of the desert or of the "landscapes of fear."[55] A real achievement of late-twentieth-century historical and archaeological studies has been to demonstrate that actual early medieval woodlands were quite unlike that terrible wilderness. In fact, nowadays some scholars see signs of a "little cultural revolution" in the tenacious *integration* of woods into early medieval economic horizons.[56] Populated, utilized, and humanized territories, filled with herdsmen and their flocks, with hunters trapping game, with lumberjacks seeking firewood, with bee-keepers and berry pickers, as well of course as with a few holy people in search of solitude, such woods in Italy (and also in other parts of Europe) were an economic space, a type of landscape filled more with ordinary people making a living than with heroic hermits alienated from society. This is a reversal of the emphases given by prior scholarship, for in some current conceptions, Dark Age woodlands were, or maybe re-became after the imperial hiatus, rural societies' essential resource. Perhaps most importantly, the forest has been routinized somewhat, in the sense that scholars now stress how fully integrated this archetypal form of "uncultivated" land was in the agricultural routines of early medieval rural people.[57]

---

[55] Ascetics' pursuit of Egyptian solitude in Europe often led them into woods, which hagiographers duly called "desertum." R. Grégoire, "La foresta come esperienza religiosa," in L'ambiente vegetale nell'alto medioevo, Settimane del CISAM 37 (Spoleto, 1990), 663–703 (665–69), discusses Christian fears of woods. The English title of V. Fumagalli's essays on medieval attitudes to nature was borrowed from Y. Tuan, *Landscapes of Fear* (New York, 1979).

[56] M. Montanari, "La foresta come spazio economico e culturale," in *L'uomo e spazio nell'alto medioevo*, Settimane del CISAM 50 (Spoleto, 2003), 301–40 (338): "una piccola rivoluzione culturale." M. Godelier, *L'idéal et le matériel* (Paris, 1984), 50–61, argued that cultural appreciation of woods depends on economic use of them.

[57] Wickham, "European Forests," 479–545, L'ambiente vegetale nell'alto medioevo, is a much-cited survey of early medieval engagement with woods (usefully compared with Higounet's equally

Both in a magisterial survey of western Mediterranean ecological history and in scholarly articles Oliver Rackham has sought to describe the nature of this humanized forest.[58] To Rackham, variable but continuous maintenance for millennia has meant that Mediterranean woods were not densely packed with great trunks, but filled with clearings and isolated trees, an arrangement favorable to the growth of grasses various domestic animals liked to graze on, as well as to healthy trees with ample root space. This was as true in medieval times as it had been beforehand or was to be subsequently, an outcome of people's ongoing engagement with their arboreal resources and of pastoral strategies. Rackham's "savanna" may not match the Italian evidence perfectly (he drew many of his examples for it from Iberia), but it helpfully complicates the dense and impenetrable savagery we imagine in early medieval "uncultivated" landscapes, reminding us of how much maintenance uncultivation required. A good example of such anthropogenic woodland in early medieval Italy is Prato Spilla, the high Apennine site whose very long pollen deposition sequence allows inferences about Dark Age forest use: it had a "wooded meadow system" that was savanna-like in Rackham's sense, and was created by axes, firebrands, and hoes.[59] Though that wood developed in specific economic and strategic conditions (on a borderland at the time of Lombard settlement in the area), it is a nice demonstration of what an actual early medieval woodland in Italy was like. It was peopled.

People in the woods worked to maintain them, and it is hard to discern any post-Roman catastrophe for Italian woodlands. The traditional argument that in a period of superfluity, when there were more than enough trees available for the needs of a reduced population, there were no inducements to take care of a cheap resource, implied that a kind of "tragedy of the commons" ensued. Yet there is evidence of perfectly reasonable "forestry" practices in early medieval administrative documents, and these are confirmed to some extent by records of ash deposits that reveal changes in post-classical forest-burning patterns. For the Carolingian ruler of Italy Lothair I sought to restrain the practice of "starting a fire in the woods" by means of fines, beatings, and forcible

---

good survey ["Les forêts"] of twenty-five years before). The high-quality collection by Andreolli and Montanari, *Il bosco nel medioevo*, marked a turning point in Italian studies of post-classical woods. A good synthesis is B. Andreolli, "L'uso del bosco e degli incolti," in *Storia dell'agricoltura italiana*, 5 vols., Vol. II, ed. G. Pinto and M. Ambrosoli (Florence, 2002), 123–44.

[58] Grove and Rackham, *The Nature*, 46, 61, 191–95, 210–13; O. Rackham, "Savanna in Europe," in *The Ecological History of European Forests*, ed. C. Watkins and K. Kirby (Wallingford, 1998), 1–24. See also H. Allen, "Vegetation and Ecosystem Dynamics," in *The Physical Geography of the Mediterranean*, ed. J. Woodward (Oxford, 2009), 203–07 (206).

[59] See n. 52 above.

head shavings.[60] The capitulary in question, of 840, suggests governors' willingness to take stewardship of woods seriously; Lothair considered burning them "anywhere within the boundaries of the realm" as an offense. In this case, exceptionally, Carolingian conservation does not seem motivated by hunting and the desire to protect land where that important aristocratic activity could take place.[61] The attempt to regulate forest-burning falls within a period when bog deposits show lower influxes of charcoal dust (indicating less woodland combustion) across Italy.[62] It is certainly suggestive that in the period between 500 and 900 there were fewer forest fires than before or after, though assuredly it was not just because Lothair discouraged them. For the capitulary also reveals that somewhere in the kingdom of Italy people sought to create clearings with fire, either to benefit animals like sheep or deer (through the grasses that would grow where trees had burned) or perhaps to facilitate their cultivation of specific plants, which need not exclude trees.[63]

All in all, the Carolingian law shows as much forest management as it does mindless destruction of undervalued wilderness, spurred by its plentifulness. As woods were integral to early medieval productive strategies, a vital part of the sagacious diversification that protected peasants from the uncertainties of Mediterranean agriculture, they could not be blithely annihilated. In fact, early medieval woods functioned as the reservoir that permitted contemporary people to increase the range of foods they ate, and perhaps their standards of living too, in a medieval mirror to the "broad spectrum revolution" that had allowed some prehistoric communities to flourish by expanding the number of foods they consumed, while others floundered by specializing in a few easily obtainable foods.[64]

---

[60] *Capitularia regum Francorum 1*, MGH, Leges, Sectio II, ed. A. Boretius (Hanover, 1883), 168.3 (335): "volumus ut si quaelibet persona in finibus regni nostri ignem in silvam convivare ausa fuerit, diligenter inquiratur ..." For similar legislation, see M. McCormick, *Origins of the European Economy* (Cambridge, 2001), 730. More or less contemporary Byzantine agrarian law decriminalized forest arson: Trifone, *Storia del diritto*, 24.

[61] Here the woods seem a royal asset important because their donation could win loyalty from magnates and monasteries.

[62] B. Vannière, D. Colombaroli, E. Chapron, A. Leroux, W. Tinner, and M. Magny, "Climate versus Human-Driven Fire Regimes in Mediterranean Landscapes: The Holocene Record of Lago dell'Accesa (Tuscany, Italy)," *Quaternary Science Reviews* 27 (2008), 1181–96 (1188).

[63] An example of early medieval swidden techniques in action: G. Cherubini, "Le campagne," in *Storia della Calabria medievale*, 2 vols., ed. A. Placanica, Vol. II (Reggio, 2001), 429–66 (442).

[64] The idea that Stone Age humans raised their standards of living by increasing the kinds of food they ate, and thus made possible the first agricultural societies, derives from K. Flannery, "Origins and Effects of Early Near Eastern Domestication in Iran and the Near East," in *The Domestication and Exploitation of Plants and Animals*, ed. P. Ucko and G. Dimbleby (Chicago, 1969), 73–100. See, M. Stiner, N. Munro, and T. Surovell, "The Tortoise and the Hare: Small Game Use, the Broad-Spectrum Revolution, and Paleolithic Demography," *Current Anthropology* 41 (2000), 39–79 (39–41, 56–57).

But whether or not early medieval people enjoyed more and better nutrition than their ancestors had because they were more willing to seek it in the woods, the intensified frequentation of woodlands – widespread willingness to use the resources within them and consider woods a special type of productive space – was characteristic of early medieval Italian societies. Farmers, shepherds, hunters, charcoal-burners, and other people made their living in and through the woods, and in the process of doing so they altered the treed landscapes of the peninsula.

CHANGES IN THE WOODS

Both the traditional conception of a large-scale late antique "return" of the savage forest and the more recently established vision of early medieval woodlands as eminently humanized spaces acknowledge the vital characteristic of all medieval woods – that is to say, their dynamism. The moderate middle ground between the overwhelming wilderness and the virtual wooded factories proposed here, with a microregionalized, syncopated extension of wooded vegetation in Italy, often aligning with the interests of local inhabitants, likewise emphasizes mutability in early medieval woodland. It is important to recognize such changes as something inherent to wooded landscapes, as something we may call natural. In fact, framed in the spacious chronologies of historical-ecological studies, first-millennium changes in Italy's actual woods were a small twist in an ongoing series of adjustments in Mediterranean treed landscapes, always among the liveliest in Europe.[65]

Botanists, who have long known how far and how fast a wood can move when appropriately stimulated (most of all by climate) and who always pay attention to the complex interplay of species and modification of woodland composition over time, find this constantly evolving ecosystem unsurprising.[66] Indeed, by naturalizing "disturbance" biologists have contributed a lot to comprehension of woods' dynamism. For insofar as fires, wind storms, infestations by insects or microbes, and other such phenomena are no longer considered unfortunate departures from correct ecological patterns, Mediterranean woods no longer look like ragged, unbalanced, and endangered anemic relatives of the truly natural, more properly stable temperate or tropical woodlands further north or

---

[65] Delort and Walter, *Histoire*, 155–59; D. Galop, *La forêt, l'homme et le troupeau dans les Pyrénées* (Toulouse, 1998). R. Comba, "Castagneto e paesaggio agrario nelle valli piemontesi," in *Uomini boschi castagne*, ed. R. Comba and I. Naso (Cuneo, 2000), 21, suggested that active species introduction and protection in the first millennium decisively shaped forest history in the second.

[66] M. Davis and R. Shaw, "Range Shifts and Adaptive Responses to Quaternary Climate Change," *Science* 292 (April 27, 2001), 673–79.

south.[67] Accepting the unique dynamism of woods in Mediterranean Europe, subject to an extraordinary range of disturbances and adapted to them, allows even dramatic changes in post-classical Italian forests to look normal. If fifth-, sixth-, and seventh-century (local, erratic, non-linear) woodland growth is an episode in a longer history of changes, driven among other things by processes that are part of the ecological routine, the barbarization of Italian landscapes by trees appears less momentous. Woodland change is natural, it turns out, and not necessarily barbaric.[68]

This emergent historical-ecological concept of woods and trees as anything but static backdrops has the potential to turn them into historical agents, a return to views the ninth-century hagiographer of Barbatus would recognize. It is a productive context within which to set discussions of the extent and significance of early medieval chestnut woods, the subject of the pages that follow. Mediterranean woods of various types fit along a spectrum of natural-and-cultural forms of land use, and move along the spectrum at different moments in time with varying levels of anthropization. Post-classical chestnut woods are one of the various semi-natural formations that have occupied Italy's soil since Neolithic farming started there.[69] Such formations have been the outcome of the ongoing unstable interaction between prevailing ecological and social conditions. In a mutable landscape, the early medieval woods – simultaneously abundant and managed – represent how post-classical people adapted to the climatic, geological, vegetational, and epidemiological situation they found themselves in. The imposing stands of chestnut that first became a feature of woodlands in late Roman Italy were a characteristic vegetative adjustment to post-classical ecological and social equilibria.[70]

For the discussion to follow seeks to demonstrate that it was precisely in the waning of Rome's imperial hegemony that chestnut first prospered in Italy. The explanation advanced for this rise in fortunes

---

[67] G. Peterken, *Natural Woodland: Ecology and Conservation in Northern Temperate Regions* (Cambridge, 1996), 91–113.

[68] In the latter 1900s F. E. Clement's theories of natural succession and climax vegetation lost their appeal to European botanists, who began to accept a more linear, less cyclical evolutionary model: D. Botkin, *Discordant Harmonies: A New Ecology for the Twenty-First Century* (Oxford, 1990); F. Vera, *Grazing Ecology and Forest History* (Wallingford, 2000), 1–9. D. Moreno, *Dal documento al terreno: Storia e archeologia dei sistemi silvo-pastorali* (Bologna, 1990), 15–18, describes some of the philosophical debates surrounding this reorientation.

[69] Vera, *Grazing Ecology*, 1–9; Delort and Walter, *Histoire*, 43–44, 157–59; Grove and Rackham, *The Nature*, 57.

[70] A highly illuminating classification of land-use forms in relation to inputs of labor is D. Harris, "An Ecological Continuum of People–Plant Interaction," in *Foraging and Farming: The Evolution of Plant Exploitation* (London, 1989), 11–26 (13–20). The eco-social equilibria most relevant to post-Roman Italy derived from low population in relation to available land: see below, Chapter 2.

is predominantly demographic (as argued in Chapter 2), but it is well to consider that other factors also drove late antique Italians to establish a successful working relationship with chestnut, a type of biological "mutualism." Ruralized early medieval communities, perhaps especially those that flourished in the sixth to eighth centuries and were far less dependent on state- and market-driven economies than their Roman predecessors or Carolingian successors, forged new, closer relationships with the "uncultivated" territories, and therefore with woods. Chestnut inserted itself neatly into these post-classical economic strategies, more flexible, more reliant on local resources, and more attuned to local geographies than had been the case in the early centuries of the first millennium, when growing grains and grapes to sell in urban markets had been a priority.

As *Landscape and Change* shows in considerable detail, the chestnut was above all versatile. It could live in formations that permitted early medieval people to diversify their productive activities and rely less on cereals like wheat or on herds of cattle and flocks of sheep and goats. And of course the chestnut was not just a plant that produced things people and their domestic animals liked to eat. As a tree, it also supplied wood of various types, many of them sought after by the builders of houses, by viticulturalists, and by all who needed charcoal. It was up to the grower to shape the chestnut wood so that it produced poles rather than nuts and fit into one type of agrarian economy or another.

All of these different forms of chestnut use relied on woodlands that were rather anthropogenic, as the Lombard legislator Rothari appreciated when, in the mid seventh century, he classified the chestnut with the domestic apple, pear, and walnut, and separate from oak and beech (but also, tellingly, from olive, the most domesticated of the trees in the *Edict*).[71] Chestnut woods in fact became as widespread as they did in the early medieval landscape exactly because of their susceptibility to human care, whether the people in question were shepherds, farmers, viticulturalists, woodsmen, or (as was normal) combinations of these. The notaries whose writings make it possible to know the chestnut trees of the early medieval period took notice of them on account of the human investment in them. Documents describe chestnut trees, that is, because of their domestication.

---

[71] "Edictus Rothari," ed. F. Blühme, MGH, Leges 4 (Hanover, 1868), 3–90, Chapters 300–02 (70–71). A virtually contemporary categorization of trees from Ireland ascribed the highest nobility, and fines, to oaks (for their "dignity and acorns"): F. Kelly, "The Old Irish Tree List," *Celtica* 11(1976), 107–24 (109).

Yet the post-classical peninsula's chestnut woods were far more than an agricultural strategy, a component to an agricultural landscape, utterly tame like an apple orchard. As we shall see, chestnut trees could and did grow without any human help. Their productivity in fruits was largely indifferent to human blandishments and, realizing this, humans tended not to do much to them. Thus, the chestnut woodland remained natural, as well as cultural. Early medieval Italy's distinctive environmental hybridity, or its characteristic mixture of cultivation and uncultivation, is especially evident in its chestnut woods.

ENVIRONMENTAL HISTORY IN EARLY MEDIEVAL ITALY

Historians accustomed to "real" forests tend to find such "lopped and pollarded woodlots and macabre hunting preserves" dismaying. They are hardly forests at all, only "concentration camps for the natural world."[72] Indeed, the variably anthropogenic woods of early medieval Europe and Italy, and the chestnut groves that concern us most here, fit clumsily within the New World environmental history tradition, with its cult of unspoiled wilderness. It is therefore worth stressing that early medieval woods were certainly layered cultural artifacts, but not thereby artificial or unnatural and therefore negligible. To understand them requires thinking as the forest ecologist Peterken suggested about "relative" naturalness, or the natural within a specific cultural context.[73] As Peterken advised, a "scale of naturalness" in which neither (wholly natural or artificial) extreme exists in the field, but in which there are plenty of intermediate shades of semi-naturalness, corresponds better to historical experience than the absolute antithesis of artificial and humanized versus natural and wild.[74]

Such a view of the woods, and of the environment more generally, is quite respectable in European environmental history and has had several theorists because it matches observed practice, or past reality as the

---

[72] W. Dean, *With Broadax and Firebrand: The Destruction of the Brazilian Atlantic Forest* (Berkeley, 1995), 4.

[73] Peterken, *Natural Woodland*, 5–6, 11–16. In US environmental history the publication of R. White, *The Organic Machine* (New York, 1995) and W. Cronon, ed., *Uncommon Ground* (New York, 1996) offered an important reconceptualization of wilderness purity.

[74] H. Sukopp, "On the Study of Anthropogenic Plant Migrations in Central Europe," in *Plant Invasions: Ecological Mechanisms and Human Responses,* ed. U. Starfinger, K. Edwards, I. Kowarik, and M. Williamson (Leiden, 1998), 43–56 (46), proposed that between wild and cultivated there is a middle category of naturalized plants, poised to exploit human ecosystemic disturbances. Domesticatory relationships as degrees of manipulation: Harris, "Domesticatory Relationships," 442–46.

sources represent it.[75] Such a view both enriches environmental history everywhere and helps to make sense of the "humanized" woods, and chestnut groves, of the early Middle Ages. Among other advantages, it reveals Mediterranean forests and that particular form of them, the chestnut wood, as more than degraded forms of past, grander, "proper" vegetation, or as pale and unworthy opposites of the true forests in the Amazon or the Rockies.[76]

In treating the subject of chestnut woodlands and how they affected people while being themselves affected by people, I seek to contribute to European, and specifically Italian, environmental history. Indeed, the conviction that animates this book is that environmental conditions and "facts on the ground" – trees in particular (with their dual nature as natural organisms and cultural constructs) – matter deeply to any reconstruction of the past because of how deeply they mattered to the people who experienced that past.

Admittedly, early Middle Ages and environmental history are seldom conjugated, and even rarer are ecologically sensitive histories set in the post-classical Italian peninsula. Quite recently, an eminent practitioner of modern Italy's "territorial history," Piero Bevilacqua, noted the hegemony of urban concerns and points of view in modern Italian historiography, and the neglect of rural societies, landscapes, or environmental relationships.[77] Lacking even industrialization and the rise of capitalism as a usable narrative structure or at least cultural lightning rod, by and large medieval Italian historians have shied away from asking environmental questions about land use or even forests. Since environmental history encompasses geographical scales that transgress traditional geographical (national) boundaries, it can seem incongruous and ill-suited to medieval research, which still tends to respect such boundaries. Since it also traces developments that take much longer than human lifetimes

---

[75] R. Cevasco, "Environmental Heritage of a Past Cultural Landscape," in *Nature and History in Modern Italy*, ed. M. Armiero and M. Hall (Athens, OH, 2010), 126–40 (126), suggested an EU political context for the acceptance of "cultural landscape" in geographic and environmental discourse.

[76] See Delort and Walter, *Histoire*, 43–44, 157–59; P. Leveau, "L'archéologie des paysages et les époques historiques," in *Milieux naturels, espaces sociaux*, ed. E. Mornet and F. Morenzoni (Paris, 1997), 71–83 (76–77); Rackham, "Savanna," 1–3, 15; Moreno, *Dal documento*, 15–18. Recent studies stress the anthropogenic nature of the North American chestnut forests "discovered" and exploited by early modern Europeans: F. Paillet, "Chestnut: History and Ecology of a Transformed Species," *Journal of Biogeography* 29 (2002), 1517–30.

[77] P. Bevilacqua, "Sull'impopolarità della storia del territorio in Italia," in *Natura e società: Studi in memoria di Augusto Placanica,* ed. P. Bevilacqua and P. Tino (Rome, 2005), 7–16. Marxist historians, exemplified by E. Sereni, *Storia del paesaggio agrario italiano* (Bari, 1979 [1961]), tried the hardest to bring past countrysides into the limelight.

to come to fruition, and transcends the still-current chronological categories (ancient, medieval, modern), environmental history seems poorly
adapted to investigations focused on a mere few centuries of the first
millennium.[78] One may legitimately ask what an environmental history
of early medieval Italy should actually look like.

In attempting to answer this question we should note that any environmentally minded study of Italy and the early Middle Ages has to be
elastic in its understanding of that place and time. Post-Roman Italy did
not have the obvious and basically stable territorial definition that modern Italy has, and its mobile boundaries were porous too. Accepting that
the "Italy" of *Landscape and Change* had vague borders that expanded and
contracted, and was varyingly open to the Mediterranean and the trans-
alpine worlds, is a precondition in a study that encompasses territories
ruled by so many different authorities, none of whom were able to do so
in splendid isolation.

During the first millennium AD, on which this study focuses, "Italy"
assumed many forms. In the late third century an assortment of territories that resembles modern Italy was united by the Emperor Diocletian's
administrative reforms. That unified late imperial Italy fused lands Caesar
considered Gaul with others the Romans had called Greater Greece. It
fell away from imperial rule during the fifth century. Under the skillful
Ostrogothic King Theodoric (who died in 526), Italy came to include
portions of southern France and Dalmatia. After 554 Ostrogothic Italy
re-became a province of the eastern Roman, or Byzantine, empire, ruled
from Constantinople. But between 568 and 774 its northern and inland
southern extremities were ruled by Lombard kings and more or less subordinate dukes, while Italy's central and southeastern territories remained
solidly Byzantine. In 774 a military campaign led by the Frankish King
Charlemagne toppled the Lombard regime. Yet the incorporation in the
late 700s of the Lombard-controlled areas into a Carolingian empire ruled
from northern Francia never erased the political and administrative divisions with Byzantine-held land. Furthermore, in the eighth, ninth, and
tenth centuries the ability of both Byzantine and Carolingian authorities
to shape outcomes in Tyrrhenian southern Italy was limited most of the
time. There various local potentates held sway.

To map so much variegation in an Italy whose boundaries did not
have the indisputable solidity implied by modern cartography is very
difficult. Fortunately, although several areas of the peninsula come into
focus in this discussion of early medieval chestnuts, the Italy of this book

---

[78] Points developed by M. Armiero and M. Hall, "Il bel paese," in *Nature and History*, 1–11 (2–3).

Map 1 Early medieval Italy

is smaller than the modern nation. In fact, exigencies of source material lead to privileging two zones in discussions of chestnut, chestnut wood-lands, and human engagement with both: Campania and the Po valley.[79] So it is not just an ambiguous and shape-shifting Italy, but also a trun-cated one that occupies these pages.

In addition, the first millennium, including some "Roman time" and spilling over into the eleventh century, cannot quite contain the early medieval story of the chestnut tree's rise to prominence among all the other trees in the landscape. It is sometimes necessary to contem-plate Hellenistic history, or early modern and even twentieth-century trajectories, in order to understand the early medieval environmental transformation of woods and trees chronicled here.[80] That is the way of trees: their rhythms and life spans dwarf the accustomed chronologies of humans, and so cannot always fit neatly inside the traditional categories of past time. A Braudelian long duration that can transcend canonical time frames is necessary to comprehend the history of organisms that live as long as trees do.

The same elasticity that allows better comprehension of the geograph-ical and chronological frameworks of *Landscape and Change* is the handi-est tool for understanding this book's style of environmental history. Many classic environmentally minded histories, and maybe especially those concerned with woodland ecology, are able to discern pristine wil-derness at some early point in their narratives, and relate the changes that trees endured, or disastrously failed to endure, as humans intruded into an edenic wild woodland. But, as this introduction has sought to high-light, in the Italian peninsula the fusion between nature and culture is very ancient, something that is clearly visible in the history of the pen-insula's woodlands, and during the early Middle Ages the environment was definitely never natural in the pure sense embraced by environ-mentalists. A distinctive feature of Italian environments in history, along with an extraordinary human population density and exceptional topo-graphic instability, or fragility, is their built and anthropogenic character, which is, however, not the same as artificiality.[81] The special interest of

---

[79] Tuscany is the obvious absence here, but its chestnut woodland is already known to scholars: see C. Wickham, *The Mountains and the City: The Tuscan Appennines in the Early Middle Ages* (Oxford, 1988), 23.

[80] O. Redon, *Des forêts et des âmes: Espace et société dans la Toscane médiévale* (Saint Denis, 2008), 96, stressed the incompatibility of human and arboreal time frames. How traditional and environ-mental chronologies are incongruous is discussed by J. Le Goff in his preface to Delort and Walter, *Histoire*, 5–14 (12); and R. Hoffmann, "Medieval Christendom in God's Creation," in *Northern Europe: An Environmental History*, ed. T. Whited (Santa Barbara, 2005), 45–72 (45).

[81] Density: E. Lo Cascio and P. Malanima, "Cycles and Stability: Italian Population before the Demographic Transition (225 BC–AD 1900)," *Rivista di storia economica* 21.3 (2005), 197–232.

an environmental history set in the various landscapes of the Italian peninsula and in the post-classical centuries lies exactly in the analysis of uniquely close relationships between nature and culture, between people and ecosystems. As early medieval people, plants, animals, weather patterns, soils, and stones interacted, mutually affecting each other, they created distinctive environmental associations, neither natural nor cultural, but *both*, and in ways that set them apart from Roman and central medieval ecological arrangements.[82]

AN OUTLINE

This book also seeks to participate in the lively discussion of post-Roman economies that has taken place over the past decades. Its contribution is to introduce ecology to the picture by focusing on a particular tree, the "sweet" chestnut, here proposed as a useful case study of how dynamic and active were the woods of that remote time. In pursuit of that goal, the book's first chapter sets out the basic elements of chestnut physiology in ways historians may find unfamiliar but that hopefully will not make ecologists cringe. That chapter's main point is that botany *is* historically relevant, so it sets out chestnut's behavior and arboriculturalists' efforts to benefit from that behavior. In the following chapter (2) come analyses of how chestnut spread across Italy and (in somewhat less detail) Europe during the early Middle Ages. Buttressing both of these chapters is the belief that the trees *and* early medieval people participated in the eventful history of chestnut woods.

In Chapter 3 the cultural history of the chestnut in post-classical times receives the attention it deserves. The chapter suggests that a mounting interest in chestnut fruits, trees, and wood is traceable in early medieval texts. Such heightened cultural awareness and acceptance of the species is presented as a reflection of the new agricultural significance of a lovely tree that generously fed, sheltered, heated, and enriched people, if only they would create the right conditions for its growth.

Chapters 4 and 5 are two regional case studies. These two chapters analyze the evidence upon which the argument advanced throughout the book ultimately rests, namely that early medieval social, cultural, and economic conditions were ideal for chestnut and explain its unprecedented

Fragility: P. Bevilacqua, "The Distinctive Character of Italian Environmental History," in Armiero and Hall, *Nature and History*, 15–32 (15–18). Unartificiality: Armiero and Hall, "Il bel paese," 2–3.

[82] I. Simmons, *Environmental History* (Oxford, 1998), 54, distinguishes between natural ecosystems ("unaffected" by people), subnatural ones (some influence), semi-natural ones (structurally changed by people), and cultural ecosystems (dominated by human activity): early medieval Italy probably fluctuated between Simmons' middle two categories.

success. The evidence is best understood in specific environmental contexts. Chapter 5 presents the case from a Campanian point of view. It is grounded in the astonishingly abundant and expressive charters from the area around Naples, up to Salerno and Benevento, and traces the adventures of the chestnut in a part of the Italian peninsula where soil and climate facilitated that noble species' growth. From a late antique efflorescence in a time of diminishing population, the Campanian chestnut enjoyed prominence especially in the ninth and tenth centuries when population levels and commercial contacts revived. Chapter 6 shifts the angle of vision northwards to the Po valley, the heartland of the Lombard kingdom of/in Italy. There too chestnut found willing propagators and came to have surprising economic importance for both peasants and substantial landowners, especially in the Alpine foothills and on the flanks of the Apennines.

To finish, a concluding chapter retraces the main steps of this journey through the first millennium's chestnut woodland, and proposes a modern poet as guide to thinking about the enduring bond between people and an extraordinary tree.

Chapter 1

A NATURAL HISTORY OF THE CHESTNUT

Both the physiology of chestnut trees and the procedures of their cultivation are quite complicated. However, until the twentieth century, in the Mediterranean area both have been relatively stable, even through changing economic, social, cultural, and ecological circumstances. While unraveling some of the complexity in how chestnuts grow, and how people have grown them in Italy (and, to a lesser extent, in Europe) this chapter stresses the changelessness in the biological rhythms of *Castanea sativa*'s cycles, and in the arboricultural practices whereby people sought to foster those cycles. A Braudelian historian who read this chapter might recognize its indebtedness to Fernand Braudel's concept of enduring structure and timeless repetition in Mediterranean regions. In the following chapter, the extraordinary success of the chestnut in spreading itself throughout Italy emerges as a post-classical phenomenon, specific to a few centuries in the middle of the first millennium AD. Then two different types of time, the time of people and the time of trees, moved in marvelous synchrony. Again in Braudelian terms, a conjuncture of social, economic, and cultural processes in late antiquity created a new environmental equilibrium in which *Castanea sativa* could stretch well beyond its original homelands.

Thus, if the particular ways early medieval Europeans went about producing a livelihood are relevant to the story of chestnut's dissemination across landscapes, so too are the original particularities of *Castanea sativa*, its biological characteristics, and their response to prompts in the environment. In fact, it was the coevolution of *Castanea sativa* and post-classical *Homo sapiens* that created the novel prominence of chestnut.

An important theme both in the changelessness and in the quickly evolving history of the chestnut is work. Work of course is a cultural construct and can be variously defined; indeed, early medieval monks' novel definitions of work are among the most influential in European history, for they first made physical toil respectable among elite men.[1] But, as Richard White observed, environmentally minded writers, including historians, tend to downplay work in their narratives. In his famously titled essay "Are You an Environmentalist or Do You Work for a Living?" White argued that proper environmental history should contain human productive processes and activities as integral to any understanding of nature.[2] To understand the history of chestnuts in early medieval Italy and Europe, then, we should take the additional step of seeing the productive co-operation of trees and people as a sharing of the hard work of living. Both protagonists of this history contributed labor, as an expenditure of energy, in ways that benefited the other and motivated the other's willingness to work some more. Because of the reduced commercial activity that characterized early medieval economies at least until about 800, and especially because of reduced demographic pressure in late antique and early medieval times on the essential resource, land, the more obviously conscious partner chose to foster (by industrious tilling, planting, weeding, and so on) conditions in which the arboreal partner could get on with the task of growing. By about 1000, the twin labors of growth and cultivation had fashioned a new wooded landscape in Italy, and perhaps elsewhere as well.

THE CHESTNUT'S WORK

It is hard work being a chestnut tree. Like all trees, each year a chestnut must grow a layer of tissue around its entire mass, from the loftiest twig to the deepest root, and to do so is a huge metabolic effort.[3] It depends on the available precipitation and on the nutrients and minerals locked in the dirt beneath the tree. It depends also on the sun, whose energy the corrugated bright leaves of the chestnut must absorb. In chestnuts' leaves the marvel of photosynthesis takes place, whereby solar energy, carbon dioxide, water, and dissolved materials from the ground mix to become sugars, starches, and cellulose, ready for redistribution throughout the tree, ready in other terms to become the chestnut tree's growth and life. Hidden behind the placid immobility and tough outer bark of the chestnut tree is a huge and ongoing effort, a dynamic and complex circulation of chemicals throughout the heartwood, sapwood, and

[1] G. Ovitt, *The Restoration of Perfection: Labor and Technology in Medieval Culture* (New Brunswick, 1987).
[2] R. White, "'Are You an Environmentalist or Do You Work for a Living?': Work and Nature," in *Uncommon Ground*, ed. W. Cronon (New York, 1996), 171–85.
[3] P. Szabó, *Woodland and Forest in Medieval Hungary* (Oxford, 2005), 42.

cambium, upwards or downwards according to function, and a diligent daily harvesting of the sun's warmth and the air's carbon.

Chestnut trees live an extraordinarily long time so they clearly are very good at this work, or at balancing the several extractive processes that make up their life. Indeed, in the Mediterranean region chestnuts can live for centuries, sometimes for millennia, and even outside this climatic zone there are exceptional champions of longevity, like the Tortworth chestnut in Gloucestershire in southwest England, noted as an outstanding landscape feature in records from the time of King Stephen (d. 1154) and still vegetating today, endowed with a girth of some 36 feet (*c.* 11 m).[4] In the Mediterranean area olive trees and cypress trees are pretty much *Castanea sativa's* only competitors in the toils of long living. But if cypress and yew can live perhaps 2,000 years, and the tenacious olive can endure a millennium, chestnut tops them all, in some circumstances living through more than 3,000 seasons.[5] On the eastern slopes of Mount Etna the One Hundred Horses chestnut is supposed by some to be 4,000 years old.[6] Such fantastic longevity is a first botanical feature of the chestnut that, as we shall see in subsequent sections of this study, made a difference to its historical fortunes.

Age alters a chestnut, as it does most things. For instance, it shrivels and coarsens the tree's bark and changes its appearance. Yet throughout its life the chestnut retains unique regenerative capacities, or vitality. Indeed, the rapidity with which a chestnut seed could become a chestnut tree, or with which an established stool could send up pollards, made *Castanea sativa* stand out in the Mediterranean woodland and in fact in more northerly climes as well: in Britain the quick soaring of chestnut stems is the species' main competitive advantage over hornbeam, a rival for habitat.[7] Further south, beech trees, with whom chestnuts share a botanical family (*Fagaceae*), are far slower to grow (and live a mere three or four centuries), while oaks, with which chestnuts share some physiological requirements, are notoriously patient trees, taking much time to develop. At least for the first few centuries of its life, instead, the chestnut grows stalks able to hold up grape vines in five or ten years; stout stems that

---

[4] G. Peterken, *Natural Woodland: Ecology and Conservation in Northern Temperate Regions* (Cambridge, 1996), 23, 418; O. Rackham, *Ancient Woodland: Its History, Vegetation and Uses in England* (London, 1980), 331, measured the now hollow trunk.

[5] L. Fenaroli, *Gli alberi d'Italia* (Milan, 1967), 14. G. Bounous, *Il castagno: Coltura, ambiente ed utilizzazioni in Italia e nel mondo* (Bologna, 2002), 149, considers chestnuts' life "practically unlimited in time."

[6] Bounous, *Il castagno*, iv, measures this heroic tree's circumference at 52 m.

[7] Rackham, *Ancient Woodland*, 334.

can suspend telephone wires in less than twenty years; and trunks no one person could embrace in some thirty years.[8]

Depending on the soil and climate conditions, a chestnut tree stock or nut shoots up from the ground a quick and spectacular firework of a stem that can reach 20 m in height in a matter of a few decades, and there form a dense canopy of leaves, all busily manufacturing the stuff of life and of vegetative growth. Beyond this extraordinary speed in growing, *Castanea sativa* is extraordinarily resilient. When the legendary 1987 storm toppled many chestnuts in English woods, they impassively continued to grow, lying on their sides, as long as some roots still had purchase in the soil.[9] This spectacular ability to return to vegetative life after quite brutal shocks, cuttings included, is why ancient writers called the chestnut tree "reviving," or able to live again.[10] A tree that burned down or underwent some other form of what foresters nowadays call "disturbance" could swiftly grow back from its stool, returning to a respectable size in thirty or forty years. In this fashion, within the very long period during which an individual tree might live, it could have several different trunks, or forms, each the result of the stool's prodigious reaction to a "disturbance" that had snapped or incinerated its previous trunk.[11] Actually, in spite of people's instinctive dismay over forest fires, the chestnut seems to enjoy them. For it does quite well after fires, one of the endemic "disturbances" of the Mediterranean region, and mature trees, under whose canopy not so much fuel is likely to have built up (thus mitigating a brush fire's temperatures), recover quickly, in a classic example of environmental adaptation.[12] In the right climatic and soil conditions, a mere twenty years after a major combustion chestnut stands ten and more metres high wave in the breezes.

Mature by its fourth decade of life, a chestnut tree maintains surprising vigor for many more decades, though senility eventually will set in. A chestnut tree that has reached 200 years of life is an old tree, likely to have dead branches where it has proved unable to create the cells needed to cover another year's worth of growth.[13] In this phase the tree's crown

---

[8] E. Giordano, "Biology, Physiology, and Ecology of Chestnut," in *Proceedings of the International Congress on Chestnut*, ed. E. Antognozzi (Spoleto, n.d.), 89–93 (91); C. Bourgeois, *Le châtaignier, un arbre, un bois* (Paris, 1992), 85.

[9] O. Rackham, *Trees and Woodland in the British Landscape: Revised Edition* (London, 1990), 203.

[10] E.g., Ambrose, *Exameron*, in *Sancti Ambrosii opera*, Vol. 1, ed. C. Schenkl (Vienna, 1896), 3.13.54, where the chestnut is "nemorosa et rediviva." See Chapter 3 below.

[11] As chestnut roots are quite wide, not deep, violent wind capsizes the stool, uprooting and killing the plant: L. Fenaroli, *Il castagno* (Rome, 1945), 12; Peterken, *Natural Woodland*, 88–92.

[12] Chestnut and fire: S. Pyne, *Vestal Fire* (Seattle, 1997), 81–146; A. Grove and O. Rackham, *The Nature of Mediterranean Europe* (New Haven, 2001), 227–29; M. Buccianti, *Il castagno in provincia di Lucca* (Lucca, n.d.), 42; Peterken, *Natural Woodland*, 106–11.

[13] Szabó, *Woodland*, 42.

of leaves no longer expands and as the plant grows bigger roots and branches it attains a size where its leaves' annual production of sugars, starches, and cellulose is insufficient to cover the whole organism with a growth layer. The toil of living has by then become a struggle, and such trees are more vulnerable to meteorological or other "disturbances"; though obviously not all succumb, some do. But as just noted *Castanea* is a tree of many lives, so a possible outcome of senescence is renewal, with the same stock regenerating a new tree after the fall of the old one; in any case what some botanists refer to as "stag's head," or a restricted crown below dead branches, is not an indicator of imminent death.[14] The resilient tree is only reorganizing its resources in order to get on with the business of living.

In this sense a chestnut is a botanical phoenix. Unlike the mythical bird the chestnut preserves its vital organs from combustion underground but, thanks to this, like the bird the chestnut's life may be cyclical, with several successive trunks growing and collapsing from the same organism. Thus a lucky nut might become a millenarian burl, and during this one plant's long life the root stock might generate several distinct trunks in succession. Its capacity to reiterate itself is another important feature of chestnut physiology that had historical repercussions, as discussed in subsequent sections. But this capacity is uneven, and depends on how favorable the local conditions happen to be.

For, while the conditions *Castanea sativa* deems favorable are simple enough, they are not at all common. Chestnuts require fairly deep and particularly acidic soil, though they can put up with base and even calcareous earth if there is enough potassium in it.[15] European chestnuts also require long and warm growing seasons, with about four months of hot weather being optimal; they can survive with less, and endure quite frigid winters (they die when the temperature goes below −25 °C for any length of time), but do not flourish in places where winters are consistently cold for long periods and have trouble germinating in cold climates: to some, the 52nd parallel, or a line from Brittany to Belgrade, separates the southern zone where *Castanea sativa* grows well from the less propitious European north.[16]

---

[14] Rackham, *Trees and Woodland*, 12.

[15] V. Winiwarter, "Prolegomena to a History of Soil Knowledge in Europe," in *Soils and Societies*, ed. V. Winiwarter and J. McNeill (Isle of Harris, 2006), 208–10.

[16] A. Fauve-Chamoux, "Chestnuts," in *The Cambridge World History of Food*, 2 vols., ed. K. Kiple and K. Coneè Ornelas, Vol. 1 (Cambridge, 2000), 359–64 (360). Rackham (*Ancient Woodland*, 331), who enjoys eating the nuts off the ground after frosts, thinks botanists exaggerate English chestnuts' unproductivity (on which see M. Grieve, *A Modern Herbal: The Medicinal, Culinary, Cosmetic and Economic Properties, Cultivation and Folk-Lore of Herbs, Grasses, Fungi, Shrubs and Trees, with All Their Modern Scientific Uses*, 2 vols., Vol. 1 [New York, 1959], 194).

Aside from these temperature requirements, chestnuts have a further meteorological particularity: they need much moisture. Though sweet chestnuts, like most plants that grow in the Mediterranean, can cope with some drought, they have relatively high water requirements, so do not do well in the drier parts of the region delimited by the Romans' Inland Sea. The need for water is most acute during the summer, when a chestnut tree does most of its growing, and overall it is fair to say that minimum requirements for water are the main limiting factor to chestnut's dissemination in the temperate zone and particularly in places with "Mediterranean" climate and long summer dry spells. On the other hand, if there is the right amount of moisture, chestnut can grow in the "wrong" sorts of places, with cold winters and base soil. Yet *Castanea sativa* also falters in places with heavy precipitation, in effect growing best in those parts where annual precipitation falls in the range between 600 and 1,600 mm per year and where waterlogging is not a danger (it rots chestnut roots).[17] If chestnuts grow in areas with less precipitation, other ecological conditions, like high air moisture or stillness (the absence of wind slows transpiration), are likely the cause.[18]

When one factors together *Castanea sativa*'s various physiological predilections, the need for warmth and for wet conditions, plus soil acidity, one begins to design a quite restricted habitat.[19] Most places in the world, and even in the Mediterranean region, are too wet or dry, too hot or cold, too calcareous or too thinly endowed with topsoil to be hospitable for the chestnut.[20] The tree is astoundingly resilient, and can make do or adapt, but in natural conditions *Castanea* ends up occupying only a few corners of a meager band of territory between the Caucasus and Iberia, where its idiosyncratic needs are met. For even within this zone most lands are too high, low, hot, cold, dry, or damp for the chestnut even when the soil is right, and the plant judiciously avoids them.

In those elect terrains that chestnut trees like, the long life of the plant, sometimes subdivided into the shorter ones of successive trunks, begins with a nut. Such a nut is first of all a means of reproduction. It is

---

[17] M. Becchi, *Discorso sul castagno* (Reggio Emilia, 1996), 25; K. Browicz and J. Zieliński, *Chorology of Trees and Shrubs in South-West Asia and Adjacent Regions* (Warsaw, 1982), 32; Fauve-Chamoux, "Chestnuts," 359.

[18] J. Gandullo Gutiérrez, A. Rubio Sánchez, O. Sánchez Palomares, A. Blanco Andray, V. Gómez Sanz, and R. Elena Roselló, *Las estaciones ecológicas de los castañares españoles* (Madrid, 2004), 130–31.

[19] In these requirements there may be a trace of chestnut's origin in the subtropical plant *Castanopsis*: H. Meusel, E. Jäger, and E. Weinert, *Vergleichende Chorologie der zentraleuropäischen Flora* (Jena, 1965), 131. Or it may be a sign of the recent establishment of "Mediterranean" climate, to which "foolish" winter leaflessness is a poor response: Grove and Rackham, *The Nature*, 45.

[20] J. Rameau, D. Mansion, G. Dumé, et al., *Flore forestière française: Guide écologique illustré*, 3 vols. (Dijon, 1989–2008), Vols. II, 493; and III, 497.

the fruit of a chestnut tree and contains its seed. A chestnut falls out of its parent tree when ripe, in the Mediterranean area in practice between September and November, in October if the season has been just right. Having fallen to the ground, the nut faces the challenge of germinating, and it is a difficult challenge to confront, for the nut lacks its own means of locomotion and the place where it alights, under its parent's canopy, is really inauspicious for the purposes of growing. Not of course because the soil or climate is wrong, for otherwise the parent tree would not be there to begin with, but because the mature, seed-producing parent probably has a thick mantle of leaves on it during the summer, and the young tree, starved of sunlight needed in order to grow, would sputter out in the looming parental shadow.

Many chestnut trees grow on slopes, south-facing in colder climates, or north-facing in hot ones. In these circumstances the more rounded chestnuts that managed to shake loose of the burr might roll downhill far enough from their overbearing parent to find a sunny spot. But the statistical probability of rolling to the right place, even on hillsides, is very low. In part to obviate the reproductive disadvantage each immobile, clunky individual chestnut seed has, *Castanea sativa* is fantastically prolific, every tree producing many thousands of seeds in hopes one or two will beat the odds and germinate successfully in a propitious location. However, the chances of this happening spontaneously remain slim, and precious few natural chestnut woodlands, where *Castanea* predominates, are known. Fortunately though, chestnut is a clever and social plant, prone to forging alliances with other creatures in order to survive, and in fact to flourish. In reproduction at least the chestnut delegates some of the work to willing collaborators, some of the most important of whom, as we shall see, are human. In their absence, it relies on small herbivorous animals to disseminate its nuts, and to bring them to some of those propitious places they could never reach on their own.[21]

In Japan, where a species of chestnut called *Castanea crenata* grows spontaneously, scholars have carried out experiments to measure the range of movement of the average chestnut.[22] *Castanea crenata* is surprisingly agile, an adaptation that gives its seedlings a leg-up in the shady forest world where other species have more effective dissemination methods and less punctilious pedological and climatic expectations. The

---

[21] The strategy is common to similar trees, like oaks, for which jays are vital vectors: F.Vera, *Grazing Ecology and Forest History* (Wallingford, 2000), 376–78; W. Logan, *Oak: The Frame of Civilization* (New York, 2005), 269–75.

[22] K. Seiwa, A. Watanabe, K. Irie, H. Kanno, T. Saitoh, and S. Akasaka, "Impact of Site-Induced Mouse Caching and Transport Behaviour on Regeneration in *Castanea crenata*," *Journal of Vegetation Science* 13 (2002), 517–26.

Japanese chestnut produces nuts of varying size, for in different conditions large or small nuts have a competitive advantage. Wood mice, more than squirrels or jays, are the essential allies that select the seeds, if possible large ones, from under the parent's canopy, and carry them off to hide where the mice imagine other rodents will not find them. As it turns out, quite aside from the excess shade it preserves them from, this "lift" is a life-saver for some nuts, both because hungry rodents tend to congregate under mature chestnut trees to feast on the autumnal bounty, precluding the germination of the vast majority of nuts, and because the mass of nuts there fosters the development of density-dependent moulds that rot many of the nuts that the feasters overlook. Though some of the nuts that are carried off get eaten, wood mice seem to have a short memory span and, in the burrows where they were hidden, forgotten chestnuts often find fine growing conditions, and germinate. While the mice are shy animals who spend as much time as possible under the protective canopy of the forest, it seems they are willing to take some risks to protect very big, plump nuts, which are hidden in forest edges or in canopy gaps, exactly the kind of pleasantly sunny place *Castanea crenata* finds conducive to growth. In addition, the tidy mice hide one nut per hole, and so spare the seedling the tribulations of sibling rivalry.

In the Mediterranean region other rodents and some birds do the work of transporting chestnuts and thus allowing the species to colonize promising spaces.[23] Yet the reproductive mechanism of *Castanea sativa* remains laborious and complicated, dependent on a series of very fortunate events to produce that happy outcome: a healthy, sprouting chestnut tree. Therefore, in Italy and elsewhere in the Mediterranean region natural chestnut woodland was and is a rare thing, and its expansion even rarer, a kind of "perfect storm" of soil, climate, and small mammal co-operation that seldom prevails even in those uncommon areas that offer all the geographical ingredients *Castanea sativa* prefers. Most places, most of the time, other plants occupy the terrains favorable to the chestnut because they have more effective means of reproduction. While individual chestnut trees may rise, scattered in a woodland, the species seldom is able to prevail in consistent groupings.

In the right circumstances, once a nut germinates in a sunny spot on acidic ground where there is enough rainfall, a chestnut tree grows to maturity in about thirty or forty years. It will usually not flower for its first decade of life and tends to be sterile for a couple of years thereafter, but in youth it can nevertheless produce fruit.[24] As its grey, smooth bark turns brown and rough, the mature chestnut attains the capacity to

[23] Fenaroli, *Il castagno*, 49.   [24] Becchi, *Discorso*, 44.

reproduce, which means to drop thousands of nuts each autumn. We have seen that *Castanea* remains at the height of its vitality and productivity for a couple of centuries, though it might also live much longer than that, especially by means of growing new trunks. During this commodious life span a senior chestnut tree will have repeated a series of seasonal transformations many times over, because alongside the quasi-millennial cycle of root stocks regrowing trees, courses the annual cycle whereby the chestnut responds to the seasons. It is important to the argument of this chapter to elucidate some salient features of the annual life cycle of chestnut since these rendered the species amenable to human care and created the preconditions for chestnut's most fruitful collaboration.

In spring the chestnut is among the most prudent plants of the Mediterranean basin, one of the last trees, if not the very last, to unfurl its leaves. The latter operation mostly takes place in May, but varies with seasonal fluctuations in temperature, with exposure, and with altitude. The reason for such tardiness is that chestnuts are extremely sensitive to cold during their early vegetative period, and require average temperatures of between 8 and 16 °C for proper leaf development.[25]

In early summer, mostly in the month of June, as temperatures rise, the chestnut tree sprouts its flowers, first the male and later the female ones. As each tree makes flowers of both types in succession, it is very difficult for the tree to pollinate itself, and botanists consider *Castanea sativa* autosterile, a term to describe plants requiring communities of the same species for the successful pollination of any individual.[26] Given that *Castanea* is a tree whose seedlings need much light, the twin facts that it is gregarious and that it produces nuts most effectively in large groups (that can pollinate each other but that inevitably create large patches of shade) render the necessity of cross-pollination a significant disadvantage. It is a good slice of the explanation for the difficulties chestnut encounters when it comes to extending itself across a landscape unaided, or when it has to do all the work alone.

The odorous male chestnut blossoms spread their pollen around, both with the help of beetles and other insects and, despite chestnut pollen's heavy grains and difficulty in wafting far, with the help of the wind.[27] More or less in the same period, June and July, its leaves will turn darker

---

[25] See the useful J. Pitte, *Terres de castanide* (Paris, 1987), Fig. 1.

[26] D. Zohary and M. Hopf, *Domestication of Plants in the Old World* (Oxford, 2000), 142–45; Fauve-Chamoux, "Chestnuts," 360. Bounous, *Il castagno*, 32–34, also discusses several cultivars' infertility in the absence of trees from other breeds.

[27] Rameau *et al.*, *Flore forestière*, Vol. II, 493; Giordano, "Biology," 89; Becchi, *Discorso*, 45, who notes that insects prefer the more aromatic male flowers and seldom visit female ones. Bounous, *Il castagno*, 34, claims pollen grains may travel up to 100 km, but minimal quantities waft beyond 30 m.

green and its canopy fills in, protecting any fertilized female flowers as they become fruit. At this point the chestnuts have small, bright green, spiny outer shells (burrs, or husks) that add a further level of protection for the unripe seed.

For *Castanea*, as for any other wise organism in the Mediterranean, August, at the height of the summer heat, is not a busy month, and most fruit-ripening occurs in September. In the ripening process the nuts, anywhere between one and five within each burr, change color and texture, from a gelatinous mass of white to a brown-shelled, creamy-toned solid seed. As the seeds grow larger they burst the spiny burr and prepare for the fall to the ground. Some nuts fall off with the burr.

Ripe chestnuts fall out of the tree, with or without their prickly outer protection, in early autumn, generally in October. This is not the only aerial gift a chestnut tree would send down. For, in a normal season, a few weeks after the nuts and generally in November, *Castanea* sheds its leaves in preparation for the chill season and for some rest from its unremitting cycle of toil. While this behavior certainly helps the trees survive the winter, the deposits of leaves on the ground contribute to soil enrichment and by adding acidity make it harder for other plants' seeds to germinate near the deciduous giant. Sometimes a very rainy autumn accelerates the moment for the leaves dropping, mixing leaves and nuts on the earth, but this is not the norm.[28] What is inexorable as average daily temperatures drop below 4°C is the tree going dormant, a condition in which chestnuts remain until average daily temperatures return above 6 °C. In March, as such temperatures establish themselves, the small buds on the tree's branches are a first sign of its reawakening, but as we have already seen the prudent chestnut is not precocious in leafing, letting other plants risk the cold snaps, high winds, hail, and so on, until May when, at least in the Mediterranean region, it can seem safe to launch foliation again.

This description of the chestnut's behavior has been mostly *super*-terranean, but we should remember that much of the chestnut tree lies underground. Chestnut roots are not especially deep, but they are very extensive and they grow fast. It is their vitality that empowers the much more obvious vigor of the stems in the sunlight.[29] While their primary activity is leaching minerals and nutrients from the soil, and pumping them, along with much water, upwards to the leaves, the roots of *Castanea sativa* also develop curious co-operations with other organisms,

---

[28] Rackham, *Ancient Woodland*, 36; Pitte, *Terres*, 25.
[29] Giordano, "Biology," 90; E. Amorini, "Sustainability of Chestnut Forest Ecosystems: Is It Possible?," *Ecologia mediterranea* 26 (2000), 3–14 (9); Fenaroli, *Il castagno*, 12.

signaling again one of this plant's salient characteristics. Chestnut wood-lands are famous for their abundance in mushrooms, and while there are solid climatic and pedological reasons for this (namely the shared predilections of chestnuts and fungi), it seems *Castanea* actively fosters conditions mushrooms appreciate too.[30] Indeed, a symbiotic relationship between some fungi and chestnut roots rests on exchanges of chemicals, minerals, and carbohydrates among the organisms, and such exchanges below the surface of the soil only take place in conditions of dampness, soil composition, and temperature that also are conducive to the copious efflorescence of mushrooms above, in the topsoil.

Nor are mushrooms alone in their appreciation of the ecosystem that chestnut trees create. Because chestnut's foliation is so late, many species of grass flourish in the sunny early springtime around chest-nut trees. Distinctive, highly biodiverse plant communities are associ-ated with woods of *Castanea sativa*, as long as these are not too densely spaced.[31] Where the chestnut woodland assumed the "savanna" struc-ture that Oliver Rackham believes to have been more prevalent in the Mediterranean past than other scholars have assumed, the availability of sunshine continued beyond May when chestnuts clad themselves with their elongated almond-shaped leaves.[32] Therefore, whether only in early spring or through the summer, where there were chestnut trees there was also a rich and varied grassland, even if the trees themselves do not add much biological value to their ecosystem.[33] Such grasses could become a draw for grazers whose droppings contribute to the humus whence chestnuts draw nourishment.

The European chestnut's chief botanical asset is its formidable vigor in growth, both above the ground and below it. In the right condi-tions (admittedly rare) it sprouts stems fast and burrows roots as swiftly, becoming one of the very best producers of wood in the Mediterranean, in perfect conditions able to compete with tropical hardwood species

[30] F. Meotto, S. Pellegrino, and J. Craddock, "Ectomycorrhizal Fungi of Chestnut with Particular Reference to Choice Edible Mushrooms," in *Proceedings of the International Congress on Chestnut*, ed. E. Antognozzi (spoleto, n.d.), 403–08 (403); P. Bonuccelli, "Il castagno nella Lucchesia," *Accademia lucchese di scienze, lettere ed arti* 5 (1942), 93–116 (104); G. Bignami and A. Salsotto, *La civiltà del castagno* (Cuneo, 1983), 69; P. Dallman, *Plant Life in the World's Mediterranean Climates* (Berkeley, 1998), 39.

[31] Rackham, *Ancient Woodland*, 334, notes chestnut leaves' excellent absorption of light, and conse-quent difficulties for flora in thick woods of the species.

[32] O. Rackham, "Savanna in Europe," in *The Ecological History of European Forests*, ed. C. Watkins and K. Kirby (Wallingford, 1998), 1–24; Grove and Rackham, *The Nature*, 68, 213–14, 225; Vera, *Grazing Ecology*, 371–78; Bignami and Salsotto, *La civiltà*, 74; F. Romane and L. Valerino, "Changements du paysage et biodiversité dans les châtaigneraies cévénoles (sud de la France)," *Ecologia mediterranea* 23 (1997), 121–29 (124–26).

[33] Rackham, *Ancient Woodland*, 338.

in the quality of its wood as well as in the rate at which it grows.[34] In the early Middle Ages such tremendous regenerative powers might actually seem miraculous: a story about a dead tree returning rapidly to leafy health in Gregory of Tours' *Glory of the Martyrs* reveals some of the awe people felt before *Castanea*'s vitality.[35] But since the conditions for growth seldom are exactly right in nature, chestnut has adapted, creating alliances with other plants and animals to ensure its survival and health. While these alliances enabled chestnut to remain a (minor) presence in Mediterranean woodlands, the stringent demands for humidity and warmth, and the awkward system of reproduction, dependent on an unlikely dispersal of light-hungry seeds, made the chestnut a weak competitor against other species in the harsh world of Mediterranean botany. But chestnut's great stroke of diplomatic genius, its alliance with the most powerful of the Mediterranean's inhabitants, permitted the tree to do more than subsist in a few pockets of soil where the perfect conditions existed. Piggy-backing on humans, the most gluttonous consumers of its seeds and saplings, *Castanea sativa* went far.

WORKING WITH CHESTNUTS

A spectacular demonstration of how dependent Mediterranean chestnut woodland is on people was offered by the fate of that forest in the twentieth century. At a time when, on balance, woodland has expanded considerably in most European countries, chestnut woods have suffered a massive contraction.[36] In Switzerland, France, Iberia, and Italy the 1900s were cruel to *Castanea sativa*, not so much through the introduction of new Asian pathogens, to which, ultimately, the European chestnut has so far proved quite resistant (thanks also to the susceptibility of the Asian fungus *Endothia* or *Cryphonectria* to another parasite), nor through the industrial scale of demand for the tannin so abundant in chestnut bark, but rather through neglect.[37] The demise of traditional sweat-powered

---

[34] Fenaroli, *Il castagno*, 72–76; Amorini, "Sustainability," 10.

[35] Gregory of Tours, *Liber in gloria martyrum*, ed. B. Krusch, in *Gregorii Turonensis opera. Pars II: Miracula et opera minora*, MGH, Scriptores rerum Merovingicarum 1.2 (Hanover, 1885), 34–113, Chapter 73 (87).

[36] Buccianti, *Il castagno*, 9–13, shows that chestnut woods in Italy declined by one-third between 1955 and 1991. See also Amorini, "Sustainability," 11; Becchi, *Discorso*, 27; Bignami and Salsotto, *La civiltà*, 70. A dramatic example of recent afforestation is in A. King, "Mammal, Reptile, and Amphibian Bones," in *Excavations at the Mola di Monte Gelato*, ed. T. Potter and A. King (Rome, 1997), 383–403 (399).

[37] M. Conedera, M.C. Manetti, F. Giudici, and E. Amorini, "Distribution and Economic Potential of the Sweet Chestnut (*Castanea sativa* Mill.) in Europe," *Ecologia mediterranea* 30.2 (2004), 179–93 (182–85); Buccianti, *Il castagno*, 9, suggests new diseases encouraged owners to chop down their chestnuts; Romane and Valerino, "Changements," 123, suggest instead that liability to disease is

economies and the rise of those sustained by fossil fuels created conditions inimical to the chestnut tree in Europe particularly by emptying villages and hillsides of people, who stampeded to cities or to the lowlands where industrial agriculture had raised grain yields, in a vast mutation of settlement still visible at the beginning of the twenty-first century. Even in areas whose people stayed where their ancestors had lived, it ceased to be convenient, or economically rational, to live with the chestnut trees, and hence to foster ecosystems suitable for *Castanea sativa*.

The twentieth-century abandonment of chestnut woods happened at different moments in different places. For example, a Swiss observer bemoaned the dying off of chestnuts in the Canton Ticino already in 1919, as people turned to other occupations, but in Italy the same period saw an uptick in the acreage occupied by chestnuts, stimulated first by World War demand and then by Fascist autarchic policies.[38] But the overall effect of modernization was that in the space of two or three generations chestnuts lost their most valuable aide. People were no longer willing to help the trees grow and propagate themselves; they would no longer clear the undergrowth around the trees and break up the ground under them, nor lop stalks and branches, thus stimulating vigorous roots and stems, nor tenderly plant the most promising seeds and defend them from predators.

The result has been a drastic reduction of chestnut woods, measured in acres or individual size. Without their human Sancho Panza, chestnuts cannot compete with more precocious sprouters, and as old trees get older, reduce their crowns, fall sick, or fall over, or are cut down by their old patrons, other species eagerly occupy the spaces under and around them. A decade of neglect turns a pure, monocultural chestnut grove into a mixed woodland, and in several decades chestnuts recede to marginality, swamped by other kinds of plants, more opportunistic or simply better adapted to the prevalent soil and climate conditions. In Friuli, the northwest corner of the Italian peninsula, ash, hornbeam, maple, and black alder took advantage of opportunities, colonized small clearances

---

an effect of abandonment, not a cause. See also M. Conedera, P. Stanga, C. Lischer, and V. Stöckli, "Competition and Dynamics in Abandoned Chestnut Orchards in Southern Switzerland," *Ecologia mediterranea* 26 (2000), 110–12; D. Galop, *La forêt, l'homme et le troupeau dans les Pyrénées* (Toulouse, 1998), 223. On the revival of *Phytophthora cambivora* in the late 1900s, see Bounous, *Il castagno*, 107–11.

[38] F. Merz, *Die Edelkastanie: Ihre volkswirtschaftliche Bedeutung, ihr Anbau und ihre Bewirtschaftung* (Bern, 1919), 5–7; Bonuccelli, "Il castagno," 93. In the 1990s renewed demand drove production up again in some groves where choice varieties grow: Conedera et al., "Distribution," 186–87; Bounous, *Il castagno*, 13–15, 192. My informant Domenico Piegari also celebrated a very profitable 2006 harvest above Buccino, near Eboli.

Map 2 Areas of potential chestnut cultivation in Italy and actual cultivation in 1958

and spaces along stone walls and boundaries, and spread from there into chestnut groves, in a process still unchecked.[39] Meanwhile, in the vicinity of Lugano further west, coppices of chestnut abandoned around 1950 filled with oak and beech by 1980, as weaker *Castanea* trees grew less and all showed reduced ability to send up stems. Without their Ticinese stewards, chestnuts floundered and mixed deciduous woodland prevailed.[40] In Tuscany this pattern of decline has been carefully evaluated over a slightly longer time: at Gargonza in 1984 there were 87 percent fewer chestnut trees than 150 years earlier when a survey was made.[41]

By the nineteenth century, the ability of chestnut to work with less than perfect conditions if given some help, and the human desire for the products of chestnut's vitality, had extended *Castanea* to many areas that the tree would never have tolerated on its own. Chestnut's downward spiral thereafter need not be interpreted as an ecological catastrophe, that is, although it may actually be bad for biodiversity since the number of species in a chestnut grove is actually greater than in a neglected wood.[42] After all, woodland ecosystems and in fact nature itself are dynamic, and successive formations follow upon each other in a for now unbroken chain.[43] Still, the twentieth-century misadventures of the chestnut are a pointed reminder of how intimate had been the association between chestnut woods and human care in historical times. When one subsides, so does the other. The two go together.

There are two central reasons why people cultivate their relationship with *Castanea sativa*, namely its wood and its fruit. Depending on which of the two is the cultivator's prime goal, he or she will modulate activities, producing different outcomes, though in both cases the human exploits particular biological characteristics of *Castanea*. Thus, whether it is chestnut's fantastic prodigality in nuts, or its sensationally quick generation of wood to which people respond, theirs is an astute adaptation to natural characteristics in the plant, primarily chestnut's prodigious productivity and its toleration of some imperfections in its habitat. But the crucial

---

[39] M. Guidi and P. Piussi, "The Influence of Old Rural Land-Management Practices on the Natural Regeneration of Woodland on Abandoned Farmland in the Prealps of Friuli, Italy," in *Ecological Effects of Afforestation*, ed. C. Watkins (Wallingford, 1998), 57–67 (59–62).

[40] P. Fonti, P. Cherubini, A. Rigling, P. Weber, and G. Biging, "Tree-Rings Show Competition Dynamics in Abandoned *Castanea sativa* Coppices after Land-Use Changes," *Journal of Vegetation Science* 17 (2006), 103–12.

[41] M. Agnoletti and M. Paci, "Landscape Evolution on a Central Tuscan Estate between the 18th and 20th Centuries," in Watkins and Kirby, *The Ecological History*, 117–27 (123–24).

[42] Romane and Valerino ("Changements," 124) note that thirty-five years after a grove is abandoned biodiversity reaches a nadir.

[43] D. Botkin, *Discordant Harmonies: A New Ecology for the Twenty-First Century* (Oxford, 1990), 62: "nature undisturbed is not constant in form, structure, or proportion, but changes at every scale of time and space."

point here is that either way, whether as a maker of nuts or wood, the chestnut is not a demanding task-master, and this is as true in the age of mechanized, commercial agriculture as it was when sweat powered subsistence farms and labor inputs had to be minutely calculated in farmers' growing strategies.

To raise a useful tree or grove, the chestnut farmer needs to take some seemingly simple steps. In the twenty-first century, exactly as in the Dark Ages, cultivators must bring the tree to maturity. This is truest when one aims at inducing the tree to produce nuts, but a mature bole, or root stock, is also preferable when the object is producing chestnut wicker, or poles, or lumber (it is not essential, though, for quite serviceable stems grow from modest, youthful roots too). Hence a few initial tasks in the ongoing collaboration that raises a productive plant can be avoided if the tree in question is a wild one, found in the woods already as an adult. However, as was intimated in the previous section, people tend to find inconvenient those rather select places where *Castanea* sprouts spontaneously, so most trees are grown from a nut in places people prefer. This adds work to the task, and calls for a greater dose of patience both in the chestnut woodsman, who might expect branches for wicker after some three or four years from germination, and in the nut gatherer, whose first real crop might arrive after ten years or more.

In either case the right seed must first be chosen. This normally would happen in autumn, when the nuts are ripe. The late Roman agronomist Palladius advised that selection could rely on a kind of trial by water, in which promising nuts would sink while the ones that floated should be discarded.[44] Next, the would-be chestnut grower faced the problem of preserving the seed's vitality until the spring, when it might be planted in the soil most safely. Molds, grubs, and fungi find chestnuts just as appetizing as birds and mammals do, so preservation from autumn to spring could be tricky, and sand or clay pots or hay all had their proponents as the best means of conservation through the winter months.[45]

In spring, after the ground had been prepared and rendered malleable for young roots, sometimes by hoe, sometimes by plow, at last the cultivator could bury the nuts in holes readied for that purpose. In areas where pastoralism was important, the cultivator had to worry pre-emptively about importunate teeth chewing the young trees, and a stout fence

---

[44] *Res rustica* 12.7.1718, replicated 1,000 years later by Pietro de' Crescenzi, *Ruralia commoda*, 4 vols., ed. W. Richter and R. Richter-Bergmeier, Vol. II (Heidelberg, 1996), 5.6.2 (105). N. Kingsbury, *Hybrid: The History and Science of Plant Breeding* (Chicago, 2009), 43, observes that seed selection is done by women in traditional societies: they control plants' genetic patrimony.

[45] Becchi, *Discorso*, 50–51, 77–78.

might be needed before the tender shoots first peeped through the dirt.[46] But there was another danger, in the form of voracious voles, squirrels, and mice who like to dig up nuts to eat them before they sprout.[47] To protect against this inconvenience the planter planted more nuts than the field could really accommodate, though such tighter spacing of the seeds inevitably leads to an added inconvenience when the nuts germinate in early summer (May–June): to the extent the cultivator has succeeded in protecting the buried nuts, too many seedlings may sprout, or they may do so too densely clustered. It then becomes necessary to transplant seedlings so as not to crowd them together in patterns that create competition for light or soil nutrients as the plant grows and its canopy widens.

Transplantation should take place after a couple of years' growth, when the sapling is more secure and its root system strong enough to withstand the trial of being uprooted. In the meantime the cultivator has been busy eliminating plants that might rob the chestnuts of light or minerals in the ground, which, as already noted, is a great liability to chestnuts in wild woodlands. Spring weeding was easier if the cultivator sowed a crop in the soil the previous winter; and indeed until the seedlings are tall and leafy enough that their shade and roots discourage grain, sowing a grain crop in the chestnut nursery is a good idea.[48] In castaneiculture, as with any arboriculture, intercropping gives the farmer a chance to recover some of the losses attendant on the young trees' very low productivity.[49] But unlike such trees as the olive, whose canopy is wispy, the chestnut will preclude intercropping by its leafiness once it grows up, certainly by the time it is ten years old, if the trees are not planted far from each other.[50] In the long term, then, the most viable "intercultivation" is meadow, and it depends on wide spacing of chestnut saplings.

The productive potential of a chestnut grove depends to a large extent on the spacing of its inhabitants. This in turn depends on the intentions

---

[46] Pitte, *Terres*, 140.

[47] If the grove is to rise on a steep hillside, terracing or "semi-terracing" will further burden the cultivator. There is no evidence that Dark Age Italian chestnut woods had terracing, nor (despite P. Toubert, "Paysages ruraux et techniques de production en Italie méridionale dans la seconde moitié du XIIe siècle," in *Potere società e popolo nell'età dei due Guglielmi* [Bari, 1981], 210; and J. Martin, "L'espace cultivé," in *L'uomo e spazio nell'alto medioevo*, Settimane del CISAM 50 [Spoleto, 2003], 267) that they grew on steep, marginal land of the kind that needed terracing anyway to be exploited by people. See Pitte, *Terres*, 152; Grove and Rackham, *The Nature*, 107.

[48] Fenaroli, *Il castagno*, 117–18.

[49] Pitte, *Terres*, 165–66; K. White, *Roman Farming* (London, 1970), 227.

[50] Traditional chestnut woods are much less dense than recent plantations. But in the Colli Albani nothing (save plants able to flower and fruit before mid May) grew under chestnuts by the time they were four to five years old. In the first four years, various grasses sprouted: A. Ferrantini, "Osservazioni sulle modificazioni della vegetazione nei Colli Albani," *Bollettino della Società geografica italiana*, series 7, no. 11 (1946), 16–30 (24).

of the cultivator and her or his willingness to work, to co-operate with *Castanea* in creating more suitable growing conditions for the particular style of cultivation the cultivator envisions. Obviously, a chestnut wood geared to nut production has a different "gauge" than a wood geared to growing wood. A coppiced chestnut wood, one whose primary purpose is turning out regular crops of wicker, posts, poles, and beams, may be more thickly planted, since most trees in it will be cut down before they turn thirty, or before their canopies become massive. Competition with nearby neighbors could anyway stimulate rapid, straight-upward growth, and thereby transmit a desirable trait to the wood. Therefore twentieth-century foresters advised keeping up to 1,200 trees on a hectare of land, depending on the cutting rotation: short rotations, of less than 8 years between cuts, could envision 1,000 and more trees per hectare, but if one wanted something more than branches to weave into baskets, longer rotations and wider spacing of fewer chestnuts were needed.[51]

A chestnut wood designed instead to drop large crops of edible nuts requires older and therefore larger trees, and cultivators find that branches extending horizontally from the trunk and dense canopies are most prolific in spawning chestnuts. Thus, fewer individual trees fit on a hectare of "fruiting chestnut" woodland, and in the interest of allowing as much sunshine as possible to illuminate the leaves such woodland tends to be generously spaced.[52]

Whatever the goal, the chestnut steward has to watch over the young trees, whose death rate is high. In a young grove the work of replacing struggling or dead plants is not negligible. A fresh chestnut wood undergoes some natural initial culling that thins the grove, and usually the vacated space is such that it will have to be filled with other saplings.[53] Planting a new chestnut wood involves a lot of replanting and in effect is a multi-year process rather than a one-off event. Indeed, in a coppiced wood, even after some years, once wood harvesting is properly under way, the likelihood of having to grub out dead stools and replant seeds remains, for although cutting the plants down stimulates regrowth in most individuals, it also kills others.

A further task awaiting the castaneiculturalist during the early phase of the chestnut wood's life is pruning. This is best done in winter, the trees'

---

[51] Fenaroli, *Il castagno*, 73–75. Coppice cycles affect tree longevity, more frequent cuts reducing it (84–85).

[52] Rackham, "Savanna," 15.

[53] Pitte, *Terres*, 139–42; J. Gallardo, M. Rico, and M. González, "Some Ecological Aspects of a Chestnut Coppice Located at the Sierra de Gata Mountains (Western Spain) and Its Relationship with a Sustainable Management," *Ecologia mediterranea* 26.1 (2000), 53–59 (58); Bourgeois, *Le châtaignier*, 101, gives 90 percent death rates for saplings at age eleven, based on Périgord data.

dormant season, and it is necessary for both nut and wood producers. The selection of the best, strongest stems might follow slightly different criteria (straightness in coppices, girth for fruit-bearers), and in a coppice several stems on a single root stock might receive encouragement, but given *Castanea's* vitality, each year some new pollards need cutting if a good result, arboriculturally speaking, is to emerge. In fact, the elimination of basal pollards remains necessary even in mature woods, and thinning of the canopy gives both branches and trunk more vigor, so today foresters advise it.[54] In late medieval Tuscany it seems that cutting took place during early autumn and spring, when the plants' vegetative cycle is in full swing, with the result that the die-off rate of even mature stocks was significant.[55] This pattern would increase the laboriousness of maintenance in a coppiced wood, wherein anyway a lot of stems die naturally, adding the chore of their removal.[56]

On account of its pollination the seed of a chestnut tree is a genetic mix and does not replicate the characteristics of its parent tree: as in all fruit, the seed extremely seldom grows "true," a complete replica of the tree that generated it. In the event that the cultivator aspires to imitate perfectly the idiosyncrasies of favorite plants, for instance proven producers of nuts, trees have to be grafted in the grove's youth.[57] This was and is a technically demanding task, reserved for nut producing since it gives no advantages to the grower of wood, and in fact reduces the amount of wood on a tree and slows down its production of biomass. Regardless of which grafting method the cultivator chooses, a successful graft requires both the root stock, or bole or burl or stool, and the scion, the small budding shoot cut from another plant and surgically inserted into the stock, to be woody, and thus old enough to have bark leathery enough to be protective. The stock must have mature, reliable roots. Simplifying a bit, in a graft the stock is cut at an appropriate height and the scion placed into the fiber of the cut so both plants' cambium touch. If the graft succeeds (a big if: much depends on technique and climatic conditions at the time of grafting) the bipartite plant then gradually fuses together the tissues of two plants, healing the wounds the grafter has inflicted and uniting two

---

[54] Bourgeois, *Le châtaignier*, 46; Buccianti, *Il castagno*, 97; Becchi, *Discorso*, 74–77. Gallardo *et al.*, "Some Ecological Aspects," 58; Fenaroli, *Il castagno*, 79, 102. Canopy trimming: Amorini, "Sustainability," 12–13.

[55] O. Redon, *Des forêts et des âmes: Espace et société dans la Toscane médiévale* (Saint Denis, 2008), 108–09.

[56] Rackham, *Ancient Woodland*, 334: of the dozens of stems a large bole sprouts, barely ten survive to the seventh year.

[57] Chestnut grafting: Becchi, *Discorso*, 52–53; Pitte, *Terres*, 139–46, 167. Grafting history: J. Diamond, *Guns, Germs and Steel* (New York, 1999), 124–25; Zohary and Hopf, *Domestication*, 143–44; White, *Roman Farming*, 248, 257–59.

genetically distinct organisms. From the cultivator's point of view, grafting has the great advantage that it gives control over the characteristics of the bipartite tree, whose leaves, branches, and nuts above the incision will be genetically identical to those of the tree whence the scion has come. The choice of the scion, then, is momentous, based on a refined appreciation of characteristics in the original tree whence the scion was excised.

If the root stock is a sapling, the scion is close in diameter, and as the double-natured, grafted chestnut tree grows all that would show their artificial union would be a ringed scar in the bark, marking the cuts that joined the two plants. Since a chestnut lives a long time, and since its productivity in nuts declines after about 200 years, it is possible to renew the graft by chopping it down above the scar, then allowing the tree to generate new stems or pollards, exactly identical in genetic make-up to the first graft, but more vigorous and likely to make nuts. This is a drastic measure, risky and quite time-consuming, best avoided until the health of the old grafted tree is so weak that the loss of productivity makes it absolutely necessary. Some contemporary Italian chestnut farmers in fact prefer to remove the old tree and begin afresh with a nut in spite of the additional years of waiting that entails.

As the chestnut grove grows, grafted or ungrafted, thinned or replanted according to the vagaries of place, season, and agricultural strategy, the cultivator enters into a long-term maintenance regimen. The goal of this work is to sustain the ecosystem that suits the favored plants and delivers arboricultural advantages. The amount of time and energy this takes depends again on the type of chestnut wood one is rearing. Chestnut coppice is far less demanding, for fewer other plants grow in that dense formation, at least after two or three years from the cutting.

In fruit-growing groves, good husbandry involves a round of light tilling of the ground at the beginning of spring, or in June. This is not vital, but it facilitates moisture absorption and retention and keeps weeds at bay. Maintaining the grove might further involve making hay in the meadow that most widely spaced canopies permit to grow. This is something best done before the male chestnut flowers fall onto the ground late in June and render the hay unpalatable to most herbivores.[58] In many Mediterranean regions, by August aridity depletes grasses and it can be advisable to strip the tree of some leaves to feed animals by then short of fodder, though this is never good for the trees and early medieval documents do not attest to the practice.[59] In September, any grove that lacks fencing

---

[58] Fenaroli, *Il castagno*, 119. The catkins are furry, as well as aromatic.
[59] Pitte, *Terres*, 197. The "aerial pastures" described in early modern northern Italy were not of chestnut leaves: E. Bargioni and A. Zanzi Sulli, "The Production of Fodder Trees in Valdagno, Vicenza,

becomes vulnerable to opportunists seeking early-falling nuts, and some premodern communities addressed this problem by a sort of time-zoning, whereby normally open access to chestnut woods was limited during the two or more months when chestnuts ripened.[60] Late summer is also the last chance to clear away any tall grass, brush, or other vegetation in the chestnut grove that might hamper harvesting operations.

For though contemporary chestnut farmers use machines that literally shake the chestnuts out of the trees, and some early modern farmers resorted to beating the branches with sticks to loosen the nuts, in the long Middle Ages patience was the chestnut gatherer's main tool. In fact, chestnuts are unlike other fruits in that until they fall off the tree, either with or without their prickly burr, they are not ripe and should not be gathered.[61] And, since many groves contain mixed varieties of chestnut (cultivars) to enhance fertility by cross-pollination, in very few could the entire year's crop be relied on to fall off the trees in a day or two. Gathering the nuts from the ground, some still wrapped in their prickly burrs, can be tiresome work, yet it has to be repeated several times in the same woods because of the different rates of ripening among the different trees and indeed on the same tree. In modern groves after 10 hours of gathering fallen nuts a single gatherer has between 50 and 150 kg of nuts, depending on the season's growing conditions and on the grove's lay-out. Foresters calculate that in reasonably well kept "traditional" groves a solitary gatherer averages between 10 and 15 kg of nuts gathered every hour, though this productivity is liable to grow considerably when modern techniques and machines are applied. The whole process can stretch out over weeks, depending on climatic conditions, and this multiplies opportunities for predators, four- and two-footed.[62]

Yet all (early modern) reports concur that chestnut gathering was a joyous occasion, with gatherers of different ages and both genders joining in. It was not the end of the season's toil in the chestnut grove, since some gathered the discarded burrs as fuel, and in November the fallen leaves as litter, but it was the high point of the chestnut season, and probably very reassuring to Mediterranean people whose grain harvest, hauled in in June, might be running low by early winter.[63]

Italy," in Watkins and Kirby, *The Ecological History*, 43–52 (47–51). See also Guidi and Piussi, "The Influence," 60, 64.

[60] Pitte, *Terres*, 201; Buccianti, *Il castagno*, 83.

[61] Unripe nuts are less tasty and spoil quickly: Bounous, *Il castagno*, 125.

[62] F. Cardini, "Magia del castagno," in *Il castagno: Tradizioni e trasformazioni,* ed. R. Roda (Ferrara, 1989), 23–38 (32–33); Fauve-Chamoux, "Chestnuts," 361; H. Breisch, "Harvesting, Storage and Processing of Chestnuts in France and Italy," in *Proceedings of the International Congress on Chestnut,* ed. E. Antognazzi (Spoleto, n.d.), 429–36 (430).

[63] Pitte, *Terres*, 254–56.

The harvest sets off a chain of extracurricular activities related to the chestnut that further occupy the cultivator. Chestnuts are marvelous food fresh from the tree and modern distribution networks have popularized them most of all in that form. Fresh nuts are mostly water (up to 60 percent) but also contain healthy quantities of glucids, some protein (up to 7 percent) and fat, as well as minerals and much vitamin C: they are quite calorific, since 100 g of fresh nuts provide almost 200 kcal to their lucky eater (for comparison, 100 g of potatoes deliver 86 kcal and the same amount of walnuts 660 kcal).[64] Despite this excellent nutritional value, it was another characteristic of chestnuts that determined their past popularity. Left untreated, many nuts will germinate, spawn pests, or succumb to mold and fungi: indeed, their relative fragility makes chestnuts different from other nuts, and more like fruit.[65] Yet chestnuts keep very well if they are dried soon after falling from their branches. Though it is possible to dry them naturally, using the sun, in the Mediterranean rainy season of autumn to leave one's chestnuts outdoors for the two or three weeks required for sun-drying is a big risk. In the centuries before the light fermentation induced by immersion in water was propagated around 1700 as a way to "disinfect" the fruit and thereby conserve it, the risk-averse cultivator therefore preferred artificial drying, in fact smoking of the nuts.[66] Smoking was a slow process that required a low, cool fire and two or three weeks' time, but after chestnuts had been slowly smoked they were very easy to separate from their shiny outer shell and their inner furry skin. What remained after a slight winnowing was a hard, butter-colored, extremely durable nut that weighed only two-thirds what it did when fresh, could keep over two years, but still contained the excellent nutrition it had originally: really, only water had been lost, while the vitamins, carbohydrates, sugars, and minerals that render chestnuts a quite complete meal remained.[67]

The preserved chestnut could be boiled, exactly like the fresh one, but it could also be ground into meal, useful for porridge and also in baking, rather like corn. The same equipment used for grinding grain could grind chestnuts, though this was harder on the millstones and any mechanisms, and took more energy than grain did. Mostly this operation was left to specialists, and for early medieval Italy I know of no

[64] Fauve-Chamoux, "Chestnuts," 360. The sugar content of chestnuts is so high Napoleon considered using them to manufacture sugar to circumvent the Continental Blockade.

[65] Bounous, *Il castagno*, 133.

[66] Pitte, *Terres*, 230–35; Breisch, "Harvesting," 431–35; M. Montanari, "Un frutto ricco di storia," in *La castagna sulle tavole d'Europa* (S. Piero al Bagno, 2001), 50–63 (58).

[67] Fenaroli, *Il castagno*, 105; Becchi, *Discorso*, 41–42; Fauve-Chamoux, "Chestnuts," 360. Chestnuts are about 3 percent fat, much less than other nuts. See Bounous, *Il castagno*, 187, for a comparison with almonds.

chestnut farmers who were also millers, or millers who farmed chestnuts. Chestnut flour, the final product of grinding, kept as well as dried nuts in airtight containers, and though it lacked the gluten to rise adequately with yeast, it might still be kneaded into a passable, sweet-tasting bread, neat or mixed with the flour of a grain like rye.[68]

Artificial drying of chestnuts was a vast enhancement of the value of this food to premodern people, one that justified the toil it took to render the nuts durable. Moreover, the dried nuts freed the chestnut-eater from the finicky and surprisingly time-consuming chore of peeling the fresh nuts. According to a scholarly assessment, it took modern peasants forty minutes to remove the outer shell and inner furry skin from enough nuts to feed five people (about 2 kg), even if the nuts were boiled to ease the task.[69] About half that weight of dried nuts satisfy the same need, without requiring the shelling. Thus the techniques of drying and winnowing the chestnut crop right after harvest were labor-saving and well worth the trouble.

While preoccupied with the several phases of the nuts' processing, the cultivator may neglect the woods, dormant from late November until March, at which time another season begins, in some places with a burning of the litter that might have amassed under the trees over the winter. Overall, then, traditional chestnut cultivation occupies about seven months of the year, from the springtime attempts to improve the soil and curb weed growth, to the removal of any leaves wanted as litter in November. The most important operation, taking the nuts, is eased by ground-cover control, but that too produces desirable side-effects (hay) and in mature nut-producing groves controlled fire can do a lot of the work of transforming biomass and accelerating its absorption by the soil. Among the other labors that the chestnut grove could impose on its managers was the gathering of mushrooms and berries, and also of honey, for chestnut blossoms, particularly the earlier male ones, attract bees. In modern chestnut woods honey-making has become a surprisingly important economic activity, and in early modern France transhumant beekeepers followed the blossoming in the groves uphill, moving higher as the season warmed up.[70]

Such ancillary activities are not strictly speaking part of chestnut cultivation, just useful ecological consequences of it, and a cultivator who

[68] Pitte, *Terres*, 237–40; R. Zagnoni, "La coltivazione del castagno nella montagna fra Bologna e Pistoia nei secoli XI–XIII," in *Villaggi, boschi e campi dell'Appennino dal medioevo all'età contemporanea* (Porretta Terme, 1997), 41–57 (47–49).

[69] Fauve-Chamoux, "Chestnuts," 361.

[70] Pitte, *Terres*, 252; G. Cherubini, "La 'civiltà' del castagno in Italia alla fine del medioevo," *Archeologia medievale* 8 (1981), 247–80 (261).

wished to overlook them could do so without severe consequences once the grove was old enough. There are, however, some other ancillary activities that often accompany castaneicuture and that add somewhat to the labor of keeping a chestnut wood. In some regards the compatibility of a chestnut grove with pastoral pursuits is a distinguishing trait of this style of arboriculture, and it was certainly important to the chestnut's success in the Mediterranean region. Under the canopy of properly spaced, mature chestnut trees there tend to grow particularly biodiverse and nutritious grasses, plants that take advantage of *Castanea*'s late budding and benefit from the shade a chestnut tree makes when the summer warms up.[71] In a chestnut grove flocks of sheep and goats, and herds of cattle, find savory pasture from earliest spring through autumn, when the nuts begin to fall off the trees. In early summer chestnut trees shed their male catkins, which, as observed above, can render the pasture below both unpalatable and indigestible to ungulates, but most of the time the herbs and grasses that flourish in places where chestnuts grow offer grazers excellent nutrition. If their caretakers offer them, these animals will eat chestnut leaves, particularly if the grass has run out or dried up. Thus, with little oversight, the animals will add to the fertility of a chestnut wood without stripping it of the things people prefer. The milk cattle, goats, and sheep produced was a fine complement to the chestnuts themselves, whose main nutritional defect, from a human point of view, was their poverty in protein. Chestnut mush dressed with milk was, and is, a satisfying dish.[72]

Just as chestnut woods are nicely compatible with small-scale pastoralism and can induce cultivators to add some herding to their routines (and labors), they are also able to fit in where grains are grown. A widely spaced chestnut grove allows the cultivation of such "rustic" grains as rye, a cereal early medieval cultivators popularized.[73] Though Fernand Braudel was suspicious of such "pseudo-flours," premodern people, and some modern ones, mixed chestnuts, ground into meal, with the flour of various grains, most notably rye, and could thus fashion passable loaves from what came to be known in early modern Italy as "the tree of bread."[74] In this way, a chestnut wood could contribute important

---

[71] On such pasture: Grove and Rackham, *The Nature*, 68; Fenaroli, *Il castagno*, 118–19.

[72] On chestnut's association with the herding of goats and sheep, see below, 73–79.

[73] Examples from Umbria and the Marche: E. Brugiapaglia and J.-L. de Beaulieu, "Etude de la dynamique végétale Tardiglaciaire et Holocène en Italie centrale," *Comptes rendus de l'Académie des Sciences Paris* 321 (1995), 617–22 (621–22); from the Alpine foothills of Lombardy: R. Drescher-Schneider, "Forest, Forest Clearance and Open Land during the Time of the Roman Empire in Northern Italy," in *Evaluation of Land Surfaces Cleared from Forests in the Mediterranean Region during the Time of the Roman Empire*, ed. B. Franzel (Stuttgart, 1994), 45–58 (54). Wheat tends not to grow well in the cool places where chestnut thrives.

[74] F. Braudel, *Civilisation matérielle et capitalisme: xve–xviii siècle*, 2 vols., Vol. 1 (Paris, 1967), 84. See also M. Montanari, *L'alimentazione contadina nell'alto medioevo* (Naples, 1979), 299–300; J.-P. Delumeau,

calories to any agrarian community that favored it and was willing to shoulder some additional toil, from fencing in the sowed grove to tending to the cereal crop.

In effect, the chestnut finds a place for itself in the most varied agrarian circumstances. It is a versatile tree. Above all, it fits in because it does not demand all that much of people. The actual toils of chestnut cultivation are of course different according to the cultivators' purposes (wood or nuts), to choices about how or whether to "integrate" the trees' productivity with other compatible pursuits, and to the grove's age. Naturally, over time a chestnut wood lost any uniformity in age structure it might have had, as plants died and were replaced, but launching a new chestnut wood was always the most time-consuming and fatiguing part of the chestnut grower's routine. Much more than any other type of chestnut wood, however managed, the young grove required work. Once the roots of the trees established themselves, the work-load for people diminished, and most of the burden passed to the trees, whose biological labor the chestnut farmer simply stimulates. A mature chestnut grove geared to either nut or wood production imposed (and still does) negligible demands on the cultivator.

In a study of a medium-sized farm in the Garfagnana in northern Tuscany, Buccianti found that although mature chestnuts covered two-thirds of the available land, they absorbed only 12 percent of the annual labor the farmers invested on their farm, as measured in full days of work.[75] A similar study of central French groves suggested that 2 hectares of chestnut wood required 10 adult "male days" of work, and 100 days of female or child work to render 5.5 tons of nuts each year. Though such analyses do not calculate some ancillary tasks (like processing the nuts, or managing the hives under them), and though the late-twentieth-century situation can serve only as a rough gauge for understanding premodern chestnut cultivation's demands on labor, scholars are unanimous in noticing the favorable relation between the need for labor in a chestnut wood and the value of the products such labor extracts.

Quite aside from the pasture, mostly for sheep and cows, that a fruiting chestnut wood offers, and the ancillary woodland products (honey, berries, mushrooms), chestnut woods are a highly "efficient" way to use land. First of all there is the agrarian calendar to consider, and the uncanny way in which chestnut cultivation's main operations fit tidily into those

---

Arezzo, espace et sociétés, 2 vols., Vol. 1: *715–1230* (Rome, 1996), 69. Zagnoni, "La coltivazione del castagno," 47, treats the difficulties of grinding chestnuts.

[75] Buccianti, *Il castagno*, 18. The study period was 1978–91. Pitte, *Terres*, 195–97, suggests that twenty days per year of an adult farmer's work is the average for a hectare of wood.

periods of the year when a Mediterranean farmer, given over to grain- and vine-raising, some gathering, and small-scale animal husbandry, has more time on her or his hands. The late harvest time of chestnuts is an important advantage. A first "efficiency" of chestnut-growing, then, comes from the contribution this activity makes to distributing the phys- ical effort of food production more equally over the course of a year without interfering with other important tasks. Next, if one keeps in mind the vital distinction between agrarian yields (how much food a plot of land produces) and productivity (the difference between the food produced and the labor invested to produce it), the economic "rational- ity" of chestnut woodlands increases; for very small investments of labor, measured in food calories expended or days occupied, return very large amounts of nutritious food.[76]

As one might expect, a chestnut tree's production of nuts fluctuates with the seasonal wavering of temperature and precipitation, and also with the tree's own biological clock, following which boom years very seldom get an immediate encore.[77] The tree will also produce fewer nuts in youth and senility. Moreover, nut production depends on cultivar, on locality, and on exposure, so that chestnut productivity is a variable thing by the standards of modern industrial regularity.[78] Yet it is much less so by the standards of arable agriculture, and on average it is possible to esti- mate that 7 reasonably generous trees consistently make enough nuts to feed a person for a year, if we allow about 50 kg as the output in nuts of each tree. They do so without demanding anything like 365 days of toil in exchange.[79] Compared to most grains, and in particular to most grains that will grow where chestnuts like to live, chestnuts are a fine and emi- nently "rational" solution to the great pre-industrial question of how to produce regularly from the land the calories a local population needed to live. For whereas grain-growing is an unvarying cycle of fastidious and laborious work, renewed each year, that consumes much of the energy it

[76] J. Devroey, *Économie rurale et société dans l'Europe franque (vie–ixe siècles)*, (Paris, 2003), 115–17; J. Landers, *The Field and the Forge: Population, Production, and Power in the Pre-Industrial West* (Oxford, 2003), 58.

[77] Fenaroli, *Il castagno*, 102.

[78] Pitte, *Terres*, 26–27; Buccianti, *Il castagno*, 51–52.

[79] Cherubini, "La 'civiltà,'" 272. Mature trees produce 27–65 kg of nuts per year, but coppices much less (*c.* 7 kg according to Fenaroli, *Il castagno*, 30). Pitte, *Terres*, 199–201, calculated that an average hectare of Cevegnol chestnut wood produces 1,000 kg of nuts, or about 2 million kcal (he con- siders that 1 kg delivers 2,400 kcal, as opposed to the roughly 2,000 allowed by Fauve-Chamoux, "Chestnuts," 361). V. Hehn, *Cultivated Plants and Domesticated Animals in Their Migration from Asia to Europe* (Amsterdam, 1976), 297, reports that entire Corsican clans lived from twenty-four trees and some goats in the mid 1800s.

produces, chestnut-growing is (relatively) light work that does not erode the energy-capital it amasses.[80]

People uninvolved in chestnut cultivation have long noticed the light burden this activity imposes on its practitioners. The trope of the chestnut growers' unwillingness to work, shameful in a culture that for various reasons lionized laborious activity, was successful because it seemed to correspond to what everyone saw: chestnut cultivators enjoying abundant and nourishing food without working for it, contravening the injunctions of St. Paul in 2 Thessalonians 3.7–8 ("Neither did we eat any man's bread for nothing, but in labor and in toil we worked night and day, lest we should be chargeable to any of you") and of Genesis 3.19 ("In the sweat of thy face shalt thou eat bread until thou return to the earth out of which thou wast taken"). In a famous article published in the *Annales*, Ariane Bruneton-Governatori argued that the early modern decline of chestnut cultivation had less to do with the demand for tannin found in chestnut bark (which other scholars assumed led to widespread logging of *Castanea* and its marginalization in the 1800s) than with the unfavorable cultural image early modern writers created for chestnuts.[81] In particular she discovered that seventeenth- and eighteenth-century commentators considered chestnuts base food, primitive and rustic, and associated the savory nuts with backwards mountain folk and also with ignorance and sloth.[82]

In the twenty-first century "service economy" I inhabit, the tasks of the pre-industrial chestnut cultivator look like hard enough work. Nowadays we all know there is no such thing as a free lunch, but in the organic economy of the long Middle Ages, chestnuts were a marvel, a plant that gave good food, in goodly quantities, without absorbing all that much muscle power, and thus came as close to offering that chimerical lunch as agrarian societies could get. True, the originator of any chestnut wood had struggled mightily to get this peculiar ecosystem on its feet. True too, a very specialized know-how sustained the enhanced nut production of a grafted grove. And true, finally, that a tree's planter, or grafter, embraced a rather ample view of things, for the initial labor was a long-term investment whose benefits people living generations after him or her would enjoy: by his or her work the planter presented

---

[80] Pitte, *Terres*, 199–201.

[81] A. Bruneton-Governatori, "Alimentation et idéologie," *Annales ESC* 39 (1984), 1161–89. Physiocratic insistence that grains were the most rational food mattered too: B. Andreolli, "L'uso del bosco e degli incolti," in *Storia dell'agricoltura italiana*, 5 vols., Vol. II, ed. G. Pinto and M. Ambrosoli (Florence, 2002), 123–44 (123).

[82] See also Cherubini, "La 'civiltà,'" 258–61; Cardini, "Magia del castagno," 23.

a gift to posterity. This was facilitated by the willing collaboration of *Castanea sativa*, whose foibles the planter seconded in the early phases of growth, and whose stolid assumption of the responsibilities of production in maturity other people could live from. In the end it seemed to most that the twenty or thirty years of waiting for the grove to attain its potential were a small lapse of time measured against the centuries of reliable productivity to come.

Chapter 2

THE TRIUMPH OF A TREE

First by offering an enviable balance between available products and the work needed to obtain them, and then by striking up a long-term relationship with people, the chestnut triumphed, moving from relative obscurity in a few, select habitats to considerable importance, both ecological and economic, from southern Britain to the middle Danube, and from Atlantic Cantabria to the Caucasus. Though only a portion of the extension of chestnut's range to its furthest botanical limits took place during the first millennium, that portion was the decisive phase in the winning collaboration between chestnut and people.

This chapter outlines the expansion of *Castanea* in western Europe and especially in Italy in a new way that privileges the early Middle Ages. It moves beyond mere chronology, however. In order to bolster its claims about when chestnut expanded its range the chapter also analyzes the circumstances behind that expansion. Specific early medieval social, economic, and legal conditions combined with the botanical qualities of *Castanea sativa* to effect changes in the woods.

CHESTNUT'S SPREAD: A EUROPEAN CHRONOLOGY

Debates about how chestnuts got to where they were in the European nineteenth and early twentieth century were until recently an established tradition in botanical-historical discourse. Much scholarship aimed at proving the indigeneity or the "invasive" and "exotic" character of *Castanea* in this or that place, and at dating the arrival of the plant in different corners of Europe. The publication of a scholarly summa on chestnut cultivation and its history by Pitte in 1986 marked a turning point in the old discussions, which Pitte declared "sterile" and irresolvable.[1] Since then the

---

[1] J. Pitte, *Terres de castanide* (Paris, 1987), 47–50. On the longevity of such debates in Britain, see O. Rackham, *Ancient Woodland: Its History, Vegetation and Uses in England* (London, 1980), 329–30.

increasing refinement of palynological instruments, and the better funding for archaeobotanical studies in many parts of Europe, have led to an almost consensual outcome and the creation of an orthodox version of the deep history of the chestnut in western Eurasia. In this new version of the history of how the species got to where it is, *Castanea*'s main habitats were always in western Asia, in Georgia and on the southern Black Sea coast, but it is an indigenous species around the Bosphorus and in Tyrrhenian Italy, particularly the peninsula's western volcanic areas and the valleys of Liguria, though also east of Lake Garda and in the Emilian-Tuscan Appenines. Chestnut may further have found shelter from the last glaciation in south-central France (the Isère), maybe in the Cantabrian highlands of northwest Iberia, and in Thessaly and the Peloponnesus. Thus twentieth-century *Castanea* is a plant that has had multiple homes on northern Mediterranean hillsides for at least four millennia and therefore can claim legitimate status among that territory's autochthonous dwellers.[2]

The older accounts relied less on pollen studies and granted chestnut a far shorter tenancy in Europe. They presented *Castanea sativa* as native to the Transcaucasus and able to migrate from there with human aid only after about 1000 BC. This model set chestnut towards the end of the vast migration westward of hundreds of different plants, arboreal and not, from western Asia, or India, or China. This westward botanical drift had begun in prehistoric times and introduced many of the species we now associate with the typical Mediterranean landscape and eventually the first domesticated plants as well. This older view of how chestnut populated Europe mirrored nineteenth-century ideas about the origins of civilization and its dissemination through the channels of commerce and warfare.[3] While it is plausible that refinements in genetic mapping will revitalize the traditional view, and already some suggestive genetic affinities between

---

[2] For a synthesis: P. Krebs, M. Condera, M. Pradella, D. Torriani, M. Felber, and W. Tinner, "Quaternary Refugia of the Sweet Chestnut (*Castanea sativa* Mill.): An Extended Palynological Approach," *Vegetation History and Archaeobotany* 13 (2004), 145–60 (149–55). See also A. Paganelli and A. Miola, "Chestnut (*Castanea sativa* Mill.) as an Indigenous Species in Northern Italy," *Il Quaternario* 4 (1991), 99–106; C. Accorsi, M. Bandini Mazzanti, A. Mercuri, C. Rivalenti, and G. Trevisan Grandi, "Holocene Forest Pollen Vegetation of the Po Plain: Northern Italy (Emilia Romagna Data)," *Allionia* 24 (1996), 233–76 (240–48). An indigenist precursor was G. Negri, "Distribuzione geografica del castagno e del faggio in Italia," *L'Alpe* 18 (1931), 589–94 (589).

[3] The 1870 classic is V. Hehn, *Cultivated Plants and Domesticated Animals in Their Migration from Asia to Europe* (Amsterdam, 1976), with chestnut migrations on 298. Italy's place in chestnut migration: A. Chiarugi, "Ricerche sulla vegetazione dell'Etruria marittima," *Giornale botanico italiano* 46 (1933), 15–36 (20, 26, 33); R. Cecchini, "Origine della diffusione del castagno in Italia," *Monti e boschi* 1 (1950), 412–14 (413–14). L. Fenaroli and G. Gambi, *Alberi* (Trent, 1976), 309. Interesting general considerations: M. van der Veen, "Agricultural Innovation," *World Archaeology* 42.1 (2010), 1–12 (5–8). See also D. Zohary, "The Diffusion of South and East Asian and of African Crops into the Belt of Mediterranean Agriculture," in *Plants for Food and Medicine: Proceedings of the Joint Conference of the Society for Economic Botany and the International Society for Ethnopharmacology, London, UK, 1–6*

Anatolian varieties of chestnut and French and Italian ones receive notice, currently it is more common to find scholarly endorsements of the indigenous "origin" of chestnuts in western Europe.[4]

Prevailing teleologies and nationalist ideology shaped nineteenth- and twentieth-century views on chestnut's spread, so we should expect to discern them also in the newer indigenist views on Europe's chestnut. In the last decades of the twentieth century, European and Italian political cultures have found in regional identities an apparent antidote to the anomie of transnationalism and globalization. To label a plant as exotic and imported from beyond the locality, or to call it an invasive species, makes a statement about the past and its purity (or impurity) and therefore about the shape of the present. Indigenous plants have a right to their *Lebensraum*, like indigenous people, based on supposed centuries of continuous, indeed ancestral, presence in a place. This presence confers on the place its unique character and must be protected from outside forces. The immigrants against whom the aborigines must defend themselves and their ancient identity are also plants. In the current Italian context the palynologically proven antiquity of *Castanea sativa*'s presence in the Po valley is a claim to (vegetative) citizenship founded on a particular opinion of what is the typical and righteous landscape of the region. Current constructions of north Italian identity do not look back to Neolithic farmers in their search for legitimizing ancestry, so the chestnut does not look invasive or exotic, but part of the immemorial landscape, now in danger of being supplanted by outside forces and inside pusillanimity.[5]

July 1996, ed. H. Prendergast, N. Etkin, D. Harris, and P. Houghton (Kew, 1998), 123–34 (124–26, 131–32); W. Hondelmann, *Die Kulturpflanzen der griechisch-römischen Welt: Pflänzische Ressourcen der Antike* (Berlin, 2002), 8–10, 109; F. di Castri, "On Invading Species and Invaded Ecosystems: The Interplay of Historical Chance and Biological Necessity," in *Biological Invasions in Europe and the Mediterranean Basin*, ed. F. di Castri, A. J. Hansen, and M. Debussche (Dordrecht, 1990), 3–16 (12–13); K. Sykora, "History of the Impact of Man on the Distribution of Plant Species," in di Castri *et al.*, *Biological Invasions*, 37–50 (38); D. Zohary and M. Hopf, *Domestication of Plants in the Old World* (Oxford, 2000), 246–49; W. van Zeist, "Economic Aspects," in *Progress in Old World Palaeoethnobotany: A Retrospective View on the Occasion of 20 Years of the International Work Group for Palaeoethnobotany*, ed. W. van Zeist, K. Wasylikowa, and K.-E. Behre (Rotterdam, 1991), 109–30 (109–11); Z. Naveh and J. Vernet, "The Palaeohistory of the Mediterranean Biota," in *Biogeography of Mediterranean Invasions*, ed. R. Groves and F. di Castri (Cambridge, 1991), 19–32 (27–28).

[4] Much depends on how one defines indigeneity, or how far back one draws the line. See M. Conedera, P. Krebs, W. Tinner, M. Pradella, and D. Torriani, "The Cultivation of *Castanea sativa* (Mill.) in Europe, from Its Origin to Its Diffusion on a Continental Scale," *Vegetation History and Archaeobotany* 13 (2004), 161–79 (171). For a study suggesting eastern Turkey as *Castanea*'s homeland: M. Martin, C. Mattioni, M. Cherubini, D. Taurchini, and F. Villani, "Genetic Diversity in European Chestnut Populations," *Acta horticulturae* 866 (2009), 163–67.

[5] On the global politics of plant indigeneity, see D. Simberloff, "Confronting Introduced Species: A Form of Xenophobia," *Biological Invasions* 5 (2003), 179–92; N. Kingsbury, *Hybrid: The History and Science of Plant Breeding* (Chicago, 2009), 48–53.

Far from being sterile, then, debates on chestnut origins are vigorous and vital, propelled forward by the ideological currents in the societies that engender them. We should not expect the debates to subside: chestnuts have enough symbolic clout that they will always find space in modern discourse. Yet as the European and Italian origins of *Castanea sativa* have been pushed back in time, the problem of the species' dissemination after the last glaciation has grown larger. It is worthwhile therefore to trace the main steps in the "advent and conquests," as Marc Bloch might have called the process, of *Castanea sativa* in Europe and Italy.[6]

The diffusion of the chestnut in western Europe was certainly an artifact, produced by human efforts, but probably through a much less linear process than we might imagine. It was also probably a process that brought the tree to the limits of its ecological range much later than we might expect. In prehistoric times chestnut lurked timidly in a few appropriate sites, perhaps limited to those soils whose acidity was just right, to areas with just the right amount of precipitation, to those hillsides whose exposure and temperature range perfectly suited the species. But palaeobotanical studies of Balkan, Alpine, north Iberian, and French sites that prove that by the early Iron Age there were chestnut stands in most Mediterranean places where chestnut later became economically significant also show such a presence did not transcend marginality.[7]

Usually the establishment of Roman authority beyond the Alps receives credit for a major, decisive increase in chestnut trees in the local woodlands. This orthodoxy owes much to the prevalent conception of the impact of Roman imperialism on the various northern and western "peripheral" societies it encompassed (what historians call Romanization).[8] With the Roman legions, their roads, and towns came a new economic organization, intensified exploitation of resources, markets and trade,

---

[6] See M. Bloch, "Avènement et conquêtes du moulin à eau," *Annales d'histoire économique et sociale* 7 (1935), 538–63.

[7] Chestnuts dated 1450 BC–800 BC were even found on Menorca, hardly chestnut country: H. Sitka, "Los macrorestos botánicos de la Cova de Cárritx," in *Ideología y sociedad en la prehistoria de Menorca*, ed. V. Lull (Ciutadella, 1999), 521–31 (522) – a contaminated find or a sign of trade? Portugal: I. Figueiral, "Wood Resources in Northwest Portugal: Their Availability and Use from the Late Bronze Age to the Roman Period," *Vegetation History and Archaeobotany* 5 (1996), 121–29 (122–27). Switzerland (Böschen, near Zurich, eleventh century BC): van Zeist, "Economic Aspects," 114. Alps: J.-L. de Beaulieu, "Timberline and Human Impact in the French Alps," in *Impact of Prehistoric and Medieval Man on the Vegetation*, ed. D. Moe and S. Hicks (Strasbourg, 1990), 72. Balkans: S. Bottema, "The Holocene History of the Walnut, Sweet-Chestnut, Manna-Ash and Plane Tree in the Eastern Mediterranean," *Pallas* 52 (2000), 35–59 (42).

[8] L. Foxhall, M. Jones, and H. Forbes, "Human Ecology and the Classical Landscape," in *Classical Archaeology*, ed. S. Alcock and R. Osborne (Oxford, 2007), 91–117. P. Wells, "Production within and beyond Imperial Boundaries: Goods, Exchange, and Power in Roman Europe," in *World-Systems Theory in Practice: Leadership, Production, and Exchange*, ed. P. Kardulias (Lanham, MD, 1999), 85–111

and monetarized exchanges, a kind of ancient modernization that transformed the people who lived under Roman hegemony as much as it transformed their economic arrangements. Thus, scholars have sought, and found, traces of a reorientation of the European empire's economic and therefore ecological structures between about 100 BC and AD 100. An interesting example of this is the creation in northern Europe of novel plant communities called meadows: an outcome, it seems, of the refinement of Roman metallurgy, the introduction of the long metal blades needed to harvest hay, and Roman markets' mobilization of resources through strong demand for animal products.[9] The point is that the presumed Roman dissemination of chestnut woodland fits into a much ampler narrative of imperially sponsored economic and environmental change.[10]

Actually, whatever changes Romanization brought to productive relationships in Europe, it does not appear to have left a deep imprint on chestnut woods. Other species of tree had palynologically clear transformations, and fir and oak wood finds are common in excavated sites in Roman Europe; but chestnut pollen remained quite inconspicuous and the chestnut is elusive in both its wood and nut form in sites dated to the late Republic or early empire.[11] Along the Rhine and Danube *limes*, for instance, almost no wood of *Castanea* and a minuscule number of chestnuts or shells emerged from the extensive digs carried out after World War II. Given such small quantities, it is just as likely these traces of chestnut's presence were imported from faraway places, like the much more common date pits in tombs and middens, as that they came from local sources of supply and thus reflect any Romanization of forests.[12] Very

(95–96). See also van Zeist, "Economic Aspects," 114–16; P. Blänkle, A. Kreuz, and V. Rupp, "Archäologische und naturwissenschaftliche Untersuchungen an zwei römischen Brandgräbern in der Wetterau," *Germania* 73 (1995), 103–30 (120–21); H. Küster, "Weizen, Pfeffer, Tannenholz: Botanische Untersuchungen zur Verbreitung von Handelsgütern in römischer Zeit," *Münsterische Beitrage zur antiken Handelsgeschichte* 15 (1995), 1–26 (6–8, 14–21).

9 Foxhall *et al.*, "Human Ecology," 110.

10 H. Küster, "Botanische Untersuchungen zur Landwirtschaft in der Rhein-Donau-Provinzen vom 1. bis zum 5. Jahrhundert nach Chr.," in *Ländliche Besiedlung und Landwirtschaft in der Rhein-Donau-Provinzen des römischen Reiches*, ed. H. Bender and H. Wolff (Espelkamp, 1994), 21–35 (24–32). The narrative of Romanization is now nuanced and contested, agency being redistributed to the "Romanized" populations who modulated Rome's influence: see for instance D. Mattingly, *An Imperial Possession* (London, 2006), 353–69, with a critique of imperialist and progressivist narratives.

11 Conedera *et al.*, "The Cultivation," 174–75, with Figs. 5b and 7b.

12 A solitary mid-first-century AD nut from Straubing, near Passau: Küster, "Botanische Untersuchungen," Fig. 3.4. A nut from a first- to seventh-century tomb near Kempten: U. Willerding, "Die Pflanzenreste," in *Das römische Gräberfeld auf der Keckweise in Kempten*, ed. M. Mackenstein (Kallmünz, 1978), 183–95 (185). A sixth-century "Frankish" tomb near Krefeld had a nut too: M. Hopf, "Wallnüsse und Esskastanie in Holzschalen als Beigaben im frankischen Grab von Gellep

weak evidence of Roman-period chestnut cultivation derives also from those regions, like the wine-growing Pfalz, where chestnut woodlands became economically significant in the late medieval and early modern eras.[13] Likewise, for the Roman provinces in what is now Switzerland, whose palaeobotany is well developed, only in the southern Alps, within the Po watershed, are there sure signs from second–fourth-century contexts of the dissemination of chestnut woods.[14] For the rest, the area was poor in chestnuts or chestnut wood under the Romans.[15] In the Low Countries too the archaeobotanical data supporting chestnut's presence in Roman times is at best vestigial, and the case of Pannonia at the other end of the Rhine–Danube frontier is similar, with little to attest to chestnuts before the thirteenth century AD.[16] With only very slight exaggeration one might say that there is as much evidence for chestnuts in early Roman Egypt, where *Castanea* definitely never grew, as there is from Germania.[17]

The situation is not so different for the Gallic provinces, in some parts of which *Castanea* grew spontaneously long before the Romans got there. Some Gallo-Romans definitely employed chestnut wood in building and heating baths in the southern Massif Central, not far from that Isère where prehistorians detect very early traces of chestnut's presence. But this usage is most clear for the latest period of Roman hegemony, the fifth

(Krefeld)," *Jahrbuch des römisch-germanischen Zentralmuseums Mainz* 10 (1963), 200–03 (202–03). A useful synthesis of finds is M. Petrucci-Bavaud and S. Jacomet, "Zur Interpretation von Nahrungsbeigaben im römerzeitlichen Brandgräbern," *Ethnographisch-archäologische Zeitschrift* 38 (1997), 567–93 (579–88). See also G. Bounous, *Il castagno: Coltura, ambiente ed utilizzazioni in Italia e nel mondo* (Bologna, 2002), 243–45.

[13] J. Wilde, *Kulturgeschichte der rheinpfälzischen Baumwelt und ihrer Naturdenkmale* (Kaiserslautern, 1936), 200–05. Wilde's claim (201) that the Alsatian town of Kestenholz (Châtenois) existed in 679 depends on twelfth-century accounts of legendary donations to Ebersheim from St. Odile (*Chronicon Ebersheimense*, ed. L. Weiland, in *Chronica aevi Suevici*, MGH, Scriptores 23 [Hanover, 1874], 428). My thanks to Hans Hummer for this reference.

[14] Conedera *et al.*, "The Cultivation," 173.

[15] C. Brombacher, S. Jacomet, and M. Kühn, "Mittelalterliche Kulturpflanzen aus der Schweiz und Liechtenstein," in *Environment and Subsistence in Medieval Europe*, ed. G. de Boe and F. Verhaeghe (Zellik, 1997), 95–111; L. Fenaroli, *Il castagno* (Rome, 1945), 20; M. Irninger and M. Kühn, "Obstvielfalt: Von wilden und zahmen Früchten im Mittelalter und in früher Neuzeit," *Archäologie der Schweiz* 22 (1999), 48–56 (50–52).

[16] Netherlands: J.-P. Pals, "De introductie van cultuurgewassen in de Romeinse Tijd," in *De introductie van onze cultuurplanten en hun begeleiders, van het Neolithicum tot 1500 AD*, ed. A. Zeven (Wageningen, 1997), 25–51 (37, 51); W. Willems and L. Kooistra, "De Romeinse villa te Voerendaal: Opgraving 1987," *Archeologie in Limburg* 33 (1988), 137–47 (142); L. Kooistra, "Arable Farming in the Hey Day of the Roman Villa at Voerendaal (Limbourg, the Netherlands)," in *Palaeoethnobotany and Archaeology: International Work Group for Palaeoethnobotany* (Nitra, 1991), 165–75 (167). Pannonia: U. Willerding, "Die Paläoethnobotanik und ihre Stellung im System der Wissenschaften," *Berichte der deutschen botanischen Gesellschaft* 91 (1978), 3–30 (17). P. Szabó, *Woodland and Forest in Medieval Hungary* (Oxford, 2005), 75–77.

[17] C. de Vartavan and V. Asensi Amorós, *Codex of Ancient Egyptian Plant Remains* (London, 1997), 66.

century.[18] Pollen records suggest a minor surge of chestnut's range in the Pyrenees from the third century onwards, and in the eastern Cévennes, the region of modern France between St. Etienne and Montpellier most closely connected to chestnut cultivation, early Roman-period pollens show barely a hint of chestnut's presence.[19] Elsewhere in the territory of modern France, the best evidence for anthropogenic extension of chestnut comes from the *end* of the first millennium: at the remarkable site of Charavines near Grenoble, it is clear from fruit, wood, and especially pollen finds, facilitated by a lake's transgression and the formation of a bog, that tenth-century cultivators found chestnuts appealing, and cleared other trees to foster their favorite, but were the first people to do so in the area. As they used little chestnut wood, the uptick in pollen deposits suggests the Charaviners fostered *Castanea* for its fruit.[20] Further south in Languedoc chestnut was not a significant land use before the twelfth century.[21]

Across the Pyrenees, in northwestern Iberia, where a few chestnuts that had survived the last glaciation grew in selected microecologies from at least 2000 BC, the pollen evidence suggests that the great leap forward of the species came after AD 100, mostly in late Roman times, and that by 1000 *Castanea* was the significant arboreal presence it has remained in Galicia until today.[22] In some parts of that province, chestnut pollen first appears in bogs in the sixth century, though in samples from Roman settlements apparently earlier deposits have also been found.[23]

---

[18] P. Poirier, "Architecture, combustibles, et environnement des thermes de Chassenon," *Aquitania* 16 (1999), 179–81 (180–81).

[19] D. Galop, *La forêt, l'homme et le troupeau dans les Pyrénées* (Toulouse, 1998), 201, 210, 245; C. Lefebvre, *Oppida helvica* (Paris, 2006), 469. See also A. Durand and M. Ruas, "La forêt languedocienne (fin VIIIe siècle–XIe siècle)," in *Les forêts d'Occident du moyen âge à nos jours*, ed. A. Corvol-Dessert (Toulouse, 2004), 163–80 (169, 179–80); C. Flahaut, *La distribution géographique des végétaux dans la région méditerranéenne française* (Paris, 1937), 53.

[20] M. Colardelle and E. Verdal, eds., *Les habitats du lac de Paladru (Isère) dans leur environnement* (Paris, 1993), 75–76, 79–81, 91, 238. A rise in chestnut pollens occurred at Charavines in Roman times, when the site was deserted.

[21] A. Durand, *Les paysages médiévaux du Languedoc (Xe–XIIe siècles)* (Toulouse, 1998), 342–49; M. Ruas, "Aspects of Early Medieval Farming from Sites in Mediterranean France," *Vegetation History and Archaeobotany* 14 (2005), 400–15.

[22] Conedera *et al.*, "The Cultivation," 165, 170; L. Santos, J. Romani, and G. Jalut, "History of Vegetation during the Holocene in the Courel and Queixa Sierras, Galicia, Northwest Iberian Peninsula," *Journal of Quaternary Science* 15 (2000), 621–32 (627–31); M. Aira Rodríguez, P. Saa, and P. López, "Cambios del paisaje durante el Holoceno," *Revue de paléobiologie* 11 (1992), 243–54 (251–53); M. Aira Rodríguez, "La vegetación gallega durante la época de ocupación romana a través del estudio del polen fosil," *Lucus Augusti* 1 (1996), 24–45 (30, 34–37, 40); M. Sánchez Goñi, *De la taphonomie pollinique à la reconstruction de l'environnement* (Oxford, 1993), 42–45.

[23] A. Martínez Cortizas, T. Mighall, X. Pontevedra Pombal, J. Novoa Munfoz, E. Peiteado Varelal, and R. Pifneiro Rebolol, "Linking Changes in Atmospheric Dust Deposition, Vegetation Change and Human Activities in Northwest Spain during the Last 5,300 Years," *The Holocene* 15 (2005),

A post-Roman acceleration in the distribution of chestnut receives confirmation from Britain, an area of well-developed classical archaeology. In the south of Britain, modern coppices have been reasonably successful, enough that foresters consider *Castanea* naturalized there.[24] But the commonplace that Roman troops brought the chestnut to Britain rests on wobbly foundations. It is surprising how scant are signs of ancient chestnut, or its products, and none of them are unequivocally related (by palynology) to local production during Roman times.[25] Two chestnuts found in the well of an affluent third–fourth-century villa in Essex that definitely imported its olives and mackerel are best read as exotic food bought at market, not the fruit of local orchards.[26] Since Romanization receives credit for introducing fifty new species of plant, from lettuce to walnut, to the Isles, the absence of convincing insular evidence for *Castanea sativa* is conspicuous.[27] Della Hooke found in Anglo-Saxon glossaries basic familiarity with chestnut, and indeed they use a word for it (*cystbéam*, *cystel*) that is etymologically related to the Latin one. But *Castanea* remains one of Anglo-Saxon England's "missing trees," extremely rarely mentioned in the sources, and the later Saxon glossaries show not that the Romans had made the plant common but rather that the cultural renown of this essence went beyond its botanical range by the end of the first millennium AD. British charters and place-names only begin to indicate some presence of chestnut trees in southern England from high

698–706 (701, 703). The pollens at Lucus Augusti, where *Castanea* prevailed, were poorly dated but seem "Roman": M. Aira Rodríguez and P. Uzquiano, "Análisis polínico e identificación de carbones en necrópolis gallegas de época romana," *Lucus Augusti* 1 (1996), 49–52.

[24] O. Rackham, *Trees and Woodland in the British Landscape: Revised Edition* (London, 1990), 7. C. Stace, *New Flora of the British Isles* (Cambridge, 2010), 289, adds the Channel Islands as another site of naturalization, where chestnut sets its own seeds.

[25] For Roman introduction see Fenaroli, *Il castagno*, 21; G. Peterken, *Natural Woodland: Ecology and Conservation in Northern Temperate Regions* (Cambridge, 1996), 336, 389, 418; G. Peterken, *Woodland Conservation and Management* (Cambridge, 1993), 141, 177–78; I. Richardson, "Chestnuts," in *The Oxford Encyclopedia of Trees of the World* (New York, 1983), 133–35; M. Grieve, *A Modern Herbal: The Medicinal, Culinary, Cosmetic and Economic Properties, Cultivation and Folk-Lore of Herbs, Grasses, Fungi, Shrubs and Trees, with All Their Modern Scientific Uses*, 2 vols. (New York, 1959), 193–95; W. Linnard, *Welsh Woods and Forests: A History* (Llandysul, 2000), 15–16. Recent skepticism is in P. Pugsley, *Roman Domestic Wood* (Oxford, 2003); and J. Greig, "Archaeobotanical and Historical Records Compared: A New Look at the Taphonomy of Edible and Other Useful Plants from the 11th to the 18th Centuries AD," *Circaea* 12 (1996), 211–47 (220).

[26] P. Murphy, U. Albarella, M. Germany, and A. Locker, "Production, Imports and Status: Biological Remains from a Late Roman Farm at Great Holts Farm, Boreham, Essex, UK," *Environmental Archaeology* 5 (2000), 35–48 (41–45).

[27] M. van der Veen, A. Livarda, and A. Hill, "New Food Plants in Roman Britain: Dispersal and Social Access," *Environmental Archaeology* 13.1 (2008), 10–36. M. van der Veen, "Food as Embodied Material Culture," *Journal of Roman Archaeology* 31 (2008), 83–110 (83), rejects the concept of Romanization to understand British botanical change (too affected by status) but attributes to Roman times "the first serious diversification of the plant component in British diet" since the Neolithic.

medieval times. In the twelfth century nuts were tithed in the Forest of Dean, and coppiced poles of chestnut appear in contracts in the following century.[28] Overall, the naturalization of the chestnut in southeastern Britain seems not to date to the Roman empire.

In light of the widespread presumption that there are many signs of how Roman modifications of the landscape gave chestnuts a leg-up in Europe, disappointingly little concrete evidence for this supposed expansion of *Castanea sativa* has survived. Of course, chestnuts and their shells *are* perishable, chestnut pollen *is* hard to distinguish from other tree pollens without powerful microscopes and an awareness of the problem, and there are all sorts of reasons why the Romans might have shunned chestnut wood, however abundant it was in their empire's wildwoods. Yet what archaeological data there is points to a very modest impact from Romanization on chestnut woodland in Europe. Insofar as the Roman empire mattered to the European diffusion of *Castanea*, it was the time after the high imperial phase that witnessed the most changes in the land.

CHESTNUT'S SPREAD: ITALY

Decoupling Roman influence and chestnut's diffusion in Rome's western provinces calls into question modern scholarship that assigns to the Romans the protagonist's role in the dissemination of the chestnut in Italy.[29] Reflecting earlier uncertainties on the origins of the chestnut's presence in the peninsula, there are two different versions of this story, but they are in harmony on the Roman chronology for the occupation of so many mid-altitude sites by woods of *Castanea sativa*. In one version of events, albeit one we have seen is no longer espoused by the majority of experts, the chestnut was an exotic import to Italy, brought from the eastern Mediterranean in the wake of Rome's imperial conquests there, probably at the very end of the first millennium BC. According to this narrative, Roman generals returned victorious from the Black Sea,

---

[28] D. Hooke, *Trees in Anglo-Saxon England* (Woodbridge, 2010), 275, lists chestnut as a "missing tree" in the English written tradition. Relying on H. Godwin, *The History of the British Flora* (Cambridge, 1975), 276–77 (who relied on some prewar excavations), Rackham, *Trees and Woodland* 41, 98–99, and *Ancient Woodland*, 330, refers to five Roman-era finds of chestnut wood (which, Rackham observes, often gets confused with oak). See also Greig, "Archaeobotanical and Historical Records," 220.

[29] E.g., Hehn, *Cultivated Plants*, 294–98; Pitte, *Terres*, 58–60; D. Magri and L. Sadori, "Late Pleistocene Pollen Stratigraphy at Lago di Vico, Central Italy," *Vegetation History and Archaeobotany* 8 (1999), 247–60 (258); W. van Zeist, "Aperçu sur la diffusion des végétaux cultivés dans la région méditerranéenne," in *Colloque de la Fondation L. Emberger sur la mise en place, l'évolution et la caractérisation de la flore et de la végétation circum-méditerranéenne* (Montpellier, 1980), 129–43 (138).

or maybe northern Greece, with saplings of the promising plant among their spoils, rather as they brought to Italy many other species of tree, from cherry to apricot.[30]

We have already noted that more indigenist reconstructions of chestnut's European and Italian history have prevailed in the last few decades. In fact, palynologists have quite conclusively demonstrated that the pollen of *Castanea sativa* filled the air in various parts of the Italian peninsula long before Roman hegemony.[31] A few lucky finds of prehistoric chestnut wood seem to confirm that chestnut trees have graced Italian hillsides since the last glaciation, and indeed in southern Italy around Mount Vulture, in the Vezza valley in northern Tuscany, and in the Euganean hills just southeast of Venice, chestnut trees also managed to survive that very big chill.[32]

It is still possible to accept the foreign origin of *Castanea sativa* by postulating that while this species existed in the prehistoric peninsula, it did so in inferior wild varieties. Thus Roman imperialism and Roman markets could have catalyzed the introduction to Italian arboriculture of a superior variety of chestnut tree, producing better nuts or (more likely, since, as we shall see in Chapter 3, the Romans did not value chestnuts as food) more wood with fewer defects than the scraggly local kinds did.[33] While it is feasible that Roman Italy saw not the introduction of the species but the dissemination of a particular domesticated variety of *Castanea sativa*, it is not certain nor really demonstrable on present evidence: so

---

[30] P. Horden and N. Purcell, *The Corrupting Sea* (Oxford, 2000), 259; A. Grove and O. Rackham, *The Nature of Mediterranean Europe* (New Haven, 2001), 67.

[31] See R. Nisbet, "Alcuni aspetti della storia naturale del castagno," in *Uomini boschi castagne*, ed. R. Comba and I. Naso (Cuneo, 2000), 9–17 (10–12); M. Kelly and B. Huntley, "An 11,000-Year Record of Vegetation and Environment from Lago di Martignano, Latium, Italy," *Journal of Quaternary Science* 6 (1991), 209–24 (220); Accorsi *et al.*, "Holocene Forest Pollen," 243–48; M. Buccianti, *Il castagno in provincia di Lucca* (Lucca, n.d.), 7; D. Magri, "Late Quaternary Vegetation History at Lagaccione near Lago di Bolsena (Central Italy)," *Review of Palaeobotany and Palynology* 106 (1999), 171–208 (200).

[32] Krebs *et al.*, "Quaternary Refugia," 154–55. In the valle del Vezza of northwest Tuscany chestnuts prevail even after clear-cutting, so ideal is the setting: Buccianti, *Il castagno*, 7. See also P. Kaltenrieder, G. Procacci, B. Vannière, and W. Winner, "Vegetation and Fire History of the Euganean Hills (*Colli Euganei*) as Recorded by Lateglacial and Holocene Sedimentary Series from Lago della Costa," *The Holocene* 20.5 (2010), 679–95 (688–89). Bronze Age sites with chestnut charcoals: L. Castelletti and A. Maspero, "Antracologia degli insediamenti paleolitici nella Penisola Italiana," *Bulletin de la Société botanique de France: Actualités botaniques* 139 (1992), 297–309 (304); E. Lopane, M. Bandini Mazzanti, and C. Accorsi, "Pollini e semi/frutti dell'abitato etrusco-celtico di Pianella di Monte Savino," in *Studi in ricordo di Daria Bertolani Marchetti*, ed. C. Accorsi (Modena, 1998), 359–65 (361); R. Nisbet, "Le analisi antracologiche," in *Belmonte: Alle radici della storia*, ed. M. Cima (Cuorgné, 1986), 69–73 (71–72).

[33] Van Zeist, "Economic Aspects," 113; L. Castelletti, E. Castiglioni, and M. Rottoli, "L'agricoltura dell'Italia settentrionale dal Neolitico al medioevo," in *Le piante coltivate e la loro storia*, ed. O. Failla and G. Forni (Milan, 2001), 33–84 (68); Negri, "Distribuzione geografica," 590.

far, no-one has managed to distinguish between archaeological pollen, wood, and nuts of wild and cultivated trees, nor between the cultivars, so the exact role of Roman farmers in the dissemination of the exotic or native chestnut in Italy cannot be ascertained archaeobotanically. This is unfortunate, for it leaves an aspect of *Castanea*'s early history in Italy a bit ambiguous. Yet whether the chestnuts leap-frogged Mediterranean regions in the holds of Roman veterans' home-bound ships, or whether they simply crept out of their refuges scattered around the peninsula (egged on by cultivators), most scholars think that the empire was the chestnut's great benefactor. Regardless of its origins, then, the chestnut is held to have made its great leap forward and become a significant presence in the Italian landscape under Roman tutelage.[34]

However, Roman control in Italy lasted an extraordinarily long time, well over 600 years. To understand chestnut's Italian history requires pinning down the chronology of *Castanea*'s conquest of Roman Italy with more precision. The usual pollen deposits and a few macro-fossil finds show that though the advent of *Castanea sativa* was far older, its conquests in the peninsula came *after* the first two centuries AD, after the high tide of the empire's power, that is. Indeed, several studies have indicated that the bulk of the preserved wood and nuts, and the denser accumulations of chestnut pollens, cluster in the *late* Roman period. In Tuscany, in the Alps, and elsewhere, the signs of chestnut in deposits in bogs and in the settlements of people grow in visibility really only from the third century on. Cores and samples taken in the Alban hills close to Rome, and in both northern and southern ends of Tyrrhenian Italy (Liguria and Calabria), also show chestnut made inroads after Rome's heyday in the peninsula.[35] As we shall see in detail in subsequent chapters (4 and 5), the same pattern emerges from analysis of the archaeobotanical data from both Campania and Lombardy. Naturally, this chronology is somewhat imprecise, reliant on carbon dating, and subject to revisions and corrections as further pollen diagrams are created and other fossilized botanical remains emerge. But its broad outlines seem secure. All told, it is clear

---

[34] Montanari instead suggests the domestication of wild chestnuts took place in the High Middle Ages: M. Montanari, *Uomini terre boschi nell'occidente medievale* (Catania, 1992), 52.

[35] L. Sadori and F. Susanna, "Hints of Economic Change during the Late Roman Empire Period in Central Italy," *Vegetation History and Archaeobotany* 14 (2005), 386–94 (390–92); J. Lowe, C. Accorsi, M. Bandini Mazzanti, *et al.*, "Pollen Stratigraphy of Sediment Sequences from Lakes Albano and Nemi (near Rome) and from the Central Adriatic," *Memorie dell'Istituto italiano di idrobiologia* 55 (1996), 71–98 (71, 91–92); F. di Rita and D. Magri, "Holocene Drought, Deforestation, and Evergreen Vegetation in the Central Mediterranean: A 5,500-Year Record from Lago Alimini Piccolo, Apulia, Southeast Italy," *The Holocene* 19.2 (2009), 295–306 (298); G. Noyé, "Economia e società nella Calabria bizantina," in *Storia della Calabria medievale*, 2 vols., ed. A. Placanica, Vol. II (Reggio, 2001), 579–655 (582).

that not the prosperous and confident Romans of the high empire, but the subjects of the embattled later one, propagated *Castanea*. Just as in other parts of the western Roman empire, the archaeobotanical picture that emerges for Italy is one in which late antiquity was the decisive time for the spread of the chestnut landscape.[36] This finding raises the question of why a plant with a rather low profile in high imperial Italy found so much space as Roman authority waned.

CONTEXTS FOR CHESTNUT'S SPREAD

Many arboreal species flourished in late antique Italian landscapes, when the "return of nature" got under way. Yet most of the vegetation that swallowed up formerly cultivated spaces did so spontaneously and did not need any human encouragement other than suspension of plowing and weeding. *Castanea*, on the contrary, we have seen to be a weak competitor among plants in level Mediterranean playing fields, and to need people's help, except in a few rare ecosystems. While other forms of arboriculture in Italy, like viticulture or olive-growing, suffered reductions and became unsustainable, chestnut expanded briskly, bucking the trend.[37] In a literal sense *Castanea* waxed against the grain of Italy's agricultural history.

A simple climatic explanation for this unexpected success of chestnut is insufficient. In part this is because the European climate's oscillations during the first millennium AD are still imperfectly understood, and palaeoclimate scholarship has yet to attain the microhistorical scale required to attach climate change to vegetation history. It is also because facts on the ground, like the appearance of chestnut pollens in sixth-century sites of northern Italy or the use of chestnut beams in contemporary buildings in the south, are hard to connect to large-scale phenomena that are in fact composites of averages, and thus not accurate expressions of past weather in any real place. *Castanea sativa* has furthermore proved itself largely indifferent to climate fluctuations, as long as it receives some assistance from its human sidekicks: over the past 2,000 years it endured the Roman

---

[36] Conedera *et al.*, "The Cultivation," 176–77, most forcefully made this case. See also J. Quirós Castillo, "Cambios y trasformaciones en el paysaje del Appennino toscano entre la Antigüedad Tardía y la Edad Media," *Archeologia medievale* 25 (1998), 177–97 (180); R. Drescher-Schneider, "Forest, Forest Clearance and Open Land during the Time of the Roman Empire in Northern Italy," in *Evaluation of Land Surfaces Cleared from Forests in the Mediterranean Region during the Time of the Roman Empire*, ed. B. Frenzel (Stuttgart, 1994), 45–58 (47). A useful synthesis demonstrating the absence of chestnuts in Roman burials in northern Italy is M. Rottoli and E. Castiglioni, "Plant Offerings from Roman Cremations in Northern Italy," *Vegetation History and Archaeobotany* 20.5 (2011), 495–506.

[37] V. Sirago, *L'Italia agraria sotto Traiano* (Louvain, 1958), 212–30, 267–68, 304–05.

warm period; the cooler, damper post-classical phase; the medieval warm period; and the Little Ice Age. The rise and fall of chestnut pollen levels in Italian sites does not correspond to all of this change in climate. Chestnut is an adaptable plant that can live in somewhat different climatic conditions, as long as it gets some help from its human friends, so climatologists currently accept it expanded both in the warmer and the cooler climatic periods. Therefore, the growth of chestnut woodland in Italy as the empire fell to pieces does not seem to have much to do with climatic factors.[38] Early medieval climate can at the very most be a partial explanation for chestnut's conquests.

Students of chestnut's history often express the conviction that the fortunes of this species have a lot to do with demography. As Cherubini stated most lucidly, when there are more people around or mouths to feed, in a pre-industrial, agrarian economy the imperatives of production lead to there being more chestnut trees too, particularly on "marginal" terrains.[39] Thus, the rise and fall of *Castanea* depends on population levels. This was something Braudel adumbrated already in 1967 in his meditation on the food alternatives available to Mediterranean people, with its notable aphorism on the choice between grain and meat depending on the number of people.[40] Subsequently, the correlation between a growing population, pressure on "marginal" lands, and the extension of chestnut groves has become almost an axiom of chestnut studies, often with justification.[41] For in periods like the High Middle Ages the expansion of arable into ever-increasing areas (what specialists sometimes call cerealization), including some where sowing was inadvisable, and the more intensive exploitation of lightly utilized land were the only options open when human numbers rose and there were neither fossil fuels nor chemical fertilizers to support the rise.[42] However, the correlation between

[38] That climate does induce mobility in trees' range is shown by M. Davis and R. Shaw, "Range Shifts and Adaptive Responses to Quaternary Climate Change," *Science* 292 (April 27, 2001), 673–79 (675–77).

[39] G. Cherubini, "La 'civiltà' del castagno in Italia alla fine del medioevo," *Archeologia medievale* 8 (1981), 247–80 (268–69).

[40] F. Braudel, *Civilisation matérielle et capitalisme: XVe–XVIIIe siècle*, 2 vols., Vol. 1 (Paris, 1967), 81: "céréales ou viande, l'alternative dépend du nombre des hommes." It is worth noting that chestnuts occupied an "ambiguous" position between cereals and meat. They are neither, though they resemble grain (in bread or porridge form) and integrate with shepherding and hunting.

[41] See for instance C. Wickham, *The Mountains and the City: The Tuscan Appennines in the Early Middle Ages* (Oxford, 1988), 21–23; R. Comba, "Châtaigneraie et paysage agraire dans les vallées piémontaises (XIIe–XIIIe siècles)," in *Castrum 5: Archéologie des espaces agraires méditerranéens au Moyen Age*, ed. A Bazzana (Madrid, 1999), 255–63 (256–57).

[42] Productive choices in "organic economies" are well explained by J. Landers, *The Field and the Forge: Population, Production, and Power in the Pre-Industrial West* (Oxford, 2003), 19–62. E. Boserup, *The Conditions of Agricultural Growth* (Chicago, 1965), is basic here.

population and chestnuts is not direct and linear. As we have observed, in the increasingly densely populated twentieth century Mediterranean chestnut waned, and in the relatively populous Italy of the high empire chestnut failed to wax. Moreover, the thirteenth-century demographic peaks appear to correspond to chestnut regression in some classic chestnut country, like the peninsula of Sorrento and Liguria.[43]

The relationship between expanding chestnut woodland and demography is more complex than it looks, then. A growing number of people is only one of several means whereby this species moves forward and colonizes landscapes. In fact, the period during which chestnut progressed most dramatically in Italy, the period between the third and seventh centuries, appears to have been one of diminishing human presence. Of course, late antique and early medieval demography is understudied, especially in proportion to its potential importance for understanding these periods, and scholars' understanding of post-classical population levels is imperfect at best. As for any time before the triumph of modern bureaucratic regimes and their prodigious statistical reach, very few reliable numbers are available for post-classical times, and like most premodern demography outside Egypt, statistics are basically educated guesses.[44] Still, almost everyone who has looked into the matter agrees that late ancient population levels were lower in most parts of the Roman empire than they had been during the first centuries of the first millennium.[45]

Italy is, in fact, a poster child for the demographic decline of late Roman times.[46] The population of Rome itself notoriously plummeted, but more sharply than anywhere else because the metropolis depended on supplies imported from far away.[47] More representative areas of the peninsula no doubt underwent distinct processes in response to the regional ecological conditions and economic trends, but the overall effect was the

---

[43] See for example M. Quaini, "Per lo studio dei caratteri originali del paesaggio agrario della Liguria pre-industriale," in *I paesaggi rurali Europei* (Perugia, 1975), 451–69 (469); M. del Treppo and A. Leone, *Amalfi medievale* (Naples, 1977), 32–34.

[44] J. Russell, "The Ecclesiastical Age: A Demographic Interpretation of the Period 200–900 AD," in *Medieval Demography* (New York, 1987), 100–02; and J. Russell, *Late Ancient and Medieval Population Control* (Philadelphia, 1985), 36–37, 125–35, 170–76.

[45] E.g., J. Dupâquier, *Des origines aux prémices de la révolution démographique*, Vol. 1 of *Histoire des populations de l'Europe*, 3 vols., ed. J. Bardet and J. Dupâquier (Paris, 1997–99), 31–32. D. Harrison, "Plague, Settlement, and Structural Change at the Dawn of the Middle Ages," *Scandia* 59.1 (1993), 15–48 (28–33), strikes a discordant note on demographic decline.

[46] G. Pinto and E. Sonnino, "L'Italie," in *Histoire des populations*, ed. J. Bardet and J. Dupâquier (Paris, 1997) Vol. 1, 485–508 (485–87).

[47] It is wrongheaded to take the Eternal City as a weathervane: in most cities local supplies always were the lifeline. See L. Gatto, "Riflettendo sulla consistenza demografica della Roma altomedievale," in *Roma medievale: Aggiornamenti*, ed. P. Delogu (Florence, 1998), 143–55; J. Durliat, *De la ville antique à la ville byzantine* (Rome, 1990), 91–121. R. Meneghini and R. Santangeli-Valenziani, *Roma nell'alto medioevo* (Rome, 2004), 21–24, summarize.

same as that observed in Rome, and after the year 400 the numbers of people in Italy shrank, with an acceleration in the later sixth century.[48]

In a powerful and sweeping reconstruction of Italian demography over the past two millennia, Lo Cascio and Malanima argued that beyond Rome's limits, Italy's pre-industrial "carrying capacity" of about 15 million people continued to be the decisive limiting factor for population levels throughout the Middle Ages. According to them, drastic population drops should not be part of Italian demographic reconstructions, and a gentle curve, graded ever so slightly downwards but made of several smaller undulations, would represent more accurately on graphs what happened between antiquity and the Middle Ages.[49] Lo Cascio and Malanima's gradualism is healthy, but even their attenuated series of fluctuations do not erase the impression that the number of inhabitants in the peninsula shrank substantially after about AD 180, though it helpfully avoids catastrophism and turns the late antique demographic trend into one of *several* cyclical adjustments to a basic level of *c.* 10 million inhabitants, expanding under Augustus or the High Middle Ages, and shrinking (to 8 million, for Lo Cascio and Malanima) during the Dark Ages.

Similarly innovative ways of reconstructing post-classical demographics are based on archaeology and therefore are less concerned with precise numerical calculations of millions of dwellers and more focused on trends (birth rates, average life spans, nuptuality, etc.) discernible in much smaller communities that archaeologists have actually investigated. They do not alter the general estimation of decline after the third century and demographic nadir in the seventh, though there may have been some resurgences between these chronological terminals.[50] Computer-assisted analysis now enables "microdemography" to connect all available data about individuals' life cycles in order to understand entire demographic systems, and suggests post-classical villagers were healthier than we once thought, but it does not change the sense of declining human numbers. At present, then, once we recognize the limitations of current demographic

---

[48] C. Wickham, *Framing the Early Middle Ages* (Oxford, 2005), 547–50, stresses the variation of demographic patterns across space.

[49] E. Lo Cascio and P. Malanima, "Cycles and Stability: Italian Population before the Demographic Transition (225 BC–AD 1900)," *Rivista di storia economica* 21.3 (2005), 197–332 (208–10), with "carrying capacity" evaluated on 211–13; see also E. Lo Cascio, "Il rapporto uomini-terra nel paesaggio dell'Italia romana," *Index* 32 (2004), 107–21 (112–16).

[50] In general see M. Livi-Bacci, "Macro versus Micro," in *Convergent Issues in Genetics and Demography*, ed. J. Adams, M. Livi-Bacci, E. Thompson, *et al.* (New York, 1990), 15–25; L. Del Panta and E. Sonnino, "Introduzione," in K. Beloch, *Storia della popolazione d'Italia* (Florence, 1994), xxiv–xxvi. Fine examples of early medieval Italian microdemography are F. Giovannini, *Natalità, mortalità e demografia dell'Italia medievale sulla base dei dati archeologici* (Oxford, 2001); I. Barbiera and G. Dalla-Zuanna, "Le dinamiche della popolazione nell'Italia medievale," *Archeologia medievale* 34 (2007), 19–42.

reconstructions, the fact remains that the late Roman advance of chestnut woods took place at a time when, as far as anyone can see, there were
fewer humans around, not more, to take care of the trees.

The paradox of a tree whose success depends on people flourishing
at a time when by all accounts people were dwindling in Italy, and were
fewer than they had been for several centuries, is even more puzzling if
one considers that arboriculture is a style of land use generally associated
with quiet and stable times.[51] It is true that until the Gothic Wars erupted
in Italy in the 530s Italy *had* enjoyed a comparatively quiet and stable
late antiquity, and it is likewise true that the sweeping generalizations of
hindsight are a luxury no-one in the third, fifth, or sixth centuries could
afford: viewed from within late antiquity, any springtime was as hopeful as had been such seasons under Augustus, and likely was perceived as
equally stable. But it is also true that compared to the secure centuries of
Roman hegemony, Italian late antiquity was still a much more "interesting" time than most people care to inhabit. Quite aside from the various
barbarian incursions, and the more important settlement of immigrants
in the peninsula, from the Diocletianic period onwards Italy was provin-
cialized, lost its fiscal and military privileges, may have suffered serious
epidemics, and was torn by religious sectarianism. The centuries between
200 and 600, within which the best evidence for *Castanea sativa*'s establishment in Italy clusters, are hardly the tranquil idyll arboriculturalists are
supposed to seek for their hopeful investment of labor in the land. For, as
Cicero famously said in the *Tusculan Disputations* (1.14), any tree-planter
"plants trees so another age may benefit."[52]

Three characteristics of chestnut trees help to unravel the paradox of
chestnut's late antique extension in the depopulated Italian landscape.
The first and most important characteristic is the low level of labor a
chestnut grove requires for its ordinary maintenance once it has gotten
going. As we saw in Chapter 1 above, the laborious first two or three
years after a seedling is planted are followed by many decades during
which the chestnut demands little attention, extremely little if juxta-
posed with some of the other sources of carbohydrates in Mediterranean
farming. In periods of labor scarcity chestnut trees are rather more efficient ways for a landowner or cultivator to procure profit or calories and
nutrition than are cereals. By the tenth year after the seed germinates,
and often somewhat before, crops begin to reward the planter for her

---

[51] A commonplace nicely expressed by O. Redon, *Des forêts et des âmes: Espace et société dans la Toscane
médiévale* (Saint Denis, 2008), 99.

[52] The aphorism "serit arbores quae alteri saeclo prosint" is widely known. Cicero ascribed it to
Statius and used it as proof that humans always worry about the future. He also cited it in *De
senectute* 24, contrasting arboricultural to agricultural time.

or his patience, and for the minimal work done in the grove. If a farmer planted a grove as a young person, at the end of the same farmer's life the grove was attaining its potential and showering him or her with nuts, not to mention several incidental products. Above all, in the interval between implantation and maturity the chestnut trees had not demanded much upkeep or labor, relative to other agricultural occupations, and in a population slump this would be a decisive consideration.[53] Chestnuts made land productive that otherwise, for lack of workers, might not have been. Because of their autonomous growth after their infancy, chestnuts were at least as well suited to times of scanty population as they were to times of demographic exuberance. Their willingness to do a lot of the work themselves for their allies and patrons outfitted them to do well in the underpopulated Dark Ages.

The second characteristic that tailored the majestic trees to post-classical economic conditions was *Castanea*'s reliability. We should probably not imagine that chestnuts served as an alternative to erratic grain crops, since the dips and surges in chestnut productivity from season to season generally follow those of grain in the same area, even if there is never absolute synchrony.[54] In particular, a wet early summer, the season when the tree flowers, hampers pollination and reduces fruitfulness in the autumn. But in comparison to "annual" crops sown anew each year, trees like chestnut are subject to fewer perils and are better equipped to cope with adverse conditions: a chestnut grove hardly notices the spring downpour that flattens a wheat field, or the earlier-than-usual summer drought that parches it. In this sense chestnut was a guarantee. A grove of such trees was much less fickle than other agrarian land uses, and quite consistently delivered edible crops as well as other benefits. It was surely unwise to rely exclusively on a chestnut grove for sustenance, but the early medieval art of diversification to reduce risk of shortfall gave *Castanea* unprecedented prominence because of this plant's stolid productivity. In an uncertain world, the chestnut was a sure thing.[55]

---

[53] In effect, this is a perfect inversion of Boserup's "conditions of agricultural growth." The conditions for sylvo-pastoral growth were cultivators with fewer children and more chestnuts.

[54] Pitte, *Terres*, 26; C. Bourgeois, *Le châtaignier, un arbre, un bois* (Paris, 1992), 32. See also above, 47–52.

[55] E. Giordano, "Biology, Physiology, and Ecology of Chestnut," in *Proceedings of the International Congress on Chestnut*, ed. E. Antognozzi (Spoleto, n.d.), 89–93 (93), on resilience to "avversità stagionali" (and, less persuasively, on how chestnut cultivation did not expose cultivators to as many days outside fortifications as grains did, useful in *in*-secure times). B. Andreolli, "L'uso del bosco e degli incolti," in *Storia dell'agricoltura italiana*, 5 vols., ed. G. Pinto and M. Ambrosoli, Vol. II (Florence, 2002), 123–44 (123), discusses how exploiting woods protected early medieval populations from famine.

The third quality of chestnut that outfitted it to flourish in declining and falling Roman Italy was its versatility. Here was a tree that could give food to eat, wood to warm, and even lumber for construction. It supplied props for grape vines. It facilitated the growth of other useful plants, especially grasses, and, if managed with circumspection, it did not interfere with the growth of those plants people appreciated most, like grains. Depending on what was needed in a given place, chestnuts could perform the task. From many quite different viewpoints the chestnut looked attractive, able to secure its cultivators important advantages.

Such versatility made a difference especially when farmers were growing more autarchic than they had been, which in most parts of Italy means in the fifth century. Indeed, chestnut's timeless qualities came into their own as Italy's agrarian communities were becoming ever more regionalized, more self-reliant, and less involved in commercial economies, when diversification of production was the pillar on which life rested. *Castanea sativa* was almost predestined to flourish in the emergent sylvo-pastoral economy of the sixth and seventh centuries, where people relied heavily on animal husbandry to produce essential protein and fibers, and where much reduced manpower was available, driving the pursuit of the highest returns possible on investments of labor.

Thus, the period where archaeological evidence for the "advent and conquests" of chestnut clusters is also the time of what Wickham called "the peasant mode of production."[56] According to Wickham, Italy (and, at slightly different speeds, the other western Roman provinces) went from being ruled by a strong and capable central authority in the fourth and even fifth centuries to being ruled by small-scale and divided governments with weak extractive power after 550 or so. Related to this change, after the middle of the sixth century, highly stratified Italian societies with large and burdensome elites able to lord it over peasants thanks to superior access to state resources evaporated, and the peninsula developed a simplified and more homogeneous social hierarchy, with relatively unpretentious elites.[57] The new situation left peasantries more autonomous than they had been for a very long time, more able to develop their

---

[56] Wickham, *Framing*, 536–39.

[57] *Ibid.* Chapters 7–9 carefully postulated microregional variation and a spectrum of degrees of lordly domination creating a "leopard skin" across the peninsula of more or less peasant autonomy. But Wickham's basic point of a golden age of the (Italian) peasantry from 550 to 750 remains strong, despite criticism that has asserted the enduring power of aristocracies (for which see J. Banaji, "Aristocracies, Peasantries, and the Framing of the Early Middle Ages," *Journal of Agrarian Change* 9 [2009], 59–91; M. Costambeys, "Settlement, Taxation, and the Condition of the Peasantry in Post-Roman Central Italy," *Journal of Agrarian Change* 9 [2009], 92–119; B. Shaw, "After Rome," *New Left Review* 51 [2008], 89–114).

growing strategies. In the "peasant mode of production" working less was a basic goal, and the versatile chestnut tree eased attaining it.

Since early modern times, in Europe chestnuts have been associated with peasants, even more with peasants who inhabited difficult and marginal zones, and there are sound reasons for this socio-ecological linkage. However, the chronologies of *Castanea sativa*'s expansion in Italy do not align perfectly with those of the decline and fall of the Roman state and elites. We should begin to suspect that the late antique chestnut was not purely a peasant plant. Indeed, as the several palynological studies discussed above show, already in the last two centuries of imperial rule, rural Italians extended chestnuts beyond the areas where they had grown in the time of Augustus. In other words, chestnut's adventure launched in different parts of the peninsula between the third and fifth centuries when the Roman state was still vigorous and Italy's landed elite socially and economically hegemonic. By the sixth century aristocrats were less able to shape outcomes and dictate strategies, but earlier it is clear that they too had perceived the advantages chestnuts offered.[58] Like peasants, late antique aristocrats had every reason to foster chestnut woodland, able to produce crops and spare labor at the same time.[59] During the relatively prosperous fourth century and in the more straitened circumstances thereafter, declining numbers of people meant that labor-intensive cultivations were not as remunerative as chestnut arboriculture, and property owners evidently took notice.[60] Thus, the "tree of bread" that sustained subsistence farmers also supported late Roman landowners, who reciprocated by creating the conditions for the tree to colonize Italy's landscape.

More perhaps than in other places, in Italy the economic, social, and particularly the demographic transformations of late antiquity favored *Castanea sativa*. First by solving the problems of landowners and then by sharing their work with farmers, chestnuts altered the classical landscape decisively.

THE COSTS OF ADOPTION

Like all change in environmental equilibria, the gradual adoption of *Castanea sativa* in the suitable landscapes of the Italian peninsula brought some losses, as well as gains. The chestnut's forward march in the period

---

[58] Wickham, *Framing*, 514, 517, argues that peasants always made the decisions "on the ground," but Roman agronomical manuals suggest otherwise.

[59] That the owners of chestnut woods we know about from charters are mostly members of the elite need not mean chestnuts were an aristocratic plant. Rather, ecclesiastical archives kept mostly records of aristocratic beneficence.

[60] T. Lewit, *Agricultural Production in the Roman Economy, AD 200–400* (Oxford, 1991).

AD 200–600 was part of a broader movement whereby trees increased their presence. But not all trees, equally, exploited the opportunities of that time. In fact, the assertion of chestnut came, to some extent, at the cost of a reduction of some other woody species.

The most prominent tree in early medieval Italian woods was surely the oak. Yet Nisbet and other scholars have noted that over the course of the first millennium AD oak woods ceded ground to chestnut woods in many parts of Italy.[61] The great "struggle" between these species depended on the evaluation of the relative merits of each that early medieval people made. In the first five centuries AD, oak proved more seductive and was favored by management practices. But by the year 1000 the old preponderance had been contained, and though *Castanea* was not the only beneficiary of the shift, it was one of them. Oak was far too useful to be neglected, and even in high medieval landscapes, in its several forms (some deciduous, others evergreen), *Quercus* probably remained the commonest Italian tree, certainly in those parts of the peninsula that people frequented. Still, during the early Middle Ages chestnut encroached because of how reliable and versatile it was and how many benefits it offered to people.

Usually it is impossible to discern what species of oak an early medieval document refers to, but "acorn-bearing woods" ("silvae glandiferae") were an important asset to many large landowners between the eighth and tenth centuries. Acorns were in fact the main reason oaks mattered so much. Houses, tools, and machines could be and usually were made out of oak wood, easily the most commonly found type of wood in early medieval Italian sites; but such use did not interfere with the main, porcine function of the "acorn-bearing woods." For in the early Middle Ages, everyone relied on oak woods to fatten their animals, particularly their pigs;[62] acorns were pigs' preferred pasture, and from one end of the peninsula to the other a symbiotic relationship arose between the two during the first millennium. People very rarely ate acorns themselves, virtually only during acute shortages of other foods, so pasturing pigs in oak woods released to humans in the form of pork flesh woodland resources that otherwise people could not use.[63] Indeed, it is a commonplace that early medieval measurements of woodland were never linear, and size was evaluated in terms of the number of pigs a wood of oak

[61] R. Nisbet, "Storia forestale e agricoltura a Montaldo tra età del ferro e XVI secolo," in *Montaldo di Mondovì*, ed. E. Micheletto and M. Venturino Gambari (Rome, 1991), 247–51 (247); E. Castiglioni and M. Rottoli, "Nogara, l'abitato di Mulino di Sotto," in *Nogara*, ed. F. Saggioro (Rome, 2011), 132–57 (140); Comba, "Châtaigneraie et paysage," 256.

[62] M. Baruzzi and M. Montanari, *Porci e porcari nel medioevo* (Bologna, 1981), 18–36.

[63] See Horden and Purcell, *The Corrupting Sea*, 198–99, for some general considerations.

could maintain.[64] Thus, for example, the redactors of the tenth-century inventory of Migliarina reckoned that a wood near Carpi in Emilia could furnish more or less pork to S. Giulia's Brescian nuns, depending on how good the acorn season had been.[65] As in other early medieval documents, the people who drafted this polyptych considered food for pigs the only matter of note in the nuns' woods.

Pig-rearing, already an activity worth specializing in during Roman times and still relevant in the seventh century, when Lombard legislators assigned very high wergelds to pig-herds and had a sophisticated understanding of pig husbandry and its hierarchies, became a very profitable occupation in late antique Italy.[66] For in the late empire the annona, the state system of supply of foodstuffs to Rome, began to include pork flesh and fat, twenty-five Roman pounds of it per citizen per year, alongside more traditional emoluments like grain or bread. Between the fourth and sixth centuries the occupants of well-appointed rural villas at S. Giovanni di Ruoti and S. Vincenzo al Volturno furnished first live pigs and later pork, the latter presumably cured and salted, to the still teeming and entitled City of Rome. Both S. Giovanni and S. Vincenzo were immersed in oak woodlands where pigs could find acorns, as well as other roots and grasses they liked to eat. As excavations at the Roman forum and then at these two villas in the Apennines south of Rome suggested to Barnish, those who could position themselves properly in this pig trade could amass wealth from it.[67] Thus, supplying the metropolis with pigs was big business in the fourth and fifth centuries, and the business depended ultimately upon access to oak woods. Despite the unraveling of Rome's "command economy" during the 400s, the pork trade survived, for south Italian landowners found outlets at local fairs and markets for any surplus pigs not absorbed by the fifth-century City.

The intimate relationship between oaks and pigs endured long after the unsustainable pork-procurement politics of the annona had subsided and more autarchic production prevailed. This is clear also from

[64] B. Andreolli, "Misurare la terra: Metrologie altomedievali," in *Uomo e spazio nell'alto medioevo*, Settimane del CISAM 50 (Spoleto, 2003), 151–91 (160–62); Baruzzi and Montanari, *Porci*, 29–30; Grove and Rackham, *The Nature*, 195, estimate fifty oaks in open woodland sustain one pig for a year.

[65] *Inventari altomedievali di terre, coloni e redditi*, ed. A Castagnetti, M. Luzzati, A. Vasina, and G. Pasquali (Rome, 1979), 203.

[66] "Edictus Rothari," ed. F. Blühme, in *Leges Langobardorum*, MGH, Leges 4 (Hanover, 1868), 3–90, Chapters 349–53 (80–81), discusses altercations among pig-herds over pasture and technicalities in behavior of the lead male pig (*sonorpair*); for the lead sow (*ducaria*), whose bell allowed herders to track the animals in the woods; see Baruzzi and Montanari, *Porci*, 29–32.

[67] S. Barnish, "Pigs, Plebeians, and Potentes: Rome's Economic Hinterland, c. 350–600 AD," *Papers of the British School at Rome* 55 (1987), 157–85.

several archaeological investigations carried out in very different parts of the peninsula. Thus, in the middle Po valley, at S. Michele di Trino near Vercelli, declining incidence of pig bones between late antiquity and the High Middle Ages went along with increasing willingness to fell oak woods. At Brucato in Sicily, a high medieval site excavated in the 1970s, a waste dump revealed a relatively low number of pig bones, something the excavators explained by the considerable distance from the settlement to the closest oak forest. Similarly, in northern Apulia a conscious choice to create oak pastures for pigs at the expense of more varied woodland for fuel lies behind the seventh- and eighth-century assemblages. Eighth–ninth-century "intensive" pork-raising at Monte Gelato north of Rome on model farms run by the popes depended on the local abundance of oak woods for pasture. And in the lowlands just south of Verona, the ninth- and tenth-century inhabitants of Nogara exploited their rich forests of *Quercus* by running great herds of pigs in them.[68]

Chestnut was different. Because early medieval people desired the nuts, which alas pigs also found most palatable, the management of chestnut woodland was unlike that of oak.[69] Since pigs gobbled up fallen nuts, post-classical chestnut woods were not conducive and indeed were usually detrimental to pig pasturage. Even a coppiced chestnut wood that rendered primarily poles offered a "side" crop of nuts each year, and if there were pigs around the coppice owner would enjoy very few of these fruits. In medieval Italy a regular solution was to exclude pigs from chestnut groves until well after harvest time, if they were admitted at all.[70] Another late medieval solution was draconian regulations against leading pigs into chestnut woodland during the autumn, when the

---

[68] S. Michele: A. Ferro, "La fauna," in *San Michele di Trino (VC): Dal villaggio romano al castello medievale,* 3 vols., ed. M. Negro Ponzi Mancini, Vol. II (Florence, 1999), 631–45 (632–37). Brucato: C. Bossard and P. Beck, "Le mobilier ostéologique et botanique," in *Brucato: Histoire et archéologie d'un habitat médiéval en Sicile,* 2 vols., ed. J. Pesez (Rome, 1984), Vol. II, 615–71 (620–27). Apulia: V. Caracuta and G. Fiorentino, "L'analisi archeobotanica nell'insediamento di Faragola," in *V congresso nazionale di archeologia medievale,* ed. G. Volpe and P. Favia (Florence, 2009), 717–23 (721). Monte Gelato: A. King, "Mammal, Reptile, and Amphibian Bones," in *Excavations at the Mola di Monte Gelato,* ed. T. Potter and A. King (Rome, 1997), 383–403 (385–88, 394–95, 399). Nogara: P. Baker, "Assessment of Animal Bones Excavated in 2004–2005 at Nogara (Olmo di Nogara)," in *Nogara* ed. F. Saggioro (Rome, 2011), 107–21 (111).

[69] T. Lewit, "Pigs, Presses, and Pastoralism," *Early Medieval Europe* 17.1 (2009), 77–91 (81–82), instead links resurgent chestnut woods with pig-rearing. That may have been the way classical chestnut woods were managed.

[70] Gleaning came before any hogs were admitted: Cherubini, "La 'civiltà,'" 278. Around 1300, Pietro de' Crescenzi (*Ruralia commoda,* 4 vols., ed. W. Richter and R. Richter-Bergmeier, Vol. III [Heidelberg, 1998], 9.77.2 [116]) wrote that feeding chestnuts, broad beans, and barley to pigs during fattening gave their flesh a delectable flavor, but knew this luxury was exceptional and advised stout fences around groves from "timore porcorum" (*ibid.,* Vol. II [Heidelberg, 1996], 5.6.5 [106]).

fruits' fall made them accessible to the enterprising animals.[71] But robust fencing around nut-bearing groves was a necessity even where these time-sharing practices designed to head off conflicts between pig-herds and chestnut growers had taken root. In the twentieth century the problem was still acute in the Alban hills west of Rome. The solution there was spatial zoning. Pigs were carefully restricted to mature, wood-producing chestnut coppices and never allowed into nut-producing groves.[72]

Despite such attempts to find a balance between the two occupations, large-scale pig husbandry was fundamentally incompatible with dedicated medieval chestnut-growing. Where raising swine coexisted with growing chestnuts, either one or the other was a sideline and not a major component of agrarian strategies.

Unlike pigs, other animals *could* pasture in chestnut woods because they did not compete so effectively with people for the chestnuts.[73] In modern times Ligurian goat- and sheep-rearing economies flourished in lockstep with castaneiculture. For example, early modern landowners near Genoa encouraged sheep- and goat-grazing in their chestnut groves to enhance soil fertility.[74] Further north, in the subalpine northwest of the peninsula, high medieval contracts show that most landowners preferred viticulture and chestnut woods, and as other land uses receded so did oak-dominated mixed deciduous forest. In the new landscape, sheep and goats became prevalent.[75] In much earlier times, therefore, it has seemed plausible to interpret the retreat of recorded oak woods from the hillsides of Abruzzo, and the concomitant rise in records of chestnuts and grape vines, as indications that shepherding was increasingly important while porcine pastoralism waned.[76] In the Liguro-Tuscan settlement of Filattiera, meticulously excavated during the 1990s, archaeologists noted a rise in chestnut trees over the course of the first millennium and into the eleventh century, at the expense of oaks that had fed pigs.[77]

---

[71] R. Trifone, *Storia del diritto forestale in Italia* (Florence, 1957), 66–74.

[72] A. Ferrantini, "Osservazioni sulle modificazioni della vegetazione nei Colli Albani," *Bollettino della Società geografica italiana*, series 7, no. 11 (1946), 24–26.

[73] Cherubini, "La 'civiltà,'" 262.

[74] D. Moreno, "Châtaigneraie 'historique' et châtaigneraie 'traditionelle,'" *Médiévales* 16–17 (1989), 147–69 (160).

[75] R. Comba, "Castagneto e paesaggio agrario delle valli piemontesi," in *Uomini boschi castagne*, ed. R. Comba and I. Naso (Cuneo, 2000), 21–32 (22–24); Comba, "Châtaigneraie et paysage," 260.

[76] T. Leggio, "Viabilità e forme insediative lungo la Valle del Velino tra tarda antichità e alto medioevo," in *L'Appennino in età romana e nel primo medioevo*, ed. M. Destro and E. Giorgi (Bologna, 2004), 231–48 (233), reading ninth-century charters.

[77] M. Rottoli and S. Negri, "I resti vegetali carbonizzati," in *Filattiera-Sorano*, ed. E. Giannichedda (Florence, 1998), 198–212 (202–04); and R. Giovinazzo, "I reperti faunistici," in Giannichedda, *Filattiera-Sorano*, 196–97.

Thus a pattern seems to appear: as chestnut woods advanced in the early Middle Ages, oak woods retreated. With that retreat, pigs found less favorable conditions, and cattle, sheep, or goats obtained more space.

Yet ungulates were hardly inexorable enemies of woodland, nor were pigs sponsors of conservation and traditional management practices, and post-classical change in the woods should not be mistaken for woodland degeneration.[78] Early medieval Italian vegetation was as dynamic as vegetation always is. Put simply, sheep and goats were the allies of one form of woodland, just as pigs were of another. The piecemeal, episodic replacement of oak by chestnut woods was a chapter in a long story, or really just a part of the chapter.

Whatever their foibles from a chestnut grower's point of view, particularly their voracious appetite for the same food people wanted, pigs *were* admirable creatures and their difficulties in areas of chestnut cultivation made a difference to people's livelihoods. Pigs were the most efficient transformers available in the Mediterranean of materials people could not eat into something people liked. Over the course of the same 12 months, a sow produced 1,600 kg of available flesh, mostly in the form of up to 2 litters of quick-growing piglets, while a cow managed barely 200 kg, usually a single calf. Sheep and goats likewise compared unfavorably to pigs as meat-producers.[79] To the extent that chestnut woods deprived pigs of living space, the triumph of that type of woodland, and the reduction around settlements of readily accessible oak-dominated pasture it dictated, necessarily reduced the amount of meat that the locals had readily at hand and, presumably, consumed.

Fernand Braudel, who had reservations about Mediterranean chestnut-eating habits, saw the decline of meat consumption as an inevitable corollary of rising populations and increasing reliance on arable agriculture, specifically of cereals in the premodern Mediterranean.[80] The success of *Castanea* on so many slopes in the post-classical peninsula complicates Braudel's dualism by adding a third, ambiguous ingredient, namely the chestnut, not really a cereal nor flesh, but somehow in between. Yet whenever chestnuts were abundant, and people ate a lot of them, pigs and their acorn-fed flesh were much less so. In this sense Braudel was right.

---

[78] J. Radkau, *Wood: A History* (Cambridge, 2012), 68–69, thinks pig-herding, unlike shepherding, fostered Europe's traditional woodland conservation.

[79] J. De Grossi Mazzorin and C. Minniti, "L'allevamento e l'approvvigionamento alimentare di una comunità urbana," in *Roma dall'antichità al medioevo*, 2 vols., ed. M. Arena and L. Paroli, Vol. 1 (Milan, 2001), 69–78 (71).

[80] See n. 40 above; and M. Montanari, *La faim et l'abondance: Histoire de l'alimentation en Europe* (Paris, 1995), 59–60.

Still, animals that were compatible with castaneiculture offered their owners many benefits. Because of the "renewable" nature of the products they produced (wool and milk), premodern herders tended to keep cows, sheep, and goats alive much longer than most pigs, raised exclusively to be eaten and therefore usually killed soon after they attained their adult weight. Flocks and herds were kept in chestnut woods to supply "secondary products," not meat. The ecological and economic logic of a chestnut wood was thus unlike that of an oak wood. Old cattle, incapable of work or of giving milk, and old caprovines whose milk production faltered, were of course killed and eaten, but that was just being frugal. A chestnut landscape was indeed generally a place of less meat-eating than an oak-filled one. But it was not a malnourished place. It was rather a place where dairy products integrated other foods.

A useful survey of the archaeological data on meat consumption in early medieval Europe puts these Italian trends in proper perspective.[81] Overall, early medieval people ate more meat than their ancestors or descendants. Across the continent, after the eighth century and enduring into the fourteenth at least, pigs declined in numbers and relevance, at least insofar as people's archaeologically visible refuse reveals such trends (it is striking that pigs retained all their pre-eminence in the written documents of the period).[82] Audoin-Rouzeau puts this decline in the broader context of retreating forest cover, in other words of the "great clearances" and reduction of oaken habitat for medieval pigs, semi-feral and seldom kept indoors. Naturally, cultural preferences also played a role, and monastic landlords whose herding priorities were skins more than meat, specifically skins one could write on (so not pig skins), may have weighed disproportionately in this apparent change.[83] But the Italian rise of chestnut should probably be considered an aspect in long-term change in woodlands and woodland use. From many early medieval people's point of view, it was a change well worth the sacrifice of a few hams.

---

[81] F. Audoin-Rouzeau, "Elevage et alimentation dans l'espace européen au moyen âge," in *Milieux naturels, espaces sociaux*, ed. E. Mornet and F. Morenzoni (Paris, 1997), 143–59.

[82] There are exceptions, of course: at Otranto, pork rose relative to other meats between the seventh and tenth centuries (J. Cartledge, G. Clark, and V. Higgins, "The Animal Bones: A Preliminary Assessment of the Stock Economy," in *Excavations at Otranto*, ed. F. d'Andria and D. Whitehouse, 2 vols. [Galatina, 1992], Vol. II, 317–35), and early medieval Milanese meat consumption varied by neighborhood, with pork predominant in some areas (M. Biasotti and R. Giovinazzo, "Reperti faunistici," in *Scavi MM3* 3.2, ed. D. Caporusso [Milan, 1991], 167–84 [168–78]).

[83] Parchment: G. Clarke, "Monastic Economies? Aspects of Production and Consumption in Early Medieval Central Italy," *Archeologia medievale* 14 (1997), 31–54 (44–45). At the elite, military site of S. Antonio in Liguria in about AD 600, occupants ate mostly young pork, but reduced deciduous oak woods. Here cultural considerations (prestige, for example) seem to explain the unusual data: R. Giovinazzo, "Le risorse alimentari animali," in *S. Antonino: Un insediamento fortificato nella Liguria bizantina*, ed. T. Mannoni and G. Murialdo (Bordighera, 2001), 639–56 (654–55).

AMBIGUITY AND POSSESSION: MAKING
CHESTNUTS PROPERTY

A prime explanation for the surprising far-sighted generosity of the plant-ers of chestnut groves discussed in previous segments was that *Castanea sativa*, more than other species, left the early medieval wilderness and entered human property schemes with ease. Chestnut could cross the boundaries between nature and culture (and back again to nature, if need be) readily for several reasons, not least for the botanical and economic ones that are the focus of this section. But *Castanea's* apparent agility came about also because, as discussed in the introduction to this study, early medieval "wilderness" was a lot more flexible than modern con-ceptions of pristine nature allow. In fact, post-classical wildwoods were far less tidily edged and delineated than were earlier uncultivated zones, too. The classical categories of land use, from the cultivated *ager* to the *saltus* of gathering and pasture, and to the *silva* of occasional frequenta-tion, no longer applied neatly to post-classical landscapes, if indeed they ever had applicability on the ground.[84] As Montanari put it, the "system-atic mixture of agricultural activities and exploitation of uncultivated land" characterized the early Middle Ages, with all manner of benefits for early medieval gastronomy and nutrition, especially compared to the "monophagy" of grain in Roman or high medieval times.[85] Such an agrarian style did not support well-defined compartments of landscape engagement.

Flexible land-use strategies, a hybrid cultivated–uncultivated land-scape with porous boundaries between the wild and the sown, and the liminal position of chestnut groves within both are a helpful reminder of the peculiarities of post-classical woods, "wilderness," and perhaps even nature. In such idiosyncratic post-classical circumstances we should not expect chestnut woods to behave precisely as modern ones do. For instance, early medieval charters do not locate chestnut groves within either the cultivated or uncultivated sphere at all consistently: sometimes contracts treat chestnut woods as equivalent to agricultural land, owing

[84] For classical wild landscapes: C. Delano Smith, "Where was the 'Wilderness' in Roman Times?," in *Human Landscapes in Classical Antiquity*, ed. G. Shipley and J. Salmon (London, 1996), 154–79 (166–69, 176–77). On the uncertainties of interpreting early medieval "silva," see G. Rippe, *Padou et son contado (xe–xiiie siècle)* (Rome, 2003), 58–61; P. Toubert, "Paysages ruraux et techniques de production en Italie méridionale dans la seconde moitié du xiie siècle," in *Potere, società e popolo nell'età dei due Guglielmi* (Bari, 1981), 201–29 (207–08). J. Gaulin, "Tra *silvaticus* e *domesticus:* Il bosco nella trattatistica medievale," in *Il bosco nel medioevo*, ed. M. Montanari and B. Andreolli (Bologna, 1988), 85–96 (86–89), treats early medieval distinctions between woodland types, different from earlier and later ones.

[85] Montanari, *La faim*, 44, with "le croisement systématique des activités agricoles avec les pratiques d'exploitation des terres incultes."

regular rents, and sometimes they consider chestnuts not subject to payments, and apparently available to all comers.[86] Nothing suggests that
objective differences in the management of the "silva castanearum" and
the "castanetum" determined this uncertainty. It was rather that a chestnut wood was both cultivated and uncultivated, both a subject doing its
own growing and an object being grown, both an artifact and a "wilderness," or, as Delumeau wrote of the chestnut woods east of Arezzo, "a
kind of transition" between the two.[87]

As we saw in the introductory chapter above, such indeterminacy had a
context at once ecological and cultural. For the fall of the Roman empire
and attendant transformations also transformed the landscape and, amid
the transformations, the post-classical countryside grew more wooded
than earlier ones had been. Yet in this bosky, transformed peninsula, Dark
Age chestnut woods were a form of vegetation that seldom grew wild
or uncivilized. They were humanized, managed in sophisticated ways. An
important aspect of this woodland sophistication is the chestnut groves'
legal standing.

In any study of the Dark Age history of *Castanea sativa* in Italy the
agrarian contracts that survive in numbers from the later first millennium are a capital source of evidence. The purpose of these charters, and
indeed of most medieval charters, was to record property transactions,
namely the sale, purchase, donation, or lease of people's belongings, in
the early Middle Ages, mostly of land. It is therefore unsurprising that
chestnuts appear foremost as a type of property in the surviving contracts:
it is as such that we can know them in the available sources. Nevertheless,
the ecological characteristics of *Castanea*, that is, the regular delivery for
centuries of many edible seeds and the rapid sprouting of resilient wood,
predisposed this plant to success in a particular type of economy and thus
suited chestnuts to Dark Age societies. It was not just that post-classical
production was less specialized in agriculture, more sylvo-pastoral, and
more autarchic than had been the Roman economy. At the same time
as notaries busily wrote down people's decisions to trade, sell, buy, or
rent chestnut trees, they also neglected to do the same for fir trees and
recorded very few transactions involving beech. Only certain trees, chestnuts, willows, and oaks among them, had the characteristics needed to
become early medieval property and to be singled out in the otherwise
undifferentiated "silva" of that time.

One obvious characteristic of chestnuts that lent them to becoming human possessions in the Mediterranean is their predilection for

---

[86] M. Montanari, *L'alimentazione contadina nell'alto medioevo* (Naples, 1979), 42–43, 296–97.
[87] J.-P. Delumeau, *Arezzo, espaces et sociétés*, 2 vols., Vol. 1: *715–1230* (Rome, 1996), 38.

mid-altitude hilly terrains. Fir trees tended to grow at altitudes higher than those that Italians found comfortable for year-round occupation, so did not share people's ecosystem quite as intimately as chestnuts did. Poplars in watery and flat plains likewise lived on land most people did not inhabit regularly. Thus, it makes sense that the post-classical population's drift away from the lowlands and the ongoing avoidance of the harsh highlands located Dark Age settlement in the kind of landscape that chestnuts favor and thereby conferred on chestnuts a visibility, even an economic importance, that most other species lacked. Sharing the hillsides with people predisposed chestnuts to entering civilization and becoming property.[88]

Beyond that, the economic potential in a tree that lived an enormously long time, made useful things for much of that time, and did not demand much maintenance during it conspired to move *Castanea sativa* from the few mid-altitude glades where it lived on its own, spread it across many landscapes, and turn it into an asset in Dark Age landowners' portfolios.[89] Chestnuts shifted from the (almost) wilderness to the (fairly) cultivated area, from the commons to privately held land, because they produced seeds and wood to which people assigned a role in the Italian peninsula's early medieval economy. Since they did so for many consecutive generations, they could enter into inheritance strategies and play a bigger role in claims to land than annually planted crops could. Earlier, as far as anyone can tell, chestnuts had not had the same role, so the trees had subsisted on the margins, beyond the purview of people and property, pretty much as wild trees.

In the early 1800s, in the south of the United States, the most marginal in society relied most heavily on woodland resources and became protagonists in domesticating some portions of it. Some of the most valued cultivars of pecan today descend in direct (clonal) lines from the pecans that slaves selected in the woods, took scions from, and propagated by grafting back on the farm.[90] Plumper nuts that matured sooner rewarded careful observation and intelligent use of wild resources. It is certainly an exaggeration to claim *Castanea* was the only wildwood tree, or semi-natural tree, that similarly became patrimony in the early Middle Ages (oaks are obvious competitors), but the claim does call attention to the chestnut's position as a plant that could, and no doubt

---

[88] See the provocative but convincing case made in this sense by Quirós Castillo, "Cambios."

[89] N. Peluso, "Fruit Trees and Family Trees in an Anthropogenic Forest," in *Natures Past: The Environment and Human History*, ed. P. Squatriti (Ann Arbor, 2007), 54–102 (59), notes that long-lived trees determine access to land far more than field crops do.

[90] Kingsbury, *Hybrid*, 25.

did, grow wild, and yet over which people placed property claims.[91] Putting this in a slightly different way, we could say that chestnut woods were the only portion of the post-classical wildwood to be worth intensive management and its exertions.[92] Even oak woods could not elicit the same care.

Perhaps, though, chestnuts were less portentous than they seem. To frame things in terms an economist might use, in the (relatively) wild woods of the Italian peninsula the low economic surplus people could extract justified a common property regime, for the resources were too hard to farm, and too far from consumption sites to be worth the investments in time and work that underlie appropriation.[93] That would describe the situation at least in the classical Mediterranean's wildwood. Yet it is clear from the charters that early medieval people in Italy discerned in chestnuts economic surplus sufficient to remove them from their state of propertylessness. More than other species of tree in the woods, the chestnut supported private property and its investment, or more intensive management. This was so for plain biological reasons – the differences between chestnuts and other trees – but also for socio-cultural ones, namely the possibility post-classical societies offered for privatizing common resources, specifically trees, by means of work. Thus, chestnut offered economic surplus (nuts) enough, each year and over the long term, to appeal to early medieval people. That may be why, in the first millennium charters, heavy, unwieldy chestnut wood shrinks to insignificance next to the nuts – a more manageable form of "income." Precisely this type of economic rationale is visible in the high medieval Languedoc so subtly studied by Durand. In the south of France, eleventh-century woodland clearance ended the older common property regime, restricted rights of access to surviving woods, and turned chestnut trees into regular assets for which people paid regular

[91] P. Toubert, *Les structures du Latium médiéval*, 2 vols. (Rome, 1973), Vol. I, 191–92, was the first to show how liable chestnut was to "privatizing" schemes; see also J. Martin, "L'espace cultivé," in *L'uomo e spazio nell'alto medioevo*, Settimane del CISAM 50 (Spoleto, 2003), 239–97 (240).

[92] C. Wickham, "European Forests in the Early Middle Ages," in *L'ambiente vegetale nell'alto medioevo*, Settimane del CISAM 37 (Spoleto 1990), 479–545 (544). Wickham stressed (486–87, 494–97) layered ownership rights woods made possible.

[93] M. De Moor, L. Shaw-Taylor, and P. Warde, "Comparing the Historical Commons of North West Europe: An Introduction," in *The Management of Common Land in North West Europe, c. 1500–1850* (Turnhout, 2002), 15–31 (21), with pertinent conclusions on 248–49. The economic marginality of commons is assumed: L. Bussi, "Terre comuni e usi civici dalle origini all'alto medioevo," in *Storia del Mezzogiorno*, 15 vols., ed. G. Galasso and R. Romeo, Vol. III: *Alto medioevo* (Naples, 1990), 213–55 (213). However, M. McKean, "Common Property: What Is It, What Is It Good for, and What Makes It Work?," in *People and Forests: Communities, Institutions, and Governance*, ed. C. Gibson, M. McKean, and E. Ostrom (Cambridge, MA, 2000), 27–55 (36–37), suggested that heightened demand for resources spawned common property regimes.

taxes, evidently because the "useful tree" generated economically relevant quantities of nuts for markets.[94]

Post-classical theories of property assigned great weight to use rights. Fruition of a natural resource gave the user a kind of sovereignty over the thing based on the real relation between the two.[95] Thus, on land that everyone acknowledged belonged to the fisc, or to a lordship, or was commons, an individual user might create a claim by exercising actual management power over the things, such as trees, on the land. Both Lombard law and Byzantine rural law contemplated the special case of rights to trees distinct from ownership of the land the trees grew upon, in particular for cases where people had demonstrably toiled at the tree, tending to it or actually planting it.[96] In other words, representative texts from two of the early medieval peninsula's pre-eminent legal frameworks envisioned situations in which the characteristics of chestnuts, ecological and economic, made them appetizing for any who frequented woodlands and sought to extend claims to their resources.[97] Pruning, stripping, taking the nuts, or otherwise tending to a wild chestnut tree might lay the foundations for a proprietary stake in the tree, or otherwise complicate the layering of claims to the resources of the place where it grew.[98] Though most of the known early medieval cases of trees owned by people who did not own the land they grew on involve olives, chestnuts are also recorded in such circumstances, along with some other fruit trees.[99] But whereas olive or apple trees are domesticated plants unable to live on

---

[94] Durand, *Les paysages médiévaux*, argues *Castanea* was little used in medieval building (391), but was a taxable "arbre utile" (336, 346) that endured the deforestation of the eleventh and twelfth centuries (396–401). See Bussi, "Terre comuni," 221–27, on late antique commons privatization.

[95] P. Grossi, *Il dominio e le cose: Percezioni medievali e moderne dei diritti reali* (Milan, 1992); G. Diurni, *Le situazioni possessorie nel medioevo* (Milan, 1988), 56–57, 78.

[96] To Rothari in 643 trees in others' fields ("agrum alienum aut culturam") but not in enclosures ("clausuram") could be lopped by travelers "for their own use" because they were not exclusive, private property: "Edictus Rothari," Chapter 300 (70). Compare "The Farmer's Law II," ed. W. Ashburner, *Journal of Hellenic Studies* 32 (1912), 69–95 (90), which Wickham, *Framing*, 463, ascribes to Anatolia, *c.* 650–850. See also C. Giardina, *La così detta proprietà degli alberi separata da quella del suolo in Italia* (Palermo, 1941), 70–71, 175–78, 231–41, 270–75; R. Trifone, *Storia del diritto*, 24–29; G. Bognetti, "I beni comunali e l'organizzazione del villaggio nell'Italia superiore fino al mille," *Rivista storica italiana* 77 (1965), 469–99 (481–82, 486) on Lombard legislation, esp. "Edictus Rothari," 321 and 358; Bussi, "Terre comuni," 232–37.

[97] L. Fortmann, "The Tree Tenure Factor in Agroforestry, with Particular Reference to Africa," *Agroforestry Systems* 2 (1985), 229–51 (230–39), has much of interest on this theme, based on twentieth-century African cases. For environmental perspectives on the relation between legal systems and use of natural resources: G. Corona, "The Decline of the Commons and the Environmental Balance of Early Modern Italy," in *Nature and History in Modern Italy*, ed. M. Armiero and M. Hall (Athens, OH, 2010), 89–107 (89–92).

[98] A. Casanova, *Arboriculture et société en Méditerranée à la fin du XVIII e siècle: L'exemple de la Corse* (Corte, 1998), 32–34, gives examples of such appropriations from well-documented Corsica.

[99] Giardina, *La così detta proprietà*, 215–19, 269.

their own in the woods, chestnuts retained this capacity and in fact some of the owned chestnuts displayed by early medieval Italian documents may have originated as wild plants in the unmanaged woodlands, where the seventh-century Lombard law code expected there to be plenty of strife over control of trees.[100]

In this way the presence of chestnuts in a mixed woodland, a quite natural place, one fairly far over on the scale of naturalness discussed by Peterken, could be the seed from which a property claim grew, or at any rate whence sprouted a restriction on an open-access regime that might depend on time lots.[101] This was truest in periods of loose state control over territory and relative abundance of woodland resources, such as the early Middle Ages in Italy. Chestnuts lured people into the woodland, offering desirable resources and a foreseeably long time frame within which to enjoy them. They facilitated the easy-going colonization and the partial clearances that seem to have typified early medieval agrarian strategies: when post-classical colonists selectively removed trees from a given locality a likely survivor of the process was *Castanea sativa*, able to live through fire (the easiest way to clear) and endowed with the surplus value to justify the clearance effort in the first place.[102] To remove chestnuts' competitors, plant more seedlings, perhaps graft them, and generally to work the chestnutty bits of the woodland could have altered the ecosystem just enough to entail exclusive rights of usufruct on the trees' product or even over the land where the trees grew, over both of which in the wild other locals also had held rights. The rights lasted as long as the trees lived, but in chestnuts' case that was a long time. In early medieval woodlands where rulers, local potentates, and communities all had some claims to resources, the end result might be a multilayered ownership regimen wherein chestnut woods stood out, the object of exclusive claims and private rights by local individuals or institutions, surrounded by much less intensively exploited land held in common.[103]

It is worth underlining how much of this depended on the unique botany of the chestnut. Unlike domesticated fruit trees, it lived much

---

[100] "Edictus Rothari," Chapter 240 (59), punished manipulation of boundary markers "in silva alterius."

[101] Peterken, *Natural Woodland*, 5–11 (see also above, 19). If the tree alone became private property, and the land it grew on remained in the commons, pasture under it or litter fallen from it might be openly accessible during most of the year and closed when the fruits matured: Giardina, *La così detta proprietà*, 265–66, 269–70.

[102] Chestnuts and fire: Grove and Rackham, *The Nature*, 227. Similar selective clearing in 1800s Appalachia: R. Lutts, "'Like Manna from God': The American Chestnut Trade in Southwestern Virginia," *Environmental History* 9 (2004), 497–525 (511–12).

[103] M. Montanari, *Campagne medievali: Strutture produttive, rapporti di lavoro, sistemi alimentari* (Turin, 1984), 158–60; Wickham, "European Forests," 490–97, 536–41, 544; Martin, "L'espace cultivé," 287.

longer than a person did and grew in the less anthropogenic conditions of the non-agricultural space (the *incolto*), often in woodlands. In this way chestnut offered advantages that walnut, a species incapable of growing in the woodlands, or apple, which would die after a few decades, could not.[104] Unlike its botanical relations beech or oak, chestnut grew fast and also produced more palatable fruit (though people can eat beech mast, like acorns, they generally leave them to the pigs in the Mediterranean region). Unlike firs, which grow fast and produce palatable nuts in the wild but require rigid temperatures to flourish, chestnut thrived in the mid-altitude zones of the Mediterranean where early medieval people congregated and farmed. All told, *Castanea* was without peers when it came to woodland trees of the Mediterranean area with economic potential, and was a lot more versatile than oak, the only species that could rival chestnut. It was oddly like the durian tree described by foresters in the modern woods of West Kalimantan in Indonesia, a plant whose presence in the forest practically is a record of staked claims, each tree named for its planter and first tender, and each producing fruit that generations of heirs carefully share out among themselves.[105] Exactly parallel to chestnut, durian's idiosyncratic status as property depends on its biological characteristics, especially on its longevity in a forest whose other vegetation does not match durian's multigenerational life span, and the palatability of its fruit.

But if one result of chestnut's seductive presence in the woodland could be restrictions on common access through appropriation of this peculiar resource, another result was that a wild tree might become domesticated, a cultivated plant.[106] In fact, the special character of chestnut may be discerned by viewing the plant from the opposite perspective, as a cultivated tree. For among the domesticated trees of the Mediterranean, *Castanea sativa* is almost unique in having kept its wild streak. Despite its eighteenth-century botanical name, which incorporates in itself the Latin for "cultivated" (*sativa*, whose opposite in classical Latin was, ironically, *silvestris*), chestnut retains the capacity to reproduce itself without human help and thus, like very few other tame trees (e.g., the fig), it defies the standard definition of domestication, namely dependence on people for reproduction.[107] In botanical terminology, the "mutualism" between chestnut and people is only "facultative" in that chestnut

---

[104] Giardina, *La così detta proprietà*, 21, 215–19, found early medieval olives, apples, and willows separable from the land they grew on. In modern Lombardy and Campania, chestnut is the most "separable" species (49–52).

[105] Peluso, "Fruit Trees," 54–102.

[106] Montanari, *L'alimentazione contadina*, 41, noted the tendency to classify chestnuts in the "cultum."

[107] Zohary and Hopf, *Domestication*, 142–43, note the need to change the reproductive biology of trees, from sexual to vegetative, to achieve domestication; see also D. Harris, "An Ecological Continuum

retains the ability to reproduce itself without the assistance of its human friends, though it reproduces itself more effectively with that assistance and, like people, enhances its ecological fitness through its collaborative instinct.[108]

Once again we confront the irreducibly various nature of *Castanea*, a tree that can be either wild or cultivated, forgotten and neglected in remote mountain valleys or prized personal property in manicured groves. It is certainly significant that, in the form in which early medieval notaries usually reveal the plant to us, the chestnut looks domesticated or at least quite far along on the semi-natural scale that Peterken delineated.[109] Most of the chestnut woods revealed by the early medieval Italian charters lay close to settlements, within the more humanized portion of a community's space. In the course of the early Middle Ages, as chestnut became a sought-after form of property, it received extensive care from people (to the point of modifying its genetic make-up through grafts and cultivar selection), and its various products gained value in human economies.[110] Such qualities could justify attempts to bring areas of the incolto remote from people's houses, in less manipulated landscapes, under more intensive management by raising chestnut groves there, maybe around a few grand wild trees. Thus in 1000 chestnut was a quintessential element in Italian arboriculture, present in the Alpine foothills and on the Aspromonte, everywhere nurtured by people and their industry. But chestnut at the same time remained wild, able to fend for itself without human intervention if the need arose, able to subside into the (almost) wilderness if human attentions waned and to resume the hard work of living alone, in its relatively scarce ecological niches. In sum, the chestnut was liminal, ambiguous, adaptable. This remarkable organic machine was able to weave into and out of the cultivated world, and therefore of property regimes, thanks to its vegetative and reproductive biology, and to a life span that far exceeded the ordinary fluctuations of human endeavor, and even of human civilizations.[111]

---

of People–Plant Interaction," in *Foraging and Farming: The Evolution of Plant Exploitation* (London, 1989), 11–26 (19). Chestnut and fig's exceptionalism: van Zeist, "Aperçu," 129. On the *sativus–silvestris* dualism: J. Frayn, *Subsistence Farming in Roman Italy* (London, 1979), 58.

[108] L. Lockwood, *Introduction to Population Ecology* (Malden, 2006), 188.

[109] See above, 18–20.

[110] At the same time, oats and rye, previously marginal wild plants, entered cultivation because their botanical characteristics (toughness, basically) matched socio-economic needs: Montanari, "Vegetazione e alimentazione," in *L'ambiente vegetale nell'alto medioevo*, Settimane del CISAM 37 (Spolet'o 1990), 298. The relative abundance of "wild" resources did not impair the development of a refined castaneiculture: Montanari, *Campagne medievali*, 32–3.

[111] Irninger and Kühn, "Obstvielfalt," 52–53, explain this weaving in other species in late medieval Switzerland. See also Hehn, *Cultivated Plants*, 297.

Chapter 3

THE POETICS OF THE CHESTNUT IN THE
EARLY MIDDLE AGES

The Columbian Exchange, as Alfred Crosby who first identified it in 1972 called the giant process whereby the ecological resources of Europe, Africa, and the Americas mixed together, was everything except a smooth mechanical conveyor belt for microbes, seeds, animals, and people.[1] There were innumerable blockages and trip-steps along it, and among the most intractable bottlenecks in the great early modern ecological transaction was surely human culture. A good example of how people's expectations, institutions, and social relations slowed the Exchange is visible in the adventures of the potato.[2] This bland but nutritious tuber had long been cultivated in some Andean highlands when the Europeans reached there, and it excited the curiosity of the Spanish immigrants from the start. Unsure what the potato was, how to classify it, and what to call it, sixteenth-century writers nevertheless developed a luxuriant literature about it. As the literary fortunes of *Solanum tuberosum* waxed, the actual tuber acquired a mythical reputation, particularly among the masses of people who did not know it at all. Early modern botanical publications ascribed to the humble potato (and to the sweet potato so many failed to distinguish from it) glorious properties: it was a noted aphrodisiac. But even as the botanists described such benign effects of the exotic "truffle" on people, they also warned of its dangers: it was indigestible and caused flatulence, as well as leprosy and tuberculosis. Despite the enthusiasm of a few aristocrats, then, well into the 1800s the potato was surrounded by mistrust, and in popular culture, from Latvia to Andalusia, it was seldom considered fit for human consumption. Salaman, the great twentieth-century historian of the potato, postulated that a major reason

---

[1] A. Crosby, *The Columbian Exchange: Biological and Cultural Consequences of 1492. 30th Anniversary Edition* (Westport, 2003). Crosby developed his insight further in his *Ecological Imperialism: The Biological Expansion of Europe* (Cambridge, 1986), applying it to the Pacific in the 1700s.
[2] On this topic: R. Salaman, *The History and Social Influence of the Potato* (Cambridge, 1949).

for so much hesitation was ecological: the potato is planted and disseminates itself without seeds, rendering it something of a portent in early modern agriculture as practiced in Europe.[3] With the exception of Ireland, where massive social and cultural dislocation in the 1500s predisposed seventeenth-century people to adopt the potato as the main food crop, in most of Europe the harmless and indeed basically comestible tuber was kept from fields and pantries until industrialization, the Columbian Exchange notwithstanding.

This chapter is not about early modern times, nor the potato. It aims instead to lay out the cultural history of the chestnut in Europe during the first millennium AD. Yet as John McNeill observed in an introduction to the thirtieth-anniversary edition of Crosby's *Columbian Exchange*, the great acceleration in ecological transactions among the continents after 1492 can supply a model for understanding other instances of what scientists call biological invasion.[4] It is striking how the vagaries of the potato's cultural history mirror the much earlier, and slower, dissemination of the chestnut in European written culture. If the Roman hegemony is taken as the beginning of a trans-Mediterranean Exchange, or at least as the context for easier transfers of the kind Crosby envisioned, then the chestnut begins to look a bit more like a potato (indeed, sixteenth-century writers attempting to convey what a boiled potato tastes like consistently used the cooked chestnut as their comparison[5]). In the Mediterranean Exchange facilitated by the Roman empire, the best-documented movements of disease (Antonine and Justinianic plague) and of plants (peaches, cherries, olives) go from east to west, but some animals took advantage of the Roman peace, and maybe also of its late antique collapse, to shift themselves in other directions. So for instance the porcupine, a North African mammal, appears to have crossed the Inner Sea, headed for Italy and Spain, under Roman auspices, while the rabbit spread northwards from Iberia in the same circumstances.[6]

Castanea sativa, the European chestnut, may have begun its westward march long before Rome's legions reached the Pontic Alps and

[3] *Ibid.*, 437.

[4] J. McNeill, "Foreword," in Crosby, *The Columbian Exchange*, xi–xv (xiv–xv).

[5] Salaman, *History*, 102, 104, 131, 445. See also F. Braudel, *Civilisation matérielle et capitalisme: XVe–XVIII siècle*, 2 vols. (Paris, 1967), Vol. 1, 84; and F. Merz, *Die Edelkastanie: Ihre volkswirtschaftliche Bedeutung, ihr Anbau und ihre Bewirtschaftung* (Bern, 1919), 5–6, who noted that in Switzerland acceptance of the potato and disappearance of the chestnut went together.

[6] Porcupines: J. De Grossi Mazzorin and C. Minniti, "Reperti ossei," in *Roma dall'antichità al medioevo*, ed. M. Arena, P. Delogu, L. Paroli, M. Ricci, L. Saguì, and L. Vendittelli (Rome, 2001), 328–30 (329); J. Riquelme Cantal and A. Morales Muñiz, "A Porcupine Find from Roman North Africa, with a Review of Archaeological Data from Circummediterranean Sites," *Archaeofauna* 6 (1997), 91–95. Rabbits: R. Delort, *L'uomo e gli animali dall'età della pietra a oggi* (Bari, 1987), 331–39.

Transcaucasia, on whose well-watered, north-facing slopes the tree seems to be endemic and most at home. As we noted in Chapter 2, in what is today western Bulgaria, around the Bosphorus, and in northern Greece, likewise pollens and remains of charred wood indicate the presence of the sweet chestnut in the second millennium BC. At a couple of sites in northern Italy, similar traces of chestnuts from approximately the same time have also been found. Though, as we saw earlier, the evidence for this is thin, historians assert that Roman troops disseminated chestnuts from these remote corners of the empire to the Balkans, central Europe, the rest of Italy, Gaul, and Iberia. In this version of chestnut history, between maybe 100 BC and AD 476, the chestnut astutely hitched a ride on Roman imperialism to extend its ecological range. If the chestnut actually had a much more complex relationship with Romanization, still it seems fair to say that it was a plant that first came into its own during Rome's long rule over the Mediterranean Sea.

Yet there is ample evidence, analyzed here, that the chestnut was anything but popular and common in the Roman empire, and that ancient Mediterranean people were as puzzled by this essence as early modern Europeans would be, 1,000 and more years later, by the potato.[7] Both the chestnut and the potato are useful reminders that objects are never self-evident and "obvious," but always enmeshed in a web of ideas that can hinder or facilitate their acceptance by people in ways only hindsight renders surprising. Local ideas about what things mean determine things' success or failure much more than do inherent qualities in the thing, in this case the edible tuber or nut.[8] In fact, part of the transformation of ancient into medieval Europe was the movement of the chestnut out from the margins of ancient culture. In classical antiquity the chestnut occupied a minor position as an alien plant few people knew about or cared for, but by AD 1000 the chestnut had attained agricultural and cultural prominence. Paraphrasing the famous aphorism of Lévi-Strauss, at the end of Roman hegemony the chestnut became both good to think *and* good to eat.[9] For it was during the Dark Ages that *Castanea sativa* became normal, and this revolution, similar to the introduction, reception, and dissemination of the potato in early modern Europe, had both cultural and ecological facets to it, though, unlike the crops of the

---

[7] M. Conedera, P. Krebs, W. Tinner, M. Pradella, and D. Torriani, "The Cultivation of *Castanea sativa* (Mill.) in Europe, from Its Origin to Its Diffusion on a Continental Scale," *Vegetation History and Archaeobotany* 13 (2004), 161–79, argues similarly for limited classical understanding and dissemination of chestnut.

[8] N. Thomas, *Entangled Objects: Exchange, Material Culture, and Colonialism in the Pacific* (Cambridge, MA, 1991), 29, 88–89.

[9] C. Lévi-Strauss, *Le totémisme aujourd'hui* (Paris, 1962), 128.

Atlantic Exchange, chestnuts took much more than 300 years to attain respectability and, also unlike many New World plants, they have receded back into relative obscurity in industrial times.[10] This chapter discusses the literary and cultural understandings of chestnuts in late Roman and early medieval Europe as an important indicator of the great reorientations that separated the two, and returns the chestnut tree to the cultural landscape it once dominated.

AN UNCERTAIN ORGANISM

At first glance a chestnut seems a simple thing. It has not always been so. Indeed, the number of misunderstandings, uncertainties, and ambiguities surrounding chestnut trees, wood, and fruit is one of the main themes in early castaneological literature. As we shall discover, clearing away this underbrush of ambivalence was one of the achievements of the waning Roman empire and barbarian Europe. And if there was more certainty and clarity about chestnuts in the literature of the tenth century, still throughout the first millennium writers about chestnuts betrayed some unease about the nature of *Castanea sativa*. Was it a nut at all, or was it best classified with oaks and acorns? Was chestnut lumber reliable building material and could it mysteriously communicate with people when it was about to give out and collapse? Might chestnuts actually be human food, despite the huge headaches they produced, or should these strange fruits be left to the hogs? Indeed, most fundamentally, what was the true name of this essence, and where did the name come from? These are only some of the puzzles that worried those who thought and wrote about chestnuts, revealing to us the unsure terrain *Castanea sativa* often occupied in European literature of the first millennium.

These uncertainties are visible in the pages of Roman specialist agronomical literature that fantasize about grafting chestnuts to create outlandish hybrid trees. This literature was not entirely fantasy-driven, of course. In modern agriculture, particularly fruit-growing, grafting remains a widespread technique, necessary to produce fruit with the color, flavor, size, skin-thickness, texture, time of maturation, etc. that the grafter aspires to propagate. In effect, grafting is an asexual method of reproduction, and its result is a plant with bipartite genetic character. Since plants grown from seeds, and hence from the commingling of two different

---

[10] Salaman, *History*, 437, proffers the "general rule" that before industrialization a century elapsed between the reception of a useful innovation and its widespread acceptance. The chestnut's 1,000-year struggle was clearly very pre-industrial. On chestnuts' modern marginalization: A. Bruneton-Governatori, "Alimentation et idéologie," *Annales ESC* 39 (1984), 1161–89 (1163–73).

parent-plants' genes, do not have all the qualities of the "mother" plant from which they fell, as fruit, grafting offers cultivators several advantages. As the Carolingian polymath Hrabanus Maurus put it around 840, "wild trees produce bitter and sterile fruits if left to themselves, but when they have been grafted fatten into a most sweet fruitfulness."[11]

In consequence, this arboreal surgery has been popular since people began experimenting with agriculture. In the Mediterranean, grafting surfaces frequently in the earliest agricultural texts, and in the Latin manuals of agronomy the practice seems well known and common, carried out on many different species.[12] *Castanea sativa* was not among the species that drew the attention of all the Roman agronomical writers when they thought of grafting, probably because the chestnut was a rare and marginal plant before the late Roman period (whereas early medieval agricultural contracts often mention grafted chestnut trees and groves). Neither Columella nor Gargilius, let alone Cato or Varro, discussed grafted chestnuts, and if Pliny and Palladius both did, it is still difficult to avoid the impression that grafting chestnuts was not a normal procedure in Roman Italy, the milieu reflected by the agronomical writings.

In the first century AD, Pliny knew seven cultivars of chestnut and explicitly linked two of them to the practice of grafting. Nevertheless, Pliny gave his readers the context of "wonders" within which to understand this famous detail in the *Natural History*, so the Plinian chestnut grafts were highly unusual manifestations of nature's astonishing capacities, not signs of Roman familiarity with chestnut grafts. The two grafted varieties Pliny knew were called Tereiana and Corelliana. The former had a red shell and was the result of grafting onto a Corelliana stock or bole, itself an outcome of human ingenuity and labor, in other words of an earlier selection.[13] Significantly, both cultivars got their name from the successful grafter who created the cultivar and disseminated its seeds, and to Pliny it was not the new grafted chestnut variety that mattered, but the cultivators' success, a "rare" victory of the Roman landowner over oblivion by means of a tree that perpetuated his name rather than that of a place or a god, as most tree names did.[14] Therefore, though Pliny's grafts

[11] Hrabanus Maurus, *De universo*, MPL 111 (Paris, 1864), 9–614, 13.5 (367): "ligna silvarum per se amaros et steriles inferunt fructos, sed cum fuerint insita, dulcissima ubertate pinguescunt." J. Gaulin, "Tra *silvaticus* e *domesticus*: Il bosco nella trattatistica medievale," in *Il bosco nel medioevo*, ed. M. Montanari and B. Andreolli (Bologna, 1988), 90, traces this idea to Cassiodorus. See also J. Gaulin, "Tradition et pratiques de la littérature agronomique pendant le haut moyen âge," in *L'ambiente vegetale nell'alto medioevo*, Settimane del CISAM 37 (Spoleto, 1990), 103–35 (127–29).

[12] K. White, *Roman Farming* (London, 1970), 257–58, 262.

[13] Pliny the Elder, *Historia naturalis*, 15.94.

[14] *Ibid.* 17.22. Pliny gloated over grafters' eternal fame (via the invention of new cultivars bearing their name) in 15.49.

are botanically plausible, being made from two plants of the same species, they remain fantastical. In both Tereiana and Corelliana, the chestnut had surrendered to the skill of two Roman farmers, and had become something else, as the new names signaled.

Roman agronomical writing is too often taken at face value, as accurate and detailed exposition of how one farmed at the time of a manual's composition. The sophisticated literary confections of Pliny, Varro, Cato, Columella, and Palladius actually had specific cultural and political contexts and aims. Varro, for instance, used his *De re rustica* to spar with Cicero, whose *De re publica* argued for the active, committed life of political engagement for the Roman gentry.[15] The seemingly neutral agronomical manual satirized the supposed benefits of Ciceronian political activity and mocked the empty pieties of rural "otium" with which Cicero dignified Roman political careerism. Farming was brutal, exploitative, and often futile, not at all a demonstration of Roman elite competence and control. Behind pedantic lists of agricultural activities and snippets of rustic wisdom, *De re rustica* hid a pointed assault on the values and politics of the late Republican ruling class. For Varro, agronomy was really social criticism and political philosophy.

Given the ways Roman writers could deploy agronomical advice for extra-agricultural ends, the discussion of grafting chestnut trees in the agronomical manuals should not be treated as straightforward evidence of Roman castaneiculture. In Pliny's *Natural History*, as we have seen, the discussion of grafted cultivars is also a discussion of aristocratic agriculture and fame in an empire that left few avenues for social recognition to the Roman elite. But Pliny's encyclopedia accorded to chestnut's chameleon-like ability to change nature, through the artifice of grafting, somewhat less emphasis than did the writings of Palladius some three centuries later. Palladius also laid claim to special success in grafting chestnuts. He said he had personal experience, and described his method. The Roman fantasy of de-chestnutting the chestnut was stronger in Palladius than it had been in Pliny. Palladius' claims that chestnut scions may be grafted onto pear tree stocks, or apple, prune, mulberry, almond, or willow ones, are certainly wrong, for grafts across species, like these, do not work: the scion withers or, if it lives, is sterile. Nevertheless, such claims show that in the fourth century the literate landowner enjoying a dignified rural life was as concerned with surprising hybridity as had been Roman landowners 300 years prior, when Columella lapidarily corrected the "ancients" who denied the possibility of cross-species grafts. At stake

---

[15] My interpretation here follows L. Kronenberg, *Allegories of Farming from Greece and Rome* (Cambridge, 2009), 11–13, 74–76, 90–99, 108–24.

was more than the relationship between the ancients and moderns: the discourse of graft in antiquity was about human skill, of which grafters need a huge amount, and the power of the individual over recalcitrant nature, the leitmotif of agriculture. Palladius said that his grafts permitted the farmer to remove the prickly "menacing" husks from chestnuts (when crossed with pear, prune, apple, almond), or acquire a new ornamental appearance (with apple), develop stronger branches (with prune), or make the nuts lighter (with almond), or even change the nuts' color to become a new juicier fruit (crossed with mulberry).[16] Palladius also proposed to graft chestnut scions onto river willows to render the latter fruitful, though he recognized the resultant nuts would be sour and would mature very late.[17]

None of this is botanically sound, but it worked well as a wonder-inducing narrative designed to prove Palladius' ingenuity and competence and to showcase his ability to shape his property according to his desires, in other words to be a good farmer. Abundant, husk-less, juicy, odd-colored (purple? Palladius did not specify), ornamental chestnuts were the literary embodiment of agronomical skill, a bit as discussing feats of backyard gardening might be for modern western suburbanites. But more than plump homegrown tomatoes, Palladius' grafted, hybrid plum-nuts, or chest-apples, were ultimately unreal. That only increases their interest, of course. Palladius' discussion of chestnut-grafting is in the first place a manifestation of the agronomists' fantasy world where, using the sharp tool of verbiage, men imposed their will on vegetation. In the fourth century, when Palladius wrote, the discourse of the graft could also reverberate among readers who wondered about the compatibility of barbarian settlers in the empire, and of new belief systems then implanting themselves on the old polytheistic stock. In sum, there is more to Palladius' chestnut grafts than plain arboriculture. His weird and impossible half-breed trees, covered in the authority of personal experience and scientific agriculture, finally reflect the ambiguous status of *Castanea sativa* in the Roman world, a tree whose classification was uncertain, whose nuts were rather like meat and also rather like wheat yet probably were not comestible, and whose very name created perplexities.[18]

---

[16] Palladius, *De insitione liber*, in *Opus agriculturae*, ed. R. Rodgers (Leipzig, 1975), 296–300. Though Palladius' manual is prose, the section on grafting is in verse.

[17] *Ibid.*, 301; *Opus agriculturae* 12.7, in *ibid.*, 226.

[18] R. Grand and R. Delatouche, *L'agriculture au moyen âge, de la fin de l'empire romain au XVIe siècle* (Paris, 1950), 376, note a similar taste for "doomed" grafts in late medieval manuals.

THE NAME OF THE NUT

An aspect of chestnuts' slippery nature and of the difficulty people experienced when they set about trying to understand them was the uncertainty of the plant's name.[19] Still in modern English chestnuts (or sweet chestnuts, or Spanish chestnuts) are murky, easily confused with horse chestnuts (*Aesculus hippocastanum*), to which they are, however, botanically unrelated. To compound the confusion, as in medieval Latin, from which ultimately the English derives, a single English word describes the nut and the tree, a situation with some parallels (cherry, walnut), but that produces more perplexity than it does with fruits whose wood is little used or referred to.[20] Modern scientific nomenclature (in Latin, but used in vernacular texts) also has variants that betray unsureness. Though *Castanea sativa* nowadays prevails, well into the 1900s botanical texts deployed three separate names for the same tree, depending on the nationality of the writer and loyalties to one or another eighteenth-century botanical school.[21] Such ambiguities in usage are normal when dealing with relatively new and hence unfamiliar things, cases requiring cultural adaptation, new categorizations, and new understandings.[22] Yet compared to the confusions of antiquity regarding how to call the chestnut, the modern situation is pellucid.

Probably because chestnuts as nuts and especially as trees were unfamiliar, in the ancient Mediterranean, people were not sure what the right name was for the tree or its fruits. In early Hellenistic times, when presumably chestnuts were beginning to spread in the Mediterranean area, the "father of botany" Theophrastus had set the tone. He was unable to decide how to call chestnuts, varying between "Euboean nuts," the form he tended to prefer and that suggested the nuts originated in Euboea; "diosbalanos nuts"; and "kastanean nut" (in the sense of nut from Kastania, wherever *that* was).[23] From the beginning modern scholars have linked

---

[19] R. Meiggs, *Trees and Timber in the Ancient Mediterranean World* (Oxford, 1982), 420–22, on chestnuts. G. Duchet-Suchaux, "Les noms des arbres," in *L'arbre: Histoire naturelle et symbolique de l'arbre, du bois et du fruit au Moyen Age* (Paris, 1993), 13–23, reflects on terminology.

[20] Chestnut derives from the Middle English *chasteine*, which in turn comes from Latin *castanea*. Old English *cystel* is related to both.

[21] *Castanea sativa* Miller, *Castanea vesca* Gaertner, or *Castanea vulgaris* Lamarck, or even Linnaeus' *Fagus castanea* (admittedly never very widespread): see J. Pitte, *Terres de castanide* (Paris, 1987), 13; J. Rameau, D. Mansion, G. Dumé, *et al.*, *Flore forestière française: Guide écologique illustré*, 3 vols. (Dijon, 1989–2003), Vol. I (Dijon, 1989), 403.

[22] Thomas, *Entangled Objects*, 104–06.

[23] Theophrastus, *Historia plantarum*, ed. S. Amigues, 5 vols. (Paris, 2003), 1.11.3 (Vol. I, 34); 3.3.1 (Vol. II, 7); 3.3.8 (Vol. II, 10); 4.8.11 (Vol. II, 92). There were several competing towns credited with naming the nut, from the Pontos to Thessaly and Mount Ida. In most of them it is unlikely *Castanea sativa* grew spontaneously. J. André, *L'alimentation et la cuisine à Rome* (Paris, 1961), 85, thinks the names all suggest Asia Minor origins.

so much semantic slippage to the exotic and rare status of chestnuts in the Hellenic Mediterranean, and it may indeed have that origin.[24] The naming of essences from their supposed place of origin is of course quite normal, even though the accuracy of such attributions is often questionable: in antiquity, for instance, the apricot was called Armenian plum though it grows wild only in northern China and must have originated there, while the name "portugal" still given oranges in Greece, Kurdistan, and parts of Italy is manifestly unrelated to the place where the citrus was first cultivated.[25] Thus, it is understandable that Theophrastus' doubts were not easily dispelled, and centuries later Pliny got thoroughly confused between walnuts and chestnuts when he attempted to transpose Theophrastus' wisdom into Latin.[26] Around AD 200 dinnertime conversation could still center on what the chestnut's name actually was, while a scientific writer weighed the different names circulating in the Greek-speaking world.[27]

The situation had changed little at the end of the ancient period. In the early fifth century, the setting for the highly civil mealtime conversations recorded by Macrobius in his *Saturnalia*, elegant guests could be imagined puzzling over the name of "the castanea nut."[28] These learned men referred to Virgil's *Eclogues* to prove *castanea* was the correct name, but they also knew from Oppian that chestnuts could be called "nuts of Heraclea," and that other possibilities like "Pontic nut" and "imperial walnut" existed. All their dispassionate wisdom is somewhat tarnished by the utterly misguided observation Macrobius puts in the mouths of *Saturnalia*'s conversationalists to the effect that the chestnut buds and blossoms along with the almond, one of the most precocious trees in the Mediterranean, covering itself with white flowers in January and February, even before its leaves have budded. This last comment indicates that neither Macrobius nor his readers knew or cared all that much about real chestnut trees' behavior and appearance (*Castanea sativa* blooms in late May and June, and its creamy flowers are orange-tinted); such a

---

[24] V. Hehn, *Cultivated Plants and Domesticated Animals in Their Migration from Asia to Europe* (Amsterdam, 1976), 295–96. See also J. André, *Lexique des termes de botanique en Latin* (Paris, 1956), 76, who gives eight Latin names for chestnut, five related to the Greek *kastan-*.

[25] B. Hasselrot, "L'abricot: Essai de monographie onomasiologique et sémantique," *Studia neophilologica* 13 (1940–41), 45–79 (45, 50).

[26] Meiggs, *Trees and Timber*, 421–22.

[27] Athenaeus, *The Deipnosophists*, 3 vols., trans. C. Yonge, Vol. 1, (London, 1854), 2.42–43, (87–89), offers nine names for chestnuts and worries about scholarly disagreement over whether chestnuts are actually acorns. Galen, "On the Good and Bad Humors in Foods" ("De probis pravisque alimentorum succis"), in *Claudii Galeni Opera Omnia*, 20 vols., ed. C. Kühn, Vol. VI (Hildesheim, 1965), 749–815, Cap. 4, 778.

[28] Macrobius, *Saturnalia*, ed. J. Willis (Leipzig, 1963), 3.187 (211).

cultural distance between the writers and the trees could help to explain their residual unsureness about the trees' name. However, Macrobius may also have been weighing in on an age-old debate about chestnut flowers (some thought there were none), already in full swing when Theophrastus lived, in Hellenistic times.[29]

Servius, a friend of Macrobius who figures as one of the diners in the *Saturnalia*, also wrote a famous commentary to Virgil's poems. It suggests that by AD 400 some latinophones at least had sorted out the difficulties surrounding chestnut nomenclature.[30] Servius observed that Latin speakers of Virgil's time had called chestnuts "chestnut nut" (*nux castaneae*), using the Latin word for chestnut as a qualifier, because there were many other types of nuts, or hard-shelled fruits, with which readers could mix up these ones. He praised his favorite poet for such clarifying precision: it saved readers from wrongly imagining that some other kind of nut (Servius listed hazel, walnut, and almond as possibilities) would be offered by the lovesick shepherd Corydon to the beautiful boy Alexis in the second *Bucolic*. Servius' slightly defensive explanation for Virgil's wording bypasses the problem that chestnut shells are actually much softer than almond, hazel, or walnut shells (which would remove the chestnut from the category nut, placing it with the "glandes," or acorns), but it does show that fifth-century readers might be puzzled by Virgil's failure to use a more direct expression (just "chestnuts," in Latin *castaneae*, as a noun) than he did.

In fact, another post-classical commentator on Virgil who seems to have been a contemporary of Servius and whose writings were often bundled together with Servius' by medieval copyists, Iunius Philargyrius, acknowledged the definitive change in chestnut's status from adjective to noun by using a past tense in his note to *Bucolic* 2.52. To him, Virgil had used the chestnut nut circumlocution "as chestnuts used to be called nuts."[31] Philargyrius implies that Latin had moved on, in the more than four centuries since Virgil had composed his poetry, and that in the fifth century to call a chestnut a chestnut nut sounded as awkward as it does today. Taken together, then, these commentators' evidence points to a situation where the rather clumsily over-defined chestnuts of the

---

[29] Pliny the Elder, *Historia naturalis* 16.103, knew almonds bloom first, in January. Theophrastus, *Historia Plantarum* 3.3.8 (Vol. II, 10), noted scientists' doubts about chestnut buds and flowers, to which Macrobius' certainty could be an erudite riposte. J. Frayn, *Subsistence Farming in Roman Italy* (London, 1979) 43–44, argues the unrealism of Roman poetry.

[30] *In Vergilii Bucolica et Georgica commentarii, Buc.* 2.52 ed. G. Thilo (Leipzig, 1887), 26.

[31] Servius, *Servii Grammatici qui feruntur in Vergilii Carmina commentarii*, ed. H. Hagen (Leipzig, 1902), 42. On post-classical Virgilian botany see G. Alessio, "Glossografia altomedievale alle *Georgiche*," in *L'ambiente vegetale nell'alto medioevo*, Settimane del CISAM 37 (Spoleto, 1990), 55–94 (92–93).

ancients no longer fit in comfortably, and the glosses helped people who called chestnuts simply chestnuts understand the archaism of the poet. Now that actual chestnuts were more familiar to readers of Latin it was no longer necessary to explain that chestnuts were a kind of nut, but the immortal verses of Virgil presented the former situation to readers and therefore needed glossing.

Naturally the uncertainties of the ancients were not wholly cleared up in late antiquity, a time when anything ancient was automatically excellent, even uncertainty. In the very same period when Macrobius and Servius were writing, in fact in 387, before his Christian baptism, Augustine of Hippo became involved in the discussion about the name of the nut. In light of the confusion that surrounded classical chestnut nomenclature, it is appropriate to find that for Augustine chestnuts were simply an example of equivocation. In his treatise *On Dialectics*, chestnut (*castanea*) was a word whose basic ambiguity was insurmountable, a sign of the limitations of human expression, for it could mean (and did mean) multiple things at the same time.[32] It was a tree, but really it was a nut that contained the potential to become a tree, and ultimately there was no logical proportion between the two things expressed by the one word. That which produced the chestnut somehow and unfairly had acquired its product's epithet.

While Augustine's conclusion was typically dour, namely that language was an unreliable medium for conveying truth, another conclusion also surfaces. About the year 400 one term had overtaken the others to describe *Castanea sativa*, and the simplification and clarity this implies should be related to cultural familiarity and to the greater distribution of chestnut trees and nuts, increasingly inserted in a stable semantic field by Latin speakers and writers. This new clarity was not the only possible outcome, and does not explain why, out of the several ancient possibilities, *castanea* prevailed as the name for the chestnut. *Praecoccus*, the most used Latin name for apricots, seems to have been lost in Romance languages until the crusades and the introduction into Latin Christendom of new eastern cultivars, along with an Arabized version of the fruit's old name, though apricots themselves were still cultivated in at least some parts of early medieval Europe. Thus, the survival of "kastanean nut" in the form of *castanea* in early medieval texts suggests considerable cultural continuity, as well as agricultural continuity. There are various possible reasons for the cultural acceptance of a given name for a plant, rather than another one, unrelated to the postulated geographic origins of the plant, and Spanish or Turkish names for fruits triumphed in subaltern

[32] Augustine, *De dialectica*, ed. and trans. B. Jackson and J. Pinborg (Dordrecht, 1975), 10 (116). Modern scholarship seems to have dispelled earlier doubts about Augustine's authorship of this work.

languages and cultures along with Spanish and Turkish imperialism in the early modern period.[33] In the case of chestnuts, why some names fell by the linguistic wayside and one became hegemonic is not clear. The post-classical users of the chesnut's classical name *castanea* betray no awareness that the name was toponymic, referring to the town Kastanea where the ancients sometimes thought the plant had first come under cultivation. But while they developed other, better explanations for their naming of the chestnut, they show us that the tree had lost much of its mythic allure. The new cultural clarity seems related to the new agricultural familiarity. Such familiarity might explain why the young Augustine chanced on the chestnut, rather than (say) the cherry when he sought to make an example of a thing whose name had more than one meaning in order to condemn language's limitations.

Indeed, the late antique sedimentation of name-stability is visible in a text written by one of the leading scholars of the early Middle Ages, one who ironically took quite an opposite view from Augustine on the utility of language.[34] Isidore of Seville had no doubts about the meaning of chestnut and how the word had become attached to the seed. In the vast etymological encyclopedia he assembled at the beginning of the seventh century, the bishop offered the following definition: "The Latins call chestnut 'castanea' from the Greek word. For the Greeks call it 'kastanian,' because its paired fruits are hidden away rather like testicles within the scrotum, and when they are taken out it is as if they were being castrated. The tree, as soon as it is cut, is accustomed to resprout almost like a forest."[35] Although the association of human genitals and fruits (or nuts, as English speakers will readily appreciate) is quite common across cultures, what is noteworthy here is that Isidore cast aside the ambivalence of ancient chestnut scholarship and reduced the field to one term for tree and nut.[36] The learned bishop blamed the Greek language for the odd word and more incongruously for its connotations as he saw them.

---

[33] Hasselrot, "L'abricot," 245–46. I know no archaeological attestations of early medieval apricots in Europe, and Hasselrot did not explain how he knew about pre-crusade Italian cultivation of the fruit. See A. Livarda, "Spicing up Life in Northwestern Europe: Exotic Food Plant Imports in the Roman and Medieval Worlds," *Vegetation History and Archaeobotany* 20 (2011), 143–64 (146, 161), for minimal high medieval evidence.

[34] J. Fontaine, *Isidore de Séville: Genèse et originalité de la culture hispanique au temps des Wisigoths* (Turnhout, 2000), 283–92, on Isidore's confidence in words' ability to capture things.

[35] Isidore of Seville, *Isidori hispalensis episcopi Etyologiarum sive Originum libri xx* [hereafter *Etymologiae*], 2 vols., ed. W. Lindsay (Oxford, 1911), Vol. II, 17.7.25: "Castaneam Latini a Graeco appellant vocabulo. Hanc enim Graeci kastanian vocant, propter quod fructus eius gemini in modum testiculorum intra folliculum reconditi sunt, qui dum eiciuntur quasi castrantur. Haec arbor simul ut excisa fuerit, tamquam silva expullulare consuevit."

[36] Hasselrot, "L'abricot," 239. It is worth noting that early Spanish potato nomenclature linked the tuber to testicles (Salaman, *History*, 129), and that contemporary (mostly north) Italian vernacular equates testicles and chestnuts ("marroni").

Though he borrowed the detail about the chestnut tree's phoenix-like regenerative vitality from a much-admired Genesis-commentary, the *Exameron* of Ambrose, Isidore seems to have discovered the castration etymology himself, one of the most imaginative in the seventeenth book of the *Etymologies*, dedicated to "rural things." Before him several classical authors had duly remarked on the appearance of the chestnut's external husk, called "spiny" or "hirsute" by Virgil and compared to a Roman military encampment by Pliny, but the anthropomorphic comparison had not yet occurred to anyone, perhaps because the bristly outer husk does not always wrap just two shiny nuts.[37] The closest any ancient commentator came to this association is in a passage about lumber from Pliny's *Natural History*: the Roman encyclopedist noted that chopping off branches from trees like the holm oak, the olive, the ash, and the chestnut weakened their wood and rendered it less suitable, because such lopping was like castration and "inhibited strength," a comment that does associate chestnut trees and castration, but has nothing to do with the nuts and their protective layer.[38] In other parts of the *Etymologies* Isidore showed all the etymological power of castration, claiming that to be the root behind the name for castle (*castrum*), chaste (*castus*), and beaver (*castor* in Latin), but in these instances Isidore had some classical antecedents, while his derivation of *castanea* is original.[39] Since the Latin word for chestnut is feminine, Isidore's very masculine etymology for it is especially remarkable. He was not much of a botanist, but if he had been and had known that *Castanea sativa* produces both male and female flowers in early summer, he might have appreciated the irony of his virilization of the hermaphrodite tree.

In the end only Isidore, who thought words usually derive from the nature of the thing they describe, was confident that a botanical property of the chestnut fruit explained the plant's name, though the name was Greek and the descriptive word applied to the biological characteristic was Latin (and the Greek root for castration, *eunuch-*, was utterly unrelated to the Latin one). Isidore's deeply original vision of how to call chestnuts and why they should be called thus concludes the centuries-long itinerary of the name for the chestnut in Latin. In the Dark Ages everyone

---

[37] Pliny, *Historia naturalis* 15.92; Virgil, *Bucolicae* 7.53.

[38] Pliny, *Historia naturalis* 16.206.

[39] Isidore, *Etymologiae* 9.3.44 ("castle" from castration, since women never enter them so they are sexless, with Servius as source); 10.33 ("chaste" from castration); 12.2.21 (building on Servius, beavers castrate themselves when trapped by hunters, knowing their testicles are desired for medicine-preparation: see Galen, "On Simple Medicines" in *Claudii Galeni Opera Omnia*, 20 vols., ed. C. Kühn, Vol. xii [Hildesheim, 1965], 1–377, 11.15 [337–41]); 19.27.4 (beavers self-castrate when cornered by hunters so are called "castores").

knew both what the chestnut was and what to call it, and the earlier debates about the name of the plant subsided. Even as he discarded the literary tradition that wondered about the best ways to call and classify chestnuts, Isidore offered an anatomically plausible reason for the tie between word and thing. What the late Roman commentators on Virgil had adumbrated, namely the loss of variety in chestnut's names, and the end of topographically derived (hence exoticized) names for them, as well as the end of names that stressed their nuttiness, Isidore confirmed with his uncompromising clarity. By Isidore's day a new arboreal world had grown up that crowded out the old ways of addressing *Castanea sativa*.

WRITING CHESTNUTS IN ANTIQUITY

Early medieval writers who mentioned chestnuts had at their disposal a solid corpus of ancient Latin texts containing the Roman tradition on the tree and the nut. Much of this literature was composed in two waves, either in the first century AD or in a second wind of literary interest in chestnuts at the beginning of late antiquity, in the decades around 300. As in the early medieval literature, the ancient texts responded to and cited each other, creating some stereotypes, but they also convey some idiosyncratic interpretations of the tree and its nuts.[40]

One potent strain of chestnut discourse placed the tree and especially its fruit in the picturesque but ultimately backward world of the shepherds. In this vein, Virgil's *Eclogues* were highly influential. The famous first *Bucolic* opened with the aged shepherd Tityrus offering his guest (who demurely declined the offer, having real business to attend to) a shady patch of ground on which to share an evening snack of ripe fruit, tender chestnuts, and fresh cheese. Thus, Virgil conjugated rusticity with idleness and a charming old-school kindness resigned to its own ineffectualness (Tityrus knew his simple offerings would not be accepted). This backwoods hospitality, among people whom modern times had bypassed and whose offers of "chestnut nuts" were doomed, resurfaced in another Virgilian poem when the ugly giant shepherd Corydon, mindful that a former lover once liked them, offered chestnuts to the boy of his dreams: he was duly scolded, for he should know better than to imagine his rustic gifts seductive.[41]

Following, like everyone else, in the footsteps of Virgil, Ovid represented gifts of chestnuts as mildly comical tools in the seducer's arsenal.

---

[40] Pitte, *Terres*, 60–64, 71–75.
[41] Virgil, *Bucolicae* 1.79; 2.51–56. See also 7.53, where the intention to eat the nuts is unclear.

Although Ovid moved chestnuts out of the pastoral world, the nuts are among the "rustic presents" one should pretend to have gathered on one's own suburban estate so as to impress the beloved, and in another poem chestnuts still are laughable assets of monstrous, wood-dwelling shepherds.[42] Martial too issued jocular dinner invitations to friends with the unpretentious, down-home, and unreal nature of the proposed meal made explicit by the almost-vegetarian menu that included slowly roasted chestnuts, and by the promise that none of the then-fashionable entertainments would be available.[43] Less famous first-century poets, too, like Calpurnius Siculus, deployed the chestnut within a pastoral setting and in rural people's clumsy courtships, a cultural sign of how far these people and their simple means were removed from the metropolitan consumers of the poetry.[44]

The poetic chestnut was thus a loser's food, fit for simple-minded shepherds and those out of touch with high society. Indeed, Latin prose writers, particularly the early agronomists, did not deem chestnut trees able to produce human food at all. Varro, an older contemporary of Virgil who is sometimes credited with the first Latin use of the noun *castanea* for chestnut, fed chestnuts to his snails.[45] Whereas he seems to have looked forward to eating the snails, he showed no interest in chestnuts, plants he maintained as a "bush" inside the snail-rearing pens and whose leaves he did not expect to tempt any sensible snail. Strangely, Varro advised that when the chestnut bush had no fruit, namely most of the time, the snail-rancher should toss chestnuts into the pen to fatten his wards, but he gave no instructions about how to procure them, or store them.[46] The whole scheme is impractical to the point it seems to have been a purely literary exercise, or a political statement like his intervention on grafting, but Varro does show that Roman landowners of his time, when at all familiar with chestnut "bushes," would not eat their fruit as a matter of course, though they might consider it as viable fodder.

This impression is confirmed by Palladius' systematic treatise on farming techniques, which contains much information on how to plant and grow chestnut trees. Palladius compared chestnuts to willows, canes, and oaks, but concluded that reason ("ratio") dictated for the prudent

---

[42] Ovid, *Ars amandi* 2.266–67 (potentially the sole Roman reference to chestnut commerce, so it is a pity it is obscured by irony and the incongruity of buying chestnuts at any season on Rome's main ceremonial street); Ovid, *Metamorphoses* 13.810–11.

[43] Martial, *Epigrams* 5.78.

[44] Calpurnius Siculus, *Bucoliques*, ed. J. Amat (Paris, 1991), 14–18.

[45] André, *L'alimentation*, 85

[46] Marcus Terentius Varro, *Économie rurale* [*De re rustica*], ed. C. Guiraud (Paris, 1997), 3.15.1 (36).

landowner to plant chestnuts, except on a very few kinds of soil.[47] The reason was that chestnuts grow faster and thus offered the aforementioned landowner more poles upon which to drape his or her vines. In fact, Columella calculated that a healthy *iugerum* (about 2,500 m², or an eighth of an acre) of chestnut woods with 2,880 trees on it would yield 12,000 props every 5 years, and given the resistance to rot of tannic chestnut wood, the prudent landowner would have plenty of props for his vineyard of 20 *iugera*. Hence the chestnut grove was a "dowry" for the vineyard, in the sense of a subordinate economic asset designed to support the main economic activity of the "husband," in this case a vineyard. Hence too Columella never entertained the poetic idea that the nuts themselves had any place in the endowment of the farm. Oddly, the object of the exercise of planting, tending to, and owning a chestnut tree was to make wine.[48]

Though his literary intention was different from Columella's, Pliny the Elder shared Columella's general assessment of chestnuts: the fruit was "most lowly" ("vilissima"), and it was one of the marvels of nature that such a base thing should be so meticulously wrapped and protected. Pliny suggested that roasting chestnuts rendered them slightly more pleasant to eat, and he knew of cults wherein a kind of chestnut bread was eaten by women who ritually abstained from grain for a set time in the year, to honor the cereal goddesses. Pliny further knew of seven varieties of chestnut (as we saw earlier), depending on how hard to peel they were and what other nuisances they posed to would-be eaters. But among the latter Pliny included pigs first, and to him, aside from chestnuts grown at Naples or Taranto, all the others were really best left to the swine (though he *had* heard that the Indians made oil out of chestnuts).[49]

Pliny, who had his doubts about whether chestnuts were nuts at all, analyzed the tree in his *Natural History* both in Book 16, given over to "wild" trees, and in Book 17, about trees created by human ingenuity. Though he was aware of the ambiguous position of chestnuts between nature and culture, and though he had a lot to say about this essence, the topography it prefers and its foliation habits, Pliny still did not consider

---

[47] Chestnut soil preferences: loose and dark and damp, gravelly and tufaceous, north-facing, shady and inclined. See V. Winiwarter: "Soil Scientists in Ancient Rome," in *Footprints in the Soil*, ed. B. Warkentin (Amsterdam, 2006), 3–16 (13–14); "Prolegomena to a History of Soil Knowledge in Europe," in *Soils and Societies*, ed. V. Winiwarter and J. McNeill (Isle of Harris, 2006), 208–10.

[48] Columella, *De agri cultura*, ed. H. Boyd Ash (Cambridge, MA, 1941), 4.30.1 (dowry); 4.30.2 (willows, canes); 4.33.1–2 (oaks and soils); 4.33.4 (numbers); 4.33.5 (oaks and reason).

[49] Pliny, *Historia naturalis* 15.92–3. On Indian oil: 15.28. Pliny's contemporary Dio Chrysostom (*Discourses* 7.74), writing in Greek about Euboea (sometimes held to be the place where chestnuts were first cultivated), also considered chestnuts a food pigs might disdain.

chestnuts among "the most famous trees."[50] Nevertheless he recorded how the plant was weakened by over-frequent lopping, while recognizing *Castanea sativa's* wood as reasonably strong and very long-lasting.[51] To grow a tree Pliny recommended planting the seed rather than a sapling, and grafting it in winter. A bit contradictorily Pliny thought these grafted trees should still produce poles, and though the first two years after planting were risky and had a high failure rate, thereafter chestnuts took care of themselves, their shade suppressing unwanted undergrowth and their boles continuing to grow posts for many vines. Even when Pliny discussed two celebrated cultivars from the Campanian plain, one grafted from the other ("a marvel"), quality and quantity of their production seems to have been measured in terms of wood, not nuts.[52]

If they often deemed their fruit inedible or at best negligible, Roman writers of the early empire knew groves of chestnut could be precious at least as vineyard-dowries. Thus, chestnuts' woody growth could be valuable, and in fact these trees could end up figuring in the boundary disputes of Roman landowners, presumably vintners.[53] Yet the famous vitality of chestnuts, what made their trunks grow so quickly, was not prized by architects. For whereas Hellenistic botanists had remarked on chestnut lumber's utility in construction projects (it was a considerate material that creaked ominously before collapsing, so people could get out of chestnut-roofed buildings in time), Roman writers did not agree.[54] In listing building materials Vitruvius ignored chestnut altogether, and Pliny did not place chestnuts among the trees whose wood had the "thick firmness" builders needed, though as we saw he agreed it was not poor wood either. As with other trees often lopped, he seems to have thought chestnut wood would be without strength because of its usual treatment by people, not because of its own nature.[55]

In sum, the Latin literary record gives an image of chestnuts as marginal to mainstream agricultural and cultural concerns. The primary role of *Castanea sativa* in Roman agronomical landscapes was in viticulture, as an efficient way to keep vines aloft without over-frequent, laborious, and expensive substitution of their props. As we have seen, Roman writers give the impression that the main function of chestnuts was making wine, save for a few hapless shepherds roaming the remoter byways.

[50] Pliny, *Historia naturalis* 15.92 (doubts); 16.74 (fame and topography); 16.98 (leaves).
[51] *Ibid.* 16.206; 16.212.
[52] *Ibid.* 17.148 (planting); 17.150 (shade); 17.122 (grafted "raritas").
[53] Hyginus, "De condicionibus agrorum," in *Corpus agrimensorum Romanorum*, ed. C. Thulin (Leipzig, 1913), 74–86 (76).
[54] Theophrastus, *Historia Plantarum*, 5.6.1, (Vol. III, 18).
[55] Vitruvius, *De Architectura* 2.9.5–17; Pliny, *Historia naturalis* 16.206.

The poetics of the chestnut in the early Middle Ages

By the mid third century, while the empire was convulsed by its first great political and economic crisis, there are signs of change. The successful Mauretanian farmer–politician Gargilius Martialis, polemical with his agronomical predecessors for their lack of clarity and consistency, as well as knowledge, dealt with chestnut cultivation in his treatise *De hortis* (*About Gardens*).[56] There are stands on the Atlas today, but Gargilius' North Africa was not a place where *Castanea sativa* flourished, so his sophisticated treatment of growing chestnuts may not be as empirically grounded as he claimed. Still, he distinguished (in one place) between chestnuts planted for poles (most of them) and for fruit, scornfully correcting those who thought that different cultivation techniques were necessary for each. Though overall his agronomical text was traditional, it confidently catalogued the errors and ambiguities of earlier writers on the types of soil, the topography, the climate, and the agricultural treatments best suited to *Castanea sativa* as if this were an integral part of Mediterranean agronomical wisdom, as much as was his advice on olive trees and grape vines.

Gargilius' agronomics reflected his predecessors' interest in strong, long-lasting trellises for vineyards, but another work of his opened a short treatment "about the chestnut" with the assertion that chestnuts are the strongest of foods for the body, however hard to digest. Here Gargilius discussed the medicinal uses to which the nut could be put. As a medicine, he recommended fire-roasted chestnuts with honey against coughs; alternatively, an infusion in which unskinned chestnuts were boiled was excellent against dysentery, celiac flows, and bloody coughing.[57] The cuticle between shell and nut was astringent, so a fine cure for "fluid stomachs," particularly indicated when someone overdosed on purgative substances.

The important change signaled by Gargilius' medical treatise is that chestnuts were now deemed suitable, indeed appropriate, for human consumption, even if in special and controlled circumstances. Roman agronomists and poets had established a tradition in which eating chestnuts was *déclassé*, and just a few generations before Gargilius, Athenaeus, a Greek author, had thought eating chestnuts a bad idea for health reasons: they gave people bad headaches, made them fat, were exceptionally hard to digest, and produced acute flatulence. Though Athenaeus allowed that cooking, and particularly roasting, mitigated chestnuts' toxicity, he

---

[56] Gargilius Martialis, *De hortis*, ed. I. Mazzini (Bologna, 1978), 4.4 (120; same techniques); 4.1–3 (116–18; predecessors' errors); 4.5–6 (122; soils and climates).

[57] Gargilius Martialis, *Les remèdes tirés des légumes et des fruits* [*Medicinae ex holeribus et pomis*], ed. B. Maire (Paris, 2002), 66 (76). Gargilius seems to have known Galen, "On the Good and Bad Humors," 4.

suspected that these procedures also robbed chestnuts of whatever nutri-
tive value they had, so he recommended that chestnuts only be eaten
boiled, if at all.[58]

In the medical literature there was no unanimity, and Athenaeus' contemporary, Galen, a famous doctor whose career led him to Rome as
Marcus Aurelius' physician, was more sanguine and said that chestnuts
were the only wild nuts that gave the body any sustenance, though it was
not much, and if they were more digestible than other nuts like acorns,
he dismissively lumped them with foods having "fat" humors, that tended
to be astringent, and were only eaten during famines.[59] Thus, Gargilius
marks a shift in orientation within the medical tradition that created room
for chestnuts as a controlled substance, if not quite as respectable food.
Perhaps his residual suspicion came from his notion that chestnuts were
not domesticated trees, and their fruit was wild, uncontrolled by people.

Meanwhile, chestnut medicine became a minor byline of late antique
literature. The personal physician of the last pagan Roman emperor, Julian,
for instance, thought chestnuts medically neutral, balanced between the
humors and thus useful for re-establishing an organism's equilibrium.[60]
In sixth-century writings about alimentary regimens, mostly created in
Ravenna, doctors pronounced chestnuts fine food when cooked, and
"well suited" to people, even to rulers, able to "nourish the stomach,"
though they still reported the ancient doubts: chestnuts could cause
swelling of the body and be hard to digest.[61]

Also outside the manuals of medicine, late antique chestnuts acquired
a more honorable position. Because Palladius wrote in the tradition of
Roman agronomics and referred to the issues and techniques earlier
authorities had discussed, his evaluation of chestnuts was not fundamentally innovative. However, the space and care a fourth-century agricultural
writer accorded to *Castanea sativa*, compared to Varro's snail-feed, signaled
what looks in hindsight like a considerable rise in status. For example,
Palladius expanded the Roman architect Vitruvius' list of suitable woods

[58] Athenaeus, *Deipnosophists* 2.43 (88–89).

[59] Galen, "On the Properties of Foods" ["De alimentorum facultatibus"], in *Claudii Galeni Opera Omnia*, 20 vols., ed. C. Kühn, vol. VI (Hildesheim, 1965) 2.38 (619 [classification with wild, ined-ible plants that give headaches], 620 [famines], 621 [nutritious, hard to digest]); "On the Good and Bad Humors" 4 (777 [fat humor, but good nutrition], 778 [famine], 779 [astringent but digestible]). See M. Montanari, "Un frutto ricco di storia," in *La castagna sulle tavole d'Europa* (San Piero al Bagno, 2001), 50–63. Other exotic fruits like apricots were thought toxic and dangerous: Hasselrot, "L'abricot," 235.

[60] Oribasius, *Synopsis*, ed. H. Mørland, in *Oribasius latinus*, Vol. 1 (Oslo, 1940), 2.1 (93).

[61] Anthimus, *De observatione ciborum ad Theodericum regem Francorum epistula*, ed. E. Liechtenhan (Berlin, 1963), 88 (32): "castania elixa bene apta sunt vel assa; nam cruda non bene degerentur"; "Diaeta Theodori," ed. K. Sudhoff, *Archiv für Geschichte der Medizin* 8 (1915), 377–403 (401): "cas-tanee carnem nutriunt sed inflationem faciunt, cocte minus inflacionem faciunt."

for construction to include chestnut, while noting its defect was its weight.[62] At one point in his treatment of chestnuts in Book 12 of *Opus agriculturae* (*Agricultural Work*), Palladius adopted the self-revealing mode agronomical writers sometimes used to give their assertions a more real flavor and more authority. He said he had personally grafted chestnuts by incision under the bark, and recommended the technique.[63] Though as we have seen Pliny thought grafting of wood-producing trees was possible, in this case Palladius aimed at producing better fruit, for he remarked that the technique worked well both on chestnut and on willow boles, the disadvantage of the latter being that the scion grew more slowly and produced "sour" fruit. Putting aside the question of why one would want to graft a chestnut scion onto willow stock if the results were so inferior, the passage indicates that Palladius' were not just the vineyard prop-producing machines chestnuts sometimes seem to have been in ancient agronomy.[64] Unlike most of his predecessors, Palladius also explained how to preserve chestnuts, though the ones he intended to keep may have been the ones used to start a tree. He suggested chestnuts could be kept buried in sand, in clay pots, in beechwood boxes sealed in mud or finely minced barley stalks, or in marsh-grass sacks. Regardless of which method she or he used, the would-be chestnut cultivator had to cull the seed nuts that went bad every thirty days, using flotation to determine their condition: the ones that sank were sound and still capable of germination. Perhaps this is an extension of Palladius' (and Gargilius') discussion in earlier sections of the treatise of how to keep vital seed nuts from harvest in autumn to planting in spring, but perhaps it is also a sign of the inroads chestnuts were making on the late antique table.[65] Limited understanding of chestnut preservation constricted the dissemination of the nut in the ancient world.

Indeed, at about the same time Palladius wrote, a composite miscellany of Roman recipes was assembled under the name of the Augustan-age gourmand Apicius. It contained directions for preparing a strange concoction of lentils boiled with chestnuts and spices. Such mush ("pultem") would have been a low-class food, so was enriched and ennobled with

[62] Palladius, *Opus agriculturae* 12.5, in *Opus agriculturae. De veterinaria medicina. De insitione*, ed. R. Rodgers (Leipzig, 1975), 231. See Meiggs, *Trees and Timber*, 240. Instead in the fourth century BC Theophrastus, *Historia Plantarum* 5.4.2 (Vol. III, 12); 5.4.4 (13); 5.6.1 (18); 5.7.7 (22) did not imagine eating the nuts and considered the chestnut mainly a lumber tree.

[63] Palladius, *Opus agriculturae* 12.7 (226). See above, 92.

[64] C. Bignami and A. Salsotto, *La civiltà del castagno* (Cuneo, 1983), 14, underestimate Palladius' interest in the nuts.

[65] Palladius, *Opus agriculturae* 12.7 (225–26). Compare Gargilius Martialls, *De hortis* 4.3 (120), who recognized the problem of having a "healthy and ripe" seed available to plant in February, for chestnuts easily go bad: "nux reservata difficile contra putredine vindicare."

pepper, cumin, coriander seed, mint, rue, laser root, and pennyroyal in order for the cooks who might use the recipe in high-class residences not to offend their employers (or owners, since chefs often were slaves). This solitary entry involving chestnuts among almost 500 recipes might derive from the late ancient context wherein the cookbook was assembled more than from Apicius' own century, but it anyway represents the very timid introduction of chestnuts in Roman literary gastronomy and perhaps kitchens too.[66]

In about AD 400, when Servius wrote his commentary to Virgilian poetry, the chestnut had been known within the Roman empire for about half a millennium. Servius' commentary aimed to help late Roman Latinists appreciate Virgil's Latin, and like all commentaries was declaredly derivative, so not a text in which to seek innovation. Yet Servius invited his audience not to consider chestnuts "base," which the nuts' treatment in the *Eclogues* might induce readers to do, for a select few Virgilian characters manifestly had appreciated them, notably Amaryllis, the onetime lover of the unseemly shepherd Corydon.[67] Despite Servius' protestations it seems that in the five-odd centuries during which Roman writers had been mindful of *Castanea sativa*, the tree had become somewhat more familiar, and more respectable, but had not quite shaken off a negative aura.

That is why a panoramic description by the statesman and man of letters Cassiodorus is so remarkable. In a crepuscular ancient world, Cassiodorus succeeded better than most at going about his business in the proper Roman way, as if nothing had changed since Trajan's day. Such at least is the impression he strove to create in his letters, still a favorite repository of information about Italy and the western provinces in very late antiquity. One interesting epistle is presented as a response from the Gothic ruler of Italy to the citizens of Como who had complained about the burden of maintaining the state post horses in such a trafficked, strategic location.[68] In the process of demonstrating the government's magnanimity by assuming the costs of the Como post stations, Cassiodorus found occasion to describe Como. The declared reason why Como deserved relief was the surrounding landscape's beauty, so Cassiodorus launched into an idealized account of the environs. Rimming the lake were the villas of the wealthy, immersed in an olive forest. At a higher elevation on the same slopes were leafy vineyards, but the hilltops were adorned by nature with thick chestnut woods. Cassiodorus got the local

---

[66] Apicius, *De re coquinaria*, ed. M. Milham (Leipzig, 1969), 5.2.2 (38).

[67] *In Vergilii Bucolica et Georgica commentarii*, *Buc.* 2.52, 26.

[68] Cassiodorus, *Variae*, ed. T. Mommsen, MGH, Auctores antiquissimi 12 (Berlin, 1894), 12.14 (343).

hydrology badly wrong (his rivers flowed in the wrong direction), and there is little reason to believe in the photographic accuracy of his literary description, some elements of which reflect Pliny's earlier account of the same landscape.[69] What should concern us here is the fact that an idealized postcard image of this north Italian city dwelt not on its fortifications, or markets, or monuments, nor even on a stereotyped trilogy of olives–vines–grain, but rather on its chestnuts. In Cassiodorus' depiction the chestnuts are the sole avowedly natural component, olive trees and vines emanating from the same genius that erected the villas. Nature itself instead painted the hilltops with those green "curly-haired" ornaments, chestnut woods. To a sixth-century audience this was manifestly beautiful, though if there was a chestnut forest around Lake Como in the early 500s it was surely fostered by the owners of the local vineyards as much as by natural processes.[70]

The incorporation of the chestnut wildwood in the aestheticized post-classical landscape of Cassiodorus is another demonstration of the surprising cultural mobility of a tree for which the ancients had had so little feeling. The literary tradition whereby chestnuts were almost inedible, food for animals, and supports for grapes, at most a faintly ridiculous rustic means of exchange, showed some traces of evolution after the third century, and if the precedent-bound compositions of the Romans did not permit chestnuts any radical makeovers, a tradition-conscious writer like Cassiodorus thought the trees at least beautiful, and certainly integral to the landscapes he administered until the 520s.

CHRISTIANIZING THE NUT

The power and glory of the ancient literary tradition was such that even Christian Latinists remained dazzled. A poem like Venantius Fortunatus' *For Chestnuts* is a monument to the magnetism Virgil and Ovid exercised in the fifth century.[71] Here Fortunatus continued to associate chestnuts with homespun charm and rusticity: they are "rustic donatives" Fortunatus claims to have set in a basket he wove with his own hands. Using the adjective "tender" to describe the nuts and signal his admiration for Virgil (who used the same one), Fortunatus nevertheless

---

[69] M. Baridon, *Naissance et renaissance du paysage* (Paris, 2006), 167.

[70] J. Devroey, *Économie rurale et société dans l'Europe franque (VIe–IXe siècles)* (Paris, 2003), 204, on post-classical woodland–agriculture integration.

[71] Venantius Fortunatus, *Carmina*, ed. F. Leo, MGH, Auctores antiquissimi 4.1 (Berlin, 1881), 11.13 (264). On Radegund and Agnes, and Virgilian echoes in the poem, see J. George, *Venantius Fortunatus: A Latin Poet in Merovingian Gaul* (Oxford, 1992), 161–77. I thank Giselle de Nie for this reference.

distanced himself from his pagan model by sending his chestnuts to his "dear mother and spotless sister," actually nuns at the monastery of the Holy Cross in Poitiers, thus inverting the classical link between such gifts and seduction. In sixth-century Gaul rumors had circulated about Fortunatus' friendships with aristocratic women so his chaste gift in effect corrected what a Christian audience might have worried about in the Virgilian or Ovidian imagery while retaining its overall structure. This choice may have eased the gradual rise in literary prestige of chestnuts in late antiquity, a rise that is also visible, for instance, in a poem of Paulinus of Nola that explicitly elevates *Castanea sativa* nuts above other types: as a coot is inferior to a swan, a magpie to a songbird, a shrub to a cypress tree, so is a hazelnut next to a chestnut.[72] In such hierarchies, the chestnut had overcome a very significant handicap for a late antique plant, namely the fact that it figured nowhere in the Christian scriptures.

For, unlike grapes, or almonds, or figs, chestnuts had not attracted attention or enjoyed approval in ancient Palestinian cultures. Yet in a more explicitly religious and Christian vein than in the poems of Fortunatus or Paulinus, the compositions of the Latin Church Fathers still reveal chestnuts' mounting cultural acceptance in Christian literature. Somewhat surprisingly, chestnuts appear in the chief theological text from Latin late antiquity, Augustine's "great and arduous" *City of God*. In a passage of polemic against those skeptical about the accuracy of reporting in the book of Genesis, Augustine took up the matter of the logistics on the Ark. Those who doubted Noah could stockpile fodder enough for all the couples of beasts aboard his vessel were roundly criticized. Their questions about how the patriarch had fed the carnivores, save perhaps by taking on board more than two of some kinds of herbivore, were misplaced. For Augustine noted that animals that usually feed on meat can suspend the habit and feed on figs and chestnuts for a period; and anyway there was nothing strange in a wise and prudent man as Noah evidently was stashing a sufficiency of those foodstuffs, without any meat. Furthermore, God, the ultimate supervisor of the entire operation, could easily intervene to render cereals and fruit more savory and nutritious than normal, since He had the power to free His creatures from any need to eat at all.[73]

In the *City of God* both the ambivalent position of chestnuts as vegetable but almost meat, and Augustine's casual inclusion of this nut, along with figs, as a readily available preserved food for seafarers, are

---

[72] Paulinus of Nola, *Carmina*, ed. G. de Haertel and M. Kamptner (Vienna, 1999), 11 (41). The point was to flatter the poem's dedicatee by comparing him to its author.
[73] Augustine, *Civitas Dei contra paganos* 15.27.5, with reference to *Quaestiones in Heptateuch* 1.6.

noteworthy. On the one hand, Augustine claimed that hardened carnivores also eat cereals and fruits, particularly meaty ones like figs and chestnuts, thereby testing the zoological knowledge of his readers and emphasizing chestnuts' liminality. On the other hand, Augustine's effort at plausibility, at historicizing the deluge and Noah's adventures therein depended on fifth-century audiences that were perhaps accustomed to preserved chestnuts as a maritime staple.

That animals rather than people were these nuts' designated eaters reflects the Mediterranean literary traditions Augustine knew so well. These same traditions shaped the literary approach to chestnuts of Augustine's older contemporary, Jerome. While writing his treatise *Adversus Iovinianum (Against Jovian)*, Jerome, whose emigration to Jerusalem in the late fourth century must have given some understanding of arid landscapes, took up the matter of people's different food habits in different environments. Jerome's argument aimed at demolishing the position of the unlucky Jovinian, who was evidently hostile to Christian fasting and abstention from meat.[74] Jovinian had apparently maintained that eating available food is natural to all humans, whom God intended to eat the animals in their ecosystems. Jerome reasoned that, on the contrary, no natural or universal law guides human food choices, and people arbitrarily choose what to eat and what not to eat, excluding viable foods that are presented to them. His example was the desert nomads (wasteland barbarians, more exactly) who live from camel milk and flesh but consider it unlawful ("nefas") to eat pork. To Jerome the cause of their irrational choice was that pigs are rare in the desert because there are so few acorns, chestnuts, fern roots, and suchlike for pigs to eat there. Unaccustomed to pigs for these ecological reasons, the Bedouin had made a cultural choice to shun them, just as northern people shun other unusual but perfectly edible beasts in their environments.[75] Having proved that the choice not to eat certain foods was normal human practice, Jerome considered Christian part-time vegetarianism vindicated. His demonstration, quite aside from its interesting early attestation of pre-Islamic pork-abhorrence in Arabia, reveals that Jerome expected pigs to feed on chestnuts, and places without chestnuts to be pigless. Christianity had not yet freed the chestnut of its links to fodder.

The third great Latin Father, Ambrose the bishop of Milan, evoked chestnuts in the context of his reflections on Genesis, like Augustine. Ambrose's *Exameron* went on to have a deep influence on Carolingian

---

[74] Jerome, *Adversus Iovinianum*, MPL 23 (Paris, 1845), 211–338, 2.7 (294–95).

[75] Extensive considerations on this topic, but not Jerome's text, are in C. Fabre-Vassas, *The Singular Beast* (New York, 1997).

exegesis and indeed its range and size made it a valuable tool for any Christians grappling with the Bible's first book.[76] The *Exameron* treated chestnuts were among only four species of plants when Ambrose puzzled over plant genetics and the "power" that made plants grow to resemble their parent.[77] This attestation that in the fourth century, when one needed to conjure up a prototypical tree, one thought of pears and chestnuts, is altogether original, though a modern botanist might take exception to Ambrose's claim that chestnuts do not grow from seeds, but only from the roots of parent trees.[78] Also original was Ambrose's dogged search for symbolic meaning in vegetation, for to him the vegetable world was first and foremost a salutary reminder of God's potency and foresight, and only secondarily a resource for the cold and hungry. In God's anthropocentric creation every kind of tree was useful: if it did not serve by producing fruit, it had other purposes, and even the wildest tree could be robbed of its "natural harshness" by cultivation.[79] A tree was clearly a lesson for Christians, and a model of their potential for behavioral improvement.

In the *Exameron* the distinguishing "genetic" characteristics of chestnuts are their thick foliage and the sensational vitality that permits the stump to start growing numerous new shoots again promptly after the tree is chopped down. Obviously familiar with the chestnut coppice, Ambrose commented that the disproportion in size between the chestnut stock and its coppiced stems revealed the tree's age, as did the shape of the branches (the knottier, the older) and the leaf shape and color (this last observation perhaps the least empirical). Ambrose duly noted that very ancient trees had more difficulty recovering from cuttings to develop new stems, but for young individuals such cutting was almost beneficial, a stimulant to growth and vigor. Ambrose's purpose in doing botanical thick description was Christian: he aimed to discern order and reason in God's universe, and to teach people how to behave through the example provided by diverse organisms within that universe. Yet the *Exameron* stands out in Latin literature for the acuteness of its botanical observation and its evident familiarity with *Castanea sativa*.[80]

Christian writers accepted the chestnut as an inherent, even beautiful (Cassiodorus) part of the harmonies of creation, indeed as one of very few of those parts that deserved to be individually mentioned and to

---

[76] For the chestnutty part of this influence, see Hrabanus Maurus, *Commentaria in Genesim*, MPL 107 (Paris, 1864), 2.6 (518); Walafrid Strabo, *Glossa ordinaria*, MPL 113 (Paris, 1879), 6.21–22 (106).

[77] Ambrose, *Exameron* 3.8.33, in *Sancti Ambrosii opera*, Vol. 1, ed. C. Schenkl (Vienna, 1896), 81.

[78] *Ibid*. Ambrose was ignoring the extensive agronomical literature on planting chestnuts.

[79] *Ibid*. 3.13.56 (98).

[80] *Ibid*. 3.11.52 (94; plants teach about life, the need for care and support); 3.11.47 (90; God clothed the earth with trees); 3.13.53 (95; usefulness of all trees); 3.13.54 (97; chestnut description).

represent all of them. Chestnuts were prodigiously productive, but able to generate and regenerate themselves chastely. They were seeds on which any red-meat-eater would love to feast, and if they could still function as signs of Virgilian affectation, at the end of antiquity *Castanea sativa* was probably the only tree in Europe worthy of a resurrection miracle, even if a fairly obscure one that took place in a very small town in the Pyrenees in the tumultuous sixth century.[81]

Not so long thereafter the biographer of the great Irish monastic trail-blazer Columbanus could revisit the ancient and late antique *topos* of the chestnut gift with some curious inversions. To Jonas of Bobbio the chestnut was "gentle," and was an unassuming yet worthy gift exactly like his biography of Bobbio's founder, Columbanus. Equating his own literary confection with a chestnut, perhaps to imply its core was succulent and nutritious despite outside stylistic appearances, Jonas distanced both from "exotic" plants and texts. In doing so Jonas shows once again the naturalization of the chestnut in the early Middle Ages, its removal from alien contexts and its new association with down-home forthrightness.[82] Thus, late antique writers went beyond classical Latin to probe the literary potential of chestnut trees and seeds, adding some new dimensions to the castaneological canon and leaving traces of the penetration of chestnuts in the culture, as well as in the landscapes of post-classical Europe.

CHESTNUT METAPHORS OF THE DARK AGES

Writing in the shelter of the empire's monasteries during the ninth century, Carolingian specialists in theology referred to chestnut trees and nuts with some frequency. Though "castanearios" were among the sixteen sorts of fruit-bearing tree that great optimist Charlemagne required his farm managers to plant on each of his fiscal estates (apples, pears, plums, and cherries were to be "of diverse kinds," so the total variety was actually greater), it is unlikely that most Carolingian writers, or readers, often saw real chestnut trees.[83] Still, they knew their chestnuts. This knowledge is visible on that quintessential Carolingian document, the large parchment called the Plan of St. Gall.

---

[81] Chestnuts' famous vitality made miracles that returned life to dead trees more believable: Gregory of Tours, *Liber in gloria martyrum*, ed. B. Krusch, in *Gregorii Turonensis opera. Pars II: Miracula et opera minora*, MGH, Scriptores rerum Merovingicarum 1.2 (Hanover, 1885), 34–113, Chapter 73 (87).

[82] Jonas of Bobbio, "Praefatio" to *Vita Columbani*, ed. B. Krusch MGH, Scriptores rerum Germanicarum in usum scholarum 34 (Hanover, 1905), 148. There is a reminiscence of Virgil, *Bucolicae* 7.54 here. Cf. Isidore, *Etymologiae* 17.7.26.

[83] *Capitulare de villis*, in *Capitularia regum Francorum 1*, MGH, Leges, Sectio II, ed. A. Boretius (Hanover, 1883), Chapter 70 (90). D. Campbell, "The *Capitulare de villis*, the *Brevium exempla*, and the Carolingian Court at Aachen," *Early Medieval Europe* 18 (2010), 243–64, argues this was

For a long time now scholars have been aware of the close relationship between Charlemagne's *De villis* capitulary and the Plan.[84] For instance, all fourteen species of tree in the Plan's cemetery were plants Charlemagne expected to find on his estates as outlined in the *De villis* capitulary. But the appearance of chestnuts in both Plan and capitulary probably has less to do with producing edible nuts for kings and monks than with ideology. For the Plan was drawn, most likely at Reichenau, and reworked, likely at St. Gall itself, in contexts where *Castanea sativa* struggled to grow even in early modern times, the high point for the species in northeastern Switzerland.[85]

The scribe who, as an afterthought, added the label "castenarius" to one of the small tendrils drawn in red between plots designated for the burial of monks did not employ the familiar form for chestnut in early medieval Latin. But this was not necessarily because of unfamiliarity with the tree. Though the labeler, who considered trees' labels important enough to justify his additions and corrections to the Plan, did not copy the odd orthography from the capitulary, which uses the equally unusual "castanearios," this scribe *did* retain the capitulary's masculine gender, unlike the other occurrences of chestnut trees in Carolingian Latin.[86] For in the monastic graveyard a masculine chestnut was the only appropriate kind, as it would shade only male bodies in this most hallowed and very masculine space. To fit in as wardens of "the dead bodies of the brothers," all the cemetery's trees were virilized, while at the center of the enclosure towered the feminine cross ("sanctissima crux") whose fertility in "the fruits of eternal health" contrasted with the surrounding barrenness.[87]

In fact, the Plan's masculine chestnut tree was not just singular, but also single, and hence necessarily chaste, unable to bear fruit, like most of the other trees in the cemetery.[88] In order to generate any nuts chestnut

a pragmatic document aimed at supplying the newly sedentary court in the 790s, so mentions real resources, but also finds incongruities (257–58) between known estate accounts and the ideal image in the *Capitulare de villis*. The form "castanearios" was new: André, *Lexique*, 76.

[84] B. Bischoff, "Die Entstehung des Sankt Galler Klosterplan in paläographischer Sicht," in *Mitteralterliche Studien: Ausgewählte Aufsätze zur Schriftkunde und Literaturgeschichte*, 3 vols., Vol. 1 (Stuttgart, 1966), 41–49 (44); W. Horn and E. Born, *The Plan of St. Gall*, 3 vols. (Berkeley, 1979), Vol. 1, 31. The Plan is best viewed at www.stgallplan.org/en/.

[85] T. Schlatter, "Die Kastanie (*Castanea vesca* Gärtner, *Castanea sativa* Miller) im Kanton St. Gallen," *Jahrbuch der St. Gallischen naturwissenschaftlichen Gesellschaft* (1911), 57–86 (59–63, 69–71).

[86] On the scribe's pentimenti, see L. Coon, *Dark Age Bodies: Gender and Monastic Practice in the Early Medieval West* (Philadelphia, 2011), 168. Bischoff considered the trees' names an afterthought of little importance: "Die Entstehung," 48.

[87] The Plan gives masculine forms for all the tree species, even those that are feminine in ordinary Latin.

[88] Horn and Born, *The Plan of St. Gall*, Vol. 11, 212, opine the singular form meant groups of plants, because of the space available and because (they claim) one tendril is labeled both sorb and medlar.

trees require the society of other chestnuts for pollination. By depriving the solitary chestnut tree of company, the labeler underlined the asexual (and male) nature of the community. In this way, he allowed dead monks and living trees to intertwine appositely in the eastern sector of the planned monastery, one of its most exclusive and holy portions. Yet the graveyard was unlike the rest of the monastery, where masonry mattered. Amid the tombs wood, specifically the "woods of the soil," signals a high-status space ordered around "the most holy cross," itself explicitly called a "wood" that bore fragrant fruit, though technically it was not alive.[89] Therefore, what at first sight might seem like a misspelling ("castenarius") actually was a mindful and meaningful transposition of the gender and number of real, fruiting chestnut trees into the Carolingian ascetic context.

The great monastic centers where the Carolingian Renaissance was manufactured tended to lie in the north part of Continental Europe, where *Castanea sativa* often fails to bear fruit, or does not grow at all. In consequence the chestnuts of the Carolingians, whether in capitulary or Plan, were bookish plants first and foremost. Yet precisely for that reason they are more revealing of the status chestnuts had attained in early medieval culture. By the 800s chestnuts' widespread literary acceptance reflected *Castanea sativa*'s presence on the ground in the ecologically feasible portions of the Carolingian empire, the southern ones where many powerful landowners acquired estates. It also reflected a mounting knowledge of chestnuts, the fruit of *Castanea*.

Indeed, when Hrabanus Maurus sat composing his ambitious encyclopedia *On the Natures of Things* (known since the first edition in 1467 as *About the Universe* [*De universo*]) the fruits of chestnuts were literarily familiar enough to have become metaphors and cultural references. Hrabanus, who dedicated his compilation to Louis the German, implying it was written in the mid 840s during his enforced residence at the Petersburg hermitage, wanted to do much more than simply catalogue and define all known things in his great book.[90] He aspired through it

---

This special pleading does not make sense of the tendril labeled "apple and/or pear," which suggests the tendrils are simply place-holders. In the monks' cemetery word and image do not align, and large tendrils represent small trees (quince) while chestnut or walnut are drawn in smaller. Apple, pear, plum, quince, fig, walnut, hazelnut, almond, and chestnut need cross-pollination to bear fruit. Mulberry, sorb, medlar, and peach are self-pollinators. Laurel is male or female but not grown for fruit.

[89] Unlike the living trees. *Ibid.*, Vol. III, 85, gives the best translation of "inter ligna soli haec semper sanctissima crux est in qua perpetuae poma salutis olent." See Coon, *Dark Age Bodies*, 201–04, for a gendered analysis of the cemetery, and 165–69 on the ideological purposes of the Plan.

[90] Hrabanus Maurus, *De universo*, MPL III (Paris, 1864), 19.6 (514–15). For context on Hrabanus' book: Coon, *Dark Age Bodies*, 36, 278.

also to uncover for his readers the hidden meaning of the scriptures. In this context, the nineteenth book of *On the Natures of Things* made room for the traditional observation that tree-fruits (*poma*) dressed in hard shells are called nuts, to distinguish them from soft-shelled fruits (*mala*). Hrabanus noted the weight of the putative place of origin of tree-fruits on their naming but was most concerned with the mystical meaning of such botanical phenomena. This led Hrabanus to the observation that nuts like the pine nut, hazel nut, almond, acorn, walnut, and chestnut symbolized either the Church itself or its holiest members, the saints, reasoning that the latter hid at their core "the sweetness of the fruit of virtue" rather as nuts hid in hard shells their pale and nutritious seeds. Not content with this simple association, the erstwhile abbot of Fulda suggested some further symbolic alternatives, so nuts could also signify the Incarnation or even the mystery of the Trinity, though he was less convinced of these possibilities. Always, the contrast between the unpalatable and discouraging exterior and the excellent interior led Hrabanus' thought. This reading clearly derived from the "integumentary interpretation" of things popularized by Augustine, whereby a cloak of materiality, or language, was presumed to protect the presence of deeper truth.[91] It contrasts with modern analytical metaphors for peeling away layers of meaning like layers of an onion, for an early medieval monk was sure that at the end of the peeling process, however laborious, the peeler would find something real and sustaining, something of substance. This conviction made the chestnut an appropriate tool for understanding creation.

Most of all a chestnut reminded the ninth-century polymath of reading. Specifically, it was the nut itself that helped to explain what attentive reading is. To read a text literally was equivalent to trying to eat a chestnut with the shell on, and thus ruining one's gustatory experience. An allegorical reading instead removed the shell and revealed the succulent whiteness of what was within. With this metaphor, which he did not borrow, like so much else in his exposition of reading, from Augustine, Hrabanus shows all the distance that separated ancient contemplators of chestnuts from post-classical ones.[92] He also shows how chestnuts had become a household word, a possible symbol for a mundane activity and for the human struggle to extract the real meaning from God's sometimes impenetrable Word.

---

[91] On medieval thinking about "integumentum" (literally, a cover), see J. Ross, *Figuring the Feminine* (Toronto, 2008), 25, 126–28.

[92] Hrabanus Maurus, *De ecclesiastica disciplina*, MPL 112 (Paris, 1878), 1 (1196), cites Augustine's *De catechizandis rudibus* 9 on the role of "integumentum." Though Hrabanus Maurus, *Commentarium in Matthaeum*, MPL 107 (Paris, 1864), 2.8 (842), used Augustine's oysters as metaphors for how integumentary interpretation works, with chestnuts (Augustine preferred grapes and barley as integumentary plants: *Enarrationes in Psalmos* 8.1; *De diversis quaestionibus* 61.1) he was independent.

The poetics of the chestnut in the early Middle Ages

Citing Isidore of Seville on the Greek etymology of the Latin *casta-neam*, Hrabanus accepted chestnuts' link with castration as an explanation for its classical, first Greek and then Latin name (*k/castanean*). Then, shifting his focus away from the nut to the chestnut tree, he took up his own suggestion to delve for deeper meanings: a chestnut, read properly, could mean the whole category of the chaste, whose bodily continence nevertheless was fruitful in virtue.[93] In effect, Hrabanus' empirical and otherworldly interpretation of the tree, as also of the nut, was based on the perfectly accurate botanical observation that chestnuts produce abundant fruit without visible sexual unions, and have unmatched capacity to resprout after being cut down. Hrabanus followed St. Ambrose in this, but added Isidore's castration etymology to reinforce his notion that a tree could represent those males who voluntarily became "eunuchs for God" while retaining their full reproductive powers.[94]

Overall, other Carolingian writers took less note of the chestnut tree and its fruit than Hrabanus did. For instance, Sedulius Scotus mentioned them solely because Virgil had and they offered him a useful case of a rare grammatical construction. To the great Irish-Lotharingian scholar, *Castanea sativa*'s confirmation of the order and harmony of creation seemed less relevant than the literary use of syllepsis.[95] A generation earlier, Charlemagne's friend and counselor, the Englishman Alcuin, was the first Carolingian to seize upon the metaphorical possibilities of the chestnut for audiences familiar with it. In his extensive *Commentary on Ecclesiastes* Alcuin advised that the author of the famous Hebrew book had knowingly signposted the text with clues about how to read it. The right way to read Ecclesiastes was therefore allegorical, and its pronouncements should be taken symbolically. They stood for something else, beyond the apparent grammatical meaning of the words from which they were made. Only "the simple" took such a text literally, while all others would delve beyond the deceptive exterior, surface meaning. Just as soil conceals gold, nutshells the nut, and the prickly husks hide the chestnut, so there were unexpected rewards for any who handled Ecclesiastes with all the discerning care the text required. Pealing back the "hirsute" outer cover of a chestnut seemed, around 800, an apposite way to express the act of intelligent reading. Gingerly, respectfully, in order to avoid painful punctures on the fingers, one revealed the scented nuts within, shiny

---

[93] Hrabanus, *De universo* 19.6 (514–15).

[94] Something the labeler of the Plan of St. Gall would appreciate.

[95] See Sedulius' *Collected Miscellany* of citations from books that he had liked: Sedulius Scotus: *Collectaneum miscellaneum*, ed. D. Simpson (Turnhout, 1988), 70.23 (287); and *In Donati artem maiorem*, ed. B. Löfstedt (Turnhout, 1977), 3 (364). Syllepsis occurs when a single word modifies two other ones, and must be understood differently in respect to each.

brown surprises whose further inner whiteness and sweetness Alcuin only implied. Similar respect and care, applied to penetrating the holy writ, would bring more than equal rewards.[96]

Alcuin, who migrated from York to Francia to pursue a more brilliant ecclesiastical career in the orbit of the Frankish court, grew up in a culture that prized riddles. As a poem by Theodulf of Orléans informs us, both Alcuin and his patron Charlemagne had a developed taste for these enigmas.[97] In fact, collections of clever, obscure, and charming riddles, many of insular origin, circulated widely in ninth-century Francia and probably played a major role in the teaching of that crucial foreign language for all Carolingian clerics, Latin. A dominant characteristic of early medieval riddles that set them apart from their Mediterranean antecedents was the use of humdrum subject matter, of ordinary, everyday things as the key to the puzzle. Of course, for a riddle to work, as entertainment and as didactic tool, it required writers and audience to be familiar with the things that the textual clues represented, however obliquely. The whole point was to lead readers through some difficulties to a discovery, but the possibility of discovery and the realization of the obviousness of it in hindsight depended on readers knowing, and writers expecting them to know, the ordinary object that the riddle described.[98] One of the post-classical riddlers' main objects was in fact to show the reader all the wonder that the most banal and common items could continue to contain despite their very commonness.[99] Thus *aenigmata* that sought to evoke a word or a thing by means of textual prompts without actually using the word are a measure of early medieval familiarity with things. In other terms, in the seventh and especially the eighth centuries, when several riddlers introduced the chestnut as the subject of their riddles, they signaled the common acceptance of *Castanea sativa*, not the plant's arcane and marginal position in early medieval culture. Suitability for riddles presupposed dissemination of physical chestnuts and the popularity of these chestnut riddles depended on some knowledge of chestnuts themselves.

Dark Age riddlers dwelled on the contradictory nature of the chestnut's nut, much less on the tree. Only Tatwine, a Mercian bishop contemporary with Bede, referred to the woods within which the tree could be

---

[96] Alcuin, *Commentaria super Ecclesiasten*, MPL 100 (Paris, 1863), 12.9–10 (718).

[97] Theodulf of Orléans, Carmen 25, lines 135–40, in "Theodulfi Carmina," ed. E. Dümmler, in *MGH Poetae latini aevi Carolini I*, (Berlin, 1881), 437–581 (486).

[98] G. Polara, "Aenigmata," in *Lo spazio letterario del medioevo*, 5 vols., ed. G. Cavallo, C. Leonardi, and E. Menestò, Vol. I.2 (Rome, 1993), 197–216 (208–14).

[99] Z. Pavlovskis, "The Riddler's Microcosm: From Symphosius to Boniface," *Classica et medievalia* 39 (1988), 219–51 (221).

found, but his misogynistic chestnut riddle centered on female chastity, a root for which the first five letters of the Latin *castanea* form.[100] Readers were asked to

> Write the 8 letters of the name of a wood from the woods;
> If, crazed, you remove the last 3 letters
> Then you will scarcely find one in many thousands.

Tatwine's riddle alluded to a somewhat contradictory, or at least ambiguous, nature in the chestnut. He did this obscurely, as the riddler must, without ever saying the word "chestnut," and without at all referring to the *Etymologies* of Isidore, which first linked chestnuts and (male) sexual organs. Unlike the other Dark Age chestnut riddlers, who found chestnuts' liminal status to be one of the plant's main characteristics, Tatwine inserted the chestnut into a context of sexual activity and its suspension. The Mercian bishop ultimately evoked the paradox of an asexual organism capable of surprising feats of reproductive vigor, by playing with the spelling of the chestnut's Latin name, made up of the Latin root for "chaste woman" (*casta*) and the demented word "nea," which does not exist in Latin.

Roughly at the same time two other *aenigmata* tested readers' mental nimbleness by describing the chestnut's fruit. In the so-called "Riddles of Tullius," the nut is simultaneously moist and dry, thick and thin, sweet and bitter, hard and soft, while another anonymous riddle plays with the perplexing circumstance of a mother's (the tree's) stewardship producing a bitter skin in her progeny that becomes more delicate with growth and emancipation from the mother's care.[101] The latter riddle presumed some understanding of the biology of a chestnut's maturation, a process that cures the thin skin within the shell and renders it less astringent to the human palate. This riddler, assumed to be Italian because of the number of "Mediterranean" riddles he or she composed, also delighted in the paradox of a fruit liable to produce loud sounds "from its belly" when whole, but to fall silently onto the ground when rotten (and therefore light). Further sexualizing the chestnut, he or she suggested that until "she" (*castanea* is feminine in Latin) had been undressed and touched while naked, no-one would love "her," again referring to the bad taste of chestnuts' inner skin. More modestly the "Riddles of Tullius," apparently

---

[100] "Aenigmata laureshamensia," ed. M. de Marco, in *Tatuini opera omnia* (Turnhout, 1968), 347–58 (353): "Scribitur octono silvarum grammate lignum / Ultima terna simul tuleris si grammata demens, / Milibus in multis vix postea cernitur una." Isidore of Seville (see n. 39 above) may have first tied chestnuts to chastity, but Fortunatus' poem (see n. 71) uses the pun *castitas/castanea*.

[101] "Aenigmata Tullii," ed. F. Glorie, in *Variae collectiones aenigmatum merovingicae aetatis*, 2 vols.,Vol. II (Turnhout, 1968), 547–610 (594); "Aenigmata hexasticha," ed. K. Strecker, *MGH, Poetae latini aevi Carolini* 4.2 (Berlin, 1914), 732–59 (753).

composed at Bobbio by an Irish monk, proposed chestnuts were sweet only once they had grown up in a bitter and hard prison, namely their sour-tasting inner cuticle and tough outer shell.[102]

Altogether the chestnuts of the riddles are a surprising food, apparently inedible but able to change nature when treated correctly by human patience and ingenuity. People who waited until the right moment to shell and peel the nut would delight in its sweet taste, while those without such foresight and delicacy would suffer from a bitter flavor and indigestion. In these poems the outer "hirsute" chestnut husk, a favorite characteristic of earlier poets and theologians, did not seem a clue worth giving or a feature worth dwelling on. Perhaps the nuts familiar to the riddlers had been removed enough from their places of production that their outer coverings were a remote memory, unknown, as chestnut husks are for modern supermarket consumers in most northern countries.[103] But in one respect the riddlers remained faithful to earlier literary traditions, for they consistently humanized the chestnut, endowing it with family, education, and gender, and in this they unconsciously echoed the notions of writers like Isidore of Seville, whom chestnuts reminded of the human anatomy. No doubt this association mirrored the symbiotic relationship between humans and chestnuts that had led to *Castanea sativa's* rise in the first millennium.

None of this effort to turn the plant into a person is visible in the poetry of the Carolingian period, where, all told, chestnuts have a small place. Still, chestnuts functioned metaphorically under the Carolingian dynasty's patronage, as they had before. For example, to commemorate the glorious death in battle of Duke Eric of Friuli, conqueror of the Avars and hence a prime contributor to the financial fortunes of Charlemagne, Paulinus of Aquileia composed a poem. Bishop of a major city in the duke's jurisdiction and beneficiary of Eric's patronage, Paulinus could scarcely contain his literary grief. To mark and sanctify the now unknown site where Eric died, Paulinus invited the rains never to fall there again, and wished for all forms of life there to cease. Neither grain crops nor cornflowers should germinate there, no elms should sustain vines, no fig or pomegranate trees should bear fruit, nor should "chestnuts push forward their prickly globes."[104] The incongruity of Paulinus' agricultural assortment, a literary harvest of proper classical Mediterranean plants destined to struggle in the middle Danube basin where the Avar

---

[102] For authorship, see Polara, "Aenigmata," 208.

[103] A few breeds of chestnut fall off the tree with the husks on, but cultivators remove these whether the nuts will be consumed fresh or dried.

[104] Paulinus of Aquileia, "Carmina" 2.8–9, ed. E. Dümmler, in *Poetae latini aevi Carolini* I, 123–48 (132).

campaigns had led Eric, was enhanced by chestnuts' insertion among the more canonical agricultural symbols.

Duke Eric was killed in 799, by which time, evidently, chestnuts had become a standard of agricultural productivity, an arboreal addition to the almost Virgilian agrarian trinity (wheat, vines, fruit). To convey to his Carolingian peers his idea that ordinary economic activity should cease at the place where Eric had met his death, Paulinus used chestnuts as a classical poet might have used olives. At the end of the eighth century, chestnuts were metaphors of anthropogenic fruitfulness, of agriculture as it was supposed to be, and hence were useful indications of humans' place in God's creation. The tiny, unprepossessing fruit of the chestnut tree, and the much larger but still humble tree itself, are both lessons in how "entangled" things could become in early medieval literary culture and, surely, in the material culture that underlay it too. Defying the stability of its material nature, the chestnut's mutations in post-classical culture, its ability to take on new meanings, show some of the creativity in the cultural appropriations we sometimes call the survival of the classical heritage.[105]

THE COLOR CHESTNUT

Among the signs of the mounting early medieval cultural assimilation of the chestnut as a nut is the application of the name as a chromatic term to specific items of clerical attire. At the end of the early Middle Ages, in fact, Rather of Verona thought a "chestnut" was the item of ecclesiastical clothing itself, as well presumably as a tree and a nut, and the story of how chestnut became a color and then a tunic of that color is part of the post-classical normalization of the chestnut.[106]

The history of color is surprisingly fluid, and what modern observers can assume to have been fixed and recognizable chromatic categories turn out not to have been so until recent times. Indeed, there are still no absolute measures of color, now thought to be a subjectively perceived, variable phenomenon of light, though modern Westerners probably think that chestnut is a specially lustrous and reddish tone of brown, visible in champion horses' coats or people's hair.[107] Modern governments have few doubts. The Italian state identity cards confidently call people's eyes chestnut to ease their identification by the agents of the state, a sign that no ambiguity is expected with people whose eyes are hazel, or brown.

---

[105] See Thomas, *Entangled Objects*, 19–29, 125, 209.

[106] *Die Briefe des Bischofs Rather von Verona*, ed. F. Weigle (Weimar, 1949), 19 (109).

[107] H. Pleij, *Colors, Demonic and Divine* (New York, 2004), 2.

Actually, there is no logical reason for chestnut to mean a form of brown. As we have seen, "chestnut" could apply ambiguously both to a tree and to its seed, but no part of the tree is colored chestnut-brown, including its roots, and even the nut only has a thin outer shell from which that tonality has been taken. The yellowish edible nut, the beige and grey fuzzy cuticle around it, and of course the pale brown spiny husk that envelops the shell – itself brilliant green for the first months of its existence and thus the cause for medieval gourmands' preference for "green chestnuts" – all have to be forgotten in order for chestnut to mean what it means, in coloristic terms.

Hence there was no inevitability behind chestnut's transformation into a certain kind of brown, rather than green, or grey, or creamy beige, or any other of the panoply of tones a large organism like a chestnut tree assumes at different times in its life and during different seasons. Indeed, Theophrastus in the fourth century BC thought chestnuts black, not brown, and Pliny the Elder half a millennium later agreed that "common" chestnuts were black, and that a special variety of chestnuts developed by Tereus were red.[108] Palladius seems to have considered chestnuts' hue a kind of green.[109] Other ancient descriptions of chestnuts showed no interest in their color. At some point a choice was made, presumably based upon an aspect of *Castanea sativa* that seemed most significant, most distinctive to the choosers. All told, their choice implies that the choosers were not cultivators or frequenters of the tree, but rather connoisseurs of the nut, fresh and unshelled, consumers of the woodland's bounty who did not eat the chestnut dried (hence shelled and skinned, thus yellowish) as a staple. Of course, not much can be said about who made the choice: as all the texts are ecclesiastical and in fact monastic in origin or transmission it would be perverse to ascribe the color to the ecclesiastical milieu wherein chestnut is first seen as a color. But something of when and why chestnut became the word to describe a shade of brown can be teased from the texts.

In ancient Latin there was no word for brown.[110] The color itself, obviously, existed all over the place, and it had been in the human palette since the Paleolithic, when people first made representations of reality.[111] However, brown did not strike Roman people as a distinct color. Brown

---

[108] *Historia Plantarum* 4.51 (Vol.II, 92), referring to the nut. Pliny, *Historia Naturalis*, 15.93, using "nigris" for the "*popularis*, also called cooking chestnuts" and "rubens" of the Etereiana.

[109] To change the "green" color of chestnuts, he grafted them onto mulberries, but did not explain exactly how the hybrid color would look: Palladius, *De insitione*, 299.

[110] J. André, *Etude sur les termes de couleur dans la langue latine* (Paris, 1949), 123. Greek also lacked "brown": L. James, *Light and Color in Byzantine Art* (Oxford, 1996), 49–51, 73–74. Modern surveys suggest Europeans do not like brown either: Pleij, *Colors*, 5.

[111] M. Pastoureau, *Blue: The History of a Color* (Princeton, 2001), 13–14.

was at most a kind of red, one color the Romans did have a high regard and precise terminology for, and which often appeared to be the opposite of white as one of the two basic colors.[112] Occasionally the Romans' brown was a variety of black, another basic color whose different densities, luminosities, brilliance, and textures the Romans recognized, and for which they developed a solid semantic field.[113] Probably the most convenient word on hand in Latin to express something's brownness was *pullus*, sometimes applied to textiles that were dark, drab, sheep-wool-colored; in effect a pale kind of brown modern English speakers might call "oatmeal."[114] *Caerulaeus*, usually associated with blue in classical Latin, was originally another word for a kind of waxy brown (*caera* means wax in Latin, but in English cerulean still means sky blue). Likewise wool from Canosa in Apulia, famously "fusca," was an intense purplish brown.[115] But all these words that could at a pinch mean brown could also mean other colors, and generally did so. Without being colorblind, the Romans were insensitive to brown, enough at any rate that they did not develop clear terminology for the color.[116] And, as art historians maintain on the basis of modern psychological experiments, what people can and do name becomes much more available and recognizable to them.[117]

In late antiquity it seems that people began to perceive colors more vividly, to recognize more of them, or anyway to write about them more in Latin and Greek.[118] One sign of this was the expansion in the number of primary colors attributed to the rainbow. Whereas in most ancient catalogues there were four, sometimes three, or at most five rainbow tones, the great Latin historian of the fourth century Ammianus Marcellinus pushed the number to six, with purple, violet, green, orange, yellow, and red replacing the more minimalist red, yellow, violet or white, red, black of earlier classifiers.[119] But if the history of color is not a forward progressive march towards psychedelic polychromy, and if the true

---

[112] Pleij, *Colors*, 17; Pastoureau, *Blue*, 15.

[113] M. Pastoureau, *Black: The History of a Color* (Princeton, 2009), 27–28.

[114] *Ibid.*, 35.

[115] Pastoureau, *Blue*, 26; André, *Étude*, 123–25.

[116] A. Hermann and M. Cagiano de Azevedo, "Farbe," in *Reallexikon für Antike und Christentum*, 24 vols., Vol. VII, ed. T. Klauser (Stuttgart, 1969), 386, noted Roman disinterest in color analysis. See, however, Baridon, *Naissance*, 109–10, 123–25.

[117] M. Baxandall, *Giotto and the Orators* (Oxford, 1971), 48.

[118] See P. Cox Miller, *The Corporeal Imagination* (Philadelphia, 2009), 18–19; James, *Light*, 125–26; P. Dronke, "Tradition and Innovation in Western Color Imagery," in *The Medieval Poet and His World* (Rome, 1984), 55–103 (59–60).

[119] Ammianus Marcellinus, *Rerum gestarum libri*, 2 vols., ed. C. Clark, Vol. I (Berlin, 1910), 20.11.27 (213): "lutea ... flaviscens vel fulva, punicea ... purpurea, caerulo concreta ... viridi" are visible to the mortal eye. Yet two centuries later Isidore stuck with the canonical four rainbow colors: Hermann and Cagiano de Azevedo, "Farbe," 422. See James, *Light*, 91–109, on rainbow history.

color revolution came later, in the 1200s, a deep sensitivity to color *is* visible in the late-fourth-century Latin translation of the scriptures called the Vulgate, within which Jerome inserted numerous Latin color terms where Hebrew, Aramaic, and Greek words for density, luminosity, and quality had been: in this way descriptions that a literal translator might have rendered with "shining" became "candidus" or "ruber," both words that connoted color in Latin rather than just brightness.[120]

Post-classical people took two approaches to understanding light and therefore color, both weighted with theological consequences. As God was light, any who considered color a tone of light, following pre-Christian philosophy, also considered it immaterial and divine. On earth there were in effect few clearer manifestations of God. The sixth-century Christian thinker Boethius' denial that color is identical with the substance of an object fits with this tradition, and by deriving the Latin word for color from that for heat and light Isidore of Seville also subscribed to this position.[121] But a less optimistic view, espoused by some Church Fathers, set color firmly in the material world, thereby devaluing it. In this conception, the color of an object was part of that object, lowly matter. Following this vein though with a distinct view, some post-classical writers suggested that color was not just matter, but also a deception, a falsification that enabled things to mask their true nature by enveloping themselves in a simple covering.[122] A curious outcome of this conception of color as a tricky mask was the early medieval distaste for foxes, whose main characteristic was their ability to shift color, a clear sign that they were doubly devilish; colorful, mutable fur signaled unreliable nature.[123] Regardless of whether object and color were one, and the color of things was inherent to the things or a tricky (but still material) veneer, there were sound reasons for disdaining color. Nevertheless, almost everyone could agree that color was not neutral, for to the perspicacious, color said something about the nature of the things themselves. Though there were disagreements about what exactly that meaning was, even in the negative reading of color it was still worthwhile to study things' hues.[124]

---

[120] Pastoureau, *Blue*, 19; M. Pastoureau, *Jésus chez le teinturier: Couleurs et teintures dans l'Occident médiévale* (Paris, 1997), 113–17; C. Meier and R. Suntrup, "Zum Lexikon der Farbebedeutung im Mittelalter," *Frühmittelalterliche Studien* 21 (1987), 390–478 (469–70). James, *Light*, 51–52, discusses ancient disinterest in hue as opposed to contrast, brightness, quality, and movement in color.

[121] Pastoureau, *Jésus*, 34–35. See Isidore, *Etymologiae* 19.17.1. Later medieval etymologists derived color from *celare* ("to hide").

[122] Pastoureau, *Jésus*, 33.   [123] *Ibid.*

[124] Meier and Suntrup, "Zum Lexikon," 396; Pleij, *Colors*, 10–15. S. Piccolo Paci, *Storia delle vesti liturgiche: Forma, immagine e funzione* (Milan, 2008), 210–12, 219–21, notes mounting willingness to "read" colors mystically across the early Middle Ages. Boethius, however, denied color was of one substance with the object it colored: Hermann and Cagiano de Azevedo, "Farbe," 416.

In the case of white there was some more certainty, for the Gospels encouraged its association with Easter and the Resurrection and hence with glory and dignity.[125] Probably for this reason in late antiquity the vestments of Christian clergymen officiating at Mass began to distinguish themselves from ordinary clothes by their whiteness, though white was a color very difficult to make and maintain before chemical bleaches, so in practice the priests wore what modern eyes would consider pale grey or beige outfits.[126] Long thereafter, Christian clergymen were expected to wear such white on feast days associated with virginity, which were very numerous.[127] Though Pope Gregory's *Pastoral Care* (*Liber regulae pastoralis* 2.3) allowed bishops to wear gold, purple, and red, and gave theological explanations for each, it was only in the Carolingian period that strong and bright colors appeared commonly in clerical vestments, a novel development that in fact some severe censors chastised.[128] Still, Carolingian clerics, very sensitive to liturgical aesthetics in an age when people disagreed violently about the religious use of art, wore much more glamorous, and colorful, vestments than had their predecessors – part of the early medieval assertion of color within western Christendom and the (temporary, as it turned out) marginalization of the suspicions about its materiality and duplicity.[129]

It is in fact in texts from the Carolingian epoch that chestnut first appears as a designation of color. In order for the chromatic references to have carried meaning for the readers, the semantic field of "chestnut" as a color must by 800 or so have been fairly stable and well established, even if Hrabanus Maurus did not treat "chestnut" among the colors whose meaning he unpacked for Carolingian audiences in his compendious *Allegories in the Sacred Scriptures*. The process of agreeing upon a rough average meaning for the color chestnut must therefore have unfolded in the decades, or centuries, before the Carolingian hegemony, and presumably after the end of the Roman one where other, vaguer words for

---

[125] Pastoureau, *Blue*, 32–35; Meier and Suntrup, "Zum Lexikon," 392; Dronke, "Tradition," 65–66.

[126] Piccolo Paci, *Storia*, 227–30. Before the 1800s, sunshine was the main bleaching agent.

[127] Pastoureau, *Jésus*, 69–70.

[128] Claudius of Turin knew color was matter, so base and unworthy of the officiant, and the Council of Nicea II (canon 16) discouraged priests from using excessive color when celebrating Mass: Pastoureau, *Blue*, 42; Piccolo Paci, *Storia*, 105–08. Still, the section "About Priests' Vestments," in Hrabanus, *De universo* 21.14 (568) gives a vivid sense of polychrome splendor. Walafrid Strabo, *De exordiis et incrementis quarundam in observationibus ecclesiasticis rerum*, in *Capitularia regum Francorum* 2, MGH, Leges, Sectio II, ed. A. Boretius and V. Krause (Hanover, 1897), 473–516, 2.25 (504), knew contemporary clerical fashion was less austere than it used to be. See J. Mayo, *A History of Ecclesiastical Dress* (London, 1984), 27–28; M. Müller, *Die Kleidung nach Quellen des frühen Mittelalters* (Berlin, 2003), 137–38, 156.

[129] M. Pastoureau, "L'église et la couleur des origines à la Réforme," *Bibliothèque de l'Ecole des chartes* 147 (1989), 203–30 (222–25); Pastoureau, *Jésus*, 33–38.

brown sufficed. Thus, when a perfunctory survey of ecclesiastical property at Staffelsee near "Augustana" around 810 reports "we found two chestnut capes [*castaneas planetas*], and one made of wool and dyed," we are at the end of a long, subterranean itinerary that transformed the nut into a color. Around the same time Pope Leo III, who crowned Charlemagne emperor, received letters and chestnut-tinted capes from the Patriarch of Constantinople as a token of the latter's "charity," and the Byzantine emperors themselves had sent similar gifts, likewise chestnut-colored, to Pope Hadrian, Leo's predecessor.[130] Further, in his late-ninth-century biography of Pope Gregory I, John the Deacon described the capes that some members of his hero's family could be seen wearing in frescos of the late 500s at the family mansion-monastery in downtown Rome. Except for a seventeenth-century black-and-white rendition, the frescos no longer exist,[131] but to a ninth-century observer as acute as John the Deacon there could be no doubt about what to call the color of the outer garments the males wore: they were the "color chestnut."[132]

Etymologists today generally derive trees' names from the purported color of their wood, or bark, but in the case of *Castanea sativa* an opposite current flowed, made possible by the semantic weakness of Latin around the color brown, and by the increasing importance of chestnut trees in the early medieval landscape.[133] In 965, when the restless bishop of Verona Rather wrote to a colleague in Bergamo that he was sending him a chestnut as a present, he meant an outer garment of a type that clergymen typically used, not the seed of *Castanea sativa*.[134] The nut that had become a color in the Dark Ages had transferred its name to a piece of ecclesiastical attire that, probably in the eighth century, began to be normally brown. This transfer of meaning might also explain the unique (as far as I know) occurrence of the use of the word Castanea as a female name, in an inventory of the year 945 from Tivoli. Perhaps by the tenth

---

[130] Staffelsee: *Capitularia regum Francorum 1*, MGH, Leges, Sectio II, ed. A. Boretius (Hanover, 1883), 128 (251); Leo III, *Epistulae*, MPL 102 (Paris, 1865), 1023–70 (1067); Anastasius the Librarian, *Synodus octava generalis*, MPL 129 (Paris, 1879), 1–196 (192–93). *Planeta* was a Greek term assimilated into Latin. Gifts of clothes created special bonds: Piccolo Paci, *Storia*, 90–91.

[131] H. Leclercq and F. Cabrol, eds., *Dictionnaire d'archéologie chrétienne et de liturgie*, 15 vols. (Paris, 1907–53), Vol. VI.2 (1761).

[132] "[C]astanei coloris": *Sancti Gregorii Magni vita*, MPL 75 (Paris, 1849), 4.83–4 (229–31). It is a good question what a sixth-century observer might have called the color, though my argument requires that it would not have been chestnut. John was the rare early medieval author to use *planeta* as a general term for cloak, wearable by civilians like Gregory's parents. Other writers reserved for clergy: Du Cange, s.v. "planeta" and "casula." Hrabanus, *De universo* 21, ignored it. A "planeta de castanea" was inventoried in an Amalfitan church in 993: *CP* 38.

[133] Duchet-Suchaux, "Les noms des arbres," 15.   [134] See n. 106 above.

century this was the best way to call a woman with strikingly brown features.[135]

The journey of the word chestnut from ambivalent marker of an exotic plant and its seed to adjectival qualifier for items in the clerical wardrobe, and onto those items themselves, reflects a process of cultural assimilation whose contours we can still discern. As the plant became more common, and thereby more familiar, its semantic field in Latin first stabilized, then grew. Just as in high medieval Europe the same word could designate a dye source, a color, and cloth dyed that color, so in the early Middle Ages a nut, and tree, became a color and a special item of attire.[136] In a philosophical world that deemed color a component of a thing's nature that revealed that nature, it was logical for the seed called chestnut to become also the color chestnut, transferring from the brown nut into chromatic abstraction a property of the nut that was inseparable from the nut itself. As many capes were in fact this color, a Veronese bishop could think that the cape's name was the same as the cape's color, derived in previous times from the comparison to the well-known brown nut. In effect, the triumph of the tree on the slopes of Dark Age Europe made possible the realization of chestnut's semantic potential in other contexts, like personal names.

These transformations of the ancient brown-less world are further reflected in the application of the formerly Greek word *castanea* to the landscape of the western Mediterranean. A quick perusal of the index to the great topographical atlases of Italy at 1:200,000 scale published by the Touring Club Italiano shows that in most parts of the peninsula today many sites are named after *Castanea sativa*, quite a contrast with the *Barrington Atlas of the Greek and Roman World*'s coverage of the very same zones. In Tuscany, for which there exists a statistical survey of plant toponyms, chestnut-related place-names are not much less prevalent than vine- or olive-related names, both quite common.[137] It is notoriously difficult, if not downright impossible, to date the origins of a place-name accurately, and it is likewise difficult properly to reconstruct the motives behind the application of a particular word to a particular place.[138] Indeed, some at least of the chestnut-toponyms in the atlases occur in places

---

[135] *Inventari altomedievali di terre, coloni e redditi*, ed. A. Castagnetti, M. Luzzati, A. Vasina, and G. Pasquali (Rome, 1979), 12 (266). The widow Castanea had been rich enough to leave a watermill to the archbishops.

[136] On the usage of "scarlet" in the 1400s: Pastoureau, *Jésus*, 131.

[137] L. Cassi Curradi, "Distribuzione geografica dei toponimi derivati dalle piante coltivate in Toscana," *Rivista geografica italiana* 83 (1976), 66–72 (66–67).

[138] For a beautiful demonstration of the relation between toponymy and culture, see K. Basso, *Wisdom Sits in Places* (Albuquerque, 1996).

where the trees are unlikely to have flourished in the past 2,000 years, the length of time scholars expect toponyms to last in the human memory.[139] Thus, a place could be named after a chestnut tree because chestnuts were rare and remarkable in the region, as well as because chestnuts were common and characteristic.[140]

But for my purposes here it is the human familiarity with the name of the tree and its nut, revealed by the willingness to apply their names to the landscape, that matters. For without these two kinds of knowledge, it is hard to imagine the name of a town in Pontos, or maybe Euboea, that may have originated one of the ancients' ways of calling chestnuts, proliferating across early medieval Europe as it seems to have done. Whereas Kastania (and associated words) was a rare toponym in antiquity, it became fairly normal in the post-classical charters, duly Latinized into Castagna, Castania, Castagnola, and similar epithets, no longer a learned term, but a vernacular one that everyone understood.[141] The process becomes visible in the 700s, thanks to the expansion of charter-survival from that epoch, but presumably had begun earlier, in late antiquity. It is not a delusion created by the emergence of charter evidence: in the vicinity of Piacenza, where, as we shall see in Chapter 5, charters mention several early medieval chestnut-toponyms, the detailed toponymy in the inscription called the *tabula alimentaria* of Veleia from the height of the Roman empire contains not a single farm or glen named after *Castanea sativa*, though it preserves thousands of place-names.[142] Regardless, by the 800s chestnut was a common toponym in many parts of Italy and an established one in southern France, woven into the land itself by people's chatter, presumably marking places where, with peasants' help, the noble tree had taken

[139] G. Pellegrini, "Variazioni del paesaggio attraverso lo studio della fitotoponomastica," in *L'ambiente vegetale nell'alto medioevo*, Settimane del CISAM 37 (Spoleto, 1990), 549–84 (580–81).

[140] On the ambiguity of place-names' historical significance: *ibid.*, 582; L. Cassi, "Distribuzione geografica dei toponimi derivati dalla vegetazione in Toscana," *Rivista geografica italiana* 80 (1973), 389–432 (393, 430); A. Brugnoli and G. Varanini, "Olivi e olio nel medioevo italiano," in *Olivi e olio nel medioevo italiano* (Bologna, 2005), 3–100 (30–31). Duchet-Suchaux, "Les noms des arbres," 20–21, has no doubts about frequency–place-name correlations.

[141] For the ancient situation, see R. Talbert, ed., *Barrington Atlas of the Greek and Roman World* (Princeton, 2000), with two volumes of indexes compiled from all known sources. A Kasthaneia in Thessaly-Boeotia (now Keramidi: see *ibid.*, Vol. II, 824) appears to be the sole classical site given a chestnut-related name in the ancient Mediterranean (though André, *Lexique*, 76, mentions one in Pontos). Pliny, *Historia naturalis* 4.29, knew of a Castana in Magnesia (832), possibly this same Kasthaneia. Kastina in Epirus (814) is known only from a sixth-century text, and the Massif Central's Caistena (Vol. I, 269) is also late antique.

[142] N. Criniti: *La tabula alimentaria di Veleia* (Parma, 1991); and "Economia e società sull'Appennino piacentino: La tavola alimentare veleiate," in *Storia di Piacenza*, 6 vols., ed. F. Ghizzoni, Vol. I.2 (Piacenza, 1990), 907–1011 (946–47). G. Petracco Sicardi, "Vico Sahiloni e Silva Arimannorum," *Archivio storico per le provincie parmensi* 29 (1977), 133–44 (134, 141–44) argued for a period of rapid name-change in the 700s in this area.

root and, in at least some cases, become predominant enough to define the locality.[143] In a world whose charters reveal an astonishing intimacy between people and their landscapes, most bits of which had names, the baptism of fields, groves, and byways with chestnut trees' title was especially meaningful. The conquests of the chestnut itself and those of its word went hand in hand in the long aftermath of the Mediterranean Exchange.

[143] See below, pp. 133–34, 180–82, 189–90, and Castagnetti *et al.*, *Inventari* 11.1 (215; near Nozzano, Lucca, *c.* AD 875); *CDB* 27 (180; near Moneglia); *CDB* 92 (317; near Bobbio, AD 961); *CDL* 1, 116 (344; Castagneto della Gherardesca, AD 754); 261 (359; near Florence, AD 772); 295 (431; *c.* AD 770); *Breviarium ecclesiae ravennatis*, ed. G. Rabotti (Rome, 1985), 179 (95; near Urbino, 818–37); *I diplomi di Ugo e di Lotario di Berengario II e di Adelberto*, ed. L. Schiaparelli (Rome, 1924), 17 (48), 76 (225; near Vienne, AD 928 and 945, respectively); *Concilium Teatinum* 11, ed. A. Werminghoff, in *Concilia aevi Karolini*, Part 11, MGH, Concilia 2.2 (Hanover, 1908), 788–91, 11 (790; AD 840); Sergius III, *Epistulae* 3, MPL 131 (Paris, 1884), 973 (AD 904).

Chapter 4

CHESTNUTS IN EARLY MEDIEVAL CAMPANIA

The cultural footprint of chestnuts in Europe depended on the social and economic roles the species assumed during the first millennium. Those roles can best be understood through microregional analyses of how *Castanea sativa* became important to people. There are at least two good reasons why a case study of Campania is helpful for understanding the post-classical history of chestnuts in Italy. One reason is ecological: Campania's piedmont and its fertile volcanic lowlands, together with the Tyrrhenian coast's abundant precipitation and insolation, create ideal conditions for *Castanea sativa*.[1] The second reason is cultural: Campania's ecclesiastical institutions made and kept very good records, particularly for the years after about AD 750. It is therefore possible to analyze chestnut cultivation and the tight alliance chestnuts struck up with people during the early Middle Ages with unusual precision in Campania.

Such an analysis uncovers a surprisingly dynamic story. The social, economic, and ecological position of chestnut in Campanian landscapes changed considerably during the early medieval centuries. Human adaptations, in other words concurrent shifts in Campanian societies and economic patterns, catalyzed the changes. But the evident modifications over time, the history of Campanian chestnuts, were also very much a product of the nature of this species. Over the course of the latter part of the first millennium AD *Castanea sativa* demonstrated uncommon mutability and a capacity to adjust to different conditions. As we shall see, chestnut flourished first in the more autarchic Dark Ages and then in the more florid and lively, commercially active Campania, especially along the region's coastline and in its coastal cities, of around 1000. In this sense

---

[1] Rain and shine: M. Paci, *Ecologia forestale* (Bologna, 1997), 90. The excellent growing conditions in Campania brought about a minor resurgence of *Castanea sativa* there in the 1990s, bucking Italian trends: G. Bounous, *Il castagno: Coltura, ambiente ed utilizzazioni in Italia e nel mondo* (Bologna, 2002), 14, 208–10.

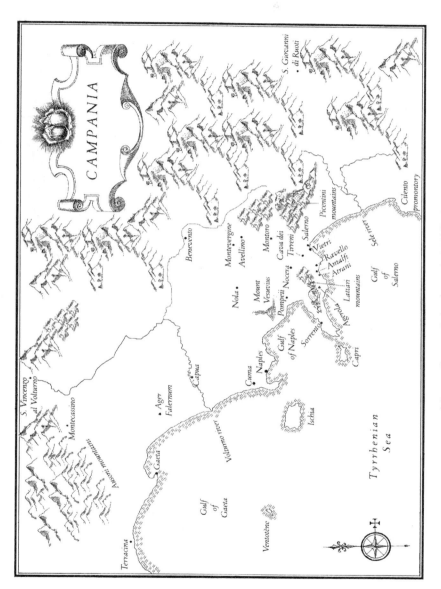

Map 3 Campania in the early Middle Ages

the chestnut retained agency in diverse circumstances thanks to its supple nature.

AN OLD STORY

The remarkable series of charters concerning the coastal lands south of Mount Vesuvius and north of the Sele river that have been preserved in the abbey of the Holy Trinity near Cava dei Tirreni offer uncommonly detailed evidence of chestnut cultivation from the 820s on. Chestnuts were present in the landscape and recorded as property virtually when the Cavese documentation begins, the earliest surviving local charter dating to 793. Through the rest of the first millennium they remained a significant element of this complex, varied, polycultural landscape, both in the fertile valleys and on hillsides draining into the Tyrrhenian around Cava. In these territories, chestnuts were constantly referred to in acts of donation, rent and sale contracts, and other legal instruments: just over 1/10 of the roughly 600 extant Cavese contracts from before 1000 refer to them.[2] The charters preserved by the other major Benedictine abbeys of the region, north and further inland from Cava, in the Apennine foothills at Montevergine near Avellino, or at San Vincenzo on the upper reaches of the Volturno river, are either not as early or not as abundant as Cava's, though they furnish plenty of material for an investigation of Campanian chestnut history. Also in these less maritime corners of Campania chestnut cultivation was significant in the early Middle Ages. Indeed, so prevalent were these woods that they extended to areas like that around Nola, which modern agronomists consider unsuited to chestnut trees.[3] For the coast around Gaeta, or in and around Amalfi, including on steep cliffs overhanging the Tyrrhenian later terraced for citrus and now filled with hotels, numerous mentions of chestnut cultivation survive in other ecclesiastical archives.[4]

---

[2] J. Martin, "Città e campagna: Economia e società (sec. VII–XIII)," in *Storia del Mezzogiorno*, 15 vols., ed. G. Galasso and R. Romeo, Vol. III: *Alto medioevo* (Naples, 1990), 259–382 (264), attributed the excellent Campanian charter record to monastic patrimonial reorganization after Saracen raids, and the end of manorialism (308).

[3] *CDV*, Vol. I, 10 (40; AD 987); 19 (72–74; AD 1001); 37 (144–45; AD 1037); *Chronicon vulturnense del Monaco Giovanni*, 3 vols., ed. V. Federici (Rome, 1925–38), Vol. I, 34 (250; c. AD 800); 60 (296; AD 833); *CDL* Vol. V, 7 (366; AD 766, but resulting from thirty years of disputes near Isernia); J.-M. Martin, E. Cuozzo, S. Gasparri, and M. Villani, eds., *Regesti dei documenti dell'Italia meridionale, 570–899* (Rome, 2002), 734 (374; c. AD 850, Nola); *I diplomi di Ugo e di Lotario di Berengario II e di Adalberto*, ed. L. Schiaparelli (Rome, 1924), 58 (173; AD 941, Celano).

[4] *CP* contains fifteen charters from 981 to 1079, and *CDA* fifteen from 939 to 1069 that are pertinent here. See also *Codex diplomaticus cajetanus*, Vol. I, ed. Monachorum S. Benedicti (Montecassino, 1887), 27 (47; AD 921); *I placiti del "Regnum Italiae,"* 3 vols., ed. C. Manaresi (Rome, 1957), Vol. II, 251 (431; AD 999). Citrus: G. Vitolo, "Il castagno nell'economia della Campania medievale," *Rassegna storica salernitana* 12 (1989), 21–34 (21).

Chestnuts in early medieval Campania

Early medieval castaneiculture was popular enough close to and far from the sea that one might say it sewed together the age-old gash dividing coast from inland zone in Campania, a region notorious for its geographical fragmentation.[5] And as chestnuts bridged the geographical divide, they did the same across the political one created by the settlement of the Lombards in the highlands of Campania in the late sixth century. But as we shall see, at the end of the early Middle Ages the coastal regions reasserted their distinctiveness, when new ways of exploiting chestnuts developed there thanks to the superior connectivity the sea guaranteed. By 1000 it was the hilly areas north of the Cilento close to the sea that had become the chestnut heartland of Campania.

We may gauge in place-names the dissemination throughout Campania of chestnut trees, woods, and specialized cultivation long before the High Middle Ages, the period often assigned this honor.[6] Sometimes a solitary tree became topographically meaningful and ended up fossilized as boundary marker in a charter, but this was rare. The enigmatic "mother chestnut" near Cava in 987 was surely a special plant, larger than others: possibly, people grafted this tree's offshoots onto wild stools or saplings to create the improved, domesticated groves of the area, or more probably the senior plant was left to produce nuts and secure genetic variety when an old grove was cut down, for this was the meaning of "matricina" in other medieval Latin documents, and the practice of managing a coppice "under standards" (larger, uncoppiced trees) was common in the Middle Ages.[7]

Far more common was the borrowing of the Latin name for chestnut groves to rechristen a field or entire locality. This habit took hold very early if a monastery at Castropiniano, east of S. Vincenzo al Volturno, was being called "in Castanieto" already when the first Gisulf was duke of Benevento, in the third quarter of the seventh century (he was the duke of Benevento whom Barbatus brought around from tree-worship to Christianity).[8] In the mid 700s a Chestnut river flowed through a Valley

---

[5] A. Giardina, "Allevamento ed economia della selva in Italia meridionale: Trasformazioni e continuità," in *Società romana e produzione schiavistica*, 3 vols., ed. A. Giardina and A. Schiavone, Vol. 1 (Bari, 1981), 87–113 (89–90); E. Savino, *Campania tardoantica (284–604)* (Bari, 2005), 155.

[6] Since A. Lizier, *L'economia rurale nell'età prenormanna nell'Italia meridionale* (Palermo, 1907), many have dated the heyday of chestnut cultivation after 1000. But see Vitolo, "Il castagno," 22, on the earlier presence.

[7] "[U]sque in ipsa castanea matrica": *CDC*, Vol. II, 394 (248); see also Vol. III, 503 (65; AD 997): "ubi proprio at castaneolu dicitur." O. Redon, *Des forêts et des âmes: Espace et société dans la Toscane médiévale* (Saint Denis, 2008), 103, 111–12, on Tuscan occurrences of "matricina." R. Keyser, "The Transformation of Traditional Woodland Management," *French Historical Studies* 32.3 (2009), 353–84 (376–77), on high medieval "coppice under standards."

[8] *Chronicon vulturnense*, Vol. III, 185 (14), refers to a "cellam sancta Marie de Castaneto quo est in Castro Piniano," a church often mentioned in the eleventh century (e.g., 25, 86). The name

of the Chestnut Grove near Vicalvi, west of the same S. Vincenzo abbey, and at roughly the same time several toponyms including chestnuts crop up in the extant land transactions.[9] By the year 1000, it seems fair to say, chestnuts had colonized the southern toponymy as thoroughly as they had the southern hillsides.[10] Since place-names do not grow up overnight but through the long sedimentation of habit, and since chestnuts also could not become the predominant feature of the landscape very fast, the evidence of toponymy indicates that this species had been significant to the locals for much time when the charters begin to show us the landscape and its designations in the eighth century.

A handful of tenth- and eleventh-century charters diligently saved from oblivion by Campanian monks contain elements that permit the reconstruction of some chestnut groves' genealogy and thus shed further light on the timing of chestnut dissemination in the area.[11] Exceptionally, notaries traced ownership of trees over three human generations, connecting property recorded in later times with trees growing in the eighth century. The dispute of 1064 between Johannes of Atri and the cleric Mascinus over land on Mount Falerio near Vietri, in which the contestants produced documents more than 200 years old to prove their right to (among other things) some chestnut groves, is a rare case where we can measure some of a Campanian chestnut wood's slow growing.[12] Johannes won in court, and asserted control over trees that were clearly very ancient. His good fortune helps us to understand the chronologies involved in Campanian castaneiculture, where *Castanea* lived on and on for generations. The dispute, however, can only indicate what might have been the case earlier, if eighth-century records were as lush or eighth-century people as litigious as eleventh-century ones.

appeared in a court case of 897 where a document supposedly of the 600s settled the case in favor of S. Vincenzo's ownership: "… olim ipsum cenobium sancte Marie constructum fuisset a domna Theoderada ducissa in Castanieto propinquo castro Piniano …" (*I placiti del "Regnum Italiae,"* Vol. I, 104 [378–79]). S. Maria was prized enough that S. Vincenzo obtained repeated confirmations of its title: *Chronicon vulturnense,* Vol. II, 91 (58); 105 (105); 115 (131); 144 (249). For context, see F. Marazzi, "The Early Medieval Alternative," in *Nourrir les cités de Méditerranée,* ed. B. Marin and C. Virlouvet (Paris, 2003), 739–67 (742).

9   *Chronicon vulturnense,* Vol. I, 16 (165): "rivus qui pergit per valle de Castanieto"; 30 (244): "rivo de Castanieto"; and Vol II (21); 34 (250); 69 (323).

10 *Inventari altomedievali di terre, coloni e redditi,* ed. A. Castagnetti, M. Luzzati, A. Vasina, and G. Pasquali (Rome, 1979), 12 (256, 262); *Codex diplomaticus cajetanus* 158 (311); *Monumenta ad neapolitani ducatus historiam pertinentia,* 2 vols., ed. B. Capasso, Vol. II.1 (Naples, 1885), 125 (91); Vol. II.2 (Naples, 1892), 31 (256), probably not of the seventh century.

11 For evidence of multigenerational investment in chestnuts, see *CDC,* Vol. I, 90 (115; AD 882); 62 (77; AD 866), which implies the "castanietu" in 57 (71; AD 859) was ancestral too; *CP* 57 (81; AD 1069); and P. Squatriti, "Trees, Nuts, and Woods at the End of the First Millennium: A Case from the Amalfi Coast," in *Ecologies and Economies in Medieval and Early Modern Europe,* ed. S. Bruce (Leiden, 2010), 25–44 (39).

12 *CDC,* Vol. VIII, 1387 (320–31).

Chestnuts in early medieval Campania

The antiquity of chestnut cultivation in the region is discernible also in the notarial terminology used to describe the woodland. Campania's early medieval agrarian contracts frequently use the term "castanietum" from the mid eighth century. The logical deduction should not be that this form of land use began then. On the contrary, when notaries could use "castanietum" without hesitation, without gloss, then the Campanians whom the notaries served already lived in landscapes where chestnut groves were familiar woods that had grown old and well established, likely with high canopy. The word "castanietum" was technical yet universally understood, requiring no definitions because everyone knew it described a specific type of woodland wherein *Castanea sativa* was the dominant if not the exclusive tenant.

Given how much human investment, and how much time, it takes in order for a chestnut stand to establish itself, the Campanian notaries' usage is most meaningful. "Castanietum" is a viable label only in a culture that had grown comfortable with this land use. "Castanietum" is also a label for a place where chestnut vegetation was economically significant enough for people to neglect other productions, both on the ground and at the notaries' desks: it was a specialized cultivation. Both the cultural acceptance and the economic exploitability rested on the ecological premise of *Castanea sativa*'s slow growth into a monopolist of the soil. Hence, when documents began to refer to "castanieta" in the eighth century, this particular form of agriculture had been around for quite a while, even if we cannot measure that "while" accurately in the early charters.

The point is reinforced if we consider that, from the early 800s, the southern charters distinguish carefully between a "castanietum" and another kind of chestnut wood, the "insitetum," or grove of grafted chestnuts.[13] This adaptation of the malleable chestnut tree to produce higher-quality nuts (however that quality was understood) was not an overnight affair, but required the pre-existence of a grove of ungrafted chestnuts onto which the selected scion could become fixed, and, indeed, perhaps on account of this filiation, some chestnut groves we know of through the charters lay next to grafted trees and woods.[14]

---

[13] Among the earliest references to grafted groves are U. Schwarz, "Regesta amalfitana, 1. Teil," *Quellen und Forschungen aus italienischen Archiven und Bibliotheken* 58 (1978), 1–136 (112–13; near Ravello, AD 875); M. Galante, *La datazione dei documenti del Codex diplomaticus cavensis. Appendice: Edizione degli inediti* (Salerno, 1980), 3 (163; Nocera, AD 882); *CDC*,Vol. 1, 12 (13; Agerola?, AD 822); 49 (61; Nocera, AD 857); 53 (66; Nocera, AD 857); 57 (71; near Pucciano, AD 859); 72 (50–51; near Nocera, AD 872); 78 (101; near Rota, AD 874); 88 (113; Nocera, AD 882); 90 (115; near Cava, AD 875). Martin, "Città e campagna," 326, sees grafting chestnuts as a *c.* 1000 improvement in southern agriculture.

[14] E.g., *CDC*,Vol. III, 495 (54; AD 996): "... castanietum ... in quo aliquante insites sunt."

Grafting anyway depended on a deep subsoil of knowledge, or astute botanical and economic evaluation of the characteristics of different individual trees, and thus could not be improvised. All chestnuts the notaries called "inserte" or "grafted" had at an early point in their lives required a precise, time-consuming, and technically demanding operation to join two different organisms in a new dual-nature plant. This operation was never extemporaneous, for the choice of a specific individual for scions came after careful observation of individual chestnuts and their growth over a long period. The procedure was an attempt to preserve genetic strains without modifying them.[15] This simple form of genetic engineering was inherently slow, and years of growing together by two organisms followed the years of resource accumulation that prepared the graft. Behind the productive asset the charters call "insitetum" or "insertetum" lay long stretches of time.

Once again it is not easy to form a precise idea of how much time went into creating a grafted chestnut grove. Unlike the finished product or "insitetum," the process of grafting rarely appears in the charters. When it does, the time allotted to create a viable grove is variable. To "graft the grafts" in 936 was expected to take six years to accomplish adequately, which meant to have securely vegetating stems on the stock; other contemporary contracts envisioned productive grafted groves after only five years, and attempted to incentivize grafting of ordinary chestnuts by granting the grafter more rights over the grafted trees than over plain chestnuts.[16] In other cases the expected lapse of time to raise grafted groves "as is right" fluctuated between ten and eight years, depending on whether woods had to be cleared and whether the root stock had to be planted or was already *in situ*. In one case, when the opinion of "good men" was sought about whether a grafted grove had been "perfected," twelve years was the lapse of time the grower had to make the grove "full."[17] Therefore, when the Campanian charters represent the grafted chestnut groves as productive and economically rewarding land, we need to recall the past work and skill that had gone into making it so, in several installments, over the course of considerable time, at the very least over several decades.

---

[15] N. Kingsbury, *Hybrid: The History and Science of Plant Breeding* (Chicago, 2009), 25.

[16] *CDC*, Vol. I, 159 (203); Vol. III, 495 (55; AD 996). Salerno's bishopric had a chestnut nursery ("biscilletum de castaneis") near Montoro in 942: Vol. I, 170 (219).

[17] Compared to planting saplings, grafting accelerates groves' productivity: Bounous, *Il castagno*, 34. Grafting seedlings avoided the lumberjack's hard work, but also lacked his rewards, for the process produced no timber. See Galante, *La datazione*, 59 (293–94; near Atrani, AD 1061); *Le pergamene degli archivi arcivescovili di Amalfi e Ravello*, 5 vols., ed. J. Mazzoleni, Vol. I (Naples, 1972), 16 (22–23; AD 1047); *CDA*, Vol. I, 45 (70; AD 1036), which contrasts "castanietum vacuum" with "plenum."

Perhaps more important here than the demonstration of the years it took to raise a grafted chestnut wood is the realization that the presence of an "insitetum" or "insertetum" on a hillside, just as much as the unexplained use of the term in the charters, implies a fully developed and even robust arboricultural system in which mature chestnuts have been protagonists for generations. Campanian notaries recorded the existence of other types of arboriculture in their landscapes – oak woods, vineyards, walnut and hazel groves are only the most prominent. Growing, tending to, and managing these trees took years of pruning, weeding, and soil preparation too, and there may have been a relationship between these various cultivations that our documents cannot reveal. Yet in the surviving charters from eighth- and ninth-century Campania the pre-eminence of chestnut-growing suggests that this sophisticated form of arboriculture had gained an economic and cultural importance only viticulture might rival. Alone among the early medieval trees we know about, chestnut was selected, grafted, transformed, and coddled so that chestnut woods were quite anthropogenic, fully managed portions of the landscape. Unlike notaries in early medieval Lombardy, southern writers and, we should imagine, southern users of documents, contrasted chestnut woods to "silva" and natural woodlands in Campania, themselves hardly wildwoods (rather, an economic zone of less defined property rights and lighter human exploitation).[18] In effect, both notarial and agricultural practices in early medieval Campania indicate the antiquity of human manipulation of chestnut woods already in the eighth century, the context of the earliest surviving documents.

In sum, the dedicated chestnut woods, grafted and ungrafted, shrouding important segments of Lombard and Byzantine Campania by 800 had not sprung up spontaneously. People who lived at some time *before* the survival rate of charters improved had disseminated chestnut woods because these had seemed to offer benefits to the trees' best friends. The right economic, demographic, and social incentives to stimulate chestnut cultivation seem to have prevailed in late antique Campania. For as this region's economy faltered, late Roman emperors repeatedly found themselves obliged to reduce its tax burden.[19] The decline of Rome as a center of consumption deprived Campania's coastal cities of an important remunerative function, namely transshipment of North African, Sicilian, and other regions' foods destined for the metropolis. Neglected by the senatorial aristocracy, depopulated to the point that numerous smaller

[18] "Silva" distinguished from "castanieta": *CDC*, Vol. II, 237 (32; AD 966). In Lombardy instead "silva castanea" prevailed.
[19] Savino, *Campania tardoantica*, 8–9, 76–77, 86.

settlements collapsed altogether in the fifth and sixth centuries while landowners could not find farmers to farm their land, Campania witnessed large-scale abandonment of arable agriculture in favor of pasture. While arable contracted, woodland advanced and agricultural production increasingly detached itself from markets. Even at Naples, the one center whose new administrative profile brought it unprecedented distinction, overall population declined between roughly 400 and 700.[20] In such a context, *Castanea sativa* offered irresistible benefits, namely abundant food for small inputs of work. It did so across the new political boundaries of the sixth century, both in barbarian-controlled upland regions and in Byzantine-run coastal sections of Campania.

Both the preconditions for chestnut's advance and the prevalence of *Castanea* were new in late antiquity. For though several parts of Campania, including the environs of Naples, had the acidic soils, high precipitation, and warm weather that suited chestnut, there is surprisingly little to indicate that the treed landscape of post-classical Campania originated in an earlier Roman agricultural landscape. Pollen remains show that *Castanea sativa* existed in Campania from remotest times, but there is much less certainty about its cultivation there.[21] Though Pliny claimed, famously, that Campanian gentlemen farmers had experimented with chestnut cultivation and created at least two cultivars by their bold grafting, for the rest nothing suggests the Roman landscape around Mount Vesuvius was densely planted with chestnuts. In fact, the celebrated and archaeologically intact Roman settlements around the volcano that have furnished endless material on living conditions in the mid first century revealed no chestnut wood to their modern excavators, and paltry amounts of the flavorful fruits of *Castanea sativa*.[22] Likewise insignificant are the chestnut

---

[20] Demography: *ibid.*, 136–37, 197; Giardina, "Allevamento," 106–07; J. Martin, "Settlement and the Agrarian Economy," in *The Society of Norman Italy*, ed. G. Loud and A. Metcalfe (Leiden, 2002), 17–45 (18–19); J. Martin, "L'évolution démographique de l'Italie méridionale du VIe au XIVe siècle," in *Demografia e società nell'Italia medievale*, ed. R. Comba and I. Naso (Cuneo, 1994), 351–62 (351–55); P. Arthur, *Naples, from Roman Town to City-State* (London, 2002), 10–11, 21–22. Pasture and wilderness advance: Savino, *Campania tardoantica*, 61–66; Lizier, *L'economia*, 29–34, 124–25; R. Cecchini, "Origine della diffusione del castagno in Italia," *Monti e boschi* 1 (1950), 412–14 (414); C. Wickham, "European Forests in the Early Middle Ages," in *L'ambiente vegetale nell'alto medioevo*, Settimane CISAM 37 (Spoleto, 1990), 479–545 (480); Arthur, *Naples*, 99, 109, 116.

[21] L. Castelletti and A. Maspero, "Antracologia degli insediamenti paleolitici nella Penisola Italiana," *Bulletin de la Société botanique de France: Actualités botaniques* 139 (1992), 297–309 (304).

[22] The modern fate of Vesuvian archaeological remains of chestnuts has been cruel, and material that may have existed until the 1800s no longer does. But the currently known finds of nuts and especially wood are extremely few: F. Meyer, "Carbonized Food Plants of Pompeii, Herculaneum, and the Villa at Torre Annunziata," *Economic Botany* 34 (1980), 401–37 (402, 413); W. Jashemski, F. Meyer, and M. Ricciardi, "Catalogue of Plants," in *The Natural History of Pompeii*, ed. W. Jashemski and F. Meyer (Cambridge, 2002), 84–180 (97–98); C. Dimbleby and E. Grüger, "Pollen Analysis of Soil Samples from the AD 79 Level: Pompeii, Oplontis, and Boscoreale," in Jashemski and Meyer,

pollens known to have deposited in the area of Pompeii under Rome's hegemony.[23] The same holds true for the area just north of the volcano, for recent construction of Naples' subway opened several downtown digs, including one in the city's main square where, in Roman times, lay Neapolis' port: there, among the harbor structures and three wrecks, extremely low levels of chestnut pollen grains collected in contexts ranging from the first through the third centuries AD.[24]

Judging from Pliny alone one might conclude that Campania was one of the high empire's cutting-edge chestnut-growing regions.[25] However, the exceptionally rich archaeological evidence shows that its more significant products were not those of woodland arboriculture and certainly not those of the chestnut tree. Thus, two farms on the northern slopes of Mount Vesuvius, both built after the great eruption of 79 that preserved so much of the Roman landscape in the area, provide especially valuable evidence of local chestnut use. Both villas used wood of *Castanea* to warm the occupants and hold up the roofs. It seems farmers managed the local chestnut woodland mostly for lumber and perhaps for stakes or poles useful in their extensive vineyards: there is no sign anyone at these sites consumed the fruit of the tree before 472, when another Vesuvian eruption buried both farms (people continued to frequent one of them until the early sixth century, when Vesuvius once again rained lapilli on the unlucky place).[26] Similarly, carbonized wood remains from Cuma, on the coast just north of Naples, indicate increases of *Castanea sativa*'s presence in the fifth century, with the species becoming locally predominant in the sixth and seventh centuries.[27] It seems then that high imperial Campania produced and exported wine and grain, and grew many other

---

Natural History, 181–216 (184, 189, 197); S. Mols, *Wooden Furniture in Herculaneum* (Amsterdam, 1999), 56, 81–83; P. Pugsley, *Roman Domestic Wood* (Oxford, 2003), 49, 103, 113.

[23] E. Grüger, B. Thulin, J. Müller, J. Schneider, J. Alefs, and F. Welter-Schultes, "Environmental Changes in and around Lake Avernus in Greek and Roman Times," in Jashemski and Meyer, *Natural History*, 240–73 (251–52); F. di Rita and D. Magri, "Holocene Drought, Deforestation, and Evergreen Vegetation in the Central Mediterranean: A 5,500-Year Record from Lago Alimini Piccolo, Apulia, Southeast Italy," *The Holocene* 19.2 (2009), 295–306 (298).

[24] E. Allevato, E. Russo Ermolli, G. Boetto, and G. Di Pasquale, "Pollen–Wood Analysis at the Neapolis Harbour Site (1st–3rd Century AD, Southern Italy) and Its Archaeological Implications," *Journal of Archaeological Science* 37 (2010), 2365–75.

[25] J. Pitte, *Terres de castanide* (Paris, 1987), 63–64.

[26] Most of the carbonized wood seems to date from the later phases of occupation: a fifth-century beam was reused as firewood: E. Allevato, M. Buonincontri, M. Vairo, et al., "Persistence of the Cultural Landscape in Campania (Southern Italy) before the AD 472 Vesuvius Eruption," *Journal of Archaeological Science* 39 (2012), 399–406 (402–03). The other recorded species of tree (beech, fir) at the site are nowadays associated with much higher altitudes in south-central Italy. See G. Di Pasquale, "Reworking the Idea of Chestnut (*Castanea sativa* Mill.). Cultivation in Roman Times: New Data from Ancient Campania," *Plant Biosystems* 144 (2010), 865–73 (867–68).

[27] Di Pasquale, "Reworking," 870.

things besides, but the products of the chestnut tree were not significant among them.

As the Roman agronomists considered chestnut trees primarily providers of poles useful for vineyards, or at most posts for construction, they would anyway have found the early medieval Campanian woodland strange. For, as we shall see, Campania's post-classical "castanieta" generally gave their tenders nuts, not wood. From Roman times, instead, there is no evidence that chestnuts were dried or otherwise preserved, and, if eaten fresh (roasted or boiled), chestnuts can only be a curiosity or a seasonal supplement to diets based on other foods, the noted "Mediterranean" triad of grain, wine, and (in Campania often imported) oil. Therefore, when the Campanian documents unveil the landscape for us in the eighth and ninth centuries, full of chestnut trees, often grafted ones, that generated fruits to be dried, we should conclude that in the centuries between the Roman heyday and the charters' emergence, that is to say between roughly 300 and 800, local chestnut cultivation had changed and extended itself dramatically.

The formation of a chestnut-filled landscape in Campania was certainly not an event. It was a gradual process to which several generations of tree-tenders contributed, for the most part unaware of the overall effect of their collective labor. A site where a few wild chestnuts grew spontaneously might be cleared of other species in the space of a few years, or decades, maybe aided by *Castanea sativa*'s good resistance to fire and mighty regenerative powers; agricultural use might prevail for a while before some new chestnut shoots, selected for their desirable qualities, received encouragement, thickening the summertime shade and extending root systems until arable farming on the plot grew difficult; then in some cases "better" types of chestnut might be grafted onto the most promising plants by another cultivator, whose successors might plant still more trees, "filling" the grove until, over the course of many decades, the site had changed appearance and function enough that it became known as a chestnut grove or, in appropriate cases, as a grafted chestnut grove.[28]

This sort of development need not be a teleological story of agricultural improvement or evolution from wilderness to manicured cultivation. On the contrary, the evidence that remains shows how different types of chestnut woods ("castanietum," "insitetum," plus woods of named

---

[28] For the notion of "empty" groves and of "filling" chestnut woodland: *CP* 35 (49; AD 1036); *CDA*, Vol. I, 45 (69–70; AD 1036); 73 (118; AD 1077); Mazzoleni, *Le pergamene*, Vol. I, 14 (19; AD 1039). Since trees, like people, die, to plant replacements even where there was no intention to increase production by filling a plot with more trees was natural.

cultivars) coexisted in Campania, without one particular form prevailing, each adjusted to specific social and economic needs and, presumably, to local ecological characteristics. In an admirable topographically grounded study of early modern chestnut cultivation, Casanova proved that eighteenth- and nineteenth-century Corsican farmers modulated their chestnut cultivations very carefully, according to the possibilities of the locale (geology) but also according to the availability of labor (which varied from generation to generation) and the opportunities offered by the market (prices, but also flukes of transportation, like the fixing of a bridge).[29] In a very small space like northern Corsica, several utterly different types of chestnut tree and grove, geared to different agricultural goals, satisfied people with wholly different aspirations, from food self-sufficiency to wood for tool-making to lumber for construction to marketable nuts.

As in early modern Corsica, so in early medieval Campania it appears that different cultivators concentrated their efforts or withheld them, chose certain cultivars or others, grafted or left trees alone, for individual and local reasons. For example, a monastery with a large endowment of chestnut trees could afford to be patient in ways a small landholder could not, so might graft cultivars that produced fewer nuts, but sweeter or of larger dimensions, and only did so after many years of waiting. The "zenzale" cultivar that appears to have been popular with substantial landlords around the year 1000 no doubt suited specific agricultural strategies, but need not have been what everyone sought.[30] A peasant with few outlets towards markets might be content with rustic or wild chestnut trees that produced small nuts but resisted pests well and required minimal contributions of work.[31] Thus, some might select for pest and disease resistance, for resilience in adverse climate, while well-off farmers might prefer breeds of chestnut with superior utility (good cooking, or grinding, or flavor characteristics) and investors might opt for trees that produced earlier or more abundant crops, or were easier to store. The cumulative result of so many divergent strategies was the well-established and variegated chestnut woodland the Campanian charters show in the last two centuries of the first millennium.

---

[29] A. Casanova, *Arboriculture et société en Méditerranée à la fin du XVIIIe siècle: L'exemple de la Corse* (Corte, 1998), 1–35; P. Bonuccelli, "Il castagno nella Lucchesia," *Accademia lucchese di scienze, lettere ed arti* 5 (1942), 93–116 (97–100), made similar points.

[30] In 983 the clergy of St. Maximus obtained one-third of the chestnuts and half of the grafted chestnuts from their holding at Pucciano (*CDC*, Vol. II, 357 [192]), showing a differential appreciation for different kinds of nuts.

[31] Kingsbury, *Hybrid*, 30, 42–43. Subsistence farmers tend to select plants whose production is reliable over plants capable of giving bumper crops but liable to failure in bad years.

LIVING WITH THE CHESTNUT

While it is impossible to know exactly who planted the chestnut groves, and this section discusses only plausible reasons why, it is perfectly clear that by the ninth century they had grown into both distinctive and desirable landscape features. The Cavese, the Amalfitans, the Beneventans, and others demonstrated a brisk interest in chestnut woodlands as property. Middle-rank landowners or higher-status ones, including rulers, clerics, and monasteries, were all involved in buying, selling, renting, and donating chestnut woods in a social configuration of chestnut cultivation that contrasts with what is known about chestnut ownership and cultivation in other times and places in Europe.[32]

In early modern Europe, probably the high tide mark in *Castanea sativa*'s European extension, chestnuts were a low-status subsistence crop, and cultivation of the productive trees was consigned to backwards people in marginal highlands, pitied for their poverty and chastised for their strange customs.[33] The enormous importance of chestnut cultivation in several parts of medieval Italy and Europe often is ascribed to monastic enterprise and farsighted administration of mid-altitude environments.[34] In Toubert's Latial hills, the chestnut grove was a marginal land use favored by high medieval people of measly status, a land reserve destined for clearance when population levels soared.[35] In early medieval Campania, however, the chestnut was valued property, worth exploiting even to people who evidently had other options and who were not all monks, but also princes, merchants, officials, and priests.[36]

Gender did not matter as much as status, for several early medieval chestnut groves belonged to women, like the widow Grisa and her daughter Iaquinta near Montevergine in the late 900s, and several groves were part of women's dotal assets, as in the case of Lioperga, who received an eighth of a grafted grove from her husband as her *Morgengabe* before 882.[37] These property transfers adumbrate early modern Campanian customs whereby nubile girls of the landed class often had chestnut groves designed to underwrite the expenses of their marriages.[38] Women's

---

[32] As noted by Martin, "Città e campagna," 276.

[33] G. Cherubini, "La 'civiltà' del castagno in Italia alla fine del medioevo," *Archeologia medievale* 8 (1981), 247–80 (258–61).

[34] Pitte, *Terres*, 86; F. Marciani, "Alcuni aspetti storici e folcloristici della castaneicoltura irpino-salernitana," *Monti e boschi* 2 (1952), 79–84 (80).

[35] P. Toubert, *Les structures du Latium médiéval*, 2 vols. (Rome, 1973), Vol. I, 260–65, 345–47.

[36] Monasteries play a big role in the Cava and Montevergine charters, as we should expect, but the appearance of other agents in these sources is more noteworthy.

[37] Chestnuts as dowry: *CDV*, Vol. x, 40 (AD 987); *CP* 119 (209; AD 1128); *CDC*, Vol. I, 84 (107; AD 880); Mazzoleni, *Le pergamene*, Vol. I, 2 (AD 988); Galante, *La datazione* 3 (163; AD 882): Lioperga's case.

[38] Marciani, "Alcuni aspetti," 81.

ownership of trees, and particularly of chestnut trees, may have been related to botany: chestnut woods did not call for socially demanding decisions and negotiations on the ground, once they had reached productive maturity, yet rendered reliable income. It seems southern gentlemen therefore considered chestnut groves the perfect property for respectable women, who would only have to measure their share of nuts in November each year, and not worry about organizing sowing, plow teams, weeding, manuring, fallow, and so on, as they would have to for arable.[39]

On both sides of the Lattari mountain watershed, in the hills of Avellino, and on the western slopes of the Picentini mountains above Salerno, we find the chestnut occupying an important position in the wooded landscape of the early Middle Ages, owned by men and women of high status. As we have seen, this was a departure from early modern patterns and a significant shift from Roman antecedents: a transformation of life, work, and environment. It seems to have taken place mostly in the second half of the first millennium, in contexts of economic retrenchment. Now the reasons for the new land-use strategies embraced in post-classical Campania require elucidation. Foremost among them was the chestnut's flexible nature. This was a plant that, once established in the landscape, could always find a role for itself, as long as its minimal environmental requirements were met.

More even than elsewhere in Italy, in Campania's ideal conditions mature chestnut trees were not intensely laborious plants to grow. It is true that around 1000, along the Amalfi coast, a farmer might confront "meager" chestnuts that required exceptional care to rejuvenate, or a landlord might make allowances for the fact that a grove of new chestnut seedlings could falter in the presence of "bitter and stony" soil, but in these cases unusually unfavorable arboricultural conditions held sway.[40] For the most part, tending a Campanian chestnut wood was not hard. Thus, an early-eleventh-century contract from Amalfi that spells out with special precision the labor obligations of a chestnut cultivator mentions the annual "clearing" and "raking" of the plot, but conceives of creating new grafts as the farmer's main burden.[41] Since many of early medieval Campania's chestnut woods were ungrafted, and many others

---

[39] Female chestnut owners: *CDC*, Vol. i, 93 (150; AD 882); 118 (180; AD 903); *CDC*, Vol. ii, 378 (228; AD 986); *CP* 5 (4; AD 981); 57 (81; AD 1069); 61 (88; AD 1039); *CDA*, Vol. i, 8 (163; AD 882).

[40] *CDA*, Vol. i, 45 (69) has "macritos arbores" in need of lopping, pruning, and grafting; Mazzoleni, *Le pergamene*, 16 (23; AD 1047), considers it possible that "abuerit ibidem asperum et petrosum ubi tigilli non profuerint ..."

[41] *CP* 35 (49; AD 1036) has "roccandum" and "rastrillandum" obligations. On the rhythms of castaneicultural work: J. Martin, "Le travail agricole," in *Terra e uomini nel Mezzogiorno normanno-svevo*, ed. G. Musca (Bari, 1987), 113–57 (131–32).

had been grafted some time ago, even this extra work concerned only some groves and only at some times. It was an exceedingly rare chore in the life of a grove.

If chestnut cultivation could be considered light work, what constituted hard work was of course not the same to everyone. Indeed, one charter from Cava dei Tirreni records a dispute in 958 between St. Maximus, the Salernitan monastery, and Amatus, the cultivator of a farm at Montoro on which there was a chestnut grove, whom the abbot accused of too-lax cultivation: the solution was to reduce the extent of the holding and introduce Domnandus, a second renter who took over half the chestnuts and lightened Amatus' work-load.[42] Amatus evidently had more than enough to do but, compared to the demands growing grain would have made on him, chestnuts were a light weight on his back, especially in relation to the rewards they offered.

But which rewards motivated late antique Campanians to turn to chestnuts and create the basis for the woodland landscape of the charters? Many parts of Campania offer *Castanea* optimal growing conditions, and the chestnut is a vigorous grower, if given a chance. Because of this, Roman agronomical manuals, some written with central Italian conditions in mind, envisioned very short coppice cycles of only five years.[43] Yet it does not appear that the late antique inhabitants of Campania invested labor and immobilized land on a large scale to increase the production of viticultural props. On the contrary, in fifth- and sixth-century Campania, even in the Ager Falernus, whose wines were highly regarded, wine lost its classical allure and market access, and therefore its capacity to orient people's productive strategies.[44] Moreover, in classical times, when educated farmers like Varro and Columella considered chestnut trees the grape vine's best friend, Campanian viticulture was healthy, though chestnut woods were few and marginal.[45]

Indeed, in early medieval Campania there is little evidence for the practice of training vines over chestnut wood supports. In the tenth century wooden poles *were* the stuff of legal disputes among people from Vietri on the Amalfi coast, and some Cavese charters explicitly refer to poles made to support vines.[46] Moreover, the transport of poles to the

---

[42] *CDC*, Vol. II, 410 (270). See Vol. II, 373 (220; AD 985) for a similar case involving a hazelnut grove.

[43] R. Meiggs, *Trees and Timber in the Ancient Mediterranean World* (Oxford, 1982), 267. Most modern Campanian chestnuts were coppiced: Pitte, *Terres*, 36–37.

[44] Savino, *Campania tardoantica*, 59–60, 330.

[45] Pitte, *Terres*, 267–71; R. Comba, "Châtaigneraie et paysage agraire dans les vallées piémontaises (XIIe–XIIIe siècles)," in *Castrum 5: Archéologie des espaces agraires méditerranéens au Moyen Age*, ed. A. Bazzana (Madrid, 1999), 255–63 (256–60); Lizier, *L'economia*, 122. G. Vitolo, "I prodotti della terra," in Musca, *Terra e uomini*, 159–85 (174), thought vineyards were planted before chestnut groves.

[46] *CDC*, Vol. II, 350 (183; "palos" dispute); 363 (202).

site where a new vineyard was to grow, deemed especially hard work that called for oxen in a charter of 913, means that people did train vines on "dead" wood, and the activity of "empoling" (a rare verb even in Latin) was required of some vintners in rented vineyards.[47] However, in those cases where the notaries noted the species of tree used to make vintners' poles, it was *oak*, not chestnut, and the custom of training vines over "live" props (trees) remained widespread in the region: it created what the charters refer to as "vined trees" all over the landscape of Campania.[48] In addition, the few chestnut groves for which we have evidence of coppicing, and thus for growing vineyard-friendly poles, were not near vineyards, as far as anyone can tell.[49] The early medieval notaries did not usually link coppiced chestnuts (in Latin, "ceppe," or "tallee") with vineyards in their writings: an exception dated to 939 concerns "that vineyard located in the chestnut grove," which Master Ursus sold to his servant Johannes as an act of charity, good for the seller's soul.[50] In those cases where there is a spatial and, maybe, a productive relationship between vineyards and chestnut groves, the chestnuts tend to be considered primarily fruit-bearers, for the landlord demanded that his tenant "properly collect the chestnuts, and dry them, and give us half the dried nuts" from his grove adjacent to his vineyard.[51] Trees trained to produce chestnuts would of course generate some usable wood, but not in the volume or the sizes a specialized viticulturalist needed. In sum, it seems that in the last centuries of the first millennium "castanieta" were seldom pole-producing coppices kept around vineyards to ease the growing of grapes, possibly because the mature chestnut woods of this region were inappropriate for that purpose.[52]

But of course chestnuts could serve vintners' purposes in more than one way. Historically, chestnut woods and viticulture collaborated over the storage, as well as the support, chestnut wood could provide. If the

---

[47] *Ibid.*, Vol. I, 113 (142; "impalare"); 132 (169; with oxcart); *CP* 18 (21).

[48] *CDC*, Vol. II, 441 (319; oak poles); 363 (202; "arbustis vitatis"). On the vineyards around Pregiato, see A. Corolla, "Il castello di S. Adiutore e le trasformazioni del territorio di Cava dei Tirreni," in *V congresso nazionale di archeologia medievale*, ed. G. Volpe and P. Favia (Florence, 2009), 355–60 (355).

[49] *CDA*, Vol. I, 38 (89; AD 1033); *CP* 12 (12; AD 1006); 40 (58; AD 1029). Coppiced chestnut wood makes fine cabinetry material, but early medieval Campanian wills do not refer to this possible outlet for chestnut coppicers' products.

[50] For "tallea" and "ceppa": *CP* 12 (12; AD 1006?). Ursus' recognition of Johannes' good service: *CDA*, Vol. V, 8–9.

[51] *CDC*, Vol. II, 260 (62–63; AD 969): "… ipso castanetum colligere sicut meruerit, et tote ipse castanee seccare, et secce ille medietatem nobis dare …" Examples of chestnut groves near vineyards: *CDC*, Vol I, 140 (179–80; AD 923); *CDA*, Vol. I, 5 (8; AD 939). H. Taviani-Carozzi, "Salerno longobarda: Una capitale principesca," in *Salerno nel medioevo*, ed. H. Taviani-Carozzi, B. Vetere, and A. Leone (Galatina, 2000), 5–53 (50–51), noted spatial links in some eleventh-century cases.

[52] Martin, "Città e campagna," 319, noted Amalfi's vines were trained very high. This required a longer coppice cycle, immobilizing land longer.

ancients stored and transported their wine mainly in earthenware containers whenever it had to move over long distances, during the early Middle Ages this custom lost currency, as in fact did most long-distance wine commerce. Though the southern metropolis, Naples, may have imported wine from around its bay in terracotta amphorae into the ninth century, and may have brought in liquids from further afield too, from the fifth century onwards the trend was negative for pottery containers; in Campania wooden barrels gradually became the standard after the third century, when fiscal wine went to Rome in wooden barrels.[53] Barrels and similar wooden receptacles do not leave as many visible, informative sherds behind when they break or are discarded, so the shift towards use of more perishable materials disappoints modern students of the circulation of commodities, yet to their first users wooden containers *were* less fragile than terracotta and could impart a pleasant taste to the liquids they contained.[54] Chestnut barrels, more even than oak, also resist corrosion admirably. Unfortunately, the barrels to which the Campanian charters refer, from 845 on, do not appear to have been fashioned from chestnut wood, though use of this material in both "buctes" (barrels) and the "organea" in which wine rested until it was ready for transport should not be ruled out.[55]

Viticulture's link with chestnut woods has been important in several regions of Italy in the past, but it does not appear to have been a primary motive either for the prodigious expansion of "castanieta" in post-classical Campania or for the maintenance of these woods after chestnuts became common. Viticulture remained a prominent land use in the early medieval region, expanding dramatically from the 900s, and chestnut wood has been the preferred material for storing and shipping Italian wine for at least the last six centuries, the better documented ones. Yet Campania's surviving early medieval charters do not consistently link vineyards and chestnut groves, either spatially or economically.[56] Though chestnut trees

---

[53] Arthur, *Naples*, 112–13, 124–30; Savino, *Campania tardoantica*, 59–60.

[54] P. Squatriti, "Water-Borne Transport and Communication in North Italy during the Early Middle Ages," in *Travel Technology and Organization in Medieval Europe*, ed. G. de Boe and F. Verhaege (Zellik, 1997), 13–20; E. Marlière, *L'outre et le tonneau dans l'Occident romain* (Montagnac, 2002); G. De Rossi, "Indicatori archeologici della produzione e diffusione del vino nella Baia di Napoli in età altomedievale," in *Paesaggi e insediamenti rurali in Italia meridionale tra tardoantico e altomedioevo*, ed. G. Volpe and M. Turchiano (Bari, 2005), 541–49 (548).

[55] *CDC*, Vol. I, 25 (29) refers to "una bote da bino" in Lucera. Salernitan landlords worried about the combustibility of their "organea": e.g., *CDC*, Vol. II, 219 (12; AD 963); 281 (89; AD 975); 363 (202; AD 984); *CDC*, Vol. III, 497 (58; AD 996). In *CDA*, Vol. I, 73 (119) the two trees "qui vobis sunt apti pro faciendum vobis exinde buctes" could be oak or chestnut. Martin, "Città e campagna," 322, mentions a thirteenth-century chestnut barrel.

[56] On viticulture, H. Taviani-Carozzi, *La principauté lombarde de Salerne*, 3 vols., Vol. I (Rome, 1991), 412–17; Corolla, "Il castello," 356–58; Martin, "Città e campagna," 317–20.

and vines can form an alliance useful to vineyard owners, this is not always the case and, as far as the charters allow us to see, not at this time and place. In fact, in the Lattari mountains north of Amalfi, viticulture's expansion occasionally took place at the *expense* of chestnut groves: in 983 Cicero of Nocera agreed to clear some "empty land" and a chestnut grove for the Salernitan church of St. Maximus, in order to create a new vineyard.[57] The same extension of vines onto hillsides formerly carrying chestnuts emerges in the valley between Vietri and Nocera in the early eleventh century as well.[58] Though in tenth-century Campania grapes did not edge out chestnuts, neither did a harmonious marriage between chestnut cultivation and viticulture, first envisioned by the ancient agronomists, drive the success of *Castanea sativa* in the region.

No better correlation exists between coast-dwelling people's requirement of wood for seafaring and the management of chestnut groves. Nowadays chestnuts are considered an upland tree, but early medieval ones could grow close to the sea, in places convenient for both lumberjacks and shipwrights. A revealing charter of 983 gives the details of a land sale at Cetara just west of Vietri, involving Count Areghis and another powerful landowner, Johannes of Amalfi. The "woods" there were distinguished from "empty land" but also from the "chestnut grove and grafted chestnut wood" that extended down to the sea. A stream along one side of the property may have helped in getting the lumber down the precipitous slopes and to the Tyrrhenian.[59]

Rising right over the water, this chestnut grove was ideally located for lumbering and transportation to Tyrrhenian shipyards. Since chestnut wood resists the corrosive action of salt water as well as it does the corrosion of acidic liquids far better than most other woods, in the early medieval western Mediterranean it was prized shipbuilding material: half a century ago Maurice Lombard noted the vivid interest south Italian trees, including chestnuts, awoke among the inhabitants of North Africa, and indeed al-Idrisi described the exceptional woods of the Sorrentine peninsula as a Mediterranean marvel, related to Sorrento's fine arsenal.[60] More recently, a twelfth-century wreck discovered in Sicily turned out to have several chestnut wood components in its hull, the result of repairs

---

[57] *CDC*, Vol. II, 358 (193–94); see also 355 (197–98).
[58] Corolla, "Il castello," 356. [59] *CDC*, Vol. II, 352 (185).
[60] M. Lombard, "Arsenaux et bois de marine dans la Méditerranée musulmane, VIIe–XIe siècles," in *Espaces et réseaux du haut moyen âge* (Paris, 1972), 107–51 (107–09, 127–28, 138); G. Pardi, *L'Italia del XII secolo: Descritta da un geografo arabo* (Florence, 1919), 106–10. See also A. Citarella, "La crisi navale araba del secolo VIII e l'origine della fortuna commerciale di Amalfi," in *Convegno internazionale 14–16 giugno 1973: Amalfi nel medioevo* (Salerno, 1977), 195–213 (203–07); and, on the later use of Tramonti chestnuts for ships, Marciani, "Alcuni aspetti," 80.

to the original frame.[61] But in the rare instances when Campanian property interests afford a glimpse into the world of boat-making, chestnut
wood is nowhere to be seen. Instead, Master Peter, "who makes lumber for boats," obtained rights over some oak woods around Cetara (the
same place where Count Areghis' chestnut grove loomed over the sea)
for the purpose of building his ships, in exchange for five gold coins.[62] In
this the tenth-century boatwright perpetuated ancient traditions of his
Campanian predecessors, who made ships of oak, with components of
cypress and fir and pine, and eschewed the wood of *Castanea sativa*.[63]

Builders of houses would appreciate the chestnut's qualities too. The
question then is whether, and when, Campanians began to use chestnut
wood in construction, and to what extent. The answer is ambiguous. The
bricks and marble of Roman constructions are what has held posterior
generations' imagination in thrall, but it is wise to remember the veritable forest of lumber that held up Roman roofing: the masonry architecture of ancient Campania *could* have created demand for chestnut lumber,
and the ancients did sometimes support roofs with chestnut beams.[64] Yet
the utter absence of any chestnut wood in the well-preserved Roman
houses around Mount Vesuvius indicates that at least until the first century chestnut was not the wood of choice, if indeed *Castanea sativa* was a
possible choice at all in the region then, given its palynologically attested
restricted range. We noted that some farmhouses on the north of Vesuvius
had chestnut roof beams; the two that have been excavated seem to have
used that wood most in the fifth century.[65]

In Naples, throughout the early Middle Ages the most populous place
in Campania, builders eschewed wood, perhaps because of Byzantine
cultural influence. Yet the Neapolitan case is an exception, related to the
city's status as an outpost of imperial interests, and Salerno's early medieval
wooden architecture was more normal.[66] Salernitan houses were regularly built of wood both in the poshest neighborhoods of the metropolis and in the outlying villages.[67] Their wooden structure was actually
essential to what seems oddest about them to modern eyes, namely their

[61] M. Bonino, "Appunti sull'impiego del legno nelle costruzioni navali tra antichità e medioevo," in *Civiltà del legno*, ed. P. Galetti (Bologna, 2004), 121–42 (130).

[62] *CDC*, Vol. II, 437 (315; AD 991).

[63] E. Allevato, E. Russo Ermolli, and G. Di Pasquale, "Woodland Exploitation and Roman Shipbuilding," *Méditerranée* 112 (2009), 33–42, on the Neapolis harbor shipwrecks of the first–second centuries.

[64] Ancient roof:. See Meiggs, *Trees and Timber*, 184, 240.

[65] Di Pasquale, "Reworking," 868; Allevato *et al.*, "Persistence," 403.

[66] Arthur, *Naples*, 31–33, 47.

[67] *CDC*, Vol. I (24; AD 844) at Sarno. On housing: J. Martin, "Quelques données textuelles sur la mai-son en Campanie et en Pouille (xe–xiie siècle)," in *Castrum 6: Maisons et espaces domestiques dans le monde méditerranéen au moyen âge*, ed. A. Bazzana and E. Hubert (Rome, 2000), 75–87 (78–80);

mobility.[68] For early medieval Campanian houses moved: several Cava charters refer to the allocation of a house's wood at the end of occupation, or simply when a contract ran out. Thus, in 934 Rodelgrimus agreed to divide with his brother Walcarius the townhouse they inherited, and upon their mother's death the division would become literal, a matter of beams and planks to be carted off. Only the roof tiles, wooden "scandole," were not to be divided: Rodelgrimus claimed them.[69] Similarly, in the year 997 a plot of land in Salerno was rented for twelve years, to build a house on "with new wood." This is a revealing formulation. It suggests that many houses were made with old, previously used wood. In 997 the builders were entitled to take half the wood with them at the contract's end, or to sell it.[70]

Barring an archaeological miracle, there is no way of knowing how much chestnut wood Campanian builders used in their recyclable houses, and the hardiness of this tannic wood before water and insects does not of course prove builders sought it. On the other hand, the fact that chestnut beams are necessarily shorter than those of other wood, like the fir the Romans preferred, because *Castanea sativa* reaches relatively modest heights – seldom more than 20 m – does not mean chestnut was unusable: early medieval houses were small, and an 8 m beam would have sufficed to span most post-classical interiors.

Elsewhere in post-classical Italy, carbonized remains of wooden structures prove chestnut wood was a popular construction material: in Tuscany the huts and sheds of agricultural settlements from the ninth century stood on beams of chestnut wood, deployed both vertically and horizontally under roofs.[71] Earlier, and closer to Campania, the simple houses in the Tolfa hills north of Rome built in the fifth century had structural components and planks of *Castanea sativa*, touted by excavators as the earliest archaeological attestation of this wood in Latium.[72] Such discoveries are still rare and the Campanian archaeology of wood

E. Hubert, "Mobilité de la population et structure des habitations à Rome et dans le Latium (IXe–XIIIe siècles)," in Comba and Naso, *Demografia*, 107–24 (112–16).

[68] Not so odd in post-Roman Italy: P. Galetti, *Abitare nel medioevo* (Florence, 1997), 93–94.

[69] *CDC*, Vol. I, 158 (202–03). This was originally their father's house, which the brothers finished and extended for their mother's dotage. Chestnut wood resists rot, and makes superior roofing material. The "scandole" may have been more valuable because they were chestnut wood.

[70] *Ibid.*, Vol. III, 508 (72–73); see also Vol. II, 372 (219); 452 (334); 432 (309); 452 (334); and Vol. III, 499 (60).

[71] M. Valenti: "Architecture and Infrastructure in the Early Medieval Village," in *Technology in Transition: AD 300–650*, ed. L. Lavan, E. Zanini, and A. Constantine Sarantis (Leiden, 2007), 451–89 (471); "La Toscana tra VI e IX secolo," in *La fine delle ville romane*, ed. G. Brogiolo (Mantua, 1996), 81–106 (83–87).

[72] L. Sadori and F. Susanna, "Hints of Economic Change during the Late Roman Empire Period in Central Italy," *Vegetation History and Archaeobotany* 14 (2005), 386–94 (392).

is underdeveloped, though the size of the roof beams in one house in the late antique Vesuvian area suggested to excavators that chestnuts were managed to produce lumber there.[73] All told, then, it is possible to say only that from the middle of the first millennium builders built with chestnut wood when they could.

One major construction project in the region involving a massive shipment of chestnut lumber was the refurbishing of the burial site of Campania's most potent saint, Januarius. According to the excavators of this Neapolitan site, in the second or third decade of the sixth century a mezzanine row of loculi was created close to St. Januarius' original tomb in the catacombs named after him on the outskirts of the city. This was done to enable further important corpses to rest in the holy space. The new tombs were accessible thanks to a wooden floor that in effect bisected the crypt, permitting access to two rows of tombs, one higher and one lower, where there had earlier been only one, and allowing more bishops of Naples to be interred next to the city's holiest patron. Sustaining the new wooden floor, a long row of chestnut beams spanned the passageway, each about 2.5 m long, with diameters of between 25 and 30 cm. The trees whence the beams were fashioned had been young and vigorous, but underground they eventually decomposed, and insects attacked them, causing the gangway to collapse, though not until they had served their purpose for a long time.[74]

In similarly prestigious ecclesiastical contexts, but about 300 years later, another builder also turned to chestnut wood. The kitchen of the great Benedictine abbey of S. Vincenzo al Volturno, in the Apennines north of Salerno, had beams made of *Castanea sativa* in it when it burned down in the Saracen raid of 881.[75] The Volturno's uplands are karstic, geologically unsuited to chestnuts' growth, but S. Vincenzo had far-flung commercial interests, and imported goods from all over southern Italy; we have seen toponymic evidence for chestnuts in the nearby hills, at Castropiniano and Vicalvi.[76] Though the source of these kitchen posts must remain uncertain for now, it is likely to have been close, given the difficulties of haulage. Other wooden elements in the abbey, like the large platform extending over the river, were not of chestnut, but of more easily procurable, local, oak.[77]

---

[73] Allevato *et al.*, "Persistence," 403–04.

[74] U. Fasola, "Le recenti scoperte nella catacomba di S. Gennaro a Napoli," *Rendiconti della Pontificia accademia romana d'archeologia* 46 (1973–74), 187–224 (221–23).

[75] F. Marazzi, C. Filippone, P. Petrone, T. Galloway, and L. Fattore, "San Vincenzo al Volturno: Scavi 2000–2002," *Archeologia medievale* 29 (2002), 209–74 (256–58).

[76] Marazzi, "The Early Medieval Alternative," 741–42, 746–48. The Matese range east of S. Vincenzo has some modern chestnut woods.

[77] F. Marazzi, personal communication.

This is not a statistically satisfactory sample, and other southern sites like the late Roman villa at S. Giovanni di Ruoti, where much evidence of wood came to light, produced no chestnut.[78] But if considered alongside the total absence of chestnut wood from the thousands of roofs engulfed by Vesuvius' eruption of AD 79, and alongside the chestnut beams in some late Roman Vesuvian villas, the post-classical archaeological evidence suggests increasing reliance on structural elements of *Castanea sativa* in Campania. That the patrons behind the building at Naples and S. Vincenzo were powerful people, and could choose the best materials, adds to the impression that during the early Middle Ages chestnut wood became a common and indeed fashionable type of lumber in urban and rural Campania.

Still, there are copious signs that construction materials were not on everyone's mind when they contemplated Amalfi's or Salerno's chestnut groves. Indeed, in the hills behind Salerno, when people chopped down lumber-worthy mature chestnut trees, as happened at Montoro in 884, the decision about whether to "work" the wood or not in order to fashion useful lumber had no obvious answer. The landlord knew that if the chestnut trunks were split, cut, or sawed, the result would be valuable "ligna da laborem," of which it was worthwhile to claim one-third. Yet there was no obligation for the cutters to treat the wood thus and create beams of respectable length – viable construction materials (or shipbuilding ones, despite the difficulties of getting logs from this upland place to the sea).[79] In fact, the owner of the wood lot left the choice of how to cut the trees, and what kind of lumber to produce, to the cutters, unconcerned with the nuances of the operation, though opportunistic enough if "construction lumber" were to emerge from the site. From situations like this one, it seems in the early medieval period producing lumber was not the priority of Campania's chestnut woodland owners.

Another vocation of chestnut wood that might have contributed to the trees' Dark Age propagation is charcoal. As chestnut wood is poor firewood, too soaked in tannin to burn well, prone to dangerous crackling and spewing of embers, it was best burned in the contained context of a charcoal pit. Peasant fireplaces of course made do, as did the fifth-century farms on Vesuvius whose fireplaces contained much fossilized wood of *Castanea*.[80] There may have been other situations where chestnut wood's inferior value outweighed its skittish combustibility, but this was not a

[78] S. Monckton, "Plant Remains," in *The Excavations at San Giovanni di Ruoti*, 3 vols., Vol. III: *The Faunal and Plant Remains*, ed. M. MacKinnon, (Toronto, 2002), 201–09 (202–03).
[79] *CDC*, Vol. I, 100 (129).   [80] Di Pasquale, "Reworking," 868–69.

commercial firewood where there were other options.[81] Perhaps for this reason in a contract whereby Mastalus of Amalfi rented a cliff side for wood-cutting, the chestnut trees were exempted, to be returned "safe" to the owner when the contract ran out.[82] Perhaps, too, the chestnut trees were old and large, daunting to any lumberjack without a chainsaw, and difficult to manage for a charcoal-maker, who preferred poles from coppiced trees, which were easier to stack in his dug-out pit and to cover over with earth in his burning mound.

Regardless, most of the inconveniences of chestnut firewood could be obviated by the partial, controlled combustion that specialists carried out in the woodlands. Chestnut charcoal was a desirable commodity in late medieval and early modern Italy and it was used in the early medieval Lombard plain. Former predilections for chestnut charcoal have left some traces on the modern toponymy of Salerno's hinterland, where the site of S. Maria Carbonara lies in an area on the western slopes of the Monti Picentini, still thickly covered with chestnut woods in 1960.[83] We can discern some traces of tenth-century use of chestnut charcoal also in a 969 charter recording the settlement of a dispute between local peasants ("omnibus hominibus de Allola quam et de Cerchi" just west of Vietri) and a kinship group of Amalfitans. The dispute centered on whether the inhabitants of the area should pay rent for arable land and a chestnut grove they used on the mountainside above the sea. Here the relevant fact is that "the chestnut grove located above Cetara" was in "the place called Carbonara," or charcoal pit, and that in their testimony the peasants called it "the chestnut grove of the charcoal pit."[84] This chestnut grove was precious enough that villagers and Amalfitan landlords thought it worth a legal wrangle, inevitably won by the Amalfitans, but neither it nor the other vestiges of chestnut charcoal in the charters make an overwhelming case for the prominence of this usage. In other words, the post-classical turn to increased reliance on chestnut woodland had a different impetus.

EATING NUTS

In the twentieth century, Campania's chestnut woods, and particularly those closer to the sea, were managed as coppices to produce poles of various sizes and construction material. The fruit or nut production was concentrated inland, around Avellino and in the Monti Picentini, where

---

[81] *CDV*, Vol. I, 19 (73; AD 1001) allows a certain John to "cappilare" chestnut trees around Montella, southeast of Avellino, "pro vestra utilitatem faciendum," possibly for firewood.

[82] *CDC*, Vol. I, 189 (255; AD 955).

[83] A. Antonietti, *Carta della utilizzazione del suolo d'Italia* (Milan, 1966), fo. 16.

[84] *CDC*, Vol. II, 261 (63–64). Another "Carvonara" near Dragonea: *CDC*, Vol. I, 182 (236).

larger chestnuts, easier to peel, grew lusciously.[85] Such clear distinctions were probably not applied during the early Middle Ages: in 962 the Salernitan monastery of St. Maximus permitted Garofalus both to gather chestnuts in its "castanietum" at Montoro *and* to cut down "the trees of the chestnut grove, within reason," considering that such culling was compatible with the renter's obligation to "vigilate over and keep safe" the owner's grove.[86] The modern territorial distinction of coastal and inland regions, each with its own style of castaneiculture, was not quite fully formed in early medieval times.

Both in the landlocked hills around S. Vincenzo, Benevento, and Avellino, and on the Sorrentine peninsula, in fact, when the actual use of Campania's "castanieta" comes into focus in the charters it appears that chestnut groves mainly produced fruit. This is even more true of "insiteta," those grafted chestnut groves whose very reason for being was superior nut production. For both kinds of grove, the nut harvest was most often the object of the written contract, as in the exemplary case of the Beneventan monastery of St. Modestus, which rented its extensive holdings at Bariano, near Mercogliano and Montevergine, in 1037 to John and Peter of Avellino. The monks withheld their chestnut grove in the agreement, and obliged the renters to offer hospitality in the form of lodging and (more worrisome) "wine to satiety" each autumn to the monastery's chestnut gatherers, and to store the crop during the gathering operation "so the chestnuts do not spoil," before they were transported to the monastery.[87]

Likewise, Campanian landowners measured the value of their chestnut woods in chestnuts rather than in loads of firewood or poles or lumber or pigs to pasture. In this regard too a Montevergine charter is instructive. In the shadow of the year 1000, when the mother and daughter Grisa and Iaquinta set about dividing the family patrimony in preparation for the mother's remarriage, they divided a chestnut grove in thirds, but planned to manage it "in common," recognizing that individual trees' unequal productivity, exposure, vigor, age, and other characteristics made spatial divisions impractical.[88] The chestnut crop, itself of course variable each

---

[85] Pitte, *Terres*, 36–37; Bounous, *Il castagno*, 208–10.

[86] *CDC*, Vol. II, 217 (9). It is possible that Garofalus was renewing an aged grove whose trees' yields had waned: the stools would regenerate, becoming vigorous productive trees in two or three decades.

[87] *CDV*, Vol. I, 37 (144–45). That St. Modestus was the chestnuts' destination is not specified, but "vinum ad sufficiendum" and storage and drying in the renters' house "ut non pereent ipse castanee" are.

[88] *Ibid.*, Vol. I, 10 (37–40; AD 987). Subdivision of groves into portions was done elsewhere: *Codex diplomaticus cajetanus*, 27 (47; AD 921); Schwarz, "Regesta amalfitana," 112 (AD 875). Similar arrangements are found in more recent times: Pitte, *Terres*, 151.

year according to seasonal temperatures and precipitation, was a better way to allocate shared entitlements. Like this one, whose subdivision implies it, the overwhelming majority of Campanian chestnut groves we know about were owned and managed by men and women because they produced chestnuts.

As we have seen, how many chestnuts they produced varied. It depended on the season, on the trees' age, on the soil, and to a lesser degree on the skill and work of the cultivator. Nevertheless, landlords in early medieval Campania appear to have accorded a more generous share of the chestnut crop to cultivators than they did of the fruits of other arboricultural pursuits. The share of the chestnut harvest destined to cultivators (two-thirds) and owners (one-third) remained steady throughout the ninth and tenth centuries. Hazelnut and grape rents, instead, fluctuated, though they remained at levels less advantageous to renters (usually one-half).[89] Certainly the more lenient rental terms ninth- and tenth-century owners granted for their chestnut groves were not a recognition of superior toil cultivators invested in them, for processing the crop in early winter was no harder than preparing hazelnuts for consumption; it involved the same operations, described by notaries with the same words ("colligere" and "sechare"), and was done at more convenient times of the year, when other operations did not call out for cultivators' attention.[90] Chestnut groves did not demand the plowing that hazelnut woods sometimes did, nor the fencing that kept browsers off these bush-like trees.[91] Furthermore, raising, gathering, and drying chestnuts were downright simple compared to wine-making and -storing, complicated tasks that called for much specialized equipment even after the year's endless rounds of soil preparation, pruning, and propping.

Two possible explanations suggest themselves for the relatively low rates of chestnut rent landlords extracted from their groves. In the first place, early medieval Campania's groves were full of large and leafy trees by the ninth and tenth centuries. Under the great boughs of mature, productive

---

[89] The Cava standard division of chestnut crops is exemplified by *CDC*, Vol. II, 217 (8–9; AD 962). An exception is *CDC*, Vol. I, 140 (179; AD 923), with halving of product. See Lizier, *L'economia*, 96–99. I have found no first-millennium trace of the symbolic payment called "sabbaticum" sometimes paid by high medieval castaneiculturalists, yet it was traditional by the 1100s: M. del Treppo, "Una città del Mezzogiorno nei Secoli IX–XIV," in *Convegno internazionale 14–16 giugno 1973, Amalfi nel medioevo* (Salerno, 1977), 19–175 (42); R. Trifone, "Le prestazioni degli antichi coltivatori amalfitani e la 'sabbatatica,'" *Rivista di diritto agrario* 8 (1929), 541–51.

[90] The hazel harvest in late summer (August–September) overlapped with and hampered other agricultural operations (fruit-gathering, vintage). In October–November, when chestnuts ripened, plowing for winter grains could be done. Gendered division of labor may have eased this conflict, as women and children could gather chestnuts.

[91] *CDC*, Vol. II, 340,(168; AD 982), where the renter must "totum ipso abellanietum abtis temporibus arare et studere …"

chestnuts it would be difficult to grow crops between May and November, unless the trees had been spaced widely. But as we saw above, the repeated injunction in the contracts for the "castanietum" to be "properly filled" means that a specialized and moderately thick wood was the Campanian ideal. This matters because it implies that intercultivation was not significant in Campanian chestnut management. Indeed, few contracts for chestnut orchards refer to other sown and planted crops on the same plot of land.[92] Instead, intercultivation, and the attendant rent on sown crops, were part and parcel of the other two main forms of arboriculture in early medieval Campania: vine and hazelnut cultivation.

Elsewhere in medieval Italy, pasture was the usual way to exploit the soil under chestnuts. Yet the early medieval charters from Campania seldom refer to animals and even more seldom to pastoral activities, so it is uncertain whether flocks of sheep, or pigs or cattle munched on the wild grasses that find open chestnut glades congenial.[93] The fact that Campania's chestnut groves tended to be unfenced, openly accessible (unlike hazelnut groves), indicates that managers of chestnut woodlands did not mind animals pasturing under the trees, at least until harvest time, and that no-one expected foraging animals to be able to damage the chestnut trees, too lofty for most quadrupeds to harm.[94] Despite its low demand for labor, then, the Campanian "castanietum" tended to offer a single crop, so landlords left cultivators a higher proportion of this main crop as a form of compensation for this "loss." Such a division might also stimulate overall productivity, giving the cultivator incentives to increase yields.[95]

A second explanation for the relative leniency of chestnut landlords in first-millennium Campania is not incompatible with this first one. The striking stability in rental terms, from the earliest charters onwards, indicates that the division of chestnut crops into two unequal portions was traditional, established generations before the charters were written, when fruiting groves began to establish their presence in the landscape. If this were the case, the "traditional" division of the chestnut crop

---

[92] *Ibid.*, Vol. II, 261 (64; AD 969) has people sowing ("seminavimus") in a chestnut orchard.

[93] *Ibid.*, Vol. III, 459 (1; AD 993) refers to pigs and goats a shepherd tended; *CDV*, Vol. I, 19 (74, AD 1001) shows pigs in a wood with a "castanietum."

[94] In *CDC*, Vol. I, 100 (129; AD 884) only cutting chestnuts down created the conditions for a "clusamen." An exception is the "clusura" with "castanietum" in Vol. II, 260 (62).

[95] Like other *meridionalisti*, Martin, "Città e campagna," 306–08, assumes lopsided sharecropping was an attempt to boost production. Yet the same two-thirds–one-third division applied to old and young groves, whose productive potential was unalike. Cultivators had less control over trees' productivity in mature groves, unsusceptible to more intensive husbandry. Though fruiting was unrelated to what people did under the canopy, extra labor did increase growth and thus nut production in new plantations.

(two-thirds–one-third) in Campania in the ninth and tenth centuries represented a living fossil, probably a fossil of the more relaxed tenurial arrangements and growing strategies that arose after the crisis of the sixth century.[96] The generous and undemanding trees themselves immobilized a landscape as the generations of early grove planters had imagined it, reliably turning out savory food for cultivators who did not need to do so much more than scoop up the nuts in autumn.

THE CHESTNUT'S METAMORPHOSIS

By the tenth century Campania's chestnuts were a venerable presence, an astute exploitation of certain steep slopes even, but to remain a cultivation that suited the economic, social, and demographic conditions chestnuts had to change. Although castaneiculture sometimes has seemed the most static, conservative form of cultivation, in this particular corner of the Mediterranean, at this time, the chestnut was anything but immobile.[97] It took a certain vegetative athleticism for *Castanea sativa* to perform the feat of transforming itself enough to find a new niche in the ever-shifting ecology and economy of Campania, but the chestnut is nothing if not adaptable, as it had demonstrated in late antiquity when it first became a significant Campanian tree. At the end of the first millennium the supple nature of the chestnut proved to be the species' greatest asset once again.

Signs of this apparently stolid plant's reinvention as a viable market-integrated crop range from the many grafted groves producing more prized nuts, to the chestnut rents deposited in the hulls of ships, and most immediately to the crop's capacity to convert itself into cash according to a landowner's whim. Indeed, after about 950, large landowners like the church of St. Maximus in Salerno began to require coin rents in contracts with chestnut gatherers, and thus to push chestnuts into the moneyed world of the market. Already during the ninth century Campania distinguished itself in Europe as the sort of place where rulers' diplomatic treaties included stipulations about the movements of merchants and their wares across borders, and by the tenth century, particularly along the Tyrrhenian coast, trade and markets were gathering steam.[98] It therefore made sense in 968 for the priest Maraldus

---

[96] In a period like the 500–700 one described by C. Wickham, *Framing the Early Middle Ages* (Oxford, 2005), 259–302, 534, 576–77.

[97] A. Bruneton-Governatori, "Alimentation et idéologie," *Annales ESC* 39 (1984), 1161–89 (1164); Vitolo, "Il castagno," 22.

[98] "Sicardi principis pactio cum Neapolitanis," ed. G. Waitz, in *Leges Langobardorum*, MGH, Leges 4 (Hanover, 1868), 216–21, §5 (219). On southern Italy's trade, see also M. McCormick, *Origins of the European Economy* (Cambridge, 2001), 433–43, 502–08, 511–15, 519–21, 541–45, 614–30. On local

to postpone to November 3, after the predicted end of the season, his choice of whether to take the rent for his chestnut grove in kind or cash, presumably on the basis of the quality and size of the chestnut crop and market conditions each year.[99]

Not content with this shift from their former existence as subsistence to new life as commercial crop, in the decades around 1000, near Amalfi, chestnuts had also multiplied themselves. This achievement was unique to the species, and something neither hazelnuts nor walnuts could manage. For by the late tenth century on the Sorrentine peninsula chestnuts were classified into several categories, of which at least four were prized by landowners, while hazels stayed hazels, and walnuts plain walnuts.[100] The formation of distinct chestnut cultivars was an outcome neither of chance nor poverty, for many of the landowners involved in contracts referring to them had varied assets and other options: they *chose* to foster chestnut trees that produced nuts with particular characteristics, though they chose within situations not of their own making, often in chestnut woods that were outcomes of natural selection.

What they chose, and what grafters selected to propagate, cannot now be known, for when the various cultivars began to be named in the charters they were already old and traditional, and no notary needed to introduce them with an explanatory clause. But we may imagine that the qualities that elevated different kinds of *Castanea sativa* above the naturally occurring trees in Campania were like the qualities geneticists have observed farmers select in other domesticates elsewhere.[101] Campania's environment had already winnowed the region's chestnuts with pests, diseases, droughts, frosts, and gales, and here locality mattered, so the "landraces" that prevailed on the peninsula of Sorrento were not the same as those that prevailed further inland, where hydrology and microclimate advised farmers to seek somewhat different personalities in the trees they grafted. Yet the early medieval landowners that we know from the charters sought among these naturally selected populations less trees with steady nut production than trees whose nuts ripened at more convenient times, or had superior flavor, or were easier to consume, or resisted rot.

---

production strategies and markets, see A. Di Muro, *Economia e mercato nel Mezzogiorno longobardo* (Salerno, 2009), 22–76.

[99] Money rents, though other crops are also involved: *CDC*, Vol. 1, 189 (244; AD 955); Vol. 11, 264 (67; AD 971). Maraldus: Vol. 11, 256 (57). G. Loud, "The Monastic Economy in the Principality of Salerno during the Eleventh and Twelfth Centuries," *Papers of the British School at Rome* 71 (2003), 141–79 (161–63), sees cash rents rise in the eleventh century.

[100] Vitolo, "I prodotti," 179; Martin, "Città e campagna," 320. To reach four, we can add "rubulie" (Galante, *La datazione* 59 [293]) to the three cultivars discussed just below. Some ordinary "inserte" seem a cultivar too, and "nzerte" is a known modern variety (Bounous, *Il castagno*, 212).

[101] Kingsbury, *Hybrid*, 30, 39–43.

By the tenth century the twin constraints of nature and culture had created identifiable chestnut varieties well known to the locals and desired by the elites whose maneuvers the documents record.[102]

The variegated world of chestnut cultivars is nicely illustrated in a charter of 1036 wherein the clergy of the Amalfitan church of S. Lorenzo spelled out the terms of their long-term lease of chestnut groves in detail, so as to ensure that chestnuts from grafted trees of three distinct breeds ("verole," "zenzale," and "vallanie") reached the church. The clergymen also demanded that their tenant, Leo, bring a fixed quantity of "green chestnuts" to S. Lorenzo, by which they signified chestnuts that Leo had plucked from the trees before they fell off, ripe and brown, onto the ground where the bulk of the chestnut crop was gathered.[103] Alongside several others, this case reveals a coastland world where cultivators, notaries, and landowners shared an acute sensibility to the different qualities of different kinds of chestnuts, a connoisseurship that the charters only reveal to us in the 900s but that rested on generations of sedimented familiarity.

Grafting chestnuts to create cultivars with specific characteristics was, as we have seen, an ancient practice, known to Pliny. Yet only in the Campanian charters of the late first millennium did chestnut-grafting attain such a high level of dissemination that no-one saw any need to gloss the practice. That casual attitude is related to widespread proficiency with the art. In the extant documents, it appears that the coastal lands north of Salerno were the vanguard of the grafting movement, for the named cultivars occur most often in charters about those areas.[104] The surviving charters also leave the impression that whereas grafted chestnuts were normal as early as 822, it was only some decades later that the specified breeds became household words: the earliest attested "serola" grove, in a wood near Ravello, dates to 875.[105] To keep the Campanian situation in perspective it is well to recall that elsewhere in the Italian peninsula documentation for grafted cultivars comes from a century or two later.[106]

---

[102] Martin, "Città e campagna," 326, on the "palumbola" cultivar of Avellino. On Campanian cultivars in general, see Vitolo, "I prodotti," 175–76. In the twentieth century the inland zone that lagged behind the coast in the early Middle Ages has instead been the leader of Campanian castaneiculture: Bounous, *Il castagno*, 210. On landraces, see Kingsbury, *Hybrid*, 40–53.

[103] *CP* 35 (49–50). See Squatriti, "Trees," 37, on green chestnuts and their preservation.

[104] Before 1000, inland woods had "inserte," not named cultivars: see for example *CDV*, 19 (73; 1001).

[105] Schwarz, "Regesta amalfitana," 112.

[106] But the oldest named cultivar I know is from the Garfagnana: "billitane" nuts occur there in 816. See B. Andreolli, *Contadini su terre di signori: Studi sulla contrattualistica agraria dell'Italia medievale* (Bologna, 1999), 192–93.

Chestnuts in early medieval Campania

The precocity of this corner of the Mediterranean world's investment in grafted and named types of chestnut reflected its refined consumption patterns and commercial networks. Indeed, as Vitolo pointed out in 1987, in Campania it was market demand, more than just demographic growth, that impelled chestnuts' expansion in the high medieval period, since it seems that a growing population does not always demand more chestnuts: in the population boom of the thirteenth century Campanian chestnut cultivation actually flagged.[107]

In the Cavese documentation of the 900s there are both clear attestations to the popularity of chestnut trees, especially grafted ones, among landowners, and numerous signs that the landowners were not cultivating chestnuts quite as vigorously as their predecessors had. For one thing, compared to the number of old, established groves recorded by the charters the number of new groves, created in the ninth and tenth centuries, is negligible: around the year 1000 chestnut owners were in a sense exploiting chestnut resources accumulated over the previous centuries rather than investing, as their ancestors had, the time and labor needed to renew and extend their chestnut patrimonies.[108] Landowners who would make investments enthusiastically planted hazelnut groves, and especially vineyards, on a scale that has had scholars speaking of viticultural intensification.[109] We have already noted how, to make room for hazels or vines, on occasion the extirpation of "castanieta" recommended itself to the owners of land. Particularly in the last decades before 1000, when woodland clearance, vineyard-planting, and other means of increasing the productivity of agri- and horticultural exploitations preoccupied Salerno's landed people, the neglect of chestnut groves looks significant.[110] But even in 884 St. Maximus' agent, the priest Maghenolf, arranged to "cut down the chestnuts" in order to enclose the land and "plant a hazelnut grove properly" at a farm near Montoro, a sure sign that "a plot of land with chestnuts" was not as desirable as a hazel grove "well worked and cultivated above and below."[111] Probably hazelnuts and wine had more commercial potential than did other crops, and as we have seen they did not preclude other cultivations on their same plots.

---

[107] Vitolo, "I prodotti," 178. In modern conditions, cultivar variety typified areas where chestnuts were subsistence, monotony areas with commercial vocation: Pitte, *Terres*, 185.

[108] Del Treppo, "Una città," 46; Lizier, *L'economia*, 123.

[109] Lizier, *L'economia*, 120–22; Martin, "Città e campagna," 319–20.

[110] On commerce and agriculture at the turn of the millennium: Taviani-Carozzi, *La principauté*, 415–18; Taviani-Carozzi, "Salerno longobarda," 46–51; Martin, "Settlement," 44; P. Skinner, "The Tyrrhenian Coastal Cities under the Normans," in *The Society of Norman Italy*, ed. G. Loud and A. Metcalfe (Leiden, 2002), 75–96 (90–92).

[111] *CDC*, Vol. 1, 100 (128–29), whose new hazel grove will replace the former trees after the last chestnut crop.

This intensification of investment in vines and hazels along the coast between Vesuvius and the Cilento opened a new phase in Campania's first-millennium landscape and land-use history. It was more than a simple reaction to market imperatives or opportunistic heightened exploitation by rapacious pre-industrial Mediterranean elites. A conjuncture of technological, economic, and demographic conditions lay behind it, rather as occurred centuries later, when southern latifundists discovered the profitability of citrus-growing and coordinating productions in the highlands and on the coast.[112] The increase in acreage dedicated to vineyards and hazelnut woods in the 900s, and later to other plants, came mostly at the expense of uncultivated land, some of it wooded. It did not create a less tree-covered terrain, since landlords in effect substituted one or two species for the greater variety of trees and shrubs that grew beforehand, and anyway were far from endangering the old variety in a landscape still nicely wooded.[113] In this transition the chestnut woods that had sprung up since late antiquity, grafted and ungrafted, mostly stayed where they were, as long-lived trees can do, and in a sense anchored a landscape whose new-found commercial dynamism depended on good coastal communications and a growing population.[114] The more market-oriented and labor-intensive cultivations visible in the charters of the late first millennium redesigned the territory and devalued but did not evict chestnuts.

In fact, *Castanea sativa*, one of Campanian people's most trusted allies in the hard work of early medieval living, found a new niche for itself in these altered circumstances. The chestnut tree of course continued to offer what it had for centuries: simple, reliable, nutritious, and undemanding crops, with manifold side-perks. But now other characteristics in chestnuts became paramount. Foremost, the fruit could last a long time, if it was properly treated after the harvest. Smoked, it became light and hard and therefore could move without spoilage from the places of production to those of consumption while retaining and even enhancing its value. For the dried nut lost weight and volume, kept well, traveled well, and ground into tasty meal in the same mills that prepared grain for human consumption. Since by 1000 many of the chestnuts in circulation in Campania had acquired "improved" characteristics through grafting,

---

[112] P. Bevilacqua, *Terre del grano, terre degli alberi: L'ambiente nella storia del Mezzogiorno* (Rionero, 1992), 73–94, describes how railways and market access made possible irrigation, terracing, and clearances that revolutionized Campania's coastal agriculture.

[113] *CDC*, Vol. II, 214 (5; AD 962) exemplifies colonization without deforestation. Vol. II, 318 (139; AD 980) instead involved the destruction of tree cover. Bevilacqua, *Terre del grano*, 26–29, warns against the "meridionalista" trope of deforestation.

[114] Martin, "Città e campagna," 260, 263–64, 282.

and may have been larger, easier to shell or easier to grind into meal, or have had other commercially desirable qualities, notably an aptitude for preservability, the late-first-millennium chestnut was a marketable commodity.[115] In addition, because of the trees' growth cycle, dried chestnuts appeared on the market in midwinter (December at the earliest), when southern grain stocks, amassed in June, might be running low. Thus *Castanea sativa* had prepared itself for the new conditions in the centuries before they arose. It was poised for an easy transition from a food tree for subsistence and autarchy into a player in trade circuits.

Hence we find charters around the year 1000 in which cultivators agree to dry their chestnuts "properly" and to deliver "well-dried" nuts as rent. Dried and well-dried are not defined, again because in the tenth century it went without saying what they meant. Probably the drying operation included the husking and shelling of the nuts that left them naked and pale, ready for consumers, as was customary in late medieval Europe. But though this important phase in processing the edible nuts may have been what landlords demanded in their "well-dried" nuts, in Campania another operation was crucial. After gathering the nuts and husking them, a cultivator could leave them in the open to be dried by the sun until shelling them became a manageable task. But since this took weeks and left the nuts vulnerable to animals and molds, as well as to inclement weather, artificial drying was safer. In the twelfth century smoking was the commonest preservative of chestnuts, for this accelerated drying and increased the proportion of unspoiled nuts.[116] Luckily, the extraordinary charter of 1036 involving Leo and the four cultivars of chestnut allows us to reconstruct the process of smoking much earlier.[117] In this contract Leo agreed to provide the clergyman Constantine with more than 50 kg of fresh nuts that he would transport to the church of St. Mary outside Amalfi each autumn. Leo also agreed to dry the rest of the crop "in the house which I built for the grills of the grafted chestnut grove," and to divide the dried chestnuts with the landlord in that structure. The "grates" referred to here are the earliest recorded chestnut drying racks in Campania and a place where the wood Leo was to prune from the farm's trees would facilitate the slow, low-temperature burning that late medieval and early modern castaneiculturalists recommended immediately after harvesting the chestnuts. Since the charter mentions that Leo's father, Sergius de Palumola, had also worked the same holding,

---

[115] Del Treppo, "Una città," 53.
[116] A detailed description is in *CDA*, Vol. 1, 155 (272; AD 1152) with "ipsa casa fabrita castaniara … quam ego ibidem fabricavi."
[117] *CP* 35 (49–50). See also Squatriti, "Trees," 34–42; Martin, "Le travail agricole," 135–36.

the techniques it reveals of growing, grafting, and preserving chestnuts may have originated before the year 1000.[118]

Enhancing the preservation of chestnuts by smoking them before they were shelled is a practice undocumented in antiquity. Thus, the late antique chestnut had changed character, becoming the smoked, shucked, hard chestnut of the year 1000. This new chestnut invited commercial uses. We consequently find that landlords who could had their chestnuts brought to places where they might be loaded onto boats or, in at least one case, actually shipped by sea "in your own boat" to their warehouses.[119] The year's crop could there be safely stored prior to continuing its voyage to the right place, at the right time, on the coast of Campania or beyond.

Thus, in what has been characterized as the most commercially lively corner of the western Mediterranean Sea in the late first millennium, the same *Castanea sativa* that had first risen to prominence in the shriveled commercial circumstances of late antiquity (and in a sense *because* of the shriveling) continued to be a viable agricultural plant.[120] Human work, in the form of grafting and tending groves, and technological mastery, in the form of drying, preserving, and presumably grinding techniques, coalesced with the enduring productivity of chestnut trees in a powerful combination. The growth of population and the creation of market centers that drove landlords to plant new vineyards and hazelnut groves did not drive them to abandon their old chestnuts because these could transform themselves.[121] At the end of the first millennium *Castanea sativa* fit as snugly in southern Campania's landscape, and economy, as it had 500 years earlier. The tree's fruit beguiled people who wanted to sell agricultural surplus as much as it did people with more circumscribed goals.

Chestnuts in Campania's coastlands proved capable of changing their very essence: the grafted "inserte" bore fruit whose characteristics, among which was certainly preservability, convinced people to maintain the relationship with the trees. Grafted chestnuts, divided into several categories or cultivars that emerged during the early Middle Ages, now shared the slopes with the plain trees, both producing seeds that someone

---

[118] Leo's widow Marenda still worked the farm seventy-six years later in 1112: *CP* 100 (70). This suggests Leo was young in 1036, and that Sergius' career could have begun in the 960s.

[119] *CDA*, Vol. 1, 45 (70; AD 1036): "cum naulo vestro." On Campanian coastal traffic, see del Treppo, "Una città," 34–35, 54, 71–73; Vitolo, "I prodotti," 177–78; Martin, "Città e campagna," 347–48.

[120] Wickham, *Framing*, 736–41, notes the Campanian Tyrrhenian had the most active market economy in the early medieval western Mediterranean. See also Marazzi, "The Early Medieval Alternative," 747–48; Di Muro, *Economia*, 77–123.

[121] M. del Treppo and A. Leone, *Amalfi medioevale* (Naples, 1977), 32–34, dated chestnuts' decline in the Sorrentine peninsula to the 1200s. See also Vitolo, "Il castagno," 26, 32–33.

considered worthwhile, whether to tide them over until the next grain harvest or to place on the market at the perfect time, when a ship showed up or prices rose.

In his inspiring study of landscape and agricultural change in medieval Sabina, Toubert postulated that chestnuts represented a primitive type of land use, squeezed out in the twelfth and thirteenth centuries as rational agriculture and yield-seeking became normal.[122] While the chronology visible in coastal Campania is different, and quite precocious compared to Latium (and indeed to most of Latin Europe), a similar economic trend was under way. But in Campania the process did not marginalize this characteristic early medieval form of arboriculture. The teleological connotations of Toubert's model can thus be countered by considering that chestnuts remained significant in Campania into the High Middle Ages, and indeed with ups and downs into modern times. It seems the novel reliance on *Castanea* in late antiquity endured as cultivators and landowners of the tenth century made agricultural choices in wholly unalike climatic, social, and demographic conditions.[123] Still more chestnut cultivation lay in the future, in the further commercial and capitalistic economies to come. *Castanea sativa*'s way with people was irresistible, and once this plant had proved its value and occupied the land people offered to it in late antiquity, it persisted in finding a means of recommending itself, whatever the circumstances. Few plants were more pliable, under a hard bark.

---

[122] Toubert, *Les structures*, 190–92, 261–65, 345–47.

[123] See N. Christie, *From Constantine to Charlemagne* (Aldershot, 2006), 487–89, for a recent summary of early medieval Italian climate history, with fluctuations between damp–cold (400–600) and warm–dry (800–1000) phases. On southern climate, see M. Colacino and D. Camuffo, "Il clima dell'Italia meridionale," in *Natura e società*, ed. P. Bevilacqua and P. Tino (Rome, 2005), 37–58 (42–46). I find much wisdom in P. Sereno's warnings about the dangers of linking climate change and historical/agricultural events ("Crisi climatiche e crisi di sussistenza: Qualche considerazione sulle interazioni tra ambiente geografico e agricoltura nella economia di antico regime," in *Agricoltura ambiente e sviluppo economico nella storia europea*, ed. L. Segre [Milan, 1993], 137–42).

Chapter 5

CHESTNUTS IN THE PO VALLEY

In the thick of the Patarene controversy that wracked Lombardy in the eleventh century, Abbot Andrew of Sturmi composed a biography of Ariald, a deacon very active in the early history of the *pataria* reforming sect. According to Andrew, Ariald came from a "noble" family, though one "more noble in their rectitude."[1] He had grown up in a village between Milan and Como, Cucciago: at 255 m above sea level an otherwise nondescript site in the middle valley of the Po.

Cucciago, was, however, the locus of Arialdus' family's power, where they had a "large" landholding. Thus, when Arialdus' theological enemies decided to strike down their heretical adversary, they could think of no better way to attain their goal than to girdle ("decorticare") the "innumerable chestnut trees" that the Arialdine clan held at the village. Evidently these trees were considered the bulwark of the family's economic might, along with the "vines, with which their possession also abounds." The plan involved a secret advance party's visit to the chestnut groves and vineyards, to mark the trees and vines belonging to the Patarene deacon's family. On a later night the assault proper would not mistake the right plants, nor waste precious time and energy cutting through other people's trees in what was clearly a calculated act aimed at economic devastation, based on some familiarity with both the botany and the economics of chestnut cultivation.[2]

---

[1] "Vita Sancti Arialdi auctore Andrea abbate strumensi," ed. F. Baethgen, MGH, Scriptores 30.2 (Hanover, 1934), 1047–75, 1 (1050).

[2] *Ibid.* 9 (1055). The abbot distinguished between ruining vines ("incidere") and chestnuts ("decorticare"). The latter action had Vulgate authority (Joel 1.7); it was used of plants by the Salian Law but of animals in Rothari's "Edictus" (Du Cange, *Lexicon*, s.v.), evidently to mean "skinning." In the *Vita* "decorticare" presumably meant girdling trees too large to cut down. Rothari ("Edictus Rothari," ed. F. Blühme, in *Leges Langobardorum*, MGH, Leges 4 (Hanover, 1868), 3–90, 300–02 [70–71]), punished those who would "incidere" others' chestnuts; to "capellare" oaks or beeches was acceptable, but not olives. In the eleventh-century South, to "cappillare" chestnuts warranted lawsuits: *CDC*, Vol. VII, 1387 (325).

The plan was sensible enough, but had been formulated without figuring the supernatural protections enjoyed by Arialdus' groves. On the
night when the angry clerics loyal to Milan's bishopric raided Cucciago,
they were miraculously blinded so that they could find neither the
"marked trees and vines" nor the markers the advance party had left on
the scene. Unlucky neighbors of the Arialdines found their "vines and
woods" penetrated and "cut and girdled," but the duly designated vegetation belonging to the family of Arialdus went unscathed. To underline
the wonder of the nocturnal escapade, Abbot Andrew claimed that with
his very own eyes he had seen the surviving plants "often," and that they
rendered "most abundant" fruit to their righteous cultivators up to his
own days, proving thereby the uprightness of Arialdus, deserving beneficiary of nature's arboreal bounty.

Andrew wrote the *Vita Arialdi* between about 1085 and the turn of
the twelfth century, but Ariald himself had died in 1067 and the episode
of the invisible chestnut trees took place when he was a young man,
at the beginning of the second millennium. Thus, the Arialdine groves
at Cucciago revealed by Andrew's vivid hagiography lead us back to
the early Middle Ages, when a grove that was economically significant
around 1030, a grove whose trees were dauntingly big, impossible to cut
down furtively in a single night, would have been planted. The arboreal
fortune of Arialdus had not sprung up out of nowhere; it was the inheritance of previous generations' patience and toil, of work done during
the first millennium.

Cucciago's chestnuts, property of the locally dominant family and
important to its economic as well as political fortunes, are a useful point
of entry into the curious phenomenon of chestnut cultivation in the
post-classical Po plain. Of course, Cucciago lies in one of many different
kinds of ecologies within that vast geographic area, and the Po valley is
first and foremost heterogeneous, stretching as it does from Piedmont to
the Adriatic across some 46,000 km². Yet the valley is woven together by
the great river itself, and both climate and the connectivity provided by
the Po and its many affluents justify taking the region as a whole, as early
medieval rulers did.

Today Lombardy, the portion of the Po valley where Cucciago is,
continues to produce some chestnuts, but at highish altitudes, mostly
in the foothills of the Alps. Arialdus' chestnuts suggest that early medieval agricultural strategies were distinctive and brought *Castanea sativa*
onto the valley's lower terrains, where earlier and later farmers preferred to grow grain. Indeed, much of the Po valley of early modern
times could be characterized as a "cultivated steppe," so few were its

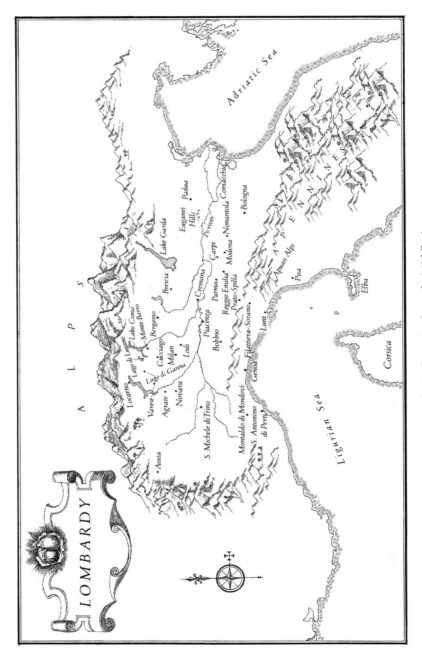

Map 4 The Po basin in the early Middle Ages

trees.[3] Arialdus' *Life* further shows that fruit-bearing chestnut groves around 1000 arose in proximity to vineyards, and that they were not fenced off and easily distinguished from neighboring groves, at least to outsiders lacking the locals' topographical intimacy. In the dark of night it might be easy to lose oneself in a Lombard chestnut wood, but the raiders from Milan knew that and had sagely tried to circumvent the difficulty by marking trees. Their farsighted planning sheds some light on Cucciago's chestnut groves, designed to produce nuts, belonging to diverse owners yet promiscuously intermingled, everyone depending on their local knowledge and custom to keep nuts, rights, and claims apart. Like the size of the trees described by Abbot Andrew, this too indicates that the chestnut woods at Cucciago were no recent upstarts, but a venerable part of the lowland landscape, maybe the result of centuries of work, agreement, arboriculture, and technique.

Through the canopy of Andrew's account we can glimpse the interweaving of human property, power relations, agricultural strategies, and chestnut botany. In other parts of the Po valley these same themes appear, not always quite as vividly as in the abbot's tale, to delineate the surprising prominence of chestnut trees in the early medieval region. Such prominence is not a natural or ecological outcome as much as it is a product of cultural and social factors, of specific choices made by farmers and landowners in places with very different ecological profiles, from the low hills of Piacenza to the ridges of the Alpine arc. In 1979, on a very useful map illustrating his groundbreaking study of peasant food systems in the early Middle Ages, Massimo Montanari highlighted the presence of chestnut groves, and rents, in Lombardy even below the 300 m contour line that botanists consider *Castanea sativa*'s altimetric limit in mainland Italy.[4] Despite Montanari's insight, the existence of chestnut groves below an altitude of 300 m in the Po valley has not yet received the attention it deserves, as an expression of agricultural and sylvicultural choices, and of patient labor, in the post-classical centuries.[5] Even the chestnut trees

---

[3] There are no chestnut woods (nor vines) recorded in the area by A. Antonietti, *Carta della utilizzazione del suolo d'Italia* (Milan, 1966), fo. 3. See Map 2, above, 40. On the Po as a "Kultursteppe": L. Castelletti, E. Castiglione, and M. Rottoli, "L'agricoltura dell'Italia settentrionale dal Neolitico al medioevo," in *Le piante coltivate e la loro storia*, ed. O. Failla and G. Forni (Milan, 2001), 33–84 (36). See F. Menant, *Campagnes lombardes du moyen âge: L'économie et la société rurales dans la région de Bergame, de Crémone et de Brescia du Xe au XIIIe siècle* (Rome, 1993), 204–17, on woodland management in the area during the High Middle Ages, and 212 on chestnuts' replacement with vines and mulberry in early modern times.

[4] M. Montanari, *L'alimentazione contadina nell'alto medioevo* (Naples, 1979), 39 (Fig. 1), 40 n. 4. See also G. Rippe, *Padou et son contado (X–XIIIe siècle)* (Rome, 2003), 63.

[5] P. Galetti, "Bosco e spazi incolti nel territorio piacentino durante l'alto medioevo," in *Il bosco nel medioevo*, ed. B. Andreolli and M. Montanari (Bologna, 1988), 201–21 (206), noted chestnuts growing at an altitude of around 100 m near Piacenza, but did not seek to interpret the fact.

growing further uphill, at more accustomed altitudes for this tree in Italy, did so earlier than we might expect and in surprisingly sophisticated systems. Inspection of their history, too, illuminates key social and economic processes that formed the Dark Age landscape of the Italian peninsula. Here, as elsewhere in Italian history, the environment coevolved with its most active and capable occupants. Here, too, as we saw earlier in the case of Campania, it was the astounding versatility of *Castanea sativa* that prompted humans to foster this plant's growth.

CHESTNUTS' LATE ANTIQUE LAUNCHING

Until the 1990s palaeobotanists assumed that the last ice age had finished off *Castanea sativa* in northern Italy, reducing the species' range to a few refuges in the central and especially southern reaches of the peninsula. As we observed in Chapter 2 above, better palynological tools, and more specialized archaeological sifting of palaeosoils, now have established a new orthodoxy, with the sweet chestnut as an indigenous species in northern Italy, able to survive the last glaciation in the Euganean hills and the highlands of the Berici, along the Brenta river, and near Lake Garda. Thus, chestnuts did not require reintroduction in the Po basin by the humans who first practiced agriculture in the region some seven millennia before Jesus.[6] That chestnuts found the Euganean and other environments congenial in prehistoric ecological conditions is not of course predictive of how things played out in later times, and in fact pollen, charcoal, and archaeological remnants show that chestnuts remained a marginal plant, weakly established in the landscapes of the Po valley, until late antiquity.[7] In other words, the great leap forward, for chestnuts, did not come until the middle of the first millennium. Before that, the plant, indigenous or not, struggled to find a secure foothold in the northern part of Italy.

At Aquileia, for instance, excavations of the Roman-era settlement turned up a single small chestnut and fragments of two more, arguably the largest such cache from the classical period anywhere north of

---

[6] For the traditional view: I. Richardson, "Chestnuts," in *The Oxford Encyclopedia of Trees of the World* (New York, 1983), 133–35.

[7] On prehistoric Euganean flora: P. Kaltenrieder, G. Procacci, B. Vannière, and W. Winner, "Vegetation and Fire History of the Euganean Hills (*Colli Euganei*) as Recorded by Lateglacial and Holocene Sedimentary Series from Lago della Costa," *The Holocene* 20.5 (2010), 679–95 (688–91). The Euganean hills do not seem to have had chestnut growth in the historical period before *c.* 1200: Rippe, *Padou*, 36–37, 63, 576. Incisive *mises à point* are M. Rottoli and S. Negri, "I resti vegetali carbonizzati," in *Filattiera-Sorano*, ed. E. Giannichedda (Florence, 1998), 198–212 (203–04); E. Castiglioni, E. Cottini, and M. Rottoli, "I resti botanici di Santa Giulia a Brescia," in *S. Giulia di Brescia*, ed. G. Brogiolo (Florence, 1999), 401–24 (415–16).

Vesuvius.[8] The Aquileian chestnuts have an even smaller profile than palm dates there, and may have been similarly exotic imports. Roman tombs near Como produced a couple more fragments and tiny bits of chestnut wood, both probably used in funerary rites.[9] A handful of Roman nuts could be gathered by bringing together finds from Locarno (second century) and Levata, near Bergamo (first–second centuries?), while there are carbonized scraps of chestnut wood, dated to the imperial period, from Angera near Varese, and from Legnano. Pollen samples from a few places, like lakes Muzzano and Segrino, indicate that *Castanea*'s puny footprint grew after the first century of the first millennium, though the pollens do not attain high concentrations before the fourth century.[10] Thus, judging from the palaeobotanical data, while *Castanea sativa* was not unknown in Roman north Italy, it was not a widespread or important tree, either in the plain or on the hills.

The late antique and early medieval material record for chestnut trees and nuts in northern Italy is far richer and indicates a more adventurous history. The record is particularly impressive if one considers that until recently archaeological attentions were focused on classical remains, and sites and structures of the "low centuries" got short shrift. Settlements like Monte Barro by Lake Como, dated to the fifth and sixth centuries, which produced much carbonized chestnut wood (structural beams) and sixty-five nuts, despite the fires that ended its settled life, suggest a shift was taking place in northern Italy's vegetation and thus in its humans' growing strategies.[11] Not very far away, but in this case within an urban community, at Brescia chestnut construction timber came to be used alongside oak and beech in the sixth century, a time when some large beams of fir were still hauled to town from the high mountains. Urban Brescian contexts returned five shelled chestnuts to their excavators, dated to the 500s, and much chestnut charcoal as well. The latter was the result of controlled combustion without air, and probably fired kilns.[12] Some such charcoal turned up in the slightly later (sixth–seventh century) layers at the site of the nunnery of S. Giulia, where much chestnut wood, shaped and notched for carpentry uses, also survived: planks and posts, but also more sophisticated panels likely for a cabinet or cupboard.

---

[8] L. Castelletti, "Contributo alle ricerche paletnobotaniche in Italia," *Istituto lombardo: Rendiconti lettere* 106 (1972), 331–74 (359, 366).

[9] E. Castiglioni, E. Cottini, and M. Rottoli, "Mariano, Via T. Grossi: Analisi archeobotaniche," in *Storia di Mariano Comense*, ed. G. Frigerio (Como, 1999), 107–12 (108–09).

[10] See the catalogue of finds in Rottoli and Negri, "I resti vegetali carbonizzati," 203.

[11] E. Castiglioni, E. Cottini, and M. Rottoli, "I resti archeobotanici," in *Archeologia a Monte Barro*, 2 vols., ed. G. Brogiolo and L. Castelletti, Vol. II (Lecco, 2001), 223–47 (224–25, 241).

[12] L. Castelletti and A. Maspero, "Analisi di resti vegetali macroscopici," in *Ricerche su Brescia altomedievale*, ed. G. Panazza and G. Brogiolo (Brescia, 1988), 125–32 (126, 129–31).

Indeed, at S. Giulia chestnut was the pre-eminent construction wood, ahead of oak, ash, and all the others.[13] Curiously, at a site so rich in finds of chestnut wood only a small number of nut fragments surfaced, but there is no doubt *Castanea sativa* had become an important presence in the hinterland of Brescia at the beginning of the Middle Ages.

In the Ligurian Apennines further west, carbonized chestnut wood fragments from the fifth and sixth centuries are an indication that the trees were locally more numerous than the hornbeams, firs, willows, poplars, and walnuts with which they shared the slopes, at the expense of the oaks that earlier inhabitants had favored.[14] If some more or less contemporary sites, recently investigated with contemporary techniques and interests, like S. Stefano Belbo near Cuneo or the high Apennine seasonal settlement at Prato Spilla, show no sign of chestnut's presence, still the post-classical centuries look like a golden age for *Castanea sativa* in the valley of the Po.[15] Chestnut's carbonized remains crop up in late antique contexts at Pontelambro, Oderzo, Angera (near Varese), Brescia (at Via A. Mario), and in burials at Trezzo close to Milan.[16] Even at the low-lying hamlet of Mulino di Sotto to the south of Verona, close to the Po, hardly the kind of place *Castanea sativa* prefers, an early medieval chestnut shell seems to suggest the plant's diffusion by the Carolingian epoch.[17] In none of these sites were chestnuts or the wood of the tree or pollens from its flowers from before the second century discovered.

Pollen profiles from varied places on both banks of the great Lombard river in fact confirm that after the second century chestnut trees spread nicely in the basin. In Piedmont the increasing prevalence of chestnut seems to have come at the expense of oakwoods, as is suggested by the relative percentages of pollen spores from Montaldo di Mondovì.[18] Near Vercelli at the western

---

[13] Castiglioni *et al.*, "I resti botanici di Santa Giulia a Brescia," 412–14, 421.

[14] Rottoli and Negri, "I resti vegetali carbonizzati," 201; L. Castelletti, "Resti vegetali macroscopici da Refondou presso Savignone," *Archeologia medievale* 3 (1976), 326–28 (327–28).

[15] Prato Spilla: G. Cruise, "Environmental Change and Human Impact in the Upper Mountain Zone of the Ligurian Apennines," *Rivista di studi liguri* 57 (1994), 175–94; J. Lowe, C. Davite, D. Moreno, and R. Maggi, "Stratigrafia pollinica olocenica e storia delle risorse boschive dell'Appennino settentrionale," *Rivista geografica italiana* 102 (1995), 267–310. Cuneo was a modern chestnut-growing center (Antonietti, *Carta della utilizzazione del suolo d'Italia*, 8); see also D. Arobba, "Analisi palinologiche," in *Montaldo di Mondovì*, ed. E. Micheletto and M. Venturino Gambari (Rome, 1991), 245–46 (245); R. Comba, "Châtaigneraie et paysage agraire dans les vallées piémontaises (xiie–xiiie siècles)," in *Castrum 5: Archéologie des espaces agraires méditerranéens au Moyen Age*, ed. A. Bazzana (Madrid, 1999), 256–57.

[16] Rottoli and Negri, "I resti vegetali carbonizzati," 202–04, with useful tables. Castelletti *et al.*, "L'agricoltura," 68, note a find at Trezzo "in Età romana."

[17] E. Castiglioni and M. Rottoli, "Nogara, l'abitato di Mulino di Sotto," in *Nogara*, ed. F. Saggioro (Rome, 2011), 123–57 (140).

[18] R. Nisbet, "Storia forestale e agricoltura a Montaldo tra età del ferro e xvi secolo," in *Montaldo di Mondovì*, ed. E. Micheletto and M. Venturino Gambari (Rome, 1991), 247–51 (247–48); R. Comba,

end of the Po's course, San Michele di Trino lay in a chestnut-rich country-side between the fifth and seventh centuries, when human activities left the deepest imprint on the landscape, or anyway on its proxy, pollen showers.[19] Further east, the mud of the two small lakes in the Lombard foothills of the Alps north of Milan, Lago di Muzzano and Lago di Segrino, preserved reveal-ing layers of deposited pollen from the first millennium. The local breezes had wafted increasingly dense amounts of chestnut pollen, beginning in the first century but reaching an apex after the third. The gradual decline of wal-nut and oak pollens at these sites coincides with *Castanea sativa's* meteoric rise, reflecting new growing strategies that included much rye.[20] Similar pat-terns are visible in the palynological record for the nearby Lago di Ganna, which is slightly higher than Segrino or Muzzano, but chestnut's predomin-ance dates to the sixth century there.[21] Much lower down and on the right bank of the Po, around Modena, some mysterious buried deposits have been interpreted as "hiding wells" by their excavators. Alongside the baskets, bowls, buckets, and other household items they contained, these wells preserved muck and hence pollens from around the year 600. In the plain environment of Modena, chestnuts cannot be expected to predominate, but *Castanea* pol-len was abundant enough to show the tree had a significant role in the land-scape of late antique Emilia.[22] Just across the Po river in equally inauspicious ecological circumstances for chestnut growth, at Nogara traces of chestnut pollen from the ninth century onwards show that not too distant from the settlement chestnut trees had begun to blossom.[23]

"Castagneto e paesaggio agrario nelle valli piemontesi," in *Uomini boschi castagne*, ed. R. Comba and I. Naso (Cuneo, 2000), 21–32 (22–3).

[19] R. Caramiello, A. Zeme, C. Siniscalco, *et al.*, "Analisi paleobotaniche e sedimentologiche: Storia forestale, clima, ed agricoltura a Trino dall'età romana al medioevo," in *San Michele di Trino (VC): Dal villaggio romano al castello medievale*, 3 vols., ed. M. Negro Ponzi Mancini, Vol. II (Florence, 1999), 577–99 (592, 596).

[20] E. Gobet, W. Tinner, P. Hubschmid, *et al.*, "Influence of Human Impact and Bedrock Differences on the Vegetational History of the Insubrian Alps," *Vegetation History and Archaeobotany* 9 (2000), 175–87 (182–84). In the High Middle Ages, chestnut plantations *reduced* peasant reliance on "lesser grains" like rye: Menant, *Campagnes lombardes*, 216.

[21] R. Schneider and K. Tobolski, "Lago di Ganna: Late-Glacial and Holocene Environments of a Lake in the Southern Alps," *Dissertationes botanicae* 87 (1985), 229–71 (248–52); R. Drescher-Schneider, "Forest, Forest Clearance and Open Land during the Time of the Roman Empire in Northern Italy," in *Evaluation of Land Surfaces Cleared from Forests in the Mediterranean Region during the Time of the Roman Empire*, ed. B. Frenzel (Stuttgart, 1994), 45–58 (51–54).

[22] C. Accorsi, M. Bandini Mazzanti, L. Forlani, *et al.*, "Archaeobotany of the Cognento Hiding Well," in *Proceedings of the 1st International Congress on Science and Technology for the Safeguard of Cultural Heritage in the Mediterranean Basin* (Palermo, 1998), 1537–44 (1538). On earlier tree cover: C. Accorsi, M. Bandini Mazzanti, A. Mercuri, C. Rivalenti, and G. Trevisan Grandi, "Holocene Forest Pollen Vegetation of the Po Plain: Northern Italy (Emilia Romagna Data)," *Allionia* 24 (1996), 233–76 (240–49).

[23] M. Marchesini, S. Marvelli, I. Gobbo, and S. Biagioni, "Paesaggio vegetale e antropico circostante l'abitato altomedievale di Nogara," in Saggioro, *Nogara*, 159–92 (177).

The overall picture rendered from the archaeobotanical records, then, is one in which Cassiodorus' fulsome praise for the green mane of chestnut leaves crowning the hills around Como becomes plausible, more than a literary trope. The pollens of *Castanea sativa* seem to become more significant in late Roman layers, and the finds of chestnut wood and fruit likewise multiply in contexts dated to after the height of the Roman empire. A sixth-century writer seeking to compliment the local readers of his prose by showing appreciation for their landscape might choose to discuss the local vegetation, whose variety was admirable. That Cassiodorus singled out the chestnut trees on slopes around Lake Como, an unclassical element in his Virgilian panorama of villas, vines, and olives, probably means such trees had "arrived" and attained the privileged status of characteristic and representative landscape feature in the northeastern Po valley by the 520s. At the beginning of the Middle Ages, then, chestnuts seemed indigenous, typical of the area around Como, at least in the eyes of a Ravennan from Calabria. That explains why, at the end of the early Middle Ages, they played such a prominent role in the life of the Patarene St. Ariald. By the eleventh century chestnuts had had several centuries to make themselves at home in northern Italy.

RISE OF A TREE: CAUSES AND EFFECTS

They did so by seducing the mammal best suited to advancing their cause, *Homo sapiens*. Without human aid, it is highly unlikely that chestnut trees in Lombardy could have become anything more than they had been since the last ice age: a sporadic presence in marginal landscapes. Of course, late antique Italy was a time and place modern commentators usually consider favorable to arboreal growth, so we might expect an increase in recorded arboreal pollens and other arboreal products around that time.[24] But not all trees did well, and, as we observed in Chapter 2, oak, a tree whose presence declined in the later first millennium, was one of the victims of early medieval afforestation.[25]

Indeed, without human aid, some species of tree vanished from late antique Lombardy, and the variety of fruit trees commonly raised by farmers definitely shrank.[26] For instance, obscurity erased the unfortunate

---

[24] E. Sereni, *Storia del paesaggio agrario italiano* (Bari, 1979), 82–84. A recent statement of orthodox forestation chronologies is M. Valenti, "Architecture and Infrastructure in the Early Medieval Village," in *Technology in Transition: AD 300–650*, ed. L. Lavan, E. Zanini, and A. Constantine Sarantis (Leiden, 2007), 451–89 (459).

[25] Castiglioni and Rottoli, "Nogara," 139–40.

[26] M. Bandini Mazzanti, G. Bosi, M. Marchesini, A. Mercuri, and C. Accorsi, "Quale frutta circolava sulle tavole emiliane-romagnole nel periodo romano?," *Atti della società dei naturalisti e matematici di Modena* 131 (2000), 63–92.

apricot, no longer able to convince anyone to invest the labor and resources to keep it alive by planting, grafting, pruning, and fertilizing it, while keeping its competitors at bay.[27] The apricot was an unusual tree in Roman Italy, rather as the chestnut had been, but one more highly prized and hence cultivated in elite gardens, unlike the chestnut. Yet after a brief high imperial apogee during which this novelty plant had been fashionable, the apricot disappeared from archaeologically known sites, and seems not to have been known to early medieval writers, either. Without human allies, *Prunus armeniaca* could not fend for itself and seems to have died off, a fate chestnuts could easily have shared had they not offered manifest advantages to their human friends. The famous list of trees Charlemagne supposedly wanted to find planted on royal estates throughout his empire included close relatives of the apricot like peach and almond, but omitted the apricot itself, apparently because no-one at the Frankish court knew it existed, despite their efforts at imperial botanico-encyclopedism. This excellent fruit had to find other routes back onto European tables, passing through the early Caliphate where, it appears, it was cultivated, selected, grafted, improved, and rechristened (*al barquq*) with the name by which it became renowned in late medieval Europe when the crusades rendered it familiar once more, but now as a new and exotic plant. The loss of its ancient name (*praecoccum*) was the toll apricot paid for its post-classical demise.

Thus, there was nothing inevitable about the survival and indeed expansion of the chestnut in late Roman and early medieval northern Italy despite the advance of woodlands and the increased reliance on "wild" resources and woods of that time. Other species were poised to exploit the opportunities created by the new social, cultural, and economic equilibria, and both ashes and beeches manifestly did so, for instance at Prato Spilla between 560 and 680, where new pastoral activities created clearings that permitted the triumph of the beech.[28] Since the chestnut tree shared many of the same needs for soil, water, and sunshine as these formidable competitors, better equipped to propagate themselves than *Castanea sativa*, it was providential that people developed a taste for the seed of the chestnut tree, and seem to have preferred it to acorns or beech mast, from late antiquity onwards. In the Po valley, chestnut imposed itself as a cultivated plant, one able to reward its cultivators with food, fodder, fuel, and construction material. It was chestnut's unique combination of utility that gave it the decisive advantage in a more self-sufficient and less populous Po valley.

---

[27] B. Hasselrot, "L'abricot: Essai de monographie onomasiologique et sémantique," *Studia neophilologica* 13 (1940–41), 45–79, 226–52.

[28] On this site, see above, 13–15, 170.

For, as we have learned, chestnut wood is fine wood, and in small sizes is most useful to country people, but beech wood made both better firewood and charcoal, while oak was the most sought-after construction material in the "world of wood."[29] In the Po area, this preference is visible at Montaldo di Mondovì, a place with many chestnuts, as we have seen, but where early medieval builders used mature oak trees for the beams that supported houses in the tenth century, and people heated themselves with an array of other species, not, it seems, with logs of chestnut. The same pattern is visible at the other end of the Po valley, at Nogara, in the ninth century.[30] The distinction between the utility of chestnut trees and that of oak and beech is sustained in the mid seventh century "Edict of Rothari," two of whose provisions have to do with these woodland trees and may be based on what actually happened around Pavia, Rothari's residence.[31] According to the categories drawn up by the Lombard legislator, chestnuts participated in the same cultural space, and maybe physical landscape too, as pears, apples, and walnuts, while oaks (of three varieties) and beeches (of two) had a separate entry and a lower "tree-geld," evidently because they were not cultivated, or were not the recipients of comparable levels of human involvement and labor. In other words, Rothari valued chestnuts as producers of fruit or nuts, while he valued oaks and beeches (less) as producers of wood. In doing so he seems to echo the preferences of the late antique arboriculturalists who so extended chestnuts' range, as well as those of the Cucciagan lineage of Arialdus.

Naturally enough, chestnut wood could and did recommend itself for some purposes during the long centuries when most utensils were made of wood. On Lake Como the wrecks of small "Byzantine" craft that plied the waters in the early medieval period were wholly made of chestnut wood, whose tannic, dense grain resists rot well.[32] Close by the same lake at Monte Barro, as we have seen, both dwellings and storehouses were built and maintained using chestnut beams, as well as oak, during the fifth and sixth centuries, and though Tuscany lies outside the Po valley zone, several early medieval buildings there were made of chestnut wood as well.[33]

If this seems an unimpressive cache of chestnut wood finds, it is well to recall that early medieval wooden construction by its very

---

[29] See P. Galetti, *Abitare nel medioevo* (Florence, 1997), 95; M. Bonino, "Appunti sull'impiego del legno nelle costruzioni navali tra antichità e medioevo," in *Civiltà del legno*, ed. P. Galetti (Bologna, 2004), 121–42 (130–34).

[30] R. Nisbet, "I macroresti vegetali," in Negro Ponzi Mancini, *San Michele di Trino*, Vol. II, 621–30 (625–27); O. Tinazzi and E. Larco, "Indagine xilotomica e dendrocronologica su elementi lignei provenienti dallo scavo 'Mulino di Sotto' di Nogara," in Saggioro, *Nogara*, 77–88 (78, 84–86).

[31] "Edictus Rothari," 300–01 (70); see Montanari, *L'alimentazione contadina*, 41.

[32] Bonino, "Appunti," 131.   [33] Valenti, "Architecture," 471.

nature lacked the capacity to leave an enduring sign of its existence. Wood is a solid material, but it deteriorates without constant care. It eventually disintegrates in most temperate climates so that it leaves few traces of itself, except when carbonized, as happened at Monte Barro, or when preserved in anaerobic conditions, like those of Lake Como. And the process of degeneration can be swift. At Montarrenti in Tuscany, between the seventh and tenth centuries the supporting posts of huts and other structures were frequently replaced, judging from the many post-holes that were dug into the floors, and even at S. Michele di Trino deteriorated structural beams were removed and recycled as firewood.[34] On top of wood's inherent long-term fragility, and resultant archaeological invisibility, the high medieval love of stone-building and overbuilding further restricted the surviving evidence, often destroying it in order to replace the wood of churches, mansions, and storerooms with masonry.[35] In fact, Carlo Citter has suggested that during the Carolingian domination of Italy increasingly assertive elites erected new buildings of stone at the expense of older wooden ones, and thereby relegated wooden structures to the social ranks that are archaeologically least visible.[36] Thus, the numerically small number of chestnut (and indeed of other) wood finds from post-classical structures needs to be calibrated with the ephemeral nature of the material and its social collocation.

The chestnut finds from post-classical contexts are perhaps best understood in juxtaposition to the truly puny known finds of chestnut wood from earlier on. For Roman-era chestnut wood is exceedingly rare in the valley of the Po, even more so than it is from other corners of the empire. Sites like Altino, where a choked canal produced a treasure trove of first-century wood remains, generated no chestnut, though much ash, cypress, fir, pine, and boxwood.[37] There are no recorded finds of chestnut wood from Roman Aquileia, either. Similarly, Roman shipwrecks found in northern Italy show Roman shipbuilders' flexibility as they adapted their skills to available species while they made and repaired boats, but the wood of *Castanea sativa* was not in their arsenal, as least

---

[34] F. Cantini, *Il castello di Montarrenti: Lo scavo archeologico (1982–1987)* (Florence, 2003), 37; Nisbet, "I macroresti," 627.

[35] A. Augenti, "Fonti archeologiche per l'uso del legno nell'edilizia medievale in Italia," in Galetti, *Civiltà del legno*, 37–69 (44–46).

[36] C. Citter, "L'Italia centrale tirrenica in età carolingia," in *V congresso nazionale di archeologia medievale*, ed. G. Volpe and P. Favia (Florence, 2009), 302–05.

[37] E. Ferrarini, "Manufatti di legno e cuoio dall'area nord del Museo di Altino," *Quaderni di archeologia del Veneto* 8 (1992), 191–206 (191–92). The "Roman period" fireplace at Belmonte (north of Turin) had chestnut charcoals, but prehistoric layers seem to have mixed in: R. Nisbet, "Le analisi antracologiche," in *Belmonte: Alle radici della storia*, ed. M. Cima (Cuorgné, 1986), 69–73 (69–71).

insofar as this is archaeologically known.[38] Roman cooping is little studied and hence imperfectly understood, yet the practitioners of this difficult craft do not appear to have used staves of chestnut even for the local, short-distance, low-value transportation that tended to rely more on barrels than amphorae in the Roman empire.[39] Thanks to the longer and deeper tradition of aesthetic interest in Roman culture, Roman furniture, cabinetry, and wooden household goods manufacture is better known, but though Roman carpenters and shoemakers employed a wondrous array of woods, the published accounts of their work show they never cut or carved any chestnut, whether in northern Italy or, for that matter, anywhere else around the Romans'Very Own Sea.[40]

In light of such sparse occurrences of chestnut wood in Roman buildings, appurtenances, tools, and machines, and of wood's low archaeological visibility, each archaeological attestation of this material from post-classical north Italian excavations gains meaning. As we saw above, the pollen counts make it appear that *Castanea sativa*'s wood was becoming more available in the middle of the first millennium AD. A look at the carbonized and otherwise preserved wood remains suggested that *Castanea sativa*'s wood was becoming more popular at the same time. In both regards the pattern is consistent: in late antiquity chestnut was a plant on the rise in the north Italian landscape. Such a rise was not happenstance, but the outcome of human choices, made in response to ecological as well as economic and cultural promptings, and like any environmental change also reflecting new social hierarchies and economic patterns.[41] It stands to reason that as Rome's hegemony waned, and early medieval commercial networks shrank, the way people treated wood and woodland resources changed too.[42] Useful wood, more than ever, was local wood, though the constraints of transportability mattered on the local scale as much as they had when wood moved across longer distances. So did the constraints of manageability in the age before

---

[38] P. DeSantis, "Le suppellettili in legno di uso quotidiano," in *Fortuna maris: La nave romana die Comacchio*, ed. F. Berti (Bologna, 1990), 105–12; and L. Castelletti, A. Maspero, S. Motella, and M. Rottoli, "Analisi silotomiche e tecnica di lavorazione del legno," in Berti, *Fortuna maris*, 150–51; E. Riccardi, "Indagine preliminare sullo scafo," in *Il relitto del Pozzino*, ed. F. Nicosia and A. Romualdi (Florence, 1990), 20–43 (23–29, 39).

[39] E. Marlière, *L'outre et le tonneau dans l'Occident romain* (Montagnac, 2002), 85–88, 184–85. Marlière found that until the second century most Roman barrels were of fir, but thereafter oak made up about one-third of known barrels (96). An excellent description of traditional cooping is W. Logan, *Oak: The Frame of Civilization* (New York, 2005), 169–81.

[40] P. Pugsley, *Roman Domestic Wood* (Oxford, 2003). One box-top of chestnut was found at Vindolanda on Hadrian's Wall (153), but is the sole exception.

[41] As proposed by M. Godelier, *L'idéel et le matériel* (Paris, 1984), 14–15, 61–72.

[42] See C. Wickham, *Framing the Early Middle Ages* (Oxford, 2005), 486, 518; M. McCormick, *Origins of the European Economy* (Cambridge, 2001), 96–115.

Andreas Stihl revolutionized the fate of all woods with his gas-powered chainsaws, indeed in an age of very few saws at all.[43]

However, northern Italians dealt with their constraints creatively. Adaptation to the geological, climatic, but also economic and social conditions of late antique life naturally took many forms. Where a calcareous soil militated against the growth of such species as *Castanea*, the locals grew, cut, and used other kinds of trees. Around the sixth- and seventh-century "Byzantine" garrison site at S. Antonino in Liguria, people favored the growth of firs, juniper, ash, holm oak, and hornbeam, and used them in building and heating. Their culling rebalanced local forest ecology, once richer in deciduous oaks. The latter receded while the other species colonized newly available hillsides.[44] In order to grow rye and fruit on the little flat ground accessible to the fortification, S. Antonino's inhabitants cleared vegetation with fire: this gave an advantage to hornbeam and ash, both of which respond well to cutting and recover readily from conflagrations, and limited oak's range. Still, holm oaks' leaves offered valuable winter fodder that, added to the acorns and the branches that became charcoal, made these trees prized at a site that relied heavily on the herding of pigs and sheep owing to the precipitous terrain and lack of water that made agriculture arduous.[45]

Just across the watershed, within the catchment basin of the Po river, the fifth-century inhabitants of S. Michele at Trino increased the amount of land on which they grew grain and pasture, launching a long early medieval phase during which the area's woodland actually receded. This site's settlement patterns suggest basic demographic continuity between the fourth and seventh centuries, so the assault on woods must have derived from increased need for land as access to markets dwindled, perhaps because of wretched road conditions.[46] Pollen spectra suggest that as woodland shrank its composition changed, too. Here also oak lost ground, while beech gained, as did elm, on a smaller scale, and firs, at higher elevations. By the tenth century S. Michele's flat landscape was

---

[43] J. McNeill, *Something New under the Sun* (New York, 2000), 307–08.

[44] E. Castiglioni, "I carboni," in *S. Antonino: Un insediamento fortificato della Liguria bizantina*, ed. T. Mannoni and G. Murialdo (Bordighera, 2001), 617–26 (620–25).

[45] P. Palazzo and G. Imperiale, "Il Finale e la formazione geomorfologica del territorio di Perti," in Mannoni and Murialdo, *S. Antonino*, 27–37 (37); D. Arobba and G. Murialdo, "Le analisi palinologiche e paleocarpologiche," in Mannoni and Murialdo, *S. Antonino*, 627–38 (632–38); R. Giovinazzo, "Le risorse alimentari animali," in Mannoni and Murialdo, *S. Antonino*, 639–56 (641–45, 654).

[46] M. Negro Ponzi Mancini, "Dalla fattoria al castello," in Negro Ponzi Mancini, *San Michele di Trino*, Vol. II, 455–548 (479–80). Contemporary Milan seems to have remained an active market for Lombardy's surplus: M. Biasotti and R. Giovinazzo, "Reperti faunistici," in *Scavi MM3* 3.2, ed. D. Caporusso (Milan, 1991), 167–84.

quite sparsely wooded, though lime and ash had become significant presences. It was likewise during the early medieval period that *Castanea* pollens attained their highest incidence in the area, even compared with high medieval contexts. In effect, the lowlanders removed oak from their territory, much of it for construction, faster than it could regenerate itself, and favored other species, notably elm and chestnut, in oak's place. The change corresponded to the need for grasses that develop lushly before chestnuts leaves grow in May; this early ground-level pasture integrated the "aerial" pasture of chestnut leaves that became relevant in summer.[47] Only after 1000 did S. Michelans' new pasturage strategies and increased reliance on beef-raising lead to a resurgence of local woods, and oaks.[48]

At S. Antonino, a tiny community, isolated and occupying a precarious site for strategic rather than economic reasons, and at S. Michele, a substantial village with access to the Po, northern Italy's main axis of communication, people fashioned different woods, co-operating with their different ecologies. Likewise the villagers at post-classical Filattiera in the hills east of modern La Spezia remade their woods according to their lights, in response to ecological and economic limitations.[49] In the fifth and sixth centuries the Filattierans' woodsmanship was sophisticated, integrated with animal husbandry and agriculture. The inhabitants used alder as firewood, a side-effect of all the hard work they were investing in clearing the most accessible, damp, low-lying flat land to sow with wheat, in a topography of steep hillsides. Like their contemporaries at S. Antonino and S. Michele, people at Filattiera also reduced the local presence of oak, at least such of it as was relatively easy to reach and transport to the Magra river. Indeed, into the sixth century these peasants seem to have exported towards the larger towns some wood, as well as the meat, milk, and wool of their flocks. Instead the Filattierans mostly left alone the tall highland species that Roman sylviculturalists had prized, so firs recovered vigorously in the area, and hornbeam also increased its presence. Both of these species had their utility, but in late antiquity a more

---

[47] Sereni, *Storia del paesaggio*, 152. See E. Bargioni and A. Zanzi Sulli, "The Production of Fodder Trees in Valdagno, Vicenza, Italy," in *The Ecological History of European Forests*, ed. C. Watkins and K. Kirby (Wallingford, 1998), 43–52 (47–51).

[48] Housing: Negro Ponzi Mancini, "Dalla fattoria," 484, 493–95. Forest composition and extent: Negro Ponzi Mancini, "Ambiente e risorse alimentari: Dati archeologici," in Negro Ponzi Mancini, *San Michele di Trino*, Vol. II, 549–73 (549–50, 567–68); and R. Caramiello *et al.*, "Analisi paleobotaniche e sedimentologiche," 592–93. Wood use: Nisbet, "I macroresti," 625–27.

[49] For what follows, see L. Gambino, "L'insediamento di Filattiera-Sorano nel quadro delle conoscenze topografiche sulla Lunigiana romana," in Giannichedda, *Filattiera-Sorano*, 238–42 (242), on market strategies; Rottoli and Negri, "I resti vegetali carbonizzati," 198–212 (199–202, with Table 37 for the drastic reduction of chestnut after the sixth century), on woodland composition and selection; R. Giovinazzo, "I reperti faunistici," in Giannichedda, *Filattiera-Sorano*, 196–97, on animal husbandry.

pragmatic, short-range enlistment of the woods' resources relieved pressure on the uplands where the straight-trunked *Abies* grew. It appears the decline and fall of the western Roman empire brought about the rise and verdant recovery of species highly sought after on Roman marketplaces, for huge, tall trees offered less to villagers than they had to Roman architects and shipwrights.

Also in the 400s and 500s *Castanea sativa*, already a dominant species, reached its highest dissemination at Filattiera, before receding along with the people who had favored it for its fruits, but also for its leaves and lumber (in one case, what seems to have been a chestnut plank was incorporated into a wattle wall). The varied agricultural economy of late antique Filattiera, incorporating animal husbandry, especially of pigs and sheep, and forestry, with arable, found in chestnut trees an invaluable bulwark. Spaced, chestnut trees favored the growth of grasses and hence of plump flocks of sheep or herds of cattle. Coppiced, chestnuts could yield marketable hardwood and small-sized lumber. Grafted, chestnuts gave nutritious and tasty nuts in late autumn that supplemented the local diet. No other tree was as generous in so many ways, and as deserving of care. Alas, at the end of the sixth century the inhabitants abandoned their simple settlement, and without its patrons chestnuts lost their privilege in this south Ligurian woodland.

The chronology of occupation at Monte Barro, overlooking Lake Como, is almost identical to Filattiera's, but the *raison d'être* of the settlement has more in common with S. Antonino. The walled site existed between the fifth and sixth centuries for military reasons, and once the Lombard kingdom redesigned the geopolitics of the Po basin, there was no longer any need for Monte Barro's watchful presence on the Alpine routes to Milan.[50] During the century and a half or so when people lived at the site, they took advantage of what woods they found there, using mature chestnut trees to fashion roof beams, walnut and alder to furnish their houses, and beech logs to warm themselves and cook.[51] All the wood was cut down during the dormant season, in winter, when such chopping has the least potential to damage the plant and can in fact stimulate its growth in the following spring. At Monte Barro people cut beeches every ten winters, a coppice cycle capable of rendering stout poles one could cut easily enough to the desired length, and fit into fireplaces. A lot of this wood appears to have ended up in Monte Barro's charcoal pits,

---

[50] G. Brogiolo, "Gli scavi a Monte Barro 1990–1997," in *Archeologia a Monte Barro*, 2 vols., ed. G. Brogiolo and L. Castelletti, Vol. II (Lecco, 2001), 21–102 (87–102).

[51] Castiglioni *et al.*, "I resti archeobotanici," 224–41; L. Castelletti, "L'economia e l'ambiente," in Brogiolo and Castelletti, *Archeologia a Monte Barro*, Vol. II, 219–22.

for archaeologists found beech charcoal in the local forge. Such charcoal has high combustion temperatures and increased reliance on this quality fuel improved smelting and metallurgy; on the other hand, it cannot have been worth the trouble, in a place of abundant wood like Monte Barro, to make charcoal for domestic purposes. Young and manageable beech poles, cut when sap did not course through them, and dense and reliable because they were taken from the north-facing slopes of the hill, were more than adequate for the Monte Barro households.

The locals, who carefully and, as one would put it today, "sustainably," stewarded their wooded resources, favored chestnuts, with olives and walnuts, as one of only three types of tree they introduced to the area. Their chestnut-tending was geared to producing nuts as well as architectural elements: in pantries remarkable both for their poverty in grains and legumes and for their abundant fruit, the Monte Barrans kept significant quantities of chestnuts in the sixth century. The inhabitants were intelligent foresters as well as vigilant soldiers, and by means of their activities they modified the woodland so as to ease people's extraction of nuts, of wood, and, through the munching of sheep, cattle, and pigs, also of fodder.

This survey of archaeologically probed woods in northern Italy proves that the triumph of the "barbaric" forest was much more than a wild "return of nature." In some places (S. Michele) woodland overall fared poorly and lost ground even as Roman civilization faltered. In all the sites discussed here people managed the woods, removing some species and encouraging others until new early medieval ecological equilibria had established themselves. Like most ecological equilibria, those in the post-classical north Italian woods were dynamic, always liable to further transformation. Yet in this naturally unstable context the wily chestnut tree did very well for itself, propagating the species to new places, consolidating and extending control of suitable landscapes, and, wherever it was geologically and climatically possible, forging a solid alliance with late Roman and post-Roman country people. Chestnut succeeded because it was malleable and able to adapt itself to different human needs at a time when access to markets for wood, lumber, fodder, and food faltered, and local supplies of all of these became paramount.

CHESTNUTS AS PROPERTY

By the 800s, the first period for which considerable charter evidence survives from the Lombard plain, chestnuts had already inscribed themselves onto the lowland terrain. Just to the west of Piacenza, "on the Lura torrent," perhaps near today's Agazzano and thus quite low, close to the Po's floor, lay a site called "Castaniola" or "Casteniola" that appeared often in the contracts of the Piacentines. Notaries drew up solemn documents there, and people's baptismal names took on the designation of being "from Casteniola," obviously a place well known and readily recognizable in the ninth century.[52] This is no longer the case, however; modern topographers have located "Castaniola"/"Casteniola" variously, in radically different ecologies. Nevertheless, the presence of the place and its toponym belies the rootedness of the chestnut in the hinterland of Piacenza, a small episcopal city on the right bank of the Po remarkable mainly for the survival of its charters and perhaps for their lay character.[53]

In none of the several charters recording "Castaniola"/"Casteniola" do chestnut trees, woods, nuts, or rents appear, yet it is fairly certain the "farm and locality" got its name from its association with *Castanea sativa*, specifically with the (feminine) nut of the tree, and got it a good deal of time before the earliest charter mentioned it in 842, just as the Carolingian empire was falling apart. By the early 800s (at the latest), chestnuts had the topographical significance needed to become *the* descriptive feature of a territory whose landowners were interested principally in wine and grain.[54]

Since the rest of the landscape around Piacenza had tended to carry the memory of its past owners' names, more than that of their cultivations or of other natural features, the Piacentines' acknowledgement of chestnuts' rootedness in their territory, by way of their toponymic usages, seems to

---

[52] *CLA* 64, ed. C. Mantegna (Zurich, 2003), 22 (80): "in fundo Castaniola"; *CLA* 65, ed. C. Mantegna (Zurich, 2004), 4 (26): "in fundo et loquo nuccopante Casteniola," where "Ioanni de Casteniola" is one of the actors; *CLA* 66, ed. C. Carbonetti Vendittelli (Zurich, 2005), 31 (102), with "Odelbertus de Casteniola"; *CLA* 69, ed. F. De Rubeis (Zurich, 2006), 33 (112): "actum Casteniola." Given the archival history of the charters, their connection to Piacenza, and their consistency in calling the place a "farm and locality," I assume they all refer to a single site. If they do not, my point about chestnuts' dissemination is reinforced.

[53] C. Manaresi (*I placiti del "Regnum Italiae,"* 3 vols., Vol. 1 [Rome, 1955], 338) thought it Castagnola di Ferriere 869 m up on the Aveto stream; Mantegna (*CLA* 65, 72) identified it with a site near Castel S. Giovanni (74 m above sea level) because stretches of a torrent there are called Lora. De Rubeis (*CLA* 69, 58) suggested Vianino (322 m above sea level) in the upper Taro valley. The hamlet Castano (180 m above sea level) on the Luretta (parts of which were called Lurone) could be Castaniola too: see L. Molossi, *Vocabolario topografico dei ducati di Parma, Piacenza, e Guastalla* (Parma, 1834), 196, 199.

[54] G. Petracco Sicardi, "Vico Sahiloni e Silva Arimannorum," *Archivio storico per le province parmensi* 29 (1977), 133–44 (134), found the early 800s a time of great toponymic upheaval around Piacenza because of new ecclesiastical landowning. *I placiti del "Regnum Italiae,"* Vol. III.1, 337 (AD 1034), and *Inventari altomedievali di terre, coloni e redditi,* ed. A. Castagnetti, M. Luzzati, A. Vasina, and G. Pasquali (Rome, 1979), 8.4 (186; AD 975) record more chestnut toponymy near Piacenza. Grain and wine rents: *CLA* 65, 4 (26; AD 842); *CLA* 69, 16 (58; AD 864). *CLA* 64, 22 (80) lists linen, beans, turnips, chicken, eggs, and oxen owed to the lords.

reflect their recognition of chestnuts' at least cultural importance. Sorb trees, wild pears, and apples also marked the land and lent their names, but in a place where field names were mostly people's names the prominence of "Castaniola"/"Casteniola" could suggest this species attained a level of visibility in the early Middle Ages other plants lacked.[55] Much the same could be said of several other Lombard place-names based on the Latin root of chestnut that the charters have preserved. An example is the "village Castaneto" in the very late-ninth-century polyptych of S. Giulia in Brescia, which paid wine, grain, and oil rents but carried in its name the memory of other cultivation. Likewise the memory of chestnut cultivation surfaces in "the little valley called Castaneto of Vilicus" named in one of Charlemagne's earliest Italian diplomas, and the settlement "Casteniade" in the vicinity of Bergamo.[56]

By the time the little chestnut of Piacenza surfaced in the surviving records of agrarian activities, people in the Po valley had been paying attention to chestnuts for some time. The sort of people whose activities are clearest in the charters are, unsurprisingly, the powerful, but it is striking how high the status of the earliest known owners of Lombardy's chestnut woods could soar. In 761 Abbess Ansilperga of S. Salvatore, the great royal nunnery at Brescia, traded a chestnut grove near Lodi with another abbess and her sister (who had married a royal official). This lowland grove (Lodi lies at 80 m above sea level) was on a "domus cultilis," a kind of model farm of the sort aristocrats interested in increasing production on their lands began to create in the 700s.

Other eighth-century chestnut woods in the northern region of the Italian peninsula have excellent social connections, though not quite as exalted: in 762 two wealthy brothers at Cividale divided a chestnut wood between two monastic houses they founded, while in May 774, just as the Lombard realm collapsed under the impetus of Charlemagne's invasion, a royal official (*gasind*) gave various churches in Bergamo much property in the nearby village of Bonate, on the Brembo river, including chestnut groves derived from both his own and his brother's share of the parental inheritance (the brother's opinion of this operation is not known).[57]

---

[55] *CLA* 68, ed. P. Degni (Zurich, 2006), 14: "ubi Pero Spino dicitur"; *CLA* 70, ed. F. De Rubeis (Zurich, 2007), 26: "ubi Sorbastrella dicitur"; 70: "loco Pomario" (near Piazzano). Other field names were owners' names in the genitive, and thus as mutable as landownership. There are no *Castanea* toponyms in the meticulous second-century inscription from Veleia in Piacentine territory (above, 128).

[56] *Inventari* 8.1, 5 (65): "vico Castaneto," now Castegnato near Brescia. In the last years of the Lombard monarchy, there was a "loco Castanieto" near a church of St. Justus of uncertain location: *CDL*, Vol. II, 295 (425). See also *CDLang* 122 (218), 250 (425; Castegnate, near Bergamo); 169 (288; near Varese); *CSMN* 57 (88; Venticolonne, AD 963); 83 (140; near Novara, AD 980).

[57] *CDL*, Vol. II, 155 (80; Ansilperga's "castaneto"); 162 (102; Cividale); 293 (431; "castanetis" at Bonate Sotto).

The attention of the Lombard aristocracy to a type of land use later linked to backwards, backwoods, low-status people may have to do with their interest in "diversifying" assets during a time when self-sufficiency usually outweighed the market. It certainly means that owning chestnuts was a normal part of the agricultural strategies of both lay people and members of the clergy who could make choices, from the highest echelons of north Italian society (Ansilperga, a king's daughter, was one of the most powerful people in the peninsula[58]) to the humbler ranks of the aristocracy. In addition, since the royal *gasind* Taido came from a lineage that for at least two generations had included chestnut groves at Bonate in its wide portfolio of economic assets, lay aristocratic control of chestnut woods goes back in time to at least the middle of the eighth century, and this in localities that seem today unsuited to such cultivation.

Later, when the records improve and allow a less socially myopic view of chestnut woods and their management, there were other kinds of owners. Though even for the ninth century we know most about the churches and monasteries through which the documents were saved from oblivion, still the charters these institutions preserved cast around some revealing glimmers of light. For instance, the Ursus, who obtained a long-term contract for several farms in Piacenza's hinterland in 827, was a layman of middling status. It mattered to him that "chestnut groves" ("castaneta") on these farms receive detailed listing – their origin in the inheritance of the landowner Gualfred was worth noting in order to forestall later disputes from Gualfred's brothers.[59] Likewise Andreverga, who sold some chestnut woods near Moneglie to Gheillone in the opening decades of the 800s, was not of exalted rank.[60] There are other chestnut owners in the 800s who did not come from Lombard society's upper tiers, either: merchants, notaries, mint masters, and judges, who, while privileged, were not necessarily insiders of Carolingian power structures.[61]

Sometimes, even in the lordly documents, we find peasants exercising rights over chestnut woods too. In the Apennines between the Ligurian Sea and the Po river the great monastery of Bobbio created a veritable chestnut empire for itself by the ninth century, when its inventories were drawn up, and allow an estimate of the monastic holdings.[62] Within these

---

[58] S. Wemple, "S. Salvatore/S. Giulia: A Case Study in the Endowment and Patronage of a Major Female Monastery in Northern Italy," in *Women of the Medieval World*, ed. J. Kirsher and S. Wemple (London, 1985), 85–102 (86–89).

[59] *CLA* 64, 10 (44).   [60] *CDB* 42 (163).

[61] *CDLang* 87 (163 and 333 [560] have "negotiator" grove-owners; 120 [216] mentions a "notarius"; in 331 [556] a "monetarius" sells a grove). More ordinary people are in 84 (158); 358 (594).

[62] M. Richter, *Bobbio in the Early Middle Ages* (Dublin, 2008), 132–37.

specialized documents, individual peasants and collectivities of cultivators appear, holding rights over the chestnut trees and their nuts, or anyway limiting the rights of the monks.[63] Carolingian and post-Carolingian Bobbio enjoyed considerable holdings in chestnut woods on both sides of the Apennine watershed the monastery straddled, some at quite high elevations (at S. Stefano d'Avete, for instance) and some at low ones (Ancarano), and extracted tons of chestnuts from them through a variety of agreements with the locals, some of whom were serfs and some free renters ("libellarii").

As this last example indicates, what remains of early medieval archives in fact reveals ecclesiastical chestnut management best. The documents from before 1000 show that even major landlords like imperial abbeys drew nuts from their holdings, becoming consumers of *Castanea sativa*'s bounty, unlike later owners who left this food to the masses.[64] Long years of experience with this cultivation meant Bobbio's ninth-century monks understood the vagaries of seasonal production: their polyptych of c. 900 claimed that the manor at Soriasco, west of Piacenza on the Versa, could gather ten modia of chestnuts and acorns "in good seasons," a phrase that shows the monastic community had had time to get used to the ups and downs in chestnuts' productivity.[65] Bobbio had varied enough holdings in different enough situations that the abbey's granary could expect relatively stable remittances and thus a reliable and calculable quantity of chestnuts for the monks' table. From the point of view of the monastic administrator worried about regular feeding of a large community, this would have been a considerable asset, a way of tempering nature's fickleness.

Similar concerns for regularity in supplies and ease of use for consumers whose spiritual activities ought not to be interrupted show through in the very late-ninth-century polyptych of the Brescian Abbey of S. Giulia, formerly Abbess Ansilperga's S. Salvatore. The free and unfree peasants who owed S. Giulia chestnuts in their rents all lived within a (long) day's walk from the city, though in unalike environmental conditions: some lived in plains, some on the edge of river valleys, and some on ridges above lakes. Only the serfs of Canelle Secco near Erbusco had to contribute "a modium of pared chestnuts," perhaps because these nuts' quality was considered finest and they were intended for the sisters' own table. In an inventory claiming 81 modia (over 4,000 kg) of nuts each year for the nuns, including 12 from the high Sabine hills that the nunnery must have sold if indeed they exacted them at all ("from the

---

[63] *Inventari* 8.1, where the "castanetum" at Caregli above Rapallo (130) produces a rent "shared" by the monks that in 852 was twice what it became the following year, according to 8.2 (151).
[64] Menant, *Campagnes lombardes*, 215–16. [65] *Inventari* 8.3 (170).

chestnut wood where they are able to gather 12 modia" is a possibilistic and indefinite formulation), this single measure, about 50 kg, of shelled and peeled nuts stands apart.[66] If considerations of chestnut quality explain why the nunnery required Canelle Seecan nuts prepared and dried, it is feasible that the other chestnuts, whose processing was not spelled out as an obligation of the cultivators, followed different, more commercial routes to Lombard consumers' tables.[67]

The monastic landowners of northern Italy, who ran veritable agricultural empires with outposts in every corner of the early medieval Po valley, shipped their produce to the abbey, as well as to warehouses in the plain's cities.[68] We have already seen it is quite likely that the great monastic chestnut magnates introduced some of their surplus nuts into circuits of exchange rather than consume them within the monastic enclosure. One of Bobbio's polyptychs from the second half of the ninth century hints at the monks' involvement in the transshipment of chestnuts from the port of Genoa. Though the evidence is not conclusive, it is suggestive: Bobbio's accountants noted that Bobbio's dependency of St. Peter's in Genoa "could collect 10 modia [about 90 kg] of chestnuts per year" for Bobbio, and added that "for the brothers' use" several commodities were purchased in Genoa and brought to the monastery, listing figs, citrons, salt, and fish sauce among the comestibles, plus pitch.[69] This association of chestnut dues and the acquisition of expensive and highly prized foods in the port city could be a clue to the ultimate fate of some, at least, of a great landowner's surplus nuts. Dried, husked, and peeled, chestnuts became the light, unspoilable, highly calorific and popular product with which the early medieval merchant dreamed of filling his hull.

Transportability distinguished the (processed) fruit of the tree *Castanea sativa* from its other main product, wood. Though monastic communities could develop an obsessive interest in wood supplies, the unwieldiness of this commodity meant that it did not circulate far from its place of origin.[70] Reduced to charcoal it was more manageable, but the cost of

---

[66] On early medieval measures: Montanari, *L'alimentazione contadina*, 167–69.

[67] *Inventari* 5 (56; "castaneas mundas modium I"). Iseo (57–58) had serfs and free rent-payers; Nuvolera (60), Nuvolento (67), and "Cervinica" (Serníga?) also paid chestnuts. "Sextuna" lay near Antrodoco (94).

[68] R. Balzaretti, "Cities, Emporia and Monasteries: Local Economies in the Po Valley, *c.* 700–875," in *Towns in Transition*, ed. N. Christie and S. Loseby (Aldershot, 1996), 213–34; Menant, *Campagnes lombardes*, 290–93.

[69] *Inventari* 8.1 (131–32). McCormick, *Origins*, 633–36, sees this document as evidence of Tyrrhenian trade.

[70] *Inventari* 5 (60) shows that cartloads of wood ("ligna carradas") were distinct from bundles of firewood ("facellas") at Nuvolera, where S. Giulia owned chestnut woods that may have produced wood, along with nuts. Santa Maria Theodote in Pavia three times confirmed its right to wood and charcoal pits in fiscal woodland during the 800s – *CDLang* 119 (215); 192 (856); 305 (517) – the

this transformation kept it out of the reach of people's fireplaces: charcoal tended to be reserved for industrial hearths and kilns. Where the owner of a chestnut grove specified that it grew next to a vineyard, and where the owner signaled the interdependence of chestnut trees and vines by listing them together in charters, we can divine a grove managed as coppice, on relatively brief rotations, with pole-cutting as often as the vineyard needed it. But such vine supports must have stayed close to the places where they grew, seldom circulating widely as commercial items.[71] In sum, the inventories and charters depict chestnuts as the primary benefit deriving from ownership and management of woods of *Castanea sativa*.

Punctilious monastic accounting was alas not universally applied in the ninth century. The famous court case of Ričana in Istria of 804 is an eloquent sign both that the new Frankish regime introduced new relations between cultivators and rulers, and of the strangely lackadaisical arrangements for exacting chestnut rents that could prevail in the ninth century. The document records the complaint lodged by the Istrians against Duke John and his men, and their local helpers, the clergy of the patriarchate of Grado. Duke and company were accused of "violence," or of careless disregard for the niceties in the agrarian pacts to which the Istrians were accustomed. The dispute had to be settled by Charlemagne's agents ("missi"), who struggled to reconstruct just what regular payments *were*, according to Istrian custom, and what were violent and novel impositions. In this sensitive situation, where precision was paramount and obligations had to be listed once and for all, accurately, the more than 200 serfs ("coloni") of the "public fisc" at Novigrad accepted that when the season was clement they owed "more than" 100 modia of grain and 200 amphorae of wine, but a vague "sufficiency" of "alnona or chestnuts." As rights of access to woods were at stake, and the Istrians' plea revolved around a return to the former gathering rights and payments to the patriarchate for woodland products, the unwillingness to stipulate a fixed quantity of chestnuts due from Novigrad, or a proportional share, means that chestnuts were not a resource comparable with grain or wine in importance, and perhaps in antiquity as well. What was sufficient was open to several interpretations, and the Carolingian ruler had proved his interpretation tended to be exploitative, yet the judges, Duke John, the

latter granting "quando necessitas imminet navem illius per Padi et Ticini portua ... discurrere liceat," a sign of how difficult wood haulage was even in the low, flat parts of the valley.
71 There were many pole-producing woods ("stalareis," from "hastalareis"), but species was unspecified. Vineyards linked to chestnut trees or woods appear in *CDLang* 358 (595; Pettenasco, on Lake Orta, AD 892); 598 (1000; Capriate d'Adda, AD 948); 679 (1179; Campione, on Lake Lugano, AD 963); 964 (1697; Gallarate, AD 999).

patriarch, and the Istrian cultivators accepted the need for annual negotiations on the meaning of "sufficient chestnuts" because no one expected these to be acrimonious. The value of chestnuts was not high enough, for chestnuts were not a commercial asset here and "sufficient" chestnuts were likely to be those the duke's household could consume, just as the duke exacted fish "for his table up to the point of satiety."[72]

Istria is at the very easternmost edge of the Po valley region, but its testimony is valuable because of its indefiniteness: chestnuts were not vital there in the early 800s. More precision regarding chestnut rents, and hence presumably more economic weight for them, emerges in the bishops of Novara's listing of privileges and immunities conceded by Italy's Carolingian rulers, squarely in the heart of the Po River valley. The earliest to survive dates from 854, but in it Louis II claims to have been moved to make his grant by the documents, signed by his ancestors Louis the Pious and Lothar, that Bishop Dodo presented.[73] Thus, the concession of all royal rights to "wine, cheese, chickens, eggs, chestnuts, and fruits of the harvest ..." derived from the early 800s. The concession implies that around Novara chestnuts were a significant enough product that they were worth recording next to wine, sown crops, and dairy products. In other terms, at the beginning of the ninth century Novaran chestnuts were a known entity, had a calculable value, and should be treated exactly like any other basic agricultural product, taxed by kings and bishops.

The treatment of chestnuts further south, on the Adriatic, was necessarily different. Yet in the flat, coastal areas where urban settlement had clustered since ancient times, chestnuts from the hills offered a means for "vertical" integration of geographically distinct economies. The evidence suggests that even in unlikely places, where no respectable chestnut tree would grow on its own, the fruit of *Castanea sativa* had made inroads. Near Faenza, where the archbishops of Ravenna owned much land after the seventh century,[74] no chestnuts appear in the rather formulaic description

---

[72] *I placiti del "Regnum Italiae,"* Vol. 1, 17 (53) records that "in Nova Civitate habet fischo publico" where "alnonas seu castaneas sufficienter" were paid, and where the fishery was worth fifty solidi per year to the duke, "absque sua mensa ad satietatem." H. Krahwinkler, *Friaul im Frühmittelalter* (Vienna, 1992), 206 suggests, "annona" for the weird "alnona." "Annona" were the victuals landlords owed serfs during their days of corvée (M. Montanari, *Contadini e città fra "Langobardia" e "Romania"* [Florence, 1988], 55–56), but in Byzantine territory these are unrecorded. Slightly more convincing is A. Guillou's suggestion (*Régionalisme et indépendence dans l'empire byzantin au VII siècle* [Rome, 1969], 297) that the term refers to the catkins of alder (in Latin *Alnus*), nutritious enough, but little used, as far as I can tell.

[73] *Ludovici II. diplomata,* ed. K. Wanner, MGH, Diplomata karolinorum (Munich, 1994), 14 (92), confirmed in 905 by Louis III (*CSMN* 25 [37]).

[74] G. Fasoli, "Il patrimonio della chiesa ravennate," in *Storia di Ravenna,* 5 vols., ed. G. Susini, Vol. II.1 (Venice, 1991), 389–400 (397–98).

of a farm Ursus, plus his wife and daughter, rented for twenty-nine years in 890. This was obviously a substantial and diverse holding. For it Ursus would pay rent in three types of grain, two different beans, wine, linen, and various other products. There were also woods on the premises, for the use of which the renters promised to hand over one chicken, a measure of "manoelictile" grain, and a modium of "cleaned chestnuts," all at the beginning of September.[75] At a time of year when chestnuts are immature, such a payment obligated Ursus and his family to keep a supply of dried and processed nuts from the previous autumn, or to procure such a product by buying it. Regardless, this unseasonable demand, associated with other symbolic offerings like one chicken and hand-selected grain, suggests that to the archbishops of Ravenna chestnuts were a delicacy, and one their pantry should not forgo. In the Apennines where Ursus toiled the situation was probably quite different. There the late autumn operations of gathering, drying, husking, and "cleaning" chestnuts were all too familiar and produced a staple, not a luxury.

Just over four years later, a large group of related women and men agreed to another twenty-nine-year pact with the Ravennan archbishopric. The farm they obtained seems to have lain near Modigliana above Forlì, at an elevation of about 500 m. It included many different types of cultivation so the contract stipulated complex arrangements for paying rent in kind. From a chestnut cultivator's point of view this contract was sensible, as rent in the nuts was due at the beginning of December, when the harvest was fresh. The archbishop made sure all "fruitful trees" on the estate were protected from cutting, and described the "chestnut woods of different kinds and ... everything pertaining to them" among the assets he let out. His scrupulous distinction between groves shows a well-developed arboricultural sensibility and awareness of the value of different cultivars of chestnut on the "Puellano" farm.

The extended family that undertook to cultivate and improve the estate accepted the obligation to bring the grain and wine they produced to their landlord's farm at S. Adriano, an arduous trek across the Tramazzo and della Valle torrents from their lands.

Among the symbolic gifts they owed were some chickens and grain, and a substantial amount (7 modia, or about 63 kg) of "fruits of the chestnut groves." But whereas the other gifts went with the rent proper to S. Adriano, "carried there by us the coloni named above," the peasants agreed to bring the chestnuts to "your archiepiscopal residence" in

---

[75] *CLA* 54, ed. G. Rabotti and F. Santoni (Zurich, 2000), 10 (73; "castanea studita").

Ravenna, almost 60 km away. In this case the fresh nuts were an especially desirable product, worthy of the archbishops' pantry.[76]

Thus, at the end of the ninth century, at the eastern end of the Po valley, in the drier lowlands where chestnut trees were not so common, the highest elite sought to secure their share of the hills' nuts for domestic consumption. The downhill movement of chestnuts, from the places where their trees grew to the places where archbishops lived, actually marked a social ascent. The peasants, who inhabited the hills and who tended and, presumably, had created the groves generations earlier with many different cultivars in them to enhance productivity and elude some of the risks of monoculture, demonstrated an astute understanding of arboriculture and the needs of *Castanea sativa*. By the ninth century equally astute and much more powerful landlords had caught on to the pleasures and advantages of living with chestnuts.

Throughout the Po valley, the tenth century was a bustling time. Quite aside from the breathtaking high political vicissitudes of the period, and the great social reorganization we now call "incastellamento," this was also a century of very diligent writers and archivists. Hence the last century assigned to the early Middle Ages in most chronologies is also the best documented for rural history. It is striking, however, that the hundreds of charters that survive from places like Verona, Piacenza, Novara, Bergamo, Brescia, and Ravenna, among others, do not trace in a new world, in castaneological terms, whatever they may teach us about the innovative doings of kings, or the unprecedented consolidation of lordship, and the subjection of rural people. The elite interest in controlling chestnut groves and acquiring chestnuts that is visible in the eighth and ninth centuries persisted. Careful management of the chestnut woodlands continued. Thanks to human labor, chestnuts grew in various and sometimes unlikely places, including low, flat, and watery ones. In sum, the evidence becomes richer but does not alter the picture of the chestnut in placid symbiosis with north Italian society.

Continuity is neatly discernible in toponymy. Tenth-century charters recording property in remote byways of the Po valley contain many references to places where chestnuts had come to designate the territory.[77]

---

[76] *Ibid.*, 19 (121). The "pomas de castanietis" echo the Lombard legal conception of pears, apples, walnuts, and chestnuts as the same (see n. 31 above). The specification that the land came "cum castanietis diversisque generibus vel cum omnibus eisdem pertinentibus" is unusual in this region, but not that the rent be "deductum per nos suprascriptis colonis." See *Le carte ravennati del decimo secolo: Archivio arcivescovile*, 3 vols., ed. R. Benericetti, Vol. III: *Aa. 976–999* (Imola, 2002), 239 (123) and 242 (132) for indications in the late 900s that chestnuts were still considered "pomas."

[77] *Codice diplomatico veronese del periodo dei re d'Italia*, ed. V. Fainelli (Venice, 1963), 211 (298; near Verona, AD 931); *Breviarium ecclesiae ravennatis*, ed. G. Rabotti (Rome, 1985), II.15 (160; south of Rimini, AD 949), III.9 (196; near Osimo, AD 980); *I placiti del "Regnum Italiae*," Vol. II.1, 252 (433;

Yet this situation was anything but new, as we saw above. Chestnuts had etched themselves and their Latin name deep onto the surface of the land before the tenth century, and indeed must have begun to do so even earlier than the time when the charter evidence begins to allow us to perceive the process. The number of chestnut toponyms that can be evinced from the charters of the 900s is greater than before, perhaps, but only in proportion to the far greater number of charters that survive from that time.

Moreover, many of the same agents (and meticulous archivists) who made possible some reconstruction of *Castanea sativa*'s incidence in eighth- and ninth-century northern Italy remained zealous stewards of the tree in the 900s. Bobbio's late-tenth-century polyptych, though less detailed than earlier ones, shows the monks managing chestnut woods on a grand scale.[78] In this document Bobbio's chestnut groves, most of them overlooking the Ligurian Sea in this accounting, were rented for returns in nuts to male and female farmers. Another Ligurian abbey, the Benedictine house on the sea's shore dedicated to St. Fructuosus, went to court in 994 to secure exclusive access to "a wood that is called Dema" that extended all the way down to the Ligurian Sea and was crossed by streams.[79] By the close of the tenth century a wood as open to logging as this one required the local marquis' special protection lest someone unlicensed should "dare to enter to pasture, or cut a tree, or remove chestnuts or other crops." From its fabulous ban of 2,000 gold coins we might legitimately conclude the mixed woodland at Dema derived special worth from its exceptional geographical and ecological situation, from its location close to waterways that made its combustible, buildable, and edible products relatively easy to remove. But chestnut trees had value in less favorable circumstances too.

In much less precipitous topography, in the lowlands east of Pavia, the nuns of S. Cristina at Corteolona owned and exploited several specialized chestnut groves, some of which produced rents in kind while others were expected to convert their nuts into other resources more congenial to

---

"loco ubi dicitur Castaneto sico," near Cremona, AD 999), Vol. II.2, 306 (616; Castagnaira, near Pavia, AD 1021), Vol. IX (671; between Bologna and Modena, AD 969); *I diplomi di Berengario I*, ed. L. Schiaparelli (Rome, 1903), 74 (205; near Cremona, AD 910); *CSMN* 57 (88; near Vigevano), 83 (140; near Novara); *CDLang* 437 (755; near Varese), 676 (1174; Cremona), 684 (1189; Melzo, near Milan), 853 (1502; Cremona), 884 (1565; Baranzate), 965 (1701; Milan); *Le carte del decimo secolo nell'archivio arcivescovile di Ravenna, 900–957*, ed. R. Benericetti (Ravenna, 1999), 64 (148) and 67 (155), both in the Montefeltro.

[78] "Castaneta" around Casarza, Moneglia, Lavagna, and Borzonasca: *Inventari* 8.4 (189–91).

[79] *I placiti del "Regnum Italiae,"* Vol. II.1, 219 (306–07; "silva que dicitur Dema"), wherein "nullus quislibet homo infra iamdicta pecia de silva audeat introire ad pascoandum nec arborem incidendum nec castanea nec alia fruges exinde tollendum."

S. Cristina.[80] In the late 900s one of the nunnery's chestnut groves near Brione was old and traditional enough to be known as the "chestnut grove of S. Cristina" – on the verge of becoming a place-name, already a recognized boundary feature. Meanwhile, in 938, Peter, a merchant of Milan, had acquired two chestnut groves around Trivolzio, in the territory of Pavia, from Ragifred and his mother Ingeltrude, plus two other groves connected with a watermill there from Ragifred alone.[81] Other laypeople, like King Berengar's "fidelis" Berctelo, or the noble Mainfred, also owned groves in the tenth century, recompenses for services rendered to Italy's rulers.[82] Among the latter, in March, 950, just months before being widowed, Adelheid received from her royal husband Lothar confirmation of rights over family property in the highland area between Modena and Bologna, including chestnut woods.[83] Clearly the family of Arialdus, who built up a chestnut fortune at Cucciago, were not alone in divining the usefulness of chestnut trees.

As in the earlier period, for the tenth century the vast majority of known owners of chestnut woods in northern Italy were clerical. In the Lombard lowlands bishops were particularly active traders in such woods, and the surviving archives give the impression the monastery of St. Ambrose in Milan held a chestnut empire in the 900s, much of it in flat and low-lying places later used as arable.[84] Abbots and clerics in Ravenna, too, carefully stewarded their chestnut resources during the tenth century. For people who dwelled in this flat and almost coastal city, "dried and properly peeled" chestnuts were a special treat in the 900s to be distinguished from ordinary rents in grains and legumes, or wine, and to be delivered to the monasteries or residences of the clergy by the peasants who gathered them.[85] Such deliveries were unnecessary for landlords who had ships and carts and dependants to bring harvested food into their warehouses, but reinforced personal ties between lords and cultivators.[86] They were especially effective in this regard because the most intimate site of the lord's superiority, his domestic table, was directly furnished by the meticulous and elaborate preparations of his dependent cultivators who lived in the hills west of the city. In this exchange, chestnuts were a delicacy whose importance derived from a certain exoticness

---

[80] *Inventari* 4 (32–38) records "castaneta" near Brione, near Menaggio, at Devio, and Bellagio on Lake Como.

[81] *I placiti del "Regnum Italiae,"* Vol. 1, 139 (522–24).

[82] *I diplomi di Berengario I* 127 (332); *I diplomi di Ugo e di Lotario di Berengario II e di Adalberto,* ed. L. Schiaparelli (Rome, 1924), 8 (269).

[83] *I diplomi di Ugo* 14 (283). [84] *CDLang* 405 (684), 446 (770), 451 (775).

[85] For example, "… castanea siccas et bene studitas …": *Le carte del decimo secolo* 39 (90).

[86] See *Le carte ravennati del decimo secolo,* Vol. II: *Aa. 957–976* (Imola, 2002), 147 (162), for "carras dominica"; and *Le carte del decimo secolo* 28 (66) for the archbishops'"navem dominicam."

in the dominant city of an area where very few chestnut groves are recorded, and where chestnuts did not play a commercial role, remaining for the most part the prerogative of the upland peasants who tended the trees.[87]

Though the bishopric of Bergamo was probably the owner of a bigger chestnut estate throughout the period, the see of Novara's tenth-century landholding was extensive in every sense of the term, and included fiscal rights over local chestnuts thanks to a concession from the Carolingian rulers of the peninsula. In the 900s the Novarese church controlled chestnut groves of more than one kind. At Oleggio on the southern edge of the modern Canton Ticino they owned "woods of chestnut" that had their own names.[88] One of these "is known as the fledgling wood" and was contiguous to two others that instead seem to have been mature stands. There were also chestnut cultivations of lesser consequence at Oleggio, where a fairly large "field having on it twelve chestnut trees and one walnut" was known as "at Briolo."[89] Across the river, around Arnate, in 976 the bishops acquired three more chestnut woods that received the designation "bearing," probably because of their age and fruitfulness.[90] In addition, through pious donations made to St. Protasius' parish by local layfolk, the bishopric also indirectly controlled various "chestnut woods" in the Val d'Ossola, a good 100 km to the north of Novara.[91] Thus, the complex machinery of episcopal administration in the 900s kept track of chestnut groves in different ecologies, purchasing some, gaining others through the generosity of the faithful, but always remaining mindful of the distinction between young and fruit-bearing trees able to contribute to the bishops' wealth, and between densely planted and sparser woodland.

Notarial practices of the tenth century perpetuated the Lombard distinction between chestnut grove ("castanetum") and chestnut wood ("silva castana" or "castanea"). In practice there does not appear to have been much difference, and the charters of the time occasionally mix the two into "chestnut grove woodland" ("silvis castanetis"). Thus, there does not transpire any "progress" from less to more intensively managed, or closely spaced, chestnut woodland over time, implying that the systems of cultivation visible in the earliest charters before 800 were already fully

---

[87] *Le carte ravennati del decimo secolo,* Vol. III, 239 (123) and 242 (132) reveal ecclesiastical landlords' slight interest for the "poma" their farms produced (dried figs and chestnuts were the exceptions).

[88] *CSMN* 73 (120): "silva castanea dicitur ad Sortexelle … silva dicitur silva longa … silva castanea dicitur novelljna …" See also Montanari, *L'alimentazione contadina,* 41–42.

[89] *CSMN* 97 (163). Given the field's size (4,300 m², as opposed to the 2,500 m² of all the chestnut groves), this was definitely an "open" wood quite like the "savanna" Rackham champions.

[90] *Ibid.* 81 (136): "silvas castaneas portatorias."   [91] *Ibid.* 117 (196), 120 (200–01).

developed and remained stable. The appearance in the tenth-century documents of more "bearing" or "gathering" woods than occurred in earlier contracts is connected to the rising number of surviving documents rather than to a new interest in chestnut crops, as opposed to wood production.[92]

A handful of tenth-century contracts permit some reconstruction of tree-spacing and woodland density. Although the surface measures are difficult to pin down accurately, the landowners who specified how many "iugium" or "tabulas" of land they were buying or selling, and numbered the chestnut trees thereon, help us in the effort of recreating the landscape. In December of 955 the widow Maria sold for two silver coins "two bearing chestnut trees" at Gazzaniga, northwest of Bergamo in the Valle Seriana, set on about 250 m² of land, a tiny parcel that did not merit the label "grove" or "wood." Neither did the larger holding on the middle Adda river of some 16,000 m² "on which there are eleven chestnut trees" in 949, obviously with a lot of living space for each tree, nor the more reasonably spaced *c.* 9,000 m² of "land with twenty chestnut trees on it" near Bergamo in 909. So it is odd to find "chestnut woods" of only some 2,500 m² with two-and-a-half chestnuts exchanged for a female slave at Lallio (around Bergamo) in the last decade of the first millennium: what constituted a chestnut wood was elastic, dependent as much on the other types of land use on the plot as on the growth of *Castanea* trees. In light of this we should be careful about assuming tall, dense, umbrageous stands of chestnut trees grew wherever the landowners noted the presence of a chestnut wood in the Po region.[93]

Diligent accounting of even a few trees on a plot, of land does, however, attest to the high value tenth-century owners placed on chestnuts. The trees' presence on the land enhanced its worth and was recorded accordingly. The Lallio charter is the only one I know where a chestnut tree was divided, but the mere possibility of such division is another clue: Lombard society considered chestnut trees precious property worth not just numbering minutely, but even splitting into fractions (in effect this meant sharing a tree's fruit and perhaps wood at harvest time, rather than segmenting the hapless tree). The same charters that betray the high worth of chestnut trees also suggest that in legal theory at least it was

---

[92] See Menant, *Campagnes lombardes*, 214. Menant found more arboricultural precision in the twelfth–thirteenth-century documents and interpreted this as an evolution. See *CDLang* for "castanetis" (430 [742]), "silvis castaneis" (435 [750]), "silva castana colectoria" (542 [925]), as well as "silvis castanetis" (464 [801]). The phrase "castaneta portatorica et alia silvata quod est aminiculalaria" (471 [815]) divides "bearing" from "wooded" groves that are coppiced ("aminicula" were poles).

[93] *CDLang* 612 (1046; Gazzaniga); 590 (1009; Adda); 433 (747; "Sporciadicia" around Bergamo); 857 (1512; Lallio).

possible to acquire the land where a chestnut wood grew without the trees above it. In practice this was not done, yet there can be little doubt about the implication of the common north Italian formula whereby owners bequeathed their chestnut woods "with the ground the wood is on" or the land "with the chestnut trees it has on it."[94] The implication remained unactualized, as far as the charters show, but the potential to separate ownership of the trees from ownership of the soil whence the trees arose can only mean that the trees were considered a special kind of asset. Chestnuts' ability to produce food, fuel, pasture, and exploitable undergrowth, all with little human effort, justified the notarial formula. Arable lands without chestnuts, or vineyards, were utterly different assets that required a wholly different investment of labor.

Overall, the period between roughly 750 and 1000 illuminated by the surviving charters emerges as a time of consolidating aristocratic property rights over a resource that had first come into its own during the Dark Ages. What may have begun the post-classical age as a marginal form of vegetation in the Po valley, remote and wild, became in the latter part of the first millennium an esteemed type of land use and cultivation. Chestnut trees crowded into veritable woods, scattered from the high hills to the more surprising low plain quite close to the Po river. People of diverse social extraction owned and managed them, both for wood and especially for the food the chestnuts offered. If chestnuts had once been the subsistence of hardscrabble villages, by the time the charters begin they were both valuable and valued commodities, sometimes inserted into trade networks. Once again the versatility of *Castanea sativa* had become utility for people as both, together, adjusted to early medieval life in the Po region.

PIRATING THE CHESTNUT

Thietmar, the bishop of the Saxon frontier outpost Merseburg, was a chronicler whose concern with Italian affairs depended on whether they generated any repercussions in the eastern German provinces where he lived and served his distant relatives, the emperors. Writing in the second decade of the eleventh century the learned historian preferred to focus on things close to home, but the interests of his Ottonian patrons sometimes led him to cast his historiographical gaze onto the peninsula. Thanks to this connection, Thietmar preserved for us, and perhaps flavored, a story set in the Ligurian Sea and that centered on the ancient Roman port city

---

[94] For example, *CDLang* 539 (919): "terra cum arboris castaneis super se abente"; 573 (978): "silva castena cum area in qua extat pecia una."

of Luni.[95] The bishop's story evokes several of the themes of this chapter and is therefore an apt way to conclude it.

According to Thietmar, during the pontificate of Pope Benedict VIII (1012–24) Islamic raiding attained unexpected levels of success in Liguria. Luni and its circumventing region fell in an incursion to a nameless "Saracen king," likely Mujahid ibn Abdullah (d. 1044), and was ruled by him "with strength and security" until the pope organized resistance and sent a huge armada to oust the usurper.[96] At first the pirate-king was indignant and wanted to stand and fight, but prudence prevailed (though Thietmar did not call it that) and in the nick of time Mujahid withdrew what troops he could to Sardinia. Still, the bulk of the Islamic force on the mainland was routed before it could make its way to that island; it was a massive defeat from which none escaped alive. Even the pirate-queen and Mujahid's vast treasure fell into the hands of the papal force (the transmission of a share of it to Thietmar's patron Henry II may explain why a bishop of Merseburg reported these events).

The defeat so disturbed the Islamic leader that he did something strange: he had "a sack of chestnuts" delivered to Pope Benedict along with a dire warning that during the next sailing season he would return to Liguria with as many fighters as there were nuts in the sack. Unfazed, the pontiff replied with a sack of his own, this one filled with millet, accompanied by the message that if Mujahid wanted another drubbing, he should indeed return next summer, confident that as many soldiers as there were grains of millet in the sack would be waiting for him to deliver it.

The conclusion that Thietmar wanted readers to draw from this episode of diplomatic derring-do was that humans have little control over outcomes on earth, except through Christian prayer. The pious, who in this case carried home much loot chanting odes of thanks to God, should earnestly pray God to avert the plague of Islamic piracy and grant "the security of peace." Audacious pirates would find themselves bested by well-directed pious supplications, but Thietmar also suggested through his account that a vigorous and decisive papacy could be an agent of such peace in this part of the Ottonian empire. Pope Benedict VIII's triumphs of arms and wit were divinely inspired, as was a geopolitical situation in which Italy and the Holy Roman empire were free of Islamic control.

Scholars of medieval chestnuts, however, should probably draw other conclusions from Thietmar's vignette. In it is visible, first of all, the

---

[95] Thietmar of Merseburg, *Chronicon*, ed. R. Holtzmann, *MGH Scriptores rerum Germanicarum* 9 (Berlin, 1935), 7.45 (453–54).
[96] On the identity of the "rex Saracenus": M. Amari, *Storia dei musulmani di Sicilia*, 3 vols., Vol. III.1 (Florence, 1868), 4–9.

normalization of chestnuts in north Italian high culture, their becoming an idiom even the "other" could speak. The chestnuts of the *Chronicon* were a message everyone understood, including aristocratic Saxon bishops and their audience. They were so humdrum and comprehensible that in Thietmar's narration they fit neatly between standard calamities such as sudden destructive tempests (7.44) and shipwrecks on Lake Constance (7.46) in a seamless flow of noteworthy events of the early eleventh century that Thietmar knew about from experience.

If Thietmar's story about the sack of chestnuts reveals the cultural currency of chestnuts in northern Italy, the *Chronicon* also indicates what the fruits of (fleeting) dominion in Liguria might be in the years around 1000. Mujahid lost an immense treasure in gold if 1,000 lb worth of it was the emperor's cut as gauged by the victorious pope, so chestnuts were not the only resource an exploitative Saracen leader might extract from the north Italian coastlands. But if chestnuts in sacks were what one might hope to get from the locals, they are significant proxies of economic life. To send a gift of chestnuts from Luni was a demonstration of dominion over local resources, as well as a claim of mastery over the Lunigiana itself. In this corner of Italy's north, around the year 1000, chestnuts were the available agricultural surplus, and therefore what the powerful vied for.

But the sack of nuts Mujahid sent to Rome is the bearer of other meanings too. The battle between papal and Islamic forces took place in summer, in June, 1016, according to Thietmar's chronology. Readers therefore knew the nuts in question were not fresh, but the dried and skinned produce of the previous autumn, reduced in bulk and so able to pack more semiotic punch into their sack. Thietmar's admonitory chestnuts thus remind us of early medieval proficiency in the elaboration of this raw agricultural material into a stable, conservable, and commercially viable product. Without the early medieval transformation of both the landscape to produce the nuts and the technologies for their preservation, the anecdote told by Thietmar is unimaginable.

The *Chronicon* implies that any provident pirate would stash at least one sack of chestnuts on board a ship fleeing Luni, and at the very least to a Saxon bishop sacks of preserved chestnuts were a likely Mediterranean cargo. For if chestnuts were Ligurians' subsistence crop they were also a seafarer's bounty in this story, linked to sailing and trade. Indeed, the bishop of Merseburg's literary chestnuts were first and foremost mobile and maritime, removed from their origin in stodgy peasant self-sufficiency. And, actually, dried chestnuts *would* have been a useful load to eleventh-century Tyrrhenian sailors, even if they did not intend to correspond with popes, for they were an easy-to-handle commodity, and one desired everywhere a ship was likely to go. Properly deciphered, then, the chestnuts of the "Saracen king" signaled his maritime prowess, commercial contacts, and frequentation of faraway markets, and thus were a warning regardless of their number.[97]

Thus, around 1000, at the time Arialdus' family chestnut groves at Cucciago were mature, nut-bearing economic assets able to underpin the ambitions of a lineage, in northern Italy *Castanea sativa* had effected a transformation of itself. The multifarious nature of the chestnut made this possible: it had an uncanny capacity to produce excellent food, which, appropriately processed, kept for months without asking its eaters to work over-hard. It could foster pastures where herds found nourishment in spring, it might sprout leaves palatable to ruminants in the meager summer season, and it supplied high-quality wood usable in fields and in people's houses. The combination of talents, rather than just one quality, raised the chestnut to unexpected pre-eminence in early medieval northern Italy.[98] A plant that came into its own in the region along with Christianity, in late antiquity, and that clearly had fit in very well with peasant subsistence strategies of the Dark Ages, soon and maybe ineluctably also became an asset in the landholding portfolios of both clerical and lay aristocrats. By the time of Mujahid and Arialdus, northern Italy's chestnuts were no longer the simple chestnuts of yore. Thanks to their opportunism, or malleability, or the almost infinite qualities people discerned in them, chestnuts were dynamic.

---

[97] In the *Chronicon*, *two* sacks carried meanings beyond the words that accompanied them. Benedict's much more homey and autarchic sack of millet was an appropriate response from a central Italian potentate to the seafarer's light, portable, nutritious chestnuts. It connected the pope to the agricultural hinterland of Italy and underlined his access to its most important resources, grain, and labor, in frightening amounts.

[98] But see M. Montanari, *Uomini terre boschi nell'occidente medievale* (Catania, 1992), 124, for a post-1000 dating of chestnut's success.

CONCLUSION: GIOVANNI PASCOLI
AND THE OLD CHESTNUT

Giovanni Pascoli is not exactly a household name in the anglophone world. Whereas in Italy generations of schoolchildren have had to master his poetry (anthologized), and a cottage industry exists in literary studies dedicated to his work, he is unfamiliar to English speakers. To tell the truth, he is not one of the most beloved poets in the Italian canon, and even in his own day critics struggled to fit his compositions into their interpretative frameworks, so his current marginality in anglophone circles has deep roots.[1] Benedetto Croce and other early-twentieth-century commentators found Pascoli's style of poetry, and some of his preferred topics, archaic and self-indulgent, which contributed to an enduring sense that Pascoli was not quite as "modern" and forward-looking as his contemporaries like D'Annunzio and Marinetti. However, most who read Pascoli's many poems find much that is worthwhile in them. And any who happen to be interested in rural subjects, and in chestnuts, find in them much that is extraordinarily pertinent.

Pascoli grew up in the Romagna, the piedmont region of hills between the Apennines and the Emilian plain in northeastern Italy. When he was eleven, in 1867, just after the unification of the kingdom of Italy, Pascoli's father was killed and his family was left in dire straits. His brothers managed to send Pascoli to school, and eventually he became a teacher in various high schools in Tuscany. After 1891 his Italian and Latin poetry gave him some fame and, having taught at the universities of Messina and Pisa, in 1905 he took over Giosuè Carducci's (his former teacher) chair in literary studies at the University of Bologna. In that city Pascoli died in 1912. Throughout his life Pascoli never attached himself to the several places he lived, sustaining instead a deep love for the countryside of his youth, and despite his poverty even maintaining a "getaway" (he called

---

[1] A point elaborated by R. LaValva, *The Eternal Child* (Chapel Hill, 1999).

it a "via di fuga" and repeatedly compared it to a bird's nest) near the Garfagnana village of Castelvecchio in northern Tuscany.

The poet's insistence on the relevance of rural things and of classical metric schemes conspired to give his poetry an old-fashioned appearance not just after his death, but even during his lifetime. The events and socio-cultural currents of around 1900 seldom occupied Pascoli's writing, which instead focused on immediately observable realities around his country house, natural processes, the repetitions of the seasons, and peasants' activities. Pascoli's broader commitment to the observation of rustic things assigned prominence to plants and botany in the corpus of Pascolian poetry, and therefore to the chestnut.

As Pascoli lived during the period when (in the historian's crystalline hindsight) chestnut lost its hallowed place in the hillside landscapes of the Italian peninsula, now two poems he dedicated to *Castanea sativa* sound more elegiac even than they were supposed to sound at the very end of the 1800s, when Pascoli wrote them. In "Il castagno" ("The Chestnut") and in "Il vecchio castagno" ("The Old Chestnut") the poet celebrated the multifarious ways in which the tree supported nineteenth-century peasant existence.[2] As food, shade, pasture, litter, fertilizer, firewood, and lumber, chestnut gave its human companions the "only plenty" that made hardscrabble lives bearable. A few lines later in "The Chestnut," Pascoli called chestnut's fruit itself "the good extra tidbit" of sustenance for peasants.[3]

Because Pascoli was punctilious about botany, chiding his literate contemporaries for not caring enough about how plants grow, and vain about his knowledge of traditional rural techniques, his poems, though they idealize rural conditions, are a useful guide into the late pre-industrial world of chestnut forestry and arboriculture.[4] But perhaps their main interest in the present context lies in the poetic conceits Pascoli adopted to express his views on *Castanea*. In "The Chestnut," the slightly earlier poem of the two, the poet addressed the tree directly. Though many a modern gardener will empathize with the practice of speaking to plants, Pascoli considered his interlocutor more than a reticent conversationalist, as he "spoke" to it in very refined verse, following strict rules of

---

[2] G. Pascoli, "Il castagno," in *Myricae* (1891); "Il vecchio castagno," in *Poemetti* (1897), both available online at www.fondazionepascoli.it/Poesie/pp21.htm and www.fondazionepascoli.it/Poesie/My189.htm.

[3] Pascoli, "Il castagno": "tu, pio castagno, solo tu, l'assai / doni al villano che non ha che il sole; / tu solo il chicco, il buon di più, tu dai / alla sua prole."

[4] In Pascoli's poetry the myth of the "home" as a safe refuge in a hostile world is strong. The chestnut that made possible the home's autonomy and supported an idealized domestic life (warmth, nourishment, shelter) was an obvious topic for a man with Pascoli's psychology. See E. Gioanola, *Giovanni Pascoli: Sentimenti filiali di un parricida* (Milan, 2000), 273–74.

meter and rhyme. In effect, "The Chestnut" elevated the mute tree to an almost human level, actually endowing it with the capacity to understand people's distinctive trait: sophisticated language.

This anthropomorphizing Pascoli pushed still further in "The Old Chestnut," whose opening stanza is in the omniscient voice of the poet, but in whose subsequent nine stanzas the chestnut itself speaks (prosopopeia, and in male tonalities). The ancient tree, whose trunk is laced by insect holes and pitted by parasites, is no longer able to give abundant nuts and so is destined to be axed down right after this last fruiting season ends. He calls out to the peasant girl Viola knitting underneath his branches while her cattle pasture, and explains his life, from its inception as a sapling, through a transplantation onto a sunnier and more promising terrain, to a grafting, and then through decades of fruitfulness. He is philosophical about things, and proud of the many annual cycles of growth by which he helped his human friends, as well as of his phenomenal endurance. Having listed the infinite services he rendered over the course of his long life, the chestnut asks Viola (by dropping a timely burr on her hand) to persuade her uncle, the tree's owner, to preserve one of his offshoots from the axe and from the flames. In this way the family's future generations will enjoy the old tree's progeny, after grafting his scion, so that Viola's children will find a tree "like his father but still more handsome."[5]

"The Old Chestnut" is a fine example of ventriloquism, with a person expressing his thoughts by ascribing them to another creature. Yet Pascoli's assigning a voice to a tree (and a lyrical voice, at that) is more radical than having a puppet speak on the end of a human arm. Pascoli's personification of the chestnut blurred the boundaries between inanimate plant and sentient human. In this manner Pascoli called into question some positivist assumptions of the nineteenth century, and of the twenty-first. For in its dialogue "The Old Chestnut" gives agency to the tree, who performs an array of tasks happily, and has a sense of justice too. The poem's message is that the multigenerational relationship between people and *Castanea* depended on both doing their part, each responsible for the other species' welfare. What a biologist might call mutualism, using a neutral term, in Pascoli's composition becomes a leveling of human and vegetative characteristics, an extreme form of democracy in which the tree is the human's equal. Curiously for a poet associated with somewhat retrograde intellectual movements, Pascoli's rejection of

---

[5] Pascoli, "Il vecchio castagno": "è come il padre, anzi più bello." In this verse the tree speaks *for* people, Viola's still unborn children.

anthropocentric views is rather avant-garde, in line with contemporary eco-criticism.[6]

Chestnut was a protagonist in early medieval Italian history as much as it was in Pascoli's rural poetry, though no-one writing in the early Middle Ages quite matched Pascoli's arboreal voice (the eighth-century riddlers mentioned in Chapter 3 came closest). Still, the mounting economic and social importance of chestnut in the latter part of the first millennium did stimulate cultural change and new ways of thinking about trees. A plant with a low classical profile gained some literary notoriety as it became more familiar to people. Late antique and early medieval authors described the tree and its fruit with precision and discernment, and turned it into a metaphor too. Thus, in order for chestnut to become, eventually, an embodiment of homey security to a writer like Pascoli, it had first to become normal in the texts of the first millennium. The crucial cultural shift from exotic and somewhat suspect tree to ordinary component of peninsular Christian landscapes took place in the early Middle Ages.

Pascoli's idea that chestnut and human mutually support each other, modifying each other's characteristics and behavior, derived from his observation of late-nineteenth-century peninsular agriculture; but the beneficial interaction of the two species Pascoli described in verse first came into being many centuries earlier, during the transformation of the late Roman world. As we have seen, specific demographic and social conditions created the space within which *Castanea sativa* could appear as an economic solution to everyday quandaries of production. Assuredly chestnut was not the only plant whose botany raised it to unprecedented relevance as woodlands grew, state authority receded, and people dwindled, and indeed by paying closer attention to vegetation's history it is possible to discover unexpected dimensions to the decline and fall of the Roman empire. To a large extent the environmental side to that story remains unwritten, but the rise of chestnut woodland discussed in the pages above is a start. Chestnut's self-assertion was one of the more dramatic and visible, as well as significant, *environmental* changes that accompanied the end of Rome's hegemony.

Castanea sativa proved itself a wily and resourceful ally of early medieval people. Once it had established its presence in the landscape, the species continued to offer solutions to its friends even as the original social and economic conditions that had facilitated chestnut's establishment faded. In the last two centuries of the first millennium, as population

---

[6] Expressed eloquently by M. Pollan, *The Botany of Desire: A Plant's-Eye View of the World* (New York, 2001).

levels recovered somewhat and the circulation of goods between regions accelerated, the tree that suited self-sufficient households and communities still managed to hold its own. As the Italian landscape changed again, and the mix of species in its vegetation began to reflect new economic priorities through more intensive agriculture, still chestnut flourished. It continued to demand little and yet to render much, and the old chestnut trees' removal did not on the whole seem worth the effort. In this second wind of castaneiculture, the fruit's preservability was the decisive fact, for it allowed people to treat what had been primarily a subsistence food also as a commercial commodity.

Most remarkable in this account is the longevity of the relationship that *Castanea* established with people. By the year 500 the entente was solid, and with only some small modifications it held up for more than a millennium, really until the industrialization of Pascoli's century. The result of people and trees interacting was not in this instance the usual catastrophe found in other environmental narratives. "Sustainable" is nowadays a loaded word in environmental circles, but the chestnut woodlands produced by the crises of late antiquity ended up being something very close to that. The idiosyncratic form of woodland, at once natural and anthropogenic, seems to have existed in equilibrium with other types of land use, for it remained a significant presence in pollen deposits and written sources throughout the first millennium. Neither a momentous "return of nature" in early medieval times, nor the "great clearances" of the High Middle Ages fundamentally altered the bond between chestnut and people. Though by the thirteenth century chestnut groves were no longer popular investments in parts of Italy, including those like Campania where such groves *had* seemed an excellent idea earlier, and though in the nineteenth century many chestnuts fell to the lumbermen, viewed over the long duration of arboreal time the chestnut enjoyed a stable history. That stability, whose premises formed in the post-classical centuries, is a demonstration of the possibilities inherent in accepting a fairly anthropomorphized natural world. The Standard Environmental Narrative of plunder and desecration is not the only story environmental historians can tell.

As an example of how neither rapacity nor deforestation are obligatory outcomes of human engagement with wooded nature, the geographically and temporally limited case study of chestnut history expands environmental history in general. It is worth underlining again that the most eventful portion in the long-term relationship between humans and chestnut trees was the early medieval one: pre-industrial, indeed "sylvo-pastoral," environments need not be static and deep changes to ecosystems can emerge from societies with limited technologies and underdeveloped states or markets. Change, the historian's most prized quarry, is very much part of the story of early medieval environments. A few years ago Julia Smith provocatively asked "did women have a transformation of the Roman world?" as a way of interjecting gender into interpretative frameworks that too seldom stretch beyond the sphere of male-dominated politics.[7] In a similar vein we can answer in the affirmative the question "did trees have a transformation of the Roman world?" This book has attempted to show that they did.

---

[7] J. Smith, "Did Women Have a Transformation of the Roman World?," *Gender and History* 12.3 (2000), 552–71.

GLOSSARY

Autosterile (cross-pollinating): plants unable to pollinate themselves, or able to do so only with great difficulty because of physical or genetic mechanisms. Many domestic plants are self-pollinating, even if their ancestors were autosterile.

Coppice: woodland managed (by regular cuts) to produce small trunks from a larger stock or stool.

Cultivar: a plant with sufficient uniformity in appearance and behavior to be distinct from others of its species, and able to produce uniform seedlings, even if these are not genetically identical.

Disturbance: naturally occurring destructive events, like blights, wind storms, or fires, that recalibrate ecological processes in woodlands and bring dynamism.

Grafting: joining together two different cultivars of a species, or of closely related species. Usually this means inserting a shoot from a desirable plant into a cut in the stem of an established plant.

Grove: a type of wooded land in which human management has deepest impact by limiting tree density and species variety.

Hybrid: the result of a cross – natural or deliberate – between two very genetically different plants (two species, or two cultivars or landraces within the same species).

Incolto: literally "the uncultivated land," or the portion of the landscape where overt cultivation did not take place and human manipulations were lightest.

Mast: seeds of trees, especially acorns, used to feed animals.

Mutualism: the relationship between two organisms that is beneficial to both and produces no disadvantages to either.

Pannage: woodland feed for pigs, usually trees' seeds (mast).

Pollard: a tree that is cut above the reach of browsing animals to produce branches useful to people, or the poles from such a tree.

Scion: the shoot or sapling of a plant that is grafted onto a rootstock of another. Scions are clones of the plant whence they were removed.

Selection: plants people judged superior and chose to privilege over others that may resemble them genetically. Also, the process of such judging and privileging.

Wildwood: a woodland little affected by human activity since prehistoric times. Since forest and wilderness are culturally loaded terms, the more neutral "wildwood" better captures the nature of early medieval Italian woodland.

BIBLIOGRAPHY

PRIMARY SOURCES

"Aenigmata hexasticha," ed. K. Strecker, *MGH, Poetae latini aevi Carolini* 4.2 (Berlin, 1914), 732–59.

"Aenigmata laureshamensia," ed. M. de Marco, in *Tatuini opera omnia* (Turnhout, 1968), 347–58.

"Aenigmata Tullii," ed. F. Glorie, in *Variae collectiones aenigmatum merovingicae aetatis*, 2 vols.,Vol. II (Turnhout, 1968), 547–610.

Ammianus Marcellinus, *Rerum gestarum libri*, 2 vols., ed. C. Clark (Berlin, 1910).

Alcuin, *Commentaria super Ecclesiasten*, MPL 100 (Paris, 1863), 666–722.

Ambrose, *Sancti Ambrosii opera*,Vol. I, ed. C. Schenkl (Vienna, 1896).

Anastasius the Librarian, *Synodus octava generalis*, MPL 129 (Paris, 1879), 1–196.

Anthimus, *De observatine ciborum ad Thoedoricum regem Francorum epistula*, ed. E. Liechtenhan (Berlin, 1963).

Antonietti, A., *Carta della utilizzazione del suolo d'Italia* (Milan, 1966).

Apicius, *De re coquinaria*, ed. M. Milham (Leipzig, 1969).

Athenaeus, *The Deipnosophists*, 3 vols.,Vol. I, trans. C.Yonge (London, 1854).

Augustine, *De dialectica*, ed. and trans. B. Jackson and J. Pinborg (Dordrecht, 1975).

Breviarium ecclesiae ravennatis, ed. G. Rabotti (Rome, 1985).

Die Briefe des Bischofs Rather von Verona, ed. F. Weigle (Weimar, 1949).

Brown, V., "New Documents at Rieti for the Monasteries of San Benedetto ad Xenodochium and Santa Sofia in Ninth Century Benevento," *Mediaeval Studies* 63 (2001), 337–51.

Calpurnius Siculus, *Bucoliques*, ed. J. Amat (Paris, 1991).

Capitularia regum Francorum 1, MGH, Leges, Sectio II, ed. A. Boretius (Hanover, 1883).

Le carte del decimo secolo nell'archivio arcivescovile di Ravenna, 900–957, ed. R. Benericetti (Ravenna, 1999).

Le carte ravennati del decimo secolo: Archivio arcivescovile, 3 vols., ed. R. Benericetti,Vol. II: *Aa. 957–976* (Imola, 2002).

Le carte ravennati del decimo secolo: Archivio arcivescovile (aa. 976–999), 3. vols., ed. R. Benericetti,Vol. III: *Aa. 976–999* (Imola, 2002).

Cassiodorus, *Variae*, ed. T. Mommsen, MGH, Auctores antiquissimi 12 (Berlin, 1894).

Bibliography

Chronicon Ebersheimense, ed. L. Weiland, *MGH, Scriptores* 23 (Hanover, 1874).

Chronicon vulturnense del Monaco Giovanni, 3 vols., ed. V. Federici (Rome, 1925–38).

CLA 54, ed. G. Rabotti and F. Santoni (Zurich, 2000).

CLA 64–65, 71, ed. C. Mantegna (Zurich, 2003–04).

CLA 66, ed. C. Carbonetti Vendittelli (Zurich, 2005).

CLA 68, ed. P. Degni (Zurich, 2006).

CLA 69–70, ed. F. De Rubeis (Zurich, 2006–07).

Codex diplomaticus cajetanus, Vol. I, ed. Monachorum S. Benedicti (Montecassino, 1887).

Codice diplomatico veronese del periodo dei re d'Italia, ed. V. Fainelli (Venice, 1963).

Columella, *Les arbres*, ed. R. Goujard (Paris, 2002).

   De agri cultura, ed. H. Boyd Ash (Cambridge, MA, 1941).

Concilium Teatinum, ed. A Werminghoff, *MGH, Concilia* 2.2 (Hanover, 1908), 788–91.

Cuozzo, E., and J. Martin, "Documents inédits ou peu connus des archives du Mont Cassin (VIIIe–Xe siècles)," *Mélanges de l'Ecole française de Rome: Moyen Age* 103 (1991), 115–210.

de' Crescenzi, Pietro, *Ruralia commoda*, 4 vols., ed. W. Richter (Heidelberg, 1995–98).

"Diaeta Theodori," ed. K. Sudhoff, *Archiv für Geschichte der Medizin* 8 (1915), 377–403.

I diplomi di Berengario I, ed. L. Schiaparelli (Rome, 1903).

I diplomi di Ugo e di Lotario di Berengario II e di Adalberto, ed. L. Schiaparelli (Rome, 1924).

I diplomi italiani di Lodovico III e di Rodolfo II, ed. L. Schiaparelli (Rome, 1910).

"Edictus Rothari," ed. F. Blühme, *MGH, Leges* 4 (Hanover, 1868), 3–90.

"The Farmer's Law II," ed. W. Ashburner, *Journal of Hellenic Studies* 32 (1912), 69–95.

Galen, "On Simple Medicines" ["De simplicium medicamentorum temperamentis ac facultatibus"], in *Claudii Galeni Opera Omnia*, 20 vols., ed. C. Kühn, Vol. XII (Hildesheim, 1965), 1–377.

   "On the Good and Bad Humors in Foods" ["De probis pravisque alimentorum succis"], in *Claudii Galeni Opera Omnia*, 20 vols., ed. C. Kühn, Vol. VI (Hildesheim, 1965), 749–815.

   "On the Properties of Foods" ["De alimentorum facultatibus"], in *Claudii Galeni Opera Omnia*, 20 vols., ed. C. Kühn, Vol. VI (Hildesheim, 1965), 453–748.

Gargilius Martialis, *De hortis*, ed. I. Mazzini (Bologna, 1978).

   Les remèdes tirés des légumes et des fruits, ed. B. Maire (Paris, 2002).

Gregory of Tours, *Liber in gloria martyrum*, ed. B. Krusch, in *Gregorii Turonensis opera. Pars II: Miracula et opera minora*. MGH, Scriptores rerum Merovingicarum 1.2 (Hanover, 1885), 34–113.

Historiae patriae monumenta, Chartarum Tomus I (Turin, 1836).

Hrabanus Maurus, *Commentaria in Genesim*, MPL 107 (Paris, 1864), 443–670.

   Commentarium in Matthaeum, MPL 107 (Paris, 1864).

   De ecclesiastica disciplina, MPL 112 (Paris, 1878), 1259D.

   De universo, MPL 111 (Paris, 1864), 9–614.

Hyginus, "De condicionibus agrorum," in *Corpus agrimensorum Romanorum*, ed. C. Thulin (Leipzig, 1913), 74–86.

Inventari altomedievali di terre, coloni e redditi, ed. A. Castagnetti, M. Luzzati, A. Vasina, and G. Pasquali (Rome, 1979).

Isidore of Seville, *Isidori hispalensis episcopi Etyologiarum sive Originum libri* XX, 2 vols., ed. W. Lindsay (Oxford, 1911).

Bibliography

Jerome, *Adversus Iovinianum*, MPL 23 (Paris, 1845), 211–338.

"Commentarius in Ecclesiasten," in *S. Hieronymi presbyteri opera*, ed. M. Adriaen, Corpus Christianorum series latina 72 (Turnhout, 1959), 246–361.

"Leges Liutprandi regis," ed. F. Bluhme, *MGH, Leges* 4 (Hanover, 1868), 96–182.

Jonas of Bobbio, *Vita Columbani*, ed. B. Krusch, *MGH, Scriptores rerum Germanicarum in usum scholarum* 34 (Hanover, 1905).

Leo III, *Epistulae*, MPL 102 (Paris, 1865), 1023–70.

Ludovici II. diplomata, ed. K. Wanner, *MGH, Diplomata karolinorum* 4 (Munich, 1994).

Macrobius, *Saturnalia*, ed. J. Willis (Leipzig, 1963).

Martin, J.-M., E. Cuozzo, S. Gasparri, and M. Villani, eds., *Regesti dei documenti dell'Italia meridionale, 570–899* (Rome, 2002).

Monumenta ad neapolitani ducatus historiam pertinentia, 2 vols., ed. B. Capasso (Naples, 1881–92).

Oribasius, *Oribasius latinus*, ed. H. Mørland (Oslo, 1940).

Palladius, *Opus agriculturae. De veterinaria medicina. De insitione*, ed. R. Rodgers (Leipzig, 1975).

Paulinus of Aquileia, "Carmina," ed. E. Dümmler, *MGH, Poetae latini aevi Carolini* 1 (Berlin, 1881), 123–48.

Paulinus of Nola, *Carmina*, ed. G. de Haertel and M. Kamptner (Vienna, 1999).

Le pergamene degli archivi arcivescovili di Amalfi e Ravello, 5 vols., ed. J. Mazzoleni, Vol. 1 (Naples, 1972).

I placiti del "Regnum Italiae," 3 vols., ed. C. Manaresi (Rome, 1955–60).

Pliny the Elder, *Historia naturalis*, ed. J. André (Paris, 2003).

Rudolf of Fulda, *Translatio S. Alexandri*, ed. G. Pertz, *MGH, Scriptores* 2 (Hanover, 1829), 673–81.

Schwarz, U., "Regesta amalfitana, 1. Teil," *Quellen und Forschungen aus italienischen Archiven und Bibliotheken* 58 (1978), 1–136.

Sedulius Scotus, *Collectaneum miscellaneum*, ed. D. Simpson (Turnhout, 1988).

In Donati artem maiorem, ed. B. Löfstedt (Turnhout, 1977).

Sergius III, *Epistulae* 3, MPL 131 (Paris, 1884).

Servius, *In Vergilii Bucolica et Georgica commentarii*, ed. G. Thilo (Leipzig, 1887).

Servii Grammatici qui feruntur in Vergilii Carmina commentarii, ed. H. Hagen (Leipzig, 1902).

"Sicardi principis pactio cum Neapolitanis," ed. G. Waitz, in *Leges Langobardorum*, MGH, Leges 4 (Hanover, 1868), 216–21.

Theodulf of Orléans, Carmen 25, lines 135–40, in "Theodulfi Carmina," ed. E. Dümmler, in *Poetae latini aevi Carolini* 1, MGH, Poetae latini aevi Carolini (Berlin, 1881), 437–581.

Theophrastus, *Recherches sur les plantes*, 5 vols., ed. S. Amigues (Paris, 2003).

Thietmar of Merseburg, *Chronicon*, ed. R. Holtzmann, *MGH Scriptores rerum Germanicarum* N.S. 9 (Berlin, 1935).

Varro, Marcus Terentius, *Economie rurale*, ed. G. Guiraud (Paris, 1997).

Venantius Fortunatus, *Carmina*, ed. F. Leo, MGH, Auctores antiquissimi 4.1 (Berlin, 1881).

Vita Barbati episcopi Beneventani, ed. G. Waitz, *MGH, Scriptores rerum Langobardicarum et Italicarum* (Hanover, 1878), 557–64.

The Vita of Constantine and the Vita of Methodius, trans. M. Kantor and R. White (Ann Arbor, 1976).

Bibliography

"Vita Sancti Arialdi auctore Andrea abbate strumensi," ed. F. Baethgen, *MGH, Scriptores* 30.2 (Hanover, 1934), 1047–75.

Walafrid Strabo, *De exordia et incrementis quarundam in observationibus ecclesiasticis rerum,* ed. A. Boretius and V. Krause, *MGH, Leges,* Sectio II, (Hanover, 1897), 473–516.

Glossa ordinaria, MPL 113 (Paris, 1879).

Willibald, *Vita Bonifatii,* ed. W. Levison, *MGH, Scriptores rerum Germanicarum in usum scholarum* 57 (Hanover, 1905), 1–58.

SECONDARY SOURCES

Accorsi, C., M. Bandini Mazzanti, L. Forlani, *et al.,* "Archaeobotany of the Cognento Hiding Well," in *Proceedings of the 1st International Congress on Science and Technology for the Safeguard of Cultural Heritage in the Mediterranean Basin* (Palermo, 1998), 1537–44.

Accorsi, C., M. Bandini Mazzanti, A. Mercuri, C. Rivalenti, and G. Trevisan Grandi, "Holocene Forest Pollen Vegetation of the Po Plain: Northern Italy (Emilia Romagna Data)," *Alliona* 24 (1996), 233–76.

Agnoletti, M., and M. Paci, "Landscape Evolution on a Central Tuscan Estate between the 18th and 20th Centuries," in *The Ecological History of European Forests,* ed. C. Watkins and K. Kirby (Wallingford, 1998), 117–27.

Aimar, A., F. d'Errico, and G. Giacobini, "Analisi dei resti faunistici," in *Montaldo di Mondovì,* ed. E. Micheletti and M. Venturino Gambari (Rome, 1991), 237–44.

Aira Rodríguez, M., "La vegetación gallega durante la época de ocupación romana a través del estudio del polen fosil," *Lucus Augusti* 1 (1996), 25–45.

Aira Rodríguez, M., and P. Uzquiano, "Análisis polínico e identificación de carbones en necrópolis gallegas de época romana," *Lucus Augusti* 1 (1996), 49–52.

Aira Rodríguez, M., P. Saa, and P. López, "Cambios del paisaje durante el Holoceno," *Revue de paléobiologie* 11 (1992), 243–54.

Alessio, G., "Glossografia altomedievale alle *Georgiche,*" in *L'ambiente vegetale nell'alto medioevo,* Settimane del CISAM 37 (Spoleto, 1990), 55–94.

Allen, H., "Vegetation and Ecosystem Dynamics," in *The Physical Geography of the Mediterranean,* ed. J. Woodward (Oxford, 2009), 203–27.

Allevato, E., M. Buonincontri, M. Vairo, *et al.,* "Persistence of the Cultural Landscape in Campania (Southern Italy) before the AD 472 Vesuvius Eruption," *Journal of Archaeological Science* 39 (2012), 399–406.

Allevato, E., E. Russo Ermolli, and G. Di Pasquale, "Woodland Exploitation and Roman Shipbuilding," *Méditerranée* 112 (2009), 33–42.

Allevato, E., E. Russo Ermolli, G. Boetto, and G. Di Pasquale, "Pollen–Wood Analysis at the Neapolis Harbour Site (1st–3rd Century AD, Southern Italy) and Its Archaeological Implications," *Journal of Archaeological Science* 37 (2010), 2365–75.

Allocati, A., "Il cartulario amalfitano detto comunemente 'Codice Perris,' e la sua edizione," in *Convegno internazionale 14–16 giugno 1973: Amalfi nel medioevo* (Salerno, 1977), 361–65.

Allsen, T., *The Royal Hunt in Eurasian History* (Philadelphia, 2006).

Amari, M., *Storia dei musulmani di Sicilia,* 3 vols., Vol. III.1 (Florence, 1868).

Amorini, E., "Sustainability of Chestnut Forest Ecosystems: Is It Possible?," *Ecologia mediterranea* 26 (2000), 3–14.

Bibliography

André, J., *L'alimentation et la cuisine à Rome* (Paris, 1961).

Etude sur les termes de couleur dans la langue latine (Paris, 1949).

Lexique des termes de botanique en Latin (Paris, 1956).

Andreolli, B., *Contadini su terre di signori: Studi sulla contrattualistica agraria dell'Italia medievale* (Bologna, 1999).

"Contratti agrari, proprietà fondiaria e lavoro contadino," in *Contadini su terre di signori* (Bologna, 1999), 17–35.

"Formule di pertinenza e paesaggio: Il castagneto nella Toscana dell'alto medioevo," in *Contadini su terre di signori* (Bologna, 1999), 191–99.

"Il linguaggio della terra," in *Comunicare e significare nell'alto medioevo: 15–20 aprile 2004*, Settimane del CISAM 52 (Spoleto, 2005), 983–1012.

"Misurare la terra: Metrologie altomedievale," in *L'uomo e spazio nell'alto medioevo*, Settimane del CISAM 50 (Spoleto, 2003), 151–91.

"L'uso del bosco e degli incolti," in *Storia dell'agricoltura italiana*, 5 vols., Vol. II, ed. G. Pinto and M. Ambrosoli (Florence, 2002), 123–44.

Andreolli, B., and M. Montanari, eds., *Il bosco nel medioevo* (Bologna, 1988).

Armiero, M., and M. Hall, "Il bel paese," in *Nature and History in Modern Italy*, ed. M. Armiero and M. Hall (Athens, OH, 2010), 1–11.

Arobba, D., "Analisi palinologiche," in *Montaldo di Mondovì*, ed. E. Micheletto and M. Venturino Gambari (Rome, 1991), 245–46.

Arobba, D., and G. Murialdo, "Le analisi palinologiche e paleocarpologiche," in *S. Antonino: Un insediamento fortificato nella Liguria bizantina*, ed. T. Mannoni and G. Murialdo (Bordighera, 2001), 627–38.

Arobba, D., P. Palazzi, and R. Caramiello, "Ricerche archeobotaniche nell'abitato medievale di Finalborgo (Savona): Primi risultati," *Archeologia medievale* 30 (2003), 247–58.

Arthur, P., "Italian Landscapes, 400–1000," in *Landscapes of Change*, ed. N. Christie (Leiden, 2006), 103–33.

Naples, from Roman Town to City-State (London, 2002).

Audoin-Rouzeau, F., "Elevage et alimentation dans l'espace européen au moyen âge," in *Milieux naturels, espaces sociaux*, ed. E. Mornet and F. Morenzoni (Paris, 1997), 143–59.

Augenti, A., "Fonti archeologiche per l'uso del legno nell'edilizia medievale in Italia," in *Civiltà del legno*, ed. P. Galetti (Bologna, 2004), 37–69.

Baker, P., "Assessment of Animal Bones Excavated in 2004–2005 at Nogara (Olmo di Nogara)," in *Nogara*, ed. F. Saggioro (Rome, 2011), 107–21.

Balzaretti, R., "Cities, Emporia and Monasteries: Local Economies in the Po Valley, c. 700–875," in *Towns in Transition*, ed. N. Christie and S. Loseby (Aldershot, 1996), 213–34.

Banaji, J., "Aristocracies, Peasantries, and the Framing of the Early Middle Ages," *Journal of Agrarian Change* 9 (2009), 59–91.

Bandini Mazzanti, M., G. Bosi, M. Marchesini, A. Mercuri, and C. Accorsi, "Quale frutta circolava sulle tavole emiliano-romagnole nel periodo romano?" *Atti della società dei naturalisti e matematici di Modena* 131 (2000), 63–92.

Barbiera, I., and G. Dalla-Zuanna, "Le dinamiche della popolazione nell'Italia medievale," *Archeologia medievale* 34 (2007), 19–42.

Bardet, J., and J. Dupâquier, eds., *Histoire des populations de l'Europe*, 3 vols. (Paris, 1997–99).

Bibliography

Bargioni, E., and A. Zanzi Sulli, "The Production of Fodder Trees in Valdagno, Vicenza, Italy," in *The Ecological History of European Forests*, ed. C. Watkins and K. Kirby (Wallingford, 1998), 43–52.

Baridon, M., *Naissance et renaissance du paysage* (Paris, 2006).

Barnish, S., "Pigs, Plebeians, and Potentes: Rome's Economic Hinterland, c. 350–600 AD," *Papers of the British School at Rome* 55 (1987), 157–85.

Basso, K., *Wisdom Sits in Places* (Albuquerque, 1996).

Baxandall, M., *Giotto and the Orators* (Oxford, 1971).

Becchi, M., *Discorso sul castagno* (Reggio Emilia, 1996).

Beinart, W., and L. Hughes, *Environment and Empire* (Oxford, 2007).

Bevilacqua, P., "The Distinctive Character of Italian Environmental History," in *Nature and History in Modern Italy*, ed. M. Armiero and M. Hall (Athens, OH, 2010), 15–32.

"Sull'impopolarità della storia del territorio in Italia," in *Natura e società: Studi in memoria di Augusto Placanica*, ed. P. Bevilacqua and P. Tino (Rome, 2005), 7–16.

Terre del grano, terre degli alberi: L'ambiente nella storia del Mezzogiorno (Rionero, 1992).

Biasotti, M., and R. Giovinazzo, "Reperti faunistici," in *Scavi MM3* 3.2, ed. D. Caporusso (Milan, 1991), 167–84.

Bignami, G., and A. Salsotto, *La civiltà del castagno* (Cuneo, 1983).

Birkhan, H., *Die Pflanzen im Mittelalter. Eine Kulturgeschichte* (Vienna, 2012).

Bischoff, B., "Die Entstehung des Sankt Galler Klosterplan in paläographischer Sicht," in *Mittelalterliche Studien: Ausgewählte Aufsätze zur Schriftkunde und Literaturegeschichte*, 3 vols., Vol. I (Stuttgart, 1966), 41–49.

Blänkle, P., A. Kreuz, and V. Rupp, "Archäologische und naturwissenschaftliche Untersuchungen an zwei römischen Brandgräbern in der Wetterau," *Germania* 73 (1995), 103–30.

Bloch, M., "Why Trees, Too, Are Good to Think With," in *The Social Life of Trees*, ed. L. Rival (Oxford, 1998), 39–55.

Bognetti, G., "I beni comunali e l'organizzazione del villaggio nell'Italia superiore fino al mille," *Rivista storica italiana* 77 (1965), 469–99.

Bonetti, E., "Pollen Sequence in the Lake Sediments," *Transactions of the American Philosophical Society* 60.4 (1970), 26–31.

Bonino, M., "Appunti sull'impiego del legno nelle costruzioni navali tra antichità e medioevo," in *Civiltà del legno*, ed. P. Galetti (Bologna, 2004), 121–42.

Bonuccelli, P., "Il castagno nella Lucchesia," *Accademia lucchese di scienze, lettere ed arti* 5 (1942), 93–116.

Boserup, E., *The Conditions of Agricultural Growth* (Chicago, 1965).

Bossard, C., and P. Beck, "Le mobilier ostéologique et botanique," in *Brucato: Histoire et archéologie d'un habitat médiéval en Sicile*, 2 vols., ed. J. Pesez, Vol. II (Rome, 1984), 615–71.

Botkin, D., *Discordant Harmonies: A New Ecology for the Twenty-First Century* (Oxford, 1990).

Bottema, S., "The Holocene History of the Walnut, Sweet-Chestnut, Manna-Ash and Plane Tree in the Eastern Mediterranean," *Pallas* 52 (2000), 35–59.

Bounous, G., *Il castagno: Coltura, ambiente ed utilizzazioni in Italia e nel mondo* (Bologna, 2002).

Bourgeois, C., *Le châtaignier, un arbre, un bois* (Paris, 1992).

Bibliography

Braudel, F., *Civilisation matérielle et capitalisme: XVe–XVIII siècle*, 2 vols. (Paris, 1967).

Breisch, H., "Harvesting, Storage and Processing of Chestnuts in France and Italy," in *Proceedings of the International Congress on Chestnut*, ed. E. Antognozzi (Spoleto, n.d.), 429–36.

Brogiolo, G., "Nuove ricerche sulla campagna dell'Italia settentrionale tra tarda antichità e altomedioevo," in *Castrum 5: Archéologie des espaces agraires méditerranéens au Moyen Age*, ed. A. Bazzana (Madrid, 1999), 153–65.

"Gli scavi a Monte Barro 1990–1997," in *Archeologia a Monte Barro*, 2 vols., ed. G. Brogiolo and L. Castelletti, Vol. II (Lecco, 2001), 21–102.

Brogiolo, G., and A. Chavarría Arnau, *Aristocrazia e campagne nell'Occidente da Costantino a Carlomagno* (Florence, 2005).

Brombacher, C., "Gemüse und Obst: Mehr als eine willkommene Abwechslung," in *Gesellschaft und Ernährung um 1000* (Vevey, 2000), 177–83.

Brombacher, C., S. Jacomet, and M. Kühn, "Mittelalterliche Kulturpflanzen aus der Schweiz und Liechtenstein," in *Environment and Subsistence in Medieval Europe*, ed. G. de Boe and F. Verhaeghe (Zellik, 1997), 95–111.

Brooks, J., C. DeCorse, and J. Walton, eds., *Small Worlds: Method, Meaning, and Narrative in Microhistory* (Santa Fe, 2008).

Browicz, K., and J. Zieliński, *Chorology of Trees and Shrubs in South-West Asia and Adjacent Regions* (Warsaw, 1982).

Brugiapaglia, E., and J.-L. de Beaulieu, "Etude de la dynamique végétale Tardiglaciaire et Holocène en Italie centrale," *Comptes rendus de l'Académie des Sciences, Paris* 321 (1995), 617–22.

Brugnoli, A., and G. Varanini, "Olivi e olio nel medioevo italiano," in *Olivi e olio nel medioevo italiano* (Bologna, 2005), 3–100.

Bruneton-Governatori, A., "Alimentation et idéologie: le cas de la châtaigne," *Annales ESC* 39 (1984), 1161–89.

Buccianti, M., *Il castagno in provincia di Lucca* (Lucca, n.d.).

Bussi, L., "Terre comuni e usi civici dalle origini all'alto medioevo," in *Storia del Mezzogiorno*, 15 vols., ed. G. Galasso and R. Romeo, Vol. III: *Alto medioevo* (Naples, 1990), 213–55.

Campbell, D., "The *Capitulare de villis*, the *Brevium exempla*, and the Carolingian Court at Aachen," *Early Medieval Europe* 18 (2010), 243–64.

Cantini, F., *Il castello di Montarrenti: Lo scavo archeologico (1982–1987)* (Florence, 2003).

Caracuta, V., and G. Fiorentino, "L'analisi archeobotanica nell'insediamento di Faragola," in *V congresso nazionale di archeologia medievale*, ed. G. Volpe and P. Favia (Florence, 2009), 717–23.

Caramiello, R., and D. Arobba, "Analisi palinologiche," in *Manuale d'archeobotanica* (Milano, 2003), 67–113.

Caramiello, R., and A. Zeme, "Analisi palinologiche," *Alba Pompeia* 13 (1992), 43.

Caramiello, R., A. Zeme, C. Siniscalco, *et al.*, "Analisi paleobotaniche e sedimentologiche: Storia forestale, clima, ed agricoltura a Trino dall'età romana al medioevo," in *San Michele di Trino (VC): Dal villaggio romano al castello medievale*, 3 vols., ed. M. Negro Ponzi Mancini, Vol. II (Florence, 1999), 577–99.

Cardini, F., "Magia del castagno," in *Il castagno: Tradizioni e trasformazioni*, ed. R. Roda (Ferrara, 1989), 23–38.

Carella, S., *Architecture religieuse haut-médiévale en Italie méridionale: Le diocèse de Bénévent* (Turnhout, 2011)

211

Bibliography

Cartledge, J., G. Clark, and V. Higgins, "The Animal Bones: A Preliminary Assessment of the Stock Economy," in *Excavations at Otranto*, 2 vols., ed. F. d'Andria and D. Whitehouse, Vol. II, (Galatina, 1992), 317–35.

Casanova, A., *Arboriculture et société en Méditerranée à la fin du XVIIIe siècle: L'exemple de la Corse* (Corte, 1998).

Cassi, L., "Distribuzione geografica dei toponimi derivati dalla vegetazione in Toscana," *Rivista geografica italiana* 80 (1973), 389–432.

Cassi Curradi, L., "Distribuzione geografica dei toponimi derivati dalle piante coltivate in Toscana," *Rivista geografica italiana* 83 (1976), 66–72.

Castelletti, L., "I carboni della vetreria di Monte Lecco," *AM* 2 (1975), 99–122.

"Contributo alle ricerche paletnobotaniche in Italia," *Istituto lombardo: Rendiconti lettere* 106 (1972), 331–74.

"L'economia e l'ambiente," in *Archeologia a Monte Barro*, 2 vols., ed. G. Brogiolo and L. Castelletti, Vol. II (Lecco, 2001), 219–22.

"Resti vegetali macroscopici da Refondou presso Savignone," *Archeologia medievale* 3 (1976), 326–28.

Castelletti, L., and A. Maspero, "Analisi di resti vegetali macroscopici," in *Ricerche su Brescia altomedievale*, ed. G. Panazza and G. Brogiolo (Brescia, 1988), 125–32.

"Antracologia degli insediamenti paleolitici nella Penisola Italiana," *Bulletin de la Société botanique de France: Actualités botaniques* 139 (1992), 297–309.

Castelletti, L., E. Castiglione, and M. Rottoli, "L'agricoltura dell'Italia settentrionale dal Neolitico al medioevo," in *Le piante coltivate e la loro storia*, ed. O. Failla and G. Forni (Milan, 2001), 33–84.

Castelletti, L., A. Maspero, S. Motella, and M. Rottoli, "Analisi silotomiche e tecnica di lavorazione del legno," in *Fortuna maris: La nave romana die Comacchio*, ed. F. Berti (Bologna, 1990), 150–51.

Castiglioni, E., "I carboni," in *S. Antonino: Un insediamento fortificato nella Liguria bizantina*, ed. T. Mannoni and G. Murialdo (Bordighera, 2001), 617–26.

Castiglioni, E., and M. Rottoli, "Nogara, l'abitato di Mulino di Sotto," in *Nogara*, ed. F. Saggioro (Rome, 2011), 123–57.

Castiglioni, E., E. Cottini, and M. Rottoli, "Mariano, Via T. Grossi: Analisi archeobotaniche," in *Storia di Mariano Comense*, ed. G. Frigerio (Como, 1999), 107–12.

"I resti archeobotanici," in *Archeologia a Monte Barro*, 2 vols., ed. G. Brogiolo and L. Castelletti, Vol. II (Lecco, 2001), 223–47.

"I resti botanici di Santa Giulia a Brescia," in *S. Giulia di Brescia*, ed. G. Brogiolo (Florence, 1999), 401–24.

Catarsi, M., "L'Appennino parmense tra età romana ed alto medioevo," in *L'Appennino in età romana e nel primo medioevo*, ed. M. Destro and E. Giorgi (Bologna, 2004), 203–18.

Cecchini, R., "Origine della diffusione del castagno in Italia," *Monti e boschi* 1 (1950), 412–14.

Cevasco, R., "Environmental Heritage of a Past Cultural Landscape," in *Nature and History in Modern Italy*, ed. M. Armiero and M. Hall (Athens, OH, 2010), 126–40.

Cherubini, G., "Le campagne," in *Storia della Calabria medievale*, 2 vols., ed. A. Placanica, Vol. II (Reggio, 2001), 429–66.

Bibliography

"La 'civiltà' del castagno in Italia alla fine del medioevo," *Archeologia medievale* 8 (1981), 247–80.

Chiarugi, A., "Ricerche sulla vegetazione dell'Etruria marittima," *Giornale botanico italiano* 46 (1933), 15–36.

Christie, N., "Barren Fields? Landscape and Settlement in Late Roman and Post-Roman Italy," in *Human Landscapes in Classical Times*, ed. G. Shipley and J. Salmon (London, 1996), 254–83.

From Constantine to Charlemagne (Aldershot, 2006).

Citarella, A., "La crisi navale araba del secolo VIII e l'origine della fortuna commerciale di Amalfi," in *Convegno internazionale 14–16 giugno 1973: Amalfi nel medioevo* (Salerno, 1977), 195–213.

Citter, C., "L'Italia centrale tirrenica in età carolingia," in *V congresso nazionale di archeologia medievale*, ed. G. Volpe and P. Favia (Florence, 2009), 302–05.

Clarke, G., "Monastic Economies? Aspects of Production and Consumption in Early Medieval Central Italy," *Archeologia medievale* 14 (1997), 31–54.

Cohen, M., *Health and the Rise of Civilization* (New Haven, 1989).

"History, Diet, and Hunter-Gatherers," in *The Cambridge History of Food*, 2 vols., ed. K. Kiple and K. Coneè Ornelas, Vol. 1 (Cambridge, 2000), 63–71.

Colacino, M., and D. Camuffo, "Il clima dell'Italia meridionale," in *Natura e società*, ed. P. Bevilacqua and P. Tino (Rome, 2005), 37–58.

Colardelle, M., and E. Verdal, eds., *Les habitats du lac de Paladru (Isère) dans leur environnement* (Paris, 1993).

Comba, R., "Castagneto e paesaggio agrario nelle valli piemontesi," in *Uomini boschi castagne*, ed. R. Comba and I. Naso (Cuneo, 2000), 21–32.

"Châtaigneraie et paysage agraire dans les vallées piémontaises (XIIe–XIIIe siècles)," in *Castrum 5: Archéologie des espaces agraires méditerranéens au Moyen Age*, ed. A. Bazzana (Madrid, 1999), 255–63.

Conedera, M., P. Krebs, W. Tinner, M. Pradella, and D. Torriani, "The Cultivation of *Castanea sativa* (Mill.) in Europe, from Its Origin to Its Diffusion on a Continental Scale," *Vegetation History and Archaeobotany* 13 (2004), 161–79.

Conedera, M., M.C. Manetti, F. Giudici, and E. Amorini, "Distribution and Economic Potential of the Sweet Chestnut (*Castanea sativa* Mill.) in Europe," *Ecologia mediterranea* 30.2 (2004), 179–93.

Conedera, M., P. Stanga, C. Lischer, and V. Stöckli, "Competition and Dynamics in Abandoned Chestnut Orchards in Southern Switzerland," *Ecologia mediterranea* 26 (2000), 101–12.

Conti, P., "Proprietà e possesso, requisizioni e confische, conduzione agraria e mobilità sociale nelle vicende degli insediamenti," in *Il territorio tra tardoantico e altomedioevo*, ed. G. Brogiolo and L. Castelletti (Florence, 1992), 7–20.

Coon, L., *Dark Age Bodies: Gender and Monastic Practice in the Early Medieval West* (Philadelphia, 2011).

Corolla, A., "Il castello di S. Adiutore e le trasformazioni del territorio di Cava dei Tirreni," in *V congresso nazionale di archeologia medievale*, ed. G. Volpe and P. Favia (Florence, 2009), 355–60.

Corona, G., "The Decline of the Commons and the Environmental Balance of Early Modern Italy," in *Nature and History in Modern Italy*, ed. M. Armiero and M. Hall (Athens, OH, 2010), 89–107.

Bibliography

Corridi, C., "Dati archeozoologici dagli scavi di Piazza della Signoria a Firenze," in *Atti del 1 Convegno nazionale di archeologia* (Florence, 1995), 331–39.

Cortonesi, A., "Fra autoconsumo e mercato: L'alimentazione rurale e urbana nel basso medioevo," in *Storia dell'alimentazione*, ed. J. Flandrin and M. Montanari (Bari, 1997), 325–35.

Costambeys, M., "Settlement, Taxation, and the Condition of the Peasantry in Post-Roman Central Italy," *Journal of Agrarian Change* 9 (2009), 92–119.

Couteaux, M., "A propos de la signification pollinique de *Castanea* en Dordogne," *Pollen et spores* 23 (1981), 433–39.

Cox Miller, P., *The Corporeal Imagination* (Philadelphia, 2009).

Criniti, N., "Economia e società sull'Appennino piacentino: La tavola alimentare veleiate," in *Storia di Piacenza*, 6 vols., ed. F. Ghizzoni, Vol. I.2 (Piacenza, 1990), 907–1011.

La tabula alimentaria di Veleia (Parma, 1991).

Cronon, W., (ed.) *Changes in the Land: Indians, Colonists, and the Ecology of New England* (New York, 1983).

ed., *Uncommon Ground* (New York, 1996).

Crosby, A., *The Columbian Exchange: Biological and Cultural Consequences of 1492. 30th Anniversary Edition* (Westport, 2003).

The Columbian Voyages, the Columbian Exchange, and Their Historians (Washington, 1987).

Ecological Imperialism: The Biological Expansion of Europe (Cambridge, 1986).

"Ecological Imperialism: The Overseas Migration of Western Europeans as a Biological Phenomenon," in *Germs, Seeds, and Animals: Studies in Ecological History* (Armonk, NY, 1994), 28–44.

Cruise, G., "Environmental Change and Human Impact in the Upper Mountain Zone of the Ligurian Apennines," *Rivista di studi liguri* 57 (1994), 175–94.

"Pollen Stratigraphy of Two Holocene Peat Sites in the Ligurian Apennines, Northern Italy," *Review of Palaeobotany and Palynology* 63 (1990), 299–313.

Cucini, C., "Topografia del territorio delle valli del Pecora e dell'Alma," in *Scarlino 1: Storia e territorio*, ed. R. Francovich (Florence, 1985), 147–320.

Cusack, C., *The Sacred Tree: Ancient and Medieval Manifestations* (Newcastle upon Tyne, 2011).

Cutini, A., "Biomass, Litterfall, and Productivity of Chestnut Coppices of Various Age at Mount Amiata," *Ecologia mediterranea* 26.1 (2000), 33–41.

Dallman, P., *Plant Life in the World's Mediterranean Climates* (Berkeley, 1998).

Daniel, G., *The Origins and Growth of Archaeology* (Harmondsworth, 1967).

Davis, M., and R. Shaw, "Range Shifts and Adaptive Responses to Quaternary Climate Change," *Science* 292 (April 27, 2001), 673–79.

Davite, C., and D. Moreno, "Des 'saltus' aux 'alpes' dans les Appenins du nord (Italie)," in *L'homme et la nature au moyen âge*, ed. M. Colardelle (Paris, 1996), 138–42.

de Beaulieu, J.-L., "Timberline and Human Impact in the French Alps," in *Impact of Prehistoric and Medieval Man on the Vegetation*, ed. D. Moe and S. Hicks (Strasbourg, 1990).

De Grossi Mazzorin, J., and C. Minniti, "L'allevamento e l'approvvigionamento alimentare di una comunità urbana," in *Roma dall'antichità al medioevo*, 2 vols., ed. M. Arena and L. Paroli, Vol. 1 (Milan, 2001), 69–78.

Bibliography

De Moor, M., L. Shaw-Taylor, and P. Warde, "Comparing the Historical Commons of North West Europe: An Introduction," in *The Management of Common Land in North West Europe*, c. *1500–1850* (Turnhout, 2002), 15–31.

"Preliminary Conclusions: The Commons of North West Europe," in *The Management of Common Land in North West Europe*, c. *1500–1850* (Turnhout, 2002), 247–65.

De Rossi, G., "Indicatori archeologici della produzione e diffusione del vino nella Baia di Napoli in età altomedievale," in *Paesaggi e insediamenti rurali in Italia meridionale tra tardoantico e altomedioevo*, ed. G. Volpe and M. Turchiano (Bari, 2005), 541–49.

de Vartavan, C., and V. Asensi Amorós, *Codex of Ancient Egyptian Plant Remains* (London, 1997).

Dean, W., *With Broadax and Firebrand: The Destruction of the Brazilian Atlantic Forest* (Berkeley, 1995).

Del Panta, L., and E. Sonnino, "Introduzione," in K. Beloch, *Storia della popolazione d'Italia* (Florence, 1994), XXIV–XXVI.

del Treppo, M., "Una città del Mezzogiorno nei secoli IX–XIV," in *Convegno internazionale 14–16 giugno 1973: Amalfi nel medioevo* (Salerno, 1977), 19–175.

del Treppo, M., and A. Leone, *Amalfi medioevale* (Naples, 1977).

Delano Smith, C., "Where was the 'Wilderness' in Roman Times?," in *Human Landscapes in Classical Antiquity*, ed. G. Shipley and J. Salmon (London, 1996), 154–79.

Delort, R., "Percevoir la nature au moyen âge," in *Campagnes médiévales*, ed. D. Mornet (Paris, 1995), 31–43.

L'uomo e gli animali dall'età della pietra a oggi (Bari, 1987).

Delort, R., and F. Walter, *Histoire de l'environnement européen* (Paris, 2001).

Delumeau, J.-P., *Arezzo, espace et sociétés*, 2 vols., Vol. 1: *715–1230* (Rome, 1996).

DeSantis, P., "Le suppellettili in legno di uso quotidiano," in *Fortuna maris: La nave romana die Comacchio*, ed. F. Berti (Bologna, 1990), 105–12.

Devroey, J., *Economie rurale et société dans l'Europe franque (VIe–IXe siècles)* (Paris, 2003).

Puissants et misérables: Système sociale et monde paysan dans l'Europe des Francs (IVe–IXe siècles) (Brussels, 2006).

di Castri, F., "On Invading Species and Invaded Ecosystems: The Interplay of Historical Chance and Biological Necessity," in *Biological Invasions in Europe and the Mediterranean Basin*, ed. F. di Castri, A. J. Hansen, and M. Debussche (Dordrecht, 1990), 3–16.

Di Pasquale, G., "Reworking the Idea of Chestnut (*Castanea sativa* Mill.). Cultivation in Roman Times: New Data from Ancient Campania," *Plant Biosystems* 144 (2010), 865–73.

di Rita, F., and D. Magri, "Holocene Drought, Deforestation, and Evergreen Vegetation in the Central Mediterranean: A 5,500-Year Record from Lago Alimini Piccolo, Apulia, Southeast Italy," *The Holocene* 19.2 (2009), 295–306.

Dimbleby, C., and E. Grüger, "Pollen Analysis of Soil Samples from the AD 79 Level: Pompeii, Oplontis, and Boscoreale," in *The Natural History of Pompeii*, ed. W. Jashemski and F. Meyer (Cambridge, 2002), 181–216.

Diurni, G., *Le situazioni possessorie nel medioevo* (Milan, 1988).

Bibliography

Doehard, R., *Le haut moyen âge occidental* (Paris, 1971).

Drescher-Schneider, R., "Forest, Forest Clearance and Open Land during the Time of the Roman Empire in Northern Italy," in *Evaluation of Land Surfaces Cleared from Forests in the Mediterranean Region during the Time of the Roman Empire*, ed. B. Frenzel (Stuttgart, 1994), 45–58.

Dronke, P., "*Arbor caritatis*," in *Medieval Studies for J. A. W. Bennet*, ed. P. Heyworth (Oxford, 1981), 207–53.

"Tradition and Innovation in Western Color Imagery," in *The Medieval Poet and His World* (Rome, 1984), 55–103.

Duchet-Suchaux, G., "Les noms des arbres," in *L'arbre: Histoire naturelle et symbolique de l'arbre, du bois et du fruit au Moyen Age* (Paris, 1993), 13–23.

Dupâquier, J., *Des origines aux prémices de la révolution démographique*, Vol. 1 of *Histoire des populations de l'Europe*, 3 vols., ed. J. Bardet and J. Dupâquier (Paris, 1997–99).

Durand, A., "Les milieux naturels autour de l'an mil: Approches paléoenvironnementales méditerranéennes," in *Hommes et sociétés dans l'Europe de l'an mil*, ed. P. Bonnassie and P. Toubert (Toulouse, 2004), 73–100.

Les paysages médiévaux du Languedoc (IXe–XIIe siècles) (Toulouse, 1998).

Durand, A., and M. Ruas, "La forêt languedocienne (fin VIIIe siècle–XIe siècle)," in *Les forêts d'Occident du moyen âge à nos jours*, ed. A. Corvol-Dessert (Toulouse, 2004), 163–80.

Durliat, J., *De la ville antique à la ville byzantine* (Rome, 1990).

Dutton, P., *Charlemagne's Mustache and Other Cultural Clusters of a Dark Age* (New York, 2004).

Fabre-Vassas, C., *The Singular Beast* (New York, 1997).

Fairhead, J., and M. Leach, "Reframing Forest History: A Radical Reappraisal of the Roles of People and Climate in West African Vegetation Change," in *Time-Scales and Environmental Change*, ed. T. Driver and G. Chapman (London, 1996), 169–95.

Fasola, U., "Le recenti scoperte nella catacomba di S. Gennaro a Napoli," *Rendiconti della Pontificia accademia romana d'archeologia* 46 (1973–74), 187–224.

Fasoli, G., "Il patrimonio della chiesa ravennate," in *Storia di Ravenna*, 5 vols., ed. G. Susini, Vol. II.1 (Venice, 1991), 389–400.

Fauve-Chamoux, A., "Chestnuts," in *The Cambridge World History of Food*, 2 vols., ed. K. Kiple and K. Coneè Ornelas, Vol. 1 (Cambridge, 2000), 359–64.

Feller, L., "Seigneurs et paysans dans le bassin Méditerranéen, vers 950–vers 1050," in *Hommes et sociétés dans l'Europe de l'an mil*, ed. P. Bonnassie and P. Toubert (Toulouse, 2004), 273–90.

Fenaroli, L., *Gli alberi d'Italia* (Milan, 1967).

Il castagno (Rome, 1945).

Guida agli alberi d'Italia (Florence, 1984).

Fenaroli, L., and G. Gambi, *Alberi* (Trent, 1976).

Ferrantini, A., "I limiti altimetrici della vegetazione nel vulcano laziale," *Rivista geografica italiana* 49 (1942), 18–34.

"Osservazioni sulle modificazioni della vegetazione nei Colli Albani," *Bollettino della Società geografica italiana*, series 7, no. 11 (1946), 16–30.

Ferrarini, E., "Manufatti di legno e cuoio dall'area nord del Museo di Altino," *Quaderni di archeologia del Veneto* 8 (1992), 191–206.

Bibliography

Ferro, A., "La fauna," in *San Michele di Trino (VC): Dal villaggio romano al castello medievale*, 3 vols., ed. M. Negro Ponzi Mancini, Vol. II (Florence, 1999), 631–45.

Figliuolo, B., "Longobardi e Normanni," in *Storia e civiltà della Campania*, ed. G. Pugliese Carratelli (Naples, 1992), 37–86.

Figueiral, I., "Wood Resources in Northwest Portugal: Their Availability and Use from the Late Bronze Age to the Roman Period," *Vegetation History and Archaeobotany* 5 (1996), 121–29.

Flahaut, C., *La distribution géographique des végétaux dans la région méditerranéenne française* (Paris, 1937).

Flandrin, J., "I tempi moderni," in *Storia dell'alimentazione*, ed. J. Flandrin and M. Montanari (Bari, 1997), 429–48.

Flannery, K., "Origins and Effects of Early Near Eastern Domestication in Iran and the Near East," in *The Domestication and Exploitation of Plants and Animals*, ed. P. Ucko and G. Dimbleby (Chicago, 1969), 73–100.

Follieri, M., D. Magri, and L. Sadori, "250,000-Year Pollen Record from Valle di Castiglione (Roma)," *Pollen et spores* 30 (1988), 329–56.

Fontaine, J., *Isidore de Séville: Genèse et originalité de la culture hispanique au temps des Wisigoths* (Turnhout, 2000).

Fonti, P., P. Cherubini, A. Rigling, P. Weber, and G. Biging, "Tree-Rings Show Competition Dynamics in Abandoned *Castanea sativa* Coppices after Land-Use Changes," *Journal of Vegetation Science* 17 (2006) 103–12.

Fortmann, L., "The Tree Tenure Factor in Agroforestry, with Particular Reference to Africa," *Agroforestry Systems* 2 (1985), 229–51.

Fortman, L., and J. Bruce, "Why Land Tenure and Tree Tenure Matter," in *Whose Trees? Proprietary Dimensions of Forestry* (Boulder, 1988), 1–9.

Fossier, R., *L'infanzia dell'Europa* (Bologna, 1987).

Fouet, G., *La villa Gallo-romaine de Montmaurin (Haut Garonne)* (Paris, 1969).

Foxhall, L., M. Jones, and H. Forbes, "Human Ecology and the Classical Landscape," in *Classical Archaeology*, ed. S. Alcock and R. Osborne (Oxford, 2007), 91–117.

Frayn, J., *Subsistence Farming in Roman Italy* (London, 1979).

Frazer, J., *The Golden Bough*, 12 vols., Vol. II (London, 1913).

Fronza, V., "Strumenti e materiali per un atlante dell'edilizia altomedievale in materiale deperibile," in *IV congresso nazionale di archeologia medievale*, ed. R. Francovich and M. Valenti (Florence, 2006), 539–45.

Frugoni, C., "Alberi in *paradiso voluptatis*," in *L'ambiente vegetale nell'alto medioevo*, Settimane del CISAM 37 (Spoleto, 1990), 725–62.

Gadgil, M., and R. Guha, *This Fissured Land: An Ecological History of India* (Berkeley, 1992).

Galante, M., *La datazione dei documenti del* Codex diplomaticus cavensis. *Appendice: Edizione degli inediti* (Salerno, 1980).

Galetti, P., *Abitare nel medioevo* (Florence, 1997).

"Bosco e spazi incolti nel territorio piacentino durante l'alto medioevo," in *Il bosco nel medioevo*, ed. B. Andreolli and M. Montanari (Bologna, 1988), 201–21.

Gallardo, J., M. Rico, and M. González, "Some Ecological Aspects of a Chestnut Coppice Located at the Sierra de Gata Mountains (Western Spain) and Its Relationship with a Sustainable Management," *Ecologia mediterranea* 26.1 (2000), 53–69.

Bibliography

Galop, D., *La forêt, l'homme et le troupeau dans les Pyrénées* (Toulouse, 1998).

Gambino, L., "L'insediamento di Filattiera-Sorano nel quadro delle conoscenze topografiche sulla Lunigiana romana," in *Filattiera-Sorano*, ed. E. Giannichedda (Florence, 1998), 238–42.

Gandullo Gutiérrez, J., A. Rubio Sánchez, O. Sánchez Palomares, A. Blanco Andray, V. Gómez Sanz, and R. Elena Roselló, *Las estaciones ecológicas de los castañares españoles* (Madrid, 2004).

Gasparri, S., *La cultura tradizionale dei Longobardi* (Spoleto, 1983).

Gatto, L., "Riflettendo sulla consistenza demografica della Roma altomedievale," in *Roma medievale: Aggiornamenti*, ed. P. Delogu (Florence, 1998), 143–55.

Gaulin, J., "Tra *silvaticus* e *domesticus*: Il bosco nella trattatistica medievale," in *Il bosco nel medioevo*, ed. M. Montanari and B. Andreolli (Bologna, 1988), 85–96.

"Tradition et pratiques de la littérature agronomique pendant le haut moyen âge," in *L'ambiente vegetale nell'alto medioevo*, Settimane del CISAM 37 (Spoleto, 1990), 103–35.

George, J., *Venantius Fortunatus: A Latin Poet in Merovingian Gaul* (Oxford, 1992).

Giardina, A., "Allevamento ed economia della selva in Italia meridionale: Trasformazioni e continuità," in *Società romana e produzione schiavistica*, 3 vols., ed. A. Giardina and A. Schiavone, Vol. I (Bari, 1981), 87–113.

Giardina, C., *La così detta proprietà degli alberi separata da quella del suolo in Italia* (Palermo, 1941).

Gioanola, E., *Giovanni Pascoli: Sentimenti filiali di un parricida* (Milan, 2000).

Giordano, E., "Biology, Physiology, and Ecology of Chestnut," in *Proceedings of the International Congress on Chestnut*, ed. E. Antognozzi (Spoleto, n.d.), 89–93.

Giovannini, F., *Natalità, mortalità e demografia dell'Italia medievale sulla base dei dati archeologici* (Oxford, 2001).

Giovinazzo, R., "I reperti faunistici," in *Filattiera-Sorano*, ed. E. Giannichedda (Florence, 1998), 196–97.

"Le risorse alimentari animali," in *S. Antonino: Un insediamento fortificato nella Liguria bizantina*, ed. T. Mannoni and G. Murialdo (Bordighera, 2001), 639–56.

Gobet, E., W. Tinner, P. Hubschmid, *et al.*, "Influence of Human Impact and Bedrock Differences on the Vegetational History of the Insubrian Alps," *Vegetation History and Archaeobotany* 9 (2000), 175–87.

Godelier, M., *L'idéal et le matériel* (Paris, 1984).

Godwin, H., *The History of the British Flora* (Cambridge, 1975).

Grand, R., and R. Delatouche, *L'agriculture au moyen âge, de la fin de l'empire romain au XVIe siècle* (Paris, 1950).

Grégoire, R., "La foresta come esperienza religiosa," in *L'ambiente vegetale nell'alto medioevo*, Settimane del CISAM 37 (Spoleto, 1990), 663–703.

Greig, J., "Archaeobotanical and Historical Records Compared: A New Look at the Taphonomy of Edible and Other Useful Plants from the 11th to the 18th Centuries AD," *Circaea* 12 (1996), 211–47.

Grieco, A., "Reflexions sur l'histoire des fruits au moyen âge," in *L'arbre: Histoire naturelle et symbolique de l'arbre, du bois et du fruit au Moyen Âge* (Paris, 1993), 145–51.

Grieve, M., *A Modern Herbal: The Medicinal, Culinary, Cosmetic and Economic Properties, Cultivation and Folk-Lore of Herbs, Grasses, Fungi, Shrubs and Trees, with All Their Modern Scientific Uses*, 2 vols. (New York, 1959).

Bibliography

Grossi, P. *Il dominio e le cose: Percezioni medievali e moderne dei diritti reali* (Milan, 1992).

Grove, A., and O. Rackham, *The Nature of Mediterranean Europe: An Ecological History* (New Haven, 2001).

Groves, R., "The Biogeography of Mediterranean Plant Invasions," in *Biogeography of Mediterranean Invasions*, ed. R. Groves and F. di Castri (Cambridge, 1991), 427–38.

Grüger, E., B. Thulin, J. Müller, J. Schneider, J. Alefs, and F. Welter-Schultes, "Environmental Changes in and around Lake Avernus in Greek and Roman Times," in *The Natural History of Pompeii*, ed. W. Jashemski and F. Meyer (Cambridge, 2002), 240–73.

Guidi, M., and P. Piussi, "The Influence of Old Rural Land-Management Practices on the Natural Regeneration of Woodland on Abandoned Farmland in the Prealps of Friuli, Italy," in *Ecological Effects of Afforestation*, ed. C. Watkins (Wallingford, 1998), 57–67.

Guillou, A., *Régionalisme et indépendence dans l'empire byzantin au VII siècle* (Rome, 1969).

Gullino, G., "La vite e il castagno in Piemonte," in *Uomini boschi castagne*, ed. R. Comba and I. Naso (Cuneo, 2000), 67–76.

Harris, D., "Domesticatory Relationships of People, Plants, and Animals," in *Redefining Nature*, ed. R. Ellen and K. Fukui (Oxford, 1996), 437–63.

"An Ecological Continuum of People–Plant Interaction," in *Foraging and Farming: The Evolution of Plant Exploitation*, ed. D. R. Harris and G. Hillman (London, 1989), 11–26.

Harrison, D., "Plague, Settlement and Structural Change at the Dawn of the Middle Ages," *Scandia* 59.1 (1993), 15–48.

Harrison, R., *Forests: The Shadow of Civilization* (Chicago, 1992).

Hasselrot, B., "L'abricot: Essai de monographie onomasiologique et sémantique," *Studia neophilologica* 13 (1940–41), 45–79, 226–52.

Hehn, V., *Cultivated Plants and Domesticated Animals in Their Migration from Asia to Europe* (Amsterdam, 1976).

Hemphill, P., "De-Forestation and Re-Forestation in a Central Italian Hinterland: Land Usage during and after the Roman Occupation," in *First Millennium Papers*, ed. R. F. J. Jones. J. H. F. Bloemers, S. L. Dyson, and M. Biddle (Oxford, 1984), 147–59.

Hermann, A., and M. Cagiano de Azevedo, "Farbe," in *Reallexikon für Antike und Christentum*, 24 vols., ed. T. Klauser, Vol. VII (Stuttgart, 1969), 386.

Higounet, C., "Les forêts de l'Europe occidentale du Ve au XIe siècle," in *Agricoltura e mondo rurale in occidente nell'alto medioevo*, Settimane del CISAM 13 (1966), 343–98.

Hoffmann, R., "Medieval Christendom in God's Creation," in *Northern Europe: An Environmental History*, ed. T. Whited (Santa Barbara, 2005), 45–72.

Hofmeister, A., "Der Übersetzer Johannes und das Geschlecht Comitis Mauronis in Amalfi," *Historische Vierteljahrschrift* 17 (1932), 225–84, 493–508, 831–33.

Hondelmann, W., *Die Kulturpflanzen der griechisch-römischen Welt: Pflänzische Ressourcen der Antike* (Berlin, 2002).

Hooke, D., *Trees in Anglo-Saxon England: Literature, Lore, and Landscape* (Woodbridge, 2010).

Bibliography

Hopf, M., "South and Southwest Europe," in *Progress in Old World Palaeoethnobotany: A Retrospective View on the Occasion of 20 Years of the International Work Group for Palaeoethnobotany*, ed. W. van Zeist, K. Wasylikowa, and K.-E. Behre (Rotterdam, 1991), 241–77.

"Walnüsse und Esskastanie in Holzschalen als Beigaben im frankischen Grab von Gellep (Krefeld)," *Jahrbuch des römisch-germanischen Zentralmuseums Mainz* 10 (1963), 200–03.

Horden, P., and N. Purcell, *The Corrupting Sea: a Study of Mediterranean History* (Oxford, 2000).

Horn, W., and E. Born, *The Plan of St. Gall*, 3 vols. (Berkeley, 1979).

Hubert, E., "Maisons urbaines et maisons rurales dans le Latium médiéval," in *Castrum 6: Maisons et espaces domestiques dans le monde méditerranéen au moyen âge*, ed. A. Bazzana and E. Hubert (Rome, 2000), 89–103.

"Mobilité de la population et structure des habitations à Rome et dans le Latium (IXe–XIIIe siècles)," in *Demografia e società nell'Italia medievale*, ed. R. Comba and I. Naso (Cuneo, 1994), 107–24.

Hughes, J., *Pan's Travail: Environmental Problems of the Ancient Greeks and Romans* (Baltimore, 1994).

Irninger, M., and M. Kühn, "Obstvielfalt: Von wilden und zahmen Früchten im Mittelalter und in früher Neuzeit," *Archäologie der Schweiz* 22 (1999), 48–56.

James, L., *Light and Color in Byzantine Art* (Oxford, 1996).

Jashemski, W., F. Meyer, and M. Ricciardi, "Catalogue of Plants," in *The Natural History of Pompeii*, ed. W. Jashemski and F. Meyer (Cambridge, 2002), 84–180.

Kaltenrieder, P., G. Procacci, B. Vannière, and W. Winner, "Vegetation and Fire History of the Euganean Hills (*Colli Euganei*) as Recorded by Lateglacial and Holocene Sedimentary Series from Lago della Costa," *The Holocene* 20.5 (2010), 679–95.

Kelly, F., "The Old Irish Tree List," *Celtica* 11 (1976), 107–24.

Kelly, M., and B. Huntley, "An 11,000-Year Record of Vegetation and Environment from Lago di Martignano, Latium, Italy," *Journal of Quaternary Science* 6 (1991), 209–24.

Keyser, R., "The Transformation of Traditional Woodland Management," *French Historical Studies* 32.3 (2009), 353–84.

King, A., "Mammal, Reptile, and Amphibian Bones," in *Excavations at the Mola di Monte Gelato*, ed. T. Potter and A. King (Rome, 1997), 383–403.

Kingsbury, N., *Hybrid: The History and Science of Plant Breeding* (Chicago, 2009).

Kooistra, L., "Arable Farming in the Hey Day of the Roman Villa at Voerendaal (Limbourg, the Netherlands)," in *Palaeoethnobotany and Archaeology: International Work Group for Palaeoethnobotany* (Nitra, 1991), 165–75.

Krahwinkler, H., *Friaul im Frühmittelalter* (Vienna, 1992).

Krebs, P., M. Condera, M. Pradella, D. Torriani, M. Felber, and W. Tinner, "Quaternary Refugia of the Sweet Chestnut (*Castanea sativa* Mill.): An Extended Palynological Approach," *Vegetation History and Archaeobotany* 13 (2004), 145–60.

Kronenberg, L., *Allegories of Farming from Greece and Rome* (Cambridge, 2009).

Küster, H., "Botanische Untersuchungen zur Landwirtschaft in den Rhein-Donau-Provinzen vom 1. bis zum 5. Jahrhundert nach Chr.," in *Ländliche Besiedlung und Landwirtschaft in der Rhein-Donau-Provinzen des römischen Reiches*, ed. H. Bender and H. Wolff (Espelkamp, 1994), 21–35.

"Kulturpflanzen," *Bauern in Bayern* (Munich, 1992), 58–63.

Bibliography

"Weizen, Pfeffer, Tannenholz: Botanische Untersuchungen zur Verbreitung von Handelsgütern in römischer Zeit," *Münsterische Beitrage zur antiken Handelsgeschichte* 15 (1995), 1–26.

Lagazzi, L., "I segni sulla terra: Sistemi di confinazione e di misurazione dei boschi nell'alto medioevo," in *Il bosco nel medioevo*, ed. B. Andreolli and M. Montanari (Bologna, 1988), 13–29.

Landers, J., *The Field and the Forge: Population, Production, and Power in the Pre-Industrial West* (Oxford, 2003).

LaValva, R., *The Eternal Child* (Chapel Hill, 1999).

Le Floc'h, E., "Invasive Plants of the Mediterranean Basin," in *Biogeography of Mediterranean Invasions*, ed. R. Groves and F. di Castri (Cambridge, 1991), 67–80.

Leclercq, H., and F. Cabrol, eds., *Dictionnaire d'archéologie chrétienne et de liturgie*, 15 vols. (Paris, 1907–53).

Le Goff, J., *La civilisation de l'Occident médiéval* (Paris, 1964).

Lefebvre, C., *Oppida helvica* (Paris, 2006).

Leggio, T., "Viabilità e forme insediative lungo la Valle del Velino tra tarda antichità e alto medioevo," in *L'Appennino in età romana e nel primo medioevo*, ed. M. Destro and E. Giorgi (Bologna, 2004), 231–48.

Leveau, P., "L'archéologie des paysages et les époques historiques," in *Milieux naturels, espaces sociaux*, ed. E. Mornet and F. Morenzoni (Paris, 1997), 71–83.

Lewit, T., *Agricultural Production in the Roman Economy, AD 200–400* (Oxford, 1991).

"Pigs, Presses, and Pastoralism," *Early Medieval Europe* 17.1 (2009), 77–91.

Linnard, W., *Welsh Woods and Forests: A History* (Llandysul, 2000).

Livarda, A., "Spicing up Life in Northwestern Europe: Exotic Food Plant Imports in the Roman and Medieval Worlds," *Vegetation History and Archaeobotany* 20 (2011), 143–64.

Livi-Bacci, M., "Macro versus Micro," in *Convergent Issues in Genetics and Demography*, ed. J. Adams, M. Livi-Bacci, E. Thompson, *et al.* (New York, 1990), 15–25.

Lizier, A., *L'economia rurale dell'età prenormanna nell'Italia meridionale* (Palermo, 1907).

Lo Cascio, E., "La dissoluzione dell'impero romano d'occidente: La 'spiegazione' demografica," in *Filosofia e storia della cultura: Studi in onore di Fulvio Tessitore*, ed. F. Tessitore, F. Cacciatore, M. Martirano, and E. Massimilla (Naples, 1999), 157–82.

"Il rapporto uomini-terra nel paesaggio dell'Italia romana," *Index* 32 (2004), 107–21.

Lo Cascio, E., and P. Malanima, "Cycles and Stability: Italian Population before the Demographic Transition (225 BC–AD 1900)," *Rivista di storia economica* 21.3 (2005), 197–232.

Lockwood, L., *Introduction to Population Ecology* (Malden, 2006).

Logan, W., *Oak: The Frame of Civilization* (New York, 2005).

Lopane, E., M. Bandini Mazzanti, and C. Accorsi, "Pollini e semi/frutti dell'abitato etrusco-celtico di Pianella di Monte Savino," in *Studi in ricordo di Daria Bertolani Marchetti*, ed. C. Accorsi (Modena, 1998), 359–65.

Lorenzi, A., "L'uomo e le foreste," *Rivista geografica italiana* 25 (1918), 141–65, 213–42; 26 (1919), 47–57.

Loud, G., "The Monastic Economy in the Principality of Salerno during the Eleventh and Twelfth Centuries," *Papers of the British School at Rome* 71 (2003), 141–79.

Bibliography

Lovejoy, A., and G. Boas, *Primitivism and Related Ideas in Antiquity* (Baltimore, 1935).

Lowe, J., C. Accorsi, M. Bandini Mazzanti, et al., "Pollen Stratigraphy of Sediment Sequences from Lakes Albano and Nemi (near Rome) and from the Central Adriatic," *Memorie dell'Istituto italiano di idrobiologia* 55 (1996), 71–98.

Lowe, J., C. Davite, D. Moreno, and R. Maggi, "Holocene Pollen Stratigraphy and Human Interference in the Woodland of the Northern Apennines, Italy," *The Holocene* 4.2 (1994), 153–64.

"Stratigrafia pollinica olocenica e storia delle risorse boschive dell'Appennino settentrionale," *Rivista geografica italiana* 102 (1995), 267–310.

Lutts, R., "'Like Manna from God': The American Chestnut Trade in Southwestern Virginia," *Environmental History* 9 (2004), 497–525.

Magri, D., "Late Quaternary Vegetation History at Lagaccione near Lago di Bolsena (Central Italy)," *Review of Palaeobotany and Palynology* 106 (1999), 171–208.

Magri, D., and L. Sadori, "Late Pleistocene Pollen Stratigraphy at Lago di Vico, Central Italy," *Vegetation History and Archaeobotany* 8 (1999), 247–60.

Marazzi, F., "The Early Medieval Alternative," in *Nourrir les cités de Mediterranée*, ed. B. Marin and C. Virlouvet (Paris, 2003), 739–67.

Marazzi, F., C. Filippone, P. Petrone, T. Galloway, and L. Fattore, "San Vincenzo al Volturno: Scavi 2000–2002," *Archeologia medievale* 29 (2002), 209–74.

Marchesini, M., S. Marvelli, I. Gobbo, and S. Biagioni, "Paesaggio vegetale e antropico circostante l'abitato altomedievale di Nogara," in *Nogara*, ed. F. Saggioro (Rome, 2011), 159–92.

Marciani, F., "Alcuni aspetti storici e folcloristici della castaneicoltura irpino-salernitana," *Monti e boschi* 2 (1952), 79–84.

Marini, S., "L'albero del ricco e l'albero del povero: Lo sfruttamento del castagno e dell'abete nel feudo di Vernio," in *L'uomo e la foresta, secc. XIII–XVIII*, ed. S. Cavaciocchi (Florence, 1996), 955–70.

Marlière, E., *L'outre et le tonneau dans l'Occident romain* (Montagnac, 2002).

Marsh, G., *Man and Nature* (Seattle, 2003).

Martin, J., "A propos de la *Vita* de Barbatus," *Mélanges de l'Ecole française de Rome* 86 (1974), 137–64.

"Capri, isola del ducato di Amalfi (X–XIII secolo)," in *Medioevo, Mezzogiorno, Mediterraneo 2*, ed. G. Rossetti and G. Vitolo (Naples, 2000), 25–42.

"Città e campagna: Economia e società (sec. VII–XIII)," in *Storia del Mezzogiorno*, 15 vols., ed. G. Galasso and R. Romeo, Vol. III: *Alto medioevo* (Naples, 1990), 259–382.

"L'espace cultivé," in *Uomo e spazio nell'alto medioevo*, Settimane del CISAM 50 (Spoleto, 2003), 239–97.

"L'évolution démographique de l'Italie méridionale du VIe au XIVe siècle," in *Demografia e società nell'Italia medievale*, ed. R. Comba and I. Naso (Cuneo, 1994), 351–62.

"L'homme et le milieu en Pouille au début du moyen âge," *Bulletin de l'Association de geographes française* 499 (1984), 15–23.

"Perception et description du paysage rural dans les actes notariés sud-italiens (IX–XIIe siècle)," in *Castrum 5: Archéologie des espaces agraires méditerranéens au Moyen Âge*, ed. A. Bazzana (Madrid, 1999), 113–27.

"Quelques données textuelles sur la maison en Campanie et en Pouille (Xe–XIIe siècle)," in *Castrum 6: Maisons et espaces domestiques dans le monde méditerranéen au moyen âge*, ed. A. Bazzana and E. Hubert (Rome, 2000), 75–87.

Bibliography

"Settlement and the Agrarian Economy," in *The Society of Norman Italy*, ed. G. Loud and A. Metcalfe (Leiden, 2002), 17–45.

"Le travail agricole," in *Terra e uomini nel Mezzogiorno normanno-svevo*, ed. G. Musca (Bari, 1987), 113–57.

Martin, M., C. Mattioni, M. Cherubini, D. Taurchini, and F. Villani, "Genetic Diversity in European Chestnut Populations," *Acta horticulturae* 866 (2009), 163–67.

Martínez Cortizas, A., T. Mighall, X. Pontevedra Pombal, J. Novoa Munfoz, E. Peiteado Varelal, and R. Pifneiro Rebolol, "Linking Changes in Atmospheric Dust Deposition,Vegetation Change and Human Activities in Northwest Spain during the Last 5,300 Years," *The Holocene* 15 (2005), 698–706.

Mattingly, D., *An Imperial Possession* (London, 2006).

Maurizio, A., *Die Getreide-Nahrung im Wandel der Zeiten* (Zurich, 1916).

Mayo, J., *A History of Ecclesiastical Dress* (London, 1984).

McCormick, M., *Origins of the European Economy: Communications and Commerce, AD 300–900* (Cambridge, 2001).

McKean, M., "Common Property: What Is It, What Is It Good for, and What Makes It Work?," in *People and Forests: Communities, Institutions, and Governance*, ed. C. Gibson, M. McKean, and E. Ostrom (Cambridge, MA, 2000), 27–55.

McNeill, J., "Foreword," in A. Crosby, *The Columbian Exchange: Biological and Cultural Consequences of 1492. 30th Anniversary Edition* (Westport, 2003), xi–xv.

The Mountains of the Mediterranean World (Cambridge, 1992).

Something New under the Sun (New York, 2000).

McNeill, J., and V. Winiwarter, "Breaking the Sod," *Science* 304 (2004), 1627–29.

Meier, C., and R. Suntrup, "Zum Lexikon der Farbebedeutung im Mittelalter," *Frühmittelalterliche Studien* 21 (1987), 390–478.

Meiggs, R., *Trees and Timber in the Ancient Mediterranean World* (Oxford, 1982).

Menant, F., *Campagnes lombardes du moyen âge: L'économie et la société rurales dans la région de Bergame, de Crémone et de Brescia du xe au xiiie siècle* (Rome, 1993).

Meneghini, R., and R. Santangeli-Valenziani, *Roma nell'alto medioevo* (Rome, 2004).

Meotto, F., S. Pellegrino, and J. Craddock, "Ectomycorrhizal Fungi of Chestnut with Particular Reference to Choice Edible Mushrooms," in *Proceedings of the International Congress on Chestnut*, ed. E. Antognozzi (Spoleto, n.d.), 403–08.

Merz, F., *Die Edelkastanie: Ihre volkswirtschaftliche Bedeutung, ihr Anbau und ihre Bewirtschaftung* (Bern, 1919).

Meusel, H., E. Jäger, and E. Weinert, *Vergleichende Chorologie der Zentraleuropäischen Flora* (Jena, 1965).

Meyer, F., "Carbonized Food Plants of Pompeii, Herculaneum, and the Villa at Torre Annunziata," *Economic Botany* 34 (1980), 401–37.

Migliario, E., "A proposito di CTh ix, 30, 1–5: Alcune riflessioni sul paesaggio italico tardoantico," *Archeologia medievale* 22 (1991), 475–85.

Molossi, L., *Vocabolario topografico dei ducati di Parma, Piacenza, e Guastalla* (Parma, 1834).

Mols, S., *Wooden Furniture in Herculaneum* (Amsterdam, 1999).

Monckton, S., "Plant Remains," in *The Excavations at San Giovanni di Ruoti*, 3 vols., Vol. iii: *The Faunal and Plant Remains*, ed. M. MacKinnon, A. Eastham, S. Monckton, et al. (Toronto, 2002), 201–09.

Montanari, M., *L'alimentazione contadina nell'alto medioevo* (Naples, 1979).

Bibliography

Campagne medievali: Strutture produttive, rapporti di lavoro, sistemi alimentari (Turin, 1984).

Contadini e città fra "Langobardia" e "Romania" (Florence, 1988).

"Dalla tarda antichità all'alto medioevo (secoli III–X)," in *Storia dell'alimentazione*, ed. J. Flandrin and M. Montanari (Bari, 1997), 211–33.

La faim et l'abondance: Histoire de l'alimentation en Europe (Paris, 1995).

"La foresta come spazio economico e culturale," in *Uomo e spazio nell'alto medioevo*, Settimane del CISAM 50 (Spoleto, 2003), 301–40.

"Un frutto ricco di storia," in *La castagna sulle tavole d'Europa* (San Piero al Bagno, 2001), 50–63.

Uomini terre boschi nell'occidente medievale (Catania, 1992).

"Vegetazione e alimentazione," in *L'ambiente vegetale nell'alto medioevo*, Settimane del CISAM 37 (Spoleto, 1990), 281–322.

Moreno, D., "Châtaigneraie 'historique' et châtaigneraie 'traditionelle,'" *Médiévales* 16–17 (1989), 147–69.

Dal documento al terreno: Storia e archeologia dei sistemi silvo-pastorali (Bologna, 1990).

"Storia delle risorse ambientali e forme di appropriazione," in *Demani civici e risorse ambientali*, ed. F. Carletti (Naples, 1993), 63–76.

Moreno, D., and G. Poggi, "Storia delle risorse boschive nelle montagne mediterranee," in *L'uomo e la foresta, secc. XIII–XVIII*, ed. S. Cavaciocchi (Florence, 1996), 635–53.

Muir, E., and G. Ruggiero, eds., *Microhistory and the Lost Peoples of Europe* (Baltimore, 1991).

Müller, M., *Die Kleidung nach Quellen des frühen Mittelalters* (Berlin, 2003).

Murphy, P., U. Albarella, M. Germany, and A. Locker, "Production, Imports and Status: Biological Remains from a Late Roman Farm at Great Hants Farm, Boreham, Essex, UK," *Environmental Archaeology* 5 (2000), 35–48.

Naveh, Z., and J. Vernet, "The Palaeohistory of the Mediterranean Biota," in *Biogeography of Mediterranean Invasions*, ed. R. Groves and F. di Castri (Cambridge, 1991), 19–32.

Negri, G., "Distribuzione geografica del castagno e del faggio in Italia," *L'Alpe* 18 (1931), 589–94.

Negro Ponzi Mancini, M., "Ambiente e risorse alimentari: Dati archeologici," in *San Michele di Trino (VC): Dal villaggio romano al castello medievale*, 3 vols., ed. M. Negro Ponzi Mancini, Vol. II (Florence, 1999), 549–73.

"Dalla fattoria al castello," in *San Michele di Trino (VC): Dal villaggio romano al castello medievale*, 3 vols., ed. M. Negro Ponzi Mancini, Vol. II (Florence, 1999), 455–548.

Nisbet, R., "Alcuni aspetti della storia naturale del castagno," in *Uomini boschi castagne*, ed. R. Comba and I. Naso (Cuneo, 2000), 9–17.

"Le analisi antracologiche," in *Belmonte: Alle radici della storia*, ed. M. Cima (Cuorgné, 1986), 69–73.

"Analisi paletnobotaniche," in *Belmonte: Alle radici della storia*, ed. M. Cima (Cuorgné, 1986), 74–79.

"I macroresti vegetali," in *San Michele di Trino (VC): Dal villaggio romano al castello medievale*, 3 vols., ed. M. Negro Ponzi Mancini, Vol. II (Florence, 1999), 621–30.

Bibliography

"Storia forestale e agricoltura a Montaldo tra età del ferro e XVI secolo," in *Montaldo di Mondovì*, ed. E. Micheletto and M. Venturino Gambari (Rome, 1991), 247–51.

Noël, R., *Les dépôts de pollens fossiles* (Turnhout, 1972).

Noyé, G., "Economia e società nella Calabria bizantina," in *Storia della Calabria medievale*, 2 vols., ed. A. Placanica, Vol. II (Reggio, 2001), 579–655.

Ovit, G., *The Restoration of Perfection: Labor and Technology in Medieval Culture* (New Brunswick, 1987).

Paci, M., *Ecologia forestale* (Bologna, 1997).

Paganelli, A., and A. Miola, "Chestnut (*Castanea sativa* Mill.) as an Indigenous Species in Northern Italy," *Il Quaternario* 4 (1991), 99–106.

Paillet, F., "Chestnut: History and Ecology of a Transformed Species," *Journal of Biogeography* 29 (2002), 1517–30.

Palazzo, P., and G. Imperiale, "Il Finale e la formazione geomorfologica del territorio di Perti," in *S. Antonino: Un insediamento fortificato nella Liguria bizantina*, ed. T. Mannoni and G. Murialdo (Bordighera, 2001), 27–37.

Pals, J.-P., "De introductie van cultuurgewassen in de Romeinse Tijd," in *De introductie van onze cultuurplanten en hun begeleiders, van het Neolithicum tot 1500 AD*, ed. A. Zeven (Wageningen, 1997), 25–51.

Pardi, G., *L'Italia del XII secolo: Descritta da un geografo arabo* (Florence, 1919).

Pastoureau, M., *Black: The History of a Color* (Princeton, 2009).

Blue: The History of a Color (Princeton, 2001).

"L'église et la couleur des origines à la Réforme," *Bibliothèque de l'Ecole des chartes* 147 (1989), 203–30.

"Introduction à la symbolique médiévale du bois," in *L'arbre: Histoire naturelle et symbolique de l'arbre, du bois et du fruit au Moyen Âge* (Paris, 1993), 13–32.

Jésus chez le teinturier: Couleurs et teintures dans l'Occident médiéval (Paris, 1997).

Pavlovskis, Z., "The Riddler's Microcosm: From Symphosius to Boniface," *Classica et medievalia* 39 (1988), 219–51 (221).

Pellegrini, G., "Variazioni del paesaggio attraverso lo studio della fitotopomastica," in *L'ambiente vegetale nell'alto medioevo*, Settimane del CISAM 37 (Spoleto, 1990), 549–84.

Peluso, N., "Fruit Trees and Family Trees in an Anthropogenic Forest," in *Natures Past: The Environment and Human History*, ed. P. Squatriti (Ann Arbor, 2007), 54–102.

Peterken, G., *Natural Woodland: Ecology and Conservation in Northern Temperate Regions* (Cambridge, 1996).

Woodland Conservation and Management (Cambridge, 1993).

Petracco Sicardi, G., "*Vico Sahiloni* e *Silva Arimannorum*," *Archivio storico per le provincie parmensi* 29 (1977), 133–44.

Petrucci-Bavaud, M., and S. Jacomet, "Zur Interpretation von Nahrungsbeigaben in römerzeitlichen Brandgräbern," *Ethnographisch-archäologische Zeitschrift* 38 (1997), 567–93.

Piccolo Paci, S., *Storia delle vesti liturgiche: Forma, immagine e funzione* (Milan, 2008).

Pinna, M., *La storia del clima* (Roma, 1984).

Pinto, G., and E. Sonnino, "L'Italie," in *Histoire des populations de l'Europe*, 3 vols., ed. J. Bardet and J. Dupâquier, Vol. I (Paris, 1997), 485–508.

Pitte, J., *Terres de castanide* (Paris, 1987).

Bibliography

Pleij, H., *Colors, Demonic and Divine* (New York, 2004).

Poirier, P., "Architecture, combustibles, et environnement des thermes de Chassenon," *Aquitania* 16 (1999), 179–81.

Polara, G., "Aenigmata," in *Lo spazio letterario del Medioevo*, 5 vols., ed. G. Cavallo, C. Leonardi, and E. Menestò, Vol. 1.2 (Rome, 1993), 197–216.

Pollan, M., *The Botany of Desire: A Plant's-Eye View of the World* (New York, 2001).

Pratesi, A., "Barbato," in *Dizionario biografico degli Italiani*, 76 vols., Vol. VI (Rome, 1961), 128–30.

Pryor, L., "Forest Plantations and Invasions in the Mediterranean Zones of Australia and South Africa," in *Biogeography of Mediterranean Invasions*, ed. R. Groves and F. di Castri (Cambridge, 1991), 405–16.

Pugsley, P., *Roman Domestic Wood* (Oxford, 2003).

Pyne, S., *Vestal Fire* (Seattle, 1997).

Quaini, M., "Per lo studio dei caratteri originali del paesaggio agrario della Liguria pre-industriale," in *I paesaggi rurali Europei* (Perugia, 1975), 451–69.

Quirós Castillo, J., "Cambios y trasformaciones en el paysaje del Appennino toscano entre la Antigüedad Tardía y la Edad Media," *Archeologia medievale* 25 (1998), 177–97.

Rackham, O., *Ancient Woodland: Its History, Vegetation and Uses in England* (London, 1980).

——— "Savanna in Europe," in *The Ecological History of European Forests*, ed. C. Watkins and K. Kirby (Wallingford, 1998), 1–24.

——— *Trees and Woodland in the British Landscape: Revised Edition* (London, 1990).

Radkau, J., *Wood: A History* (Cambridge, 2012).

Rameau, J., D. Mansion, G. Dumé, *Flore forestière française: Guide écologique illustré*, 3 vols. (Dijon, 1989–2008).

Redon, O., *Des forêts et des âmes: Espace et société dans la Toscane médiévale* (Saint Denis, 2008).

Riccardi, E., "Indagine preliminare sullo scafo," in *Il relitto del Pozzino*, ed. F. Nicosia and A. Romualdi (Florence, 1990), 20–43.

Richardson, I., "Chestnuts," in *The Oxford Encyclopedia of Trees of the World* (New York, 1983), 133–35.

Richter, M., *Bobbio in the Early Middle Ages* (Dublin, 2008).

Rinaldi, R., "L'incolto in città: Note sulle vicende del paesaggio urbano tra alto medioevo ed età comunale," in *Il bosco nel medioevo*, ed. B. Andreolli and M. Montanari (Bologna, 1988), 253–62.

Rindos, D., "Darwinism and Its Role in the Exploitation of Domestication," in *Foraging and Farming: The Evolution of Plant Exploitation* (London, 1989), 27–41.

Rippe, G., *Padou et son contado (x–xiiie siècle)* (Rome, 2003).

Riquelme Cantal, J., and A. Morales Muñiz, "A Porcupine Find from Roman North Africa, with a Review of Archaeological Data from Circummediterranean Sites," *Archaeofauna* 6 (1997), 91–95.

Rival, L., "Trees, from Symbols of Life and Regeneration to Political Artefacts," in *The Social Life of Trees* (Oxford, 1998), 1–36.

Romane, F., and L. Valerino, "Changements du paysage et biodiversité dans les châtaigneraies cévenoles (sud de la France)," *Ecologia mediterranea* 23 (1997), 121–29.

Bibliography

Ross, J., *Figuring the Feminine* (Toronto, 2008).

Rottoli, M., and E. Castiglioni, "Plant Offerings from Roman Cremations in Northern Italy," *Vegetation History and Archaeobotany* 20.5 (2011), 495–506.

Rottoli, M., and S. Negri, "I resti vegetali carbonizzati," in *Filattiera-Sorano*, ed. E. Giannichedda (Florence, 1998), 198–212.

Roubis, D., "Archeologia del paesaggio a Jure Vetere," in *Jure Vetere: Ricerche archeologiche nella prima fondazione monastica di Gioacchino di Fiore, indagine 2001–2005*, ed. C. Fonseca, D. Roubis, and F. Sogliani (Soveria Mannelli, 2007), 389–416.

Rouche, M., "Le haut moyen âge," in *Histoire des populations de l'Europe*, ed. J Bardet and J. Dupâquier (Paris, 1997), 133–67.

Ruas, M., "Aspects of Early Medieval Farming from Sites in Mediterranean France," *Vegetation History and Archaeobotany* 14 (2005), 400–15.

Rugolo, C., "Paesaggio boschivo e insediamenti umani nella Calabria medievale," in *Il bosco nel medioevo*, ed. B. Andreolli and M. Montanari (Bologna, 1988), 323–48.

Russell, J., "The Ecclesiastical Age: A Demographic Interpretation of the Period 200–900 AD," in *Medieval Demography* (New York, 1987).

Late Ancient and Medieval Population Control (Philadelphia, 1985).

Sadori, L., and F. Susanna, "Hints of Economic Change during the Late Roman Empire Period in Central Italy," *Vegetation History and Archaeobotany* 14 (2005), 386–94.

Saggioro, F., ed., *Nogara: Archeologia e storia di un villaggio medievale (Scavi 2003–2008)* (Rome, 2011).

Salaman, R., *The History and Social Influence of the Potato* (Cambridge, 1949).

Sánchez Goñi, M., *De la taphonomie pollinique à la reconstruction de l'environnement* (Oxford, 1993).

Santos, L., J. Romani, and G. Jalut, "History of Vegetation during the Holocene in the Courel and Queixa Sierras, Galicia, Northwest Iberian Peninsula," *Journal of Quaternary Science* 15 (2000), 621–32.

Savino, E., *Campania tardoantica (284–604)* (Bari, 2005).

Schama, S., *Landscape and Memory* (New York, 1995).

Schlatter, T., "Die Kastanie (*Castanea vesca* Gärtner, *Castanea sativa* Miller) im Kanton St. Gallen," *Jahrbuch der St. Gallischen naturwissenschaftlichen Gesellschaft* (1911), 57–86.

Schneider, R., and K. Tobolski, "Lago di Ganna: Late-Glacial and Holocene Environments of a Lake in the Southern Alps," *Dissertationes botanicae* 87 (1985), 229–71.

Schwarz, U., *Amalfi im frühen Mittelalter (9.–11. Jahrhundert)* (Tübingen, 1978).

Seiwa, K., A. Watanabe, K. Irie, H. Kanno, T. Saitoh, and S. Akasaka, "Impact of Site-Induced Mouse Caching and Transport Behaviour on Regeneration in *Castanea crenata*," *Journal of Vegetation Science* 13 (2002), 517–26.

Sereni, E., *Storia del paesaggio agrario italiano* (Bari, 1979).

Sereno, P., "Crisi climatiche e crisi di sussistenza: Qualche considerazione sulle interazioni tra ambiente geografico e agricoltura nella economia di antico regime," in *Agricoltura ambiente e sviluppo economico nella storia europea*, ed. L. Segre (Milan, 1993), 137–42.

Shaw, B., "After Rome," *New Left Review* 51 (2008), 89–114.

Bibliography

Simberloff, D., "Confronting Introduced Species: A Form of Xenophobia," *Biological Invasions* 5 (2003), 179–92.

Simmons, I., *Environmental History: A Concise Introduction* (Oxford, 1998).

Sirago, V., *L'Italia agraria sotto Traiano* (Louvain, 1958).

Sitka, H., "Los macrorestos botánicos de la Cova des Cárritx," in *Ideología y sociedad en la prehistoria de Menorca*, ed. V. Lull (Ciutadella, 1999), 521–31.

Skinner, P., "The Tyrrhenian Coastal Cities under the Normans," in *The Society of Norman Italy*, ed. G. Loud and A. Metcalfe (Leiden, 2002), 75–96.

Squatriti, P., "Trees, Nuts, and Woods at the End of the First Millennium: A Case from the Amalfi Coast," in *Ecologies and Economies in Medieval and Early Modern Europe*, ed. S. Bruce (Leiden, 2010), 25–44.

"Water-Borne Transport and Communication in North Italy during the Early Middle Ages," in *Travel Technology and Organization in Medieval Europe*, ed. G. de Boe and F. Verhaege (Zellik, 1997), 13–20.

Stace, C., *New Flora of the British Isles* (Cambridge, 2010).

Staffa, A., "Le campagne abruzzesi tra tarda antichità e altomedioevo," *Archeologia medievale* 27 (2000), 47–99.

Stiner, M., N. Munro, and T. Surovell, "The Tortoise and the Hare: Small Game Use, the Broad-Spectrum Revolution, and Paleolithic Demography," *Current Anthropology* 41 (2000), 39–79.

Sukopp, H., "On the Study of Anthropogenic Plant Migrations in Central Europe," in *Plant Invasions: Ecological Mechanisms and Human Responses*, ed. U. Starfinger, K. Edwards, I. Kowarik, and M. Williamson (Leiden, 1999), 43–56.

Sykora, K., "History of the Impact of Man on the Distribution of Plant Species," in *Biological Invasions in Europe and the Mediterranean Basin*, ed. F. di Castri, A. J. Hansen, and M. Debussche (Dordrecht, 1990), 37–50.

Szabó, P., *Woodland and Forest in Medieval Hungary* (Oxford, 2005).

Talbert, R., ed., *Barrington Atlas of the Greek and Roman World* (Princeton, 2000).

Taviani-Carozzi, H., *La principauté lombarde de Salerne*, 3 vols., Vol. 1 (Rome, 1991).

"Salerno longobarda: Una capitale principesca," in *Salerno nel medioevo*, ed. H. Taviani-Carozzi, B. Vetere, and A. Leone (Galatina, 2000), 5–53.

Thirgood, J., *Man and the Mediterranean Forest* (London, 1981).

Thomas, N., *Entangled Objects: Exchange, Material Culture, and Colonialism in the Pacific* (Cambridge, MA, 1991).

Tinazzi, O., and E. Larco, "Indagine xilotomica e dendrocronologica su elementi lignei provenienti dallo scavo 'Mulino di Sotto' di Nogara," in *Nogara*, ed. F. Saggioro (Rome, 2011), 77–88.

Totman, C., *The Green Archipelago: Forestry in Preindustrial Japan* (Berkeley, 1989).

Toubert, P., "Paysages ruraux et techniques de production en Italie méridionale dans la seconde moitié du XIIe siècle," in *Potere, società e popolo nell'età dei due Guglielmi* (Bari, 1981), 201–29.

Les structures du Latium médiéval, 2 vols. (Rome, 1973).

Trifone, R., "Le prestazioni degli antichi coltivatori amalfitani e la 'sabbatatica,'" *Rivista di diritto agrario* 8 (1929), 541–51.

Storia del diritto forestale in Italia (Florence, 1957).

Tuan, Y., *Landscapes of Fear* (New York, 1979).

Bibliography

Valenti, M., "Architecture and Infrastructure in the Early Medieval Village," in *Technology in Transition: AD 300–650*, ed. L. Lavan, E. Zanini, and A. Constantine Sarantis (Leiden, 2007), 451–89.

"Edilizia nel villaggio altomedievale di Miranduolo (Chiusdino, SI)," *Archeologia medievale* 35 (2008), 75–97.

"L'insediamento altomedievale," in *Poggio Imperiale a Poggibonsi*, ed. R. Francovich and M. Valenti (Florence, 1996), 79–142.

"La Toscana tra VI e IX secolo," in *La fine delle ville romane*, ed. G. Brogiolo (Mantua, 1996), 81–106.

van der Veen, M., "Agricultural Innovation," *World Archaeology* 42.1 (2010), 1–12.

"The Archaeobotany of Roman Britain," *Britannia* 38 (2007), 181–210.

"Food as Embodied Material Culture," *Journal of Roman Archaeology* 31 (2008), 83–110.

van der Veen, M., A. Livarda, and A. Hill, "New Food Plants in Roman Britain: Dispersal and Social Access," *Environmental Archaeology* 13.1 (2008), 10–36.

van Zeist, W., "Aperçu sur la diffusion des végétaux cultivés dans la région méditerranéenne," in *Colloque de la Fondation L. Emberger sur la mise en place, l'évolution et la caractérisation de la flore et de la végétation circum-méditerranéenne* (Montpellier, 1980), 129–43.

"Economic Aspects," in *Progress in Old World Palaeoethnobotany: A Retrospective View on the Occasion of 20 Years of the International Work Group for Palaeoethnobotany*, ed. W. van Zeist, K. Wasylikowa, and K.-E. Behre (Rotterdam, 1991), 109–30.

Vannière, B., D. Colombaroli, E. Chapron, A. Leroux, W. Tinner, and M. Magny, "Climate versus Human-Driven Fire Regimes in Mediterranean Landscapes: The Holocene Record of Lago dell'Accesa (Tuscany, Italy)," *Quaternary Science Reviews* 27 (2008), 1181–96.

Vera, F., *Grazing Ecology and Forest History* (Wallingford, 2000).

Vernet, J., "Man and Vegetation in the Mediterranean Area during the Last 20,000 Years," in *Biological Invasions in Europe and the Mediterranean Basin*, ed. F. di Castri, A. J. Hansen, and M. Debussche (Dordrecht, 1990), 161–68.

Vigne, J., "Small Mammal Fossil Assemblages as Indicators of Environmental Change in Northern Corsica during the Last 2,500 Years," *Journal of Archaeological Science* 23 (1996), 207–11.

Vitolo, G., "Il castagno nell'economia della Campania medievale," *Rassegna storica salernitana* 12 (1989), 21–34.

"I prodotti della terra," in *Terra e uomini nel Mezzogiorno normanno-svevo*, ed. G. Musca (Bari, 1987), 159–85.

Voisenet, J., *Bêtes et hommes dans le monde médiéval* (Turnhout, 2000).

Walsham, A., *The Reformation of the Landscape* (Oxford, 2011).

Walvin, J., *Fruits of Empire: Exotic Produce and British Taste, 1660–1800* (Houndmills, 1997).

Warde, P., "Common Rights and Common Lands in South West Germany, 1500–1800," in *The Management of Common Land in North West Europe, c. 1500–1850*, ed. M. De Moor, L. Shaw-Taylor, and P. Warde (Turnhout, 2002), 195–224.

Watkins, C., and K. Kirby, "Historical Ecology and European Woodland," in *The Ecological History of European Forests*, ed. C. Watkins and K. Kirby (Wallingford, 1998), ix–xx.

Bibliography

Wells, P., "Production within and beyond Imperial Boundaries: Goods, Exchange, and Power in Roman Europe," in *World-Systems Theory in Practice: Leadership, Production, and Exchange*, ed. P. Kardulias (Lanham, MD, 1999), 85–111.

Wemple, S., "S. Salvatore/S. Giulia: A Case Study in the Endowment and Patronage of a Major Female Monastery in Northern Italy," in *Women of the Medieval World*, ed. J. Kirsher and S. Wemple (London, 1985), 85–102.

White, K., *Roman Farming* (London, 1970).

White, R., "'Are You an Environmentalist or Do You Work for a Living?': Work and Nature," in *Uncommon Ground*, ed. W. Cronon (New York, 1996), 171–85.

The Organic Machine (New York, 1995).

Wickham, C., "Agricultura, ambiente e sviluppo economico nella storia europea: Il problema dell'alto medioevo," in *Agricultura ambiente e sviluppo nella storia europea*, ed. L. Segre (Milan, 1993), 157–61.

"European Forests in the Early Middle Ages," in *L'ambiente vegetale nell'alto medioevo*, Settimane del CISAM 37 (Spoleto, 1990), 479–545.

Framing the Early Middle Ages: Europe and the Mediterranean 400–800 (Oxford, 2005).

The Mountains and the City: The Tuscan Appennines in the Early Middle Ages (Oxford, 1988).

Wilde, J., *Kulturgeschichte der rheinpfälzischen Baumwelt und ihrer Naturdenkmale* (Kaiserslautern, 1936).

Willems, W., and L. Kooistra, "De Romeinse villa te Voerendaal: Opgraving 1987," *Archeologie in Limburg* 33 (1988), 137–47.

Willerding, U., "Die Paläoethnobotanik und ihre Stellung im System der Wissenschaften," *Berichte der deutschen botanischen Gesellschaft* 91 (1978), 3–30.

"Die Pflanzenreste," in *Das römische Gräberfeld auf der Keckweise in Kempten*, ed. M. Mackenstein (Kallmünz, 1978), 183–95.

"Zur Agrarproduktion von der jüngeren vorrömischen Eisenzeit bis ins frühe Mittelalter," *Historicum* (1996), 10–20.

Williamson, T., *Shaping Medieval Landscapes* (London, 2003).

Winiwarter, V., "Prolegomena to a History of Soil Knowledge in Europe," in *Soils and Societies*, ed. V. Winiwarter and J. McNeill (Isle of Harris, 2006), 208–10.

"Soil Scientists in Ancient Rome," in *Footprints in the Soil*, ed. B. Warkentin (Amsterdam, 2006), 3–16.

"Soils and Society: An Environmental History of Challenge and Response," *Die Bodenkultur* 57 (2006), 231–41.

Zagnoni, R., "La coltivazione del castagno nella montagna fra Bologna e Pistoia nei secoli XI–XIII," in *Villaggi, boschi e campi dell'Appennino dal medioevo all'età contemporanea* (Porretta Terme, 1997), 41–57.

Zohary, D., "The Diffusion of South and East Asian and of African Crops into the Belt of Mediterranean Agriculture," in *Plants for Food and Medicine: Proceedings of the Joint Conference of the Society for Economic Botany and the International Society for Ethnopharmacology, London, UK, 1–6 July 1996*, ed. H. Prendergast, N. Etkin, D. Harris, and P. Houghton (Kew, 1998), 123–34.

Zohary, D., and M. Hopf, *Domestication of Plants in the Old World* (Oxford, 2000).

Zotz, T., "Beobachtungen zu Königtum und Forst im früheren Mittelalter," in *Jagd und höfische Kultur im Mittelalter*, ed. W. Rösener (Göttingen, 1997), 95–122.

INDEX

Index

Index

233

Index

Januarius, Neapolitan saint, 150
Japan, 33
Japanese chestnut (*Castanea crenata*), 33–34
Jerome, saintly ascetic, 111, 124
John the Deacon, 126
Jonas of Bobbio, 113
Jovinian, demolished, 111
Julian, Roman Emperor, 106
juniper, 177

landrace, 141, 157
Languedoc, 61, 83
Latium, housing, 11n42
Lattari mountains, 143, 147
Le Goff, Jacques, 7
Legnano (MI), 169
Leo III, bishop of Rome, 126
Levata, 169
Lévi-Strauss, Claude, 90
Liguria, 56, 65, 68, 77
Ligurian Sea, 194
lime tree, 178
limes, northwestern, 59
Lo Cascio, Elio, and Paolo Malanima, 69
Locarno, 169
Lodi, 182
Lombard, Maurice, 147
Lombardy, modern chestnut production in, 165
Lothair I, Carolingian ruler, 15
Louis II, Holy Roman Emperor, 187
Louis the German, 115
Low Countries, 60
Lucretius, Roman thinker, 9
lumber, 151
Luni, 195

Macrobius, 96
Magra river, 178
Martial, 102
Martin, saintly bishop of Tours, 3
Massif Central, 60
Matese mountains, 150n76
matricina, type of tree, 133
McNeill, John, 89
meadows, *see* pasture and meadows
measures, 185n66
meat-eating, 78
Mediterranean Exchange, 88–91, 129
Menorca, 58n7
merchants, and commerce, 156
Milan, 12, 179, 191
Modena, 171
Modigliana (FC), 188
Moneglia (GE), 183
Montaldo di Mondovì (CN), 170, 174

Montanari, Massimo, 80, 167
Montarrenti (SI), 175
Monte Barro (CO), 169, 174, 179–80
Monte Gelato (RM), 12, 76
Montevergine (AV), 132, 153
Montoro (AV), 151, 159
Mujahid ibn Abdullah, 195–97
mushrooms, 37, 49
mutualism, 19, 86, 200
Muzzano, Lake, 169, 171

Naples, 138, 146, 148, 150
Napoleon, sugar scheme of, 48n64
Nocera (NA), 147
Nogara (VR), 76, 174
Nola (NA), 132
Novara, 187, 192
Novigrad, 186
nuts, symbolism of, 116

oak, 29, 33n21, 74, 77, 81, 86, 137, 145, 148, 150,
    170, 171, 172, 174, 177, 178
    of Thunor, 4
oats, 87n110
Oderzo (TV), 170
oleiculture, decline of, 66
olive, 19, 86n104, 100, 180
Otranto (LE), 79n82
Ottonians, 194
Ovid, 101
ovines, compatible with chestnuts, 77–78, 79
owls, Corsican feeding patterns of, 13

Palladius, 42, 93, 102, 106–07, 122
palynology, 13, 61, 64–66, 170, 171, 177
Pannonia, 60
Pascoli, Giovanni, 198–201
pasture and meadows, 37, 46, 50, 59, 74, 155, 178
Patarenes, 164
Paul, the Deacon, 1n11
Paulinus of Aquileia, 120
Paulinus, saintly bishop of Nola, 110
Pavia, 174
peasantry, 12, 14, 16
    economic strategies of, 72–73
pecan, 82
Peloponnesus, 56
Peterken, George, 20, 85
Pfalz, viticultural region, 60
physiocrats, deleterious influence of, 53n81
Phytophthora cambivora, 39n37
Piacenza, 128, 167, 180, 183
Picentini mountains, 143, 152
Piedmont, 170
pigs, 76n70, 155n93, 177

Made in the USA
Monee, IL
04 June 2021

70193850R00140